HAWTHORNE AND MELVILLE

HAWTHORNE
and MELVILLE

Writing a Relationship

Edited by
Jana L. Argersinger
and
Leland S. Person

THE UNIVERSITY OF GEORGIA PRESS　ATHENS AND LONDON

© 2008 by the University of Georgia Press
Athens, Georgia 30602
www.ugapress.org

Designed by Ellen Graben
Set in Minion by Graphic Composition, Inc.
Printed digitally in the United States of America

Library of Congress Cataloging-in-Publication Data

Hawthorne and Melville : writing a relationship /
edited by Jana L. Argersinger and Leland S. Person.
    xiv, 378 p. : ill. ; 23 cm.
    Includes bibliographical references (p. 345–365) and index.
    ISBN-13: 978-0-8203-2751-8 (hardcover : alk. paper)
    ISBN-10: 0-8203-2751-4 (hardcover : alk. paper)
    ISBN-13: 978-0-8203-3096-9 (pbk. : alk. paper)
    ISBN-10: 0-8203-3096-5 (pbk. : alk. paper)
    1. Hawthorne, Nathaniel, 1804–1864—Friends and associates.
2. Hawthorne, Nathaniel, 1804–1864—Relations with men. 3. Melville,
Herman, 1819–1891—Friends and associates. 4. Melville, Herman,
1819–1891—Relations with men. 5. Novelists, American—19th century—
Biography. I. Argersinger, Jana L., 1957– II. Person, Leland S.
    PS1883 .H38 2008
    813'.3—dc22
    [B]   2007044586

British Library Cataloging-in-Publication Data available

for

Robert K. Martin

for

Charlie and Forest,

friends en famille

Contents

Illustrations

Abbreviations
for Frequently Cited Sources

CE   *The Centenary Edition of the Works of Nathaniel Hawthorne,*
      ed. William Charvat et al., 23 vols. (Columbus: Ohio State
      Univ. Press, 1962–94).

Log   *The Melville Log: A Documentary Life of Herman Melville,*
      1819–1891, ed. Jay Leyda, 2 vols., paginated consecutively
      (New York: Harcourt, Brace, 1951; repr., with additional
      material, New York: Gordian Press, 1969).

WHM   *The Writings of Herman Melville,* ed. Harrison Hayford,
      Hershel Parker, and G. Thomas Tanselle, 13 vols. to date
      (Evanston and Chicago: Northwestern Univ. Press and the
      Newberry Library, 1968–).

Endnotes for individual essays provide shortened references to works
whose bibliographic information appears in full in the Works Cited list
at volume's end.

Acknowledgments

THIS VOLUME GATHERS a company of scholars in a shared sense—
if not in anything quite so paradisiacal as an infinite fraternity of
feeling—that the much-studied but potently elusive relationship between Nathaniel Hawthorne and Herman Melville has not yet yielded
up all its stories. The venture had its genesis in a lively session titled
"The Hawthorne-Melville Relationship (A Retrospect: 150 years)" that
Robert Milder organized for the American Literature Association
conference in Long Beach, California, in May 2000. From that fertile
conversation—featuring Milder, Brenda Wineapple, and Thomas R.
Mitchell—grew a special issue of *ESQ: A Journal of the American Renaissance* (vol. 46, nos. 1–2 [2000]), coedited by Robert K. Martin and
Leland S. Person. And from thence to the volume at hand, which broad-
ens the original band of three to twelve. Our greatest debt as editors is
owed, of course, to these contributors—for the fresh illumination they
bring to the subject and for the patient dedication they have accorded us
through the project's extended gestation. Thanks are also due to Mallory
Sanders, Tanya Gonzales, Albert J. von Frank, and Kristin Boudreau for
their vital support.

Versions of several essays included here have appeared elsewhere.
Professors Wineapple, Mitchell, and Milder reprise their partnership
from the 2000 *ESQ* issue courtesy of the Board of Regents of Washington State University. Professor Milder's essay also had a subsequent incarnation as chapter 6 of *Exiled Royalties: Melville and the Life We Imagine* (New York: Oxford Univ. Press, 2006). An earlier version of Robert

Sattelmeyer's contribution appeared in *ESQ* 49, no. 4 (2003): 213–47, and is printed here by permission of the Board of Regents of Washington State University. And parts of Chris Castiglia's essay find a place in chapters 1 and 7 of his *Interior States: Institutional Consciousness and the Inner Life of Democracy in the Antebellum United States* (Durham, N.C.: Duke Univ. Press, 2008). We are grateful that these publishers have given us leave to knit these materials into a new whole.

Hawthorne and Melville

Writing, Relationship, and Missing Letters

JANA L. ARGERSINGER
AND LELAND S. PERSON

WHAT'S IN A LETTER? All the world, it may sometimes seem to literary and biographical scholars intent on chasing apparitions of meaning—especially in a relationship that twines together authorial, personal, and social being as complexly as the one that took fire between Nathaniel Hawthorne and Herman Melville in 1850. But what if the letter is missing? In these critical days, we're supposed to be long habituated to the idea of absence, of spinning our own interpretive words and characters with no thought of perfect communion, no expectation that the subjects of our desires will give themselves into our embrace. Perhaps, though, we're not utterly resigned. If letters between two writers—say, a dreamed-of collaborative fiction or half an impassioned correspondence—do not now exist in full but have left undeniable traces that beckon, tease, cannot easily be ignored . . . what then?

In a gripping 1997 literary detective novel, *Quieter Than Sleep,* Emily Dickinson scholar Joanne Dobson indulges herself by "solving" arguably the greatest mystery in Dickinson studies: who is the "Master" Dickinson addresses in three famous letters? Dobson solves that mystery by having her assistant professor hero, Karen Pelletier, discover a fourth "Master" letter—addressed to none other than Henry Ward Beecher! Although Dobson does not develop the point in her novel, the appearance of such a letter would go a long way toward solving several mysteries—not only the identity of Master but the mystery of how much and what kind of sexual experience Dickinson may have had. There is no tangible evidence, of course, that missing Master letters really exist, though Dickinson scholars would undoubtedly "kill" to get their hands on a prize like this—as one of them does in Dobson's novel. Their zeal for such a missing letter rivals the desire scholars bring to the question of what Hawthorne wrote to Melville during the sixteen months (August 1850–November 1851) that the two were friends in the Berkshires. Melville apparently destroyed those letters, and missing with them, most scholars assume, is evidence that would help solve several mysteries about his relationship with Hawthorne and its literary import.

The gap that Hawthorne's missing letters leave in the historical record provides a seductive blank space on which scholars can speculate—foolscap, some would say, on which scholars (like Melville's narrator in "The Tartarus of Maids") can write their own version of "Cupid." And even if Hawthorne's letters were to turn up, of course, it is likely they would raise as many questions as they answered—as, for example, Henry James's hot letters to Hendrik Andersen, Jocelyn Persse, Hugh Walpole, and others have done on the subject of James's sexual identity and practices. Melville's writing to and about Hawthorne survives, and its frankly erotic language has provided scholars with a loaded if not smoking gun for evidencing the sexual dimensions of Melville's side of the relationship. Melville's review of Hawthorne's *Mosses from an Old Manse,* with its "astonishingly sexual image" of Hawthorne dropping "germinous seeds" into Melville's soul and then shooting his "strong New-England roots" into the "hot soil" of Melville's "Southern soul," has inspired many analyses.[1] More than a dozen of Melville's letters to the Hawthornes lend plenty of ballast to scholarly attempts to characterize Melville's feelings—especially the letter he wrote after receiving Hawthorne's praise of *Moby-Dick,* with its "pantheistic" feeling of "divine magnanimities" (*WHM,* 14:212). This is not to say that Melville scholarship finds any easy answers to the questions this fascinating relationship and particularly the 1850–51 interlude raise. As contributors to this volume amply demonstrate, Melville's language raises almost as many questions as Hawthorne's silence and missing letters. There are the questions about Hawthorne's influence on the composition of *Moby-Dick* and *Pierre* and Melville's influence on Hawthorne's writing, especially *The Blithedale Romance.* And the question of sexuality looms like a grand hooded phantom. How did Hawthorne respond to Melville's "astonishingly sexual" and physically intimate language? How might each of these men have negotiated the terms of an intense friendship? How would each have understood and characterized his own feelings and the other's? What possibilities for male-male relationships existed in mid-nineteenth-century American culture? Finally, linking the literary and the erotic, what bearing did this relationship—whatever physical and emotional forms it assumed—have on the writing each man produced?

The Scholarly Chase: First Days

At the risk of overemphasizing biographical connections between the two writers and their work, we wish to examine some of the major inter-pretations of the Hawthorne-Melville relationship.[2] As we survey read-ings of this bond, we must—especially if we wish to pursue the most provocative possibilities—face the key question not only of what sort of relation could be experienced and expressed in antebellum America but also of what sort of reading is possible at any given period in the scholarly aftermath. Reading, like the subjectivities that read, is in large part historically and culturally constructed. Robert K. Martin, whose book *The Homosexual Tradition in American Poetry* (1979) undertakes one of the first overviews of homosexuality in American literature, in a later study credits Newton Arvin as the first scholar to suggest Melville's "fundamental homosexuality" and to suggest the homoerotic dimen-sions of his attraction to Hawthorne.[3] Martin refers to Arvin's 1950 book on Melville, but it is not unreasonable to propose that Arvin also au-thored the first queer reading of Nathaniel Hawthorne. Arvin was a gay male, although still in the closet when he wrote his book on Hawthorne (in 1929). Without suggesting that Arvin's sexuality *dictated* his read-ing of Hawthorne, we want to agree with Barry Werth that Arvin read Hawthorne through the "prism of his own torments," identifying "dark strains that perhaps only someone who cloaked unwanted desires could fully detect."[4]

Arvin in 1929 describes a Hawthorne who dare not reveal himself and his deepest imaginings—a Hawthorne "in the closet," in some sense, and thus occupying a subject position very similar to Arvin's own as he reads Hawthorne. Again and again, in a book that might be subtitled (ahead of Leslie Fiedler) "Love and Guilt in an American Novelist," Arvin stresses Hawthorne's love of solitude and the guilt that love provoked. Promoting the long-lived theory of a monkish recluse, Arvin concludes: "It would have been really amazing if he had done the writing in anything but loneliness and with anything but the most jealously guarded secrecy. To such an end all the forces of his childhood and adolescence had converged."[5] Even when taking note of the marriage to Sophia, he emphasizes the way it fulfills Hawthorne's "passion for isolation" (105). Arvin sees "emotional dualism" in Hawthorne's approach to this alliance (92), his anticipation that Sophia will enter into "joint isolation" rather than share a new social life with him (94). In short, very little changes for Nathaniel. But then, Arvin suggests that intellectual curiosity as well as a desire to cure some ailment within himself propel him toward a wife in the first place: "The conviction had for some time been growing upon him that what seemed the incurable emptiness of his life was due largely to his ignorance of so deep a human experience as the love between the sexes" (76–77). Arvin, moreover, goes to some lengths to explain Sophia's special appeal. His Hawthorne, after all, feels "diffidence in the presence of all women, bred of a dozen years of the strictest celibacy" (78).

> Sophia Peabody was, in his possible sphere of acquaintance, the one woman who could have overcome the special reluctances he would have felt. How fearfully he would have shrunk from intimate relations with a woman of large physical vitality and robust emotional needs! How difficult it would have been to turn from the shadowy feminine figures of his lonely fantasies to a woman with a vigor comparable at every point with his own! And how intolerant he would have been—he who had been worshiped with strange silent devotion by his mother and two sisters—of an assertive intellect, a temper capable of disequilibrium, a tough and independent will! Sophia threatened him in none of these disastrous ways. She was, physically, of an extreme tenuity, and shivered in every wind from the east. (79)

However true such apostrophes may ring for Hawthorne, surely they reveal more about Arvin's own emotional and psychological state at the time he wrote them. The perfect woman? The slightest woman possible, as Arvin constructs her—that is, a woman of "extreme" physical "tenuity," with no "robust emotional needs," a woman less substantial than one of Hawthorne's literary creations, a woman who cannot rival his "lonely fantasies," which are consequently left, as it were, to their own devices. A woman, in short, who is not an object of physical or sexual desire—a woman and wife in name only. This is Hawthorne in the closet—covered by a marriage that does not draw on his real desires.

In 1950, Arvin will treat Herman Melville's marriage to Elizabeth Shaw in much the same way—as a puzzling event that masks other desires. "It is not easy," he professes, "to believe that Melville entered upon marriage without the most disturbing, even if unconscious, conflicts." The "truth" is that "the masculine and feminine elements in Melville's own nature were far too precariously balanced, far too unreconciled with one another, for marriage to be anything but excruciatingly problematic both for him and for his wife." Understanding homosexuality through a then-current (and latterly persistent) theory of gender inversion, Arvin also still sees it as a pathology—a "malady" that Melville did not understand. "He was conscious enough, no doubt, of the ardor and intensity of his feelings for members of his own sex, but the possibility that such emotions might have a sexual undercurrent can only with the utmost rarity, and then fleetingly, have presented itself to his consciousness."[6] Melville had homoerotic feelings, in Arvin's somewhat tortured view, but policed even his own fantasies in order to repress the thought of full-blown sexual relations. As he had with Hawthorne's marriage, Arvin pretty clearly projects not only his own internal confusions but also his socially constructed efforts to understand and express his own sexual identity.

In encouraging Arvin to undertake his Hawthorne book, Van Wyck Brooks was "convinced," Werth observes, "that the retiring young Smith instructor was one of the few people . . . capable of discerning the true Hawthorne," and he expected that Arvin would surely "'be able to do something with the relations between Hawthorne and Melville.'"[7] Arvin's treatment of the relationship changes somewhat from 1929 to 1950—a result not only of the change in focus from Hawthorne to Melville but also of the way his own sense of himself had come out during the intervening decades. Some of this change may also derive from the book he wrote in between—the book on Walt Whitman, with its explicit, if still vexed, treatment of homosexuality. In the earlier, Hawthorne-centered book, Arvin registers some surprise that a bond developed at all: "During the first summer in Lenox a friendship sprang up . . . with a suddenness and warmth unique in Hawthorne's record. . . . It was, on the surface, a singular alliance. . . . How could a life have been less like Hawthorne's than the life that Melville, his junior by fifteen years, had led?" (*Hawthorne,*

167). "Why, of all the men of letters in the world," Arvin wonders, "did Melville seize upon Nathaniel Hawthorne as the one human being to whom he could utter his deepest intentions and betray his secretest fears?" (168). Arvin's answer: Melville shared Hawthorne's reclusiveness and love of solitude. But in this 1929 version, the basis of friendship is largely intellectual and only somewhat emotional. The two men stand in similar, isolated relationship to the public world. Similarity of position breeds sympathy, in Arvin's view, especially on the younger writer's part: Melville expands in the "warmth, however moderate, of Hawthorne's friendship, and pour[s] out his doubts and anxieties and mutinous impulses to him as he would have scorned to do to any other man" (171).

Arvin does not develop his insights into Melville's outpourings in his Hawthorne book. And interestingly, he elides one of the most suggestive passages in the letter Melville wrote after receiving Hawthorne's response to *Moby-Dick,* including these telling sentences: "In me divine magnanimities are spontaneous and instantaneous—catch them while you can. The world goes round, and the other side comes up. So now I can't write what I felt. But I felt pantheistic then—your heart beat in my ribs and mine in yours, and both in God's" (*WHM,* 14:212). Arvin in 1929 ultimately dismisses Melville's likely effect on Hawthorne. What "role did this quick-flowering friendship play in [Hawthorne's] spiritual affairs"? No "full answer" can be given, "since Hawthorne's letters to Melville have been destroyed, but it is hardly likely that at this stage Hawthorne's spiritual course could be altered by any such deflecting pressure" (*Hawthorne,* 172). Whether he thinks that Hawthorne's emotional, or even sexual, "course" could have been altered by Melville's behavior—or his imagination enkindled in some new way by Melville's suggestive language—Arvin doesn't say.

When recasting the early days of this "quick-flowering friendship" in his Melville book twenty years later, on the other hand, Arvin comes a little closer to discovering the potential meanings that have intrigued more recent critics. He notes that Melville's August 1850 "meeting with the older writer" "found him in a state of quite special responsiveness; it was a cardinal moment, intellectually and emotionally, in his life." Arvin still writes somewhat euphemistically, tantalizing us with the implications of this "quite special responsiveness" and, a few sentences later, with the observation that "the current of sympathy and mutual interest had passed between them like a magnetic force." Turning to the still-stunning "germinous seeds" passage in Melville's review of *Mosses from an Old Manse,* Arvin calls attention to this "astonishingly sexual image," the only kind of image, he says, that "could adequately have expressed Melville's feeling, for the moment, of receptiveness and even passivity in the acceptance of impregnation by another mind" (*Melville,* 136–38). But he goes no further in exploring the two writers' interactions during the sixteen months they were together in the Berkshires.

F. O. Matthiessen has figured in recent years as the most famous closeted gay critic of American literature—the best example of how the pressure of the closet affects, or infects, the practices of reading and literary criticism.[8] For surely, the argument goes (either implicitly or explicitly), Matthiessen would have noted and emphasized the homoerotic dimensions of American Renaissance writing had the fear of thereby outing himself not proscribed it. We cannot know what Matthiessen would have done under different circumstances. Do gay men have to practice gay criticism? Do they have to emphasize sexuality and issues of sexual identity? No, of course not. At the same time, since Newton Arvin did discern sexual overtones in the Hawthorne-Melville relationship, it will be useful to examine other critics' readings of the same evidence at around the same time and to ask about the influence of their own experiences on their readings.

David Bergman finds in Matthiessen's *American Renaissance* (1941) a "covert celebration of the homosexual artist" and claims that the structure of the study "clearly argues for the supremacy of gay writers" (because Matthiessen prefers Melville to Hawthorne, Thoreau to Emerson, and Whitman to all others).[9] When Matthiessen takes up the Hawthorne-Melville relationship in 1941, however, he emphasizes its aesthetic dimension. In "Hawthorne and His Mosses" Melville responded to another "creative mind disclosing its own ambitions and problems in response to the profound challenge that only a fellow artist can present."[10] "Melville's efflorescence," Matthiessen claims, "came as an immediate response of his imagination to the possibilities that Hawthorne's had opened before him" (189). It is tempting to think broadly about what Matthiessen meant by "possibilities," but he goes on to tether the meaning to aesthetics and genre. Hawthorne, like Shakespeare, taught Melville about tragedy. "Melville felt himself at one with Hawthorne," Matthiessen observes and then adds, "for the strain of thought that gave rise to Hawthorne's allegories was what Melville recognized as truth" (248). Most tellingly, when Matthiessen turns to the two writers' correspondence about *Moby-Dick*, he passes over those suggestive passages in Melville's reply to Hawthorne's lost commentary that we now emphasize. Melville's "response poured out his sense of their close accord with such a flow of gratitude that at the end he pulled himself up short: 'What a pity, that, for your plain, bluff letter, you should get such gibberish!' But the experience of feeling that his aims had been understood was so beyond anything he had grown to hope for that it swept him out of control" (251). Instead of going on to quote the lines that seem to show Melville most "out of control" emotionally and even erotically—his "pantheistic" sense of hearts interchanged, or his wondering "by what right" Hawthorne drinks from his "flagon of life" with lips that supplant his own (*WHM*, 14:212)—Matthiessen continues to quote the passage with which he had started, where Melville characterizes Hawthorne's evident understanding of his paper allegory as his "glorious gratuity" (252).

In a revolutionary 1921 study—the book that resurrected Melville from scholarly limbo—Raymond Weaver begins with an excerpt from Melville's 1851 letter to Hawthorne. It is one of the more provocative passages: Melville imagines the two of them in paradise with a basket of champagne, crossing their legs in the "celestial grass that is forever tropical" and striking their glasses and heads together "till both ring musically in concert." Then, "O my dear fellow-mortal," he exclaims, "how shall we pleasantly discourse of all the things manifold which now so distress us."[11] Like Hawthorne's climactic comment on Hester and Dimmesdale in the forest—"Then, all was spoken!" (*CE*, 1:198)—Melville's allusion to "all the things manifold" entices us to imagine possibilities, even if, as responsible historians, we recognize that imaginative possibilities, like other behaviors, are limited by their cultural moment. Weaver characterizes Melville's statement as a "serene and laughing desolation" (15). In fact, he liberates the statement entirely from its object-directed context—Hawthorne fades out of the picture—and concentrates on the mood and its origins in Melville's thirty-two years of life. Weaver does note that Melville "was indebted to Nathaniel Hawthorne for the best makeshift for companionship he was ever to know," and he does note Sophia Hawthorne's "instinctive resentment of her husband's friend," her "grave and jealous suspicion of Melville" (22–23). But Sophia's jealousy is literary, in Weaver's view. Shrewdly, Sophia "resented the presence of a second luminary—treacherously veiled and of heaven knows what magnitude!—in her serene New England sky" (24).

When Weaver takes up the Melville-Hawthorne friendship in the Berkshires, he calls it an "ironical intimacy" (306), a phrase that seems to derive from his emphasis on Hawthorne's ability to feign empathy for whatever interested the people with whom he conversed. Melville, in other words, mistook Hawthorne's (feigned) interest for intimacy. Weaver's book on Melville is an act of genius—the more so because he would have had little reason to expect a sympathetic response. He is probably unfair, however, to Hawthorne, and his ideas about Hawthorne's response to Melville are perhaps ungenerous. He did not have access to Hawthorne's letter to Evert Duyckinck—the letter in which Hawthorne exclaims, "What a book Melville has written! It gives me an idea of much greater power than his preceding ones" (*CE,* 16:508). He does not comment either on Hawthorne's initial, very positive, response to Melville. Weaver concludes, in fact, that from the beginning "there had been, between Melville and Hawthorne, a profound incompatibility" (337). But he does not pursue the point, as Edwin Haviland Miller will some fifty years later. The incompatibility seems to him temperamental, and nothing more.

Lewis Mumford attends more closely to the intensity of Melville's reaction to Hawthorne in his 1929 book. Connecting Melville's responses to Shakespeare and to Hawthorne, Mumford notices how Melville suddenly felt liberated to enjoy and speak to extravagant possibilities for literary expression. "He risked much in utterance himself," Mumford observes, "and he hoped that Hawthorne would venture much in return. When they at last became friends, he contrived a hundred different ways of assaulting Hawthorne's reserve: he staggered up mountains, uncovered mounds of debris, jumped gaily off into innumerable abysses, all to excite Hawthorne to some equivalent disclosure." Like many other scholars, Mumford believes these efforts came to nothing. "He did not know at the outset of his enthusiasm for Hawthorne that nothing would ever shake that mountainous reserve, that no leaps and sorties of his would stimulate Hawthorne to put one foot before the other."[12]

Mumford certainly treats Melville more sympathetically than he does Hawthorne in his representation of the "deeper intimacy" that develops between the two (142). Melville pursues. Hawthorne remains unmoved. The opportunity for "real intercourse with Hawthorne, for talk about Time and Eternity and ultimate things, smoking a fragrant cigar, sipping brandy or cider, meant much to Melville," he observes—"far more, no doubt, than it did to Hawthorne." Melville needed the "affection of a sympathetic mind" and so "exposed the seamy depths of his own spirit" (143, 144). Mumford does not explain what he means by "seamy depths," but that doesn't really matter since Hawthorne, according to Mumford, was unable to "reciprocate" Melville's self-exposure (144). Indeed, Hawthorne remained an iceberg. "Friendship itself must have seemed a mockery," Mumford concludes, "when [Melville] found that the dearest friend and closest intellectual companion he had yet encountered was bound tight in the arctic ice" (145). Next to Edwin Haviland Miller's, Mumford's characterization of a one-sided relationship remains the most extravagant we have. While Mumford does not sexualize the friendship as Miller does, he represents it in romantic or near-romantic terms, casting Melville as the needy suitor to Hawthorne's older and frostily indifferent love object. Even though we don't have Hawthorne's letters to draw on, Mumford seems grossly unfair to him. It is the heat of Melville's responses, especially his excited reply to Hawthorne's "review" of *Moby-Dick*, that makes us think Hawthorne gave him at least a little of what he wanted.

There is no more innocent take on the Hawthorne-Melville relationship than Randall Stewart's in his 1948 literary biography. It is tempting, in fact, to think of Stewart's reading as an example of compulsory heterosexuality for the way he emphasizes the brightness of the Hawthornes' marriage and family life during their brief sojourn in the Berkshires. Stewart titles chapter 6 of his study "With Melville in the Berkshires, 1850–1851," but the spotlight is not really on Melville. "Sophia exercised her talents to their utmost toward making attractive the interior of their incommodious dwelling," Stewart writes in his second sentence, and he goes on to quote a lengthy passage from a letter Sophia wrote to her mother—an epistolary tour of the little red house.[13] Domestic bliss is the keynote here. Hawthorne plays with the children: "Twenty Days with Julian and Little Bunny," his journal account of three weeks alone with Julian during the summer of 1851, comes in for special mention—with the observation that it is "no small undertaking for the male parent to attend to the needs of a five-year-old for a period of three weeks" (103). Melville enters the story as Hawthorne's "most frequent visitor, and the most enjoyed" (107), a congeniality repaid by Hawthorne's many visits to Arrowhead—all of which Stewart summarizes briefly. During Sophia's absence the two men smoked cigars in the sitting room of the red cottage: "Such an exceptional liberty—exceptional because of Sophia's aversion, perhaps allergy to tobacco fumes—suggests an especial friendliness on Hawthorne's part" (109). Stewart's "especial friendliness" has none of the connotations of Arvin's "special responsiveness." He quotes two passages from Melville's letters. The first is Melville's scenario of the two men sitting down in paradise with a basket of champagne, which Stewart does read for what it reveals about the two men's meetings with one another, further finding that "Melville's letters to Hawthorne (which are among the most remarkable of his compositions) express a soul affinity with a frankness which might well prove embarrassing to a man of Hawthorne's reserve" (110). Second is an excerpt from Melville's ecstatic response to Hawthorne's response to *Moby-Dick*—the flagon-of-life passage in which Melville imagines Hawthorne's lips substituted for his own and extols the "infinite fraternity of feeling" that the other's letter has inspired. Melville's rhapsodic image of transmigrating hearts does not come into Stewart's treatment, but his point is clear: "[T]heir friendship, by any reasonable standards, was an eminently successful one" (111). Chastising Mumford for "representing Hawthorne, through cold unresponsiveness, as the villain in Melville's personal tragedy," he argues that Hawthorne must have been "free and cordial, if more restrained," in his letters in order to have provoked Melville's ebullient replies (111n, 111). Stewart, however, is not particularly interested in the texture of this friendship, perhaps because his subject is Hawthorne, for whom the friendship did not seem to mean as much, but perhaps also because it simply does not occur to him.

Leon Howard also skirts the issue, so obviously in a couple of places that he raises suspicions about what he really thought. He certainly acknowledges that Melville's "second growth" as a writer coincided with "Hawthorne and His Mosses" and the new friendship. He calls Melville's excitement and enthusiasm "curious," then goes on to explain it by emphasizing the "blackness" that Melville had discovered in Hawthorne's writing.[14] Reading Hawthorne's dark tales and talking with the man himself served as a "catalytic agent for the precipitation in words of a new attitude toward human nature." Comparing this new attitude to a "religious conversion," Howard stresses how "exciting and stimulating" it was for Melville, but then he roots this "excited stimulation" in the "new philosophical convictions" that were evolving in the "secret recesses" of Melville's mind (169). Howard thus abstracts Hawthorne's effect on Melville, as if separating the fiction from the man and sublimating emotion in philosophical speculation. He does cite the two most provocative passages Melville wrote about and to Hawthorne but lops them off before the most suggestive parts. He gets as far as quoting Melville's extravagant statement—"I feel that this Hawthorne has dropped germinous seeds into my soul"—but stops there, eliding the startling image of Hawthorne shooting roots into the "hot soil" of Melville's "Southern soul" (168). Similarly, when Howard quotes Melville's reaction to Hawthorne's letter about *Moby-Dick,* he includes only the first part of the famous declaration: "A sense of unspeakable security is in me at this moment, on account of your having understood the book. I have written a wicked book, and feel spotless as the lamb" (173). This extract supports Howard's view that Hawthorne's "blackness"—presumably a philosophically dark view of human nature—most attracted Melville. The personal and emotional facet of the friendship drops away, as do the sentences (which in fact bracket the section quoted) that convert Hawthorne's understanding into emotional and corporeal communion: "I felt pantheistic then—your heart beat in my ribs and mine in yours, and both in God's. . . . I would sit down and dine with you in old Rome's Pantheon. It is a strange feeling—no hopefulness is in it, no despair. Content—that is it; and irresponsibility; but without licentious inclination. I speak now of my profoundest sense of being, not of an incidental feeling" (*WHM,* 14:212). Quoting this passage with Howard's citation represented by ellipses shows very clearly how careful he was to screen out the ecstatic emotional dimensions of Melville's response.

The Scholarly Chase: Second Days

Even though Charles N. Watson had first suggested the idea, Edwin Haviland Miller shook up both Hawthorne and Melville scholars by asserting in his 1975 biography of the latter that an "advance" from Melville, which Hawthorne experienced as an "assault," ruptured the friendship. In this scenario, Hawthorne plays an elusive father figure (whom Melville feminizes as a love object) and Melville the envious son (whom Hawthorne ultimately betrays). Miller terms Melville's review of *Mosses* a "love letter," a "confession which Melville can make safely within what purports to be a book review," and he finds gender or sexual inversion implicit in its language. Hawthorne "assumes two active roles, maternal and paternal," while Melville casts himself in "two passive roles, the child and the woman, the receiver and the ravished."[15] Turning to Hawthorne and

Hawthorne's side of things in his 1991 biography, Miller develops many of the points posited in the Melville book. Hawthorne's "remarkable admission" in a August 7, 1851, letter to Horatio Bridge that he "liked" Melville "so much" he invited him to spend a few days in Lenox indicates that Hawthorne "was strongly, if perhaps ambiguously, attracted to Melville's assertive, seemingly outgoing personality."[16] It is hard to see the ambiguity in Hawthorne's enthusiasm. Indeed, the gratuitous qualification of his "liking" may derive from Miller's desire, however conditioned by social possibility, to promote the estrangement theory that has Hawthorne panicking in the face of Melville's (and presumably his own) attraction.

James R. Mellow, in *Nathaniel Hawthorne and His Times,* also emphasizes the erotic qualities of Melville's attraction to Hawthorne, even though he does not probe beneath the surface of the relationship itself. He cites the "astonishing" and "unmistakable sexual implications" of the imagery Melville employs in his review of *Mosses,* although he considers the "germinous seeds" passage "embarrassingly erotic": "In the essay's most extravagant and revealing metaphor, Melville described his response to Hawthorne's potency in a manner that was distinctly feminine and passive. In an odd merger of the agricultural and the physiological, he hinted at sexual climax."[17] Mellow's embarrassment perhaps derives from the persisting inversion paradigm he employs, in which erotic feelings for Hawthorne feminize Melville and, in turn, render him passive. Similarly, Mellow heterosexualizes the "climax" he senses in Melville's language. The possibility of a relationship and a sexual climax between men who retain their manhood in the process still seems beyond the reach of imagination in this 1980 study.

In his 1991 survey of scholarship on the Hawthorne-Melville friendship, James C. Wilson underscores the alleged "estrangement" of the two writers as well as what he repeatedly calls the possibility of "latent homosexuality" in Melville's attraction to Hawthorne.[18] Invoking the notion of latent homosexuality seems archaic, and the structure of "estrangement" begs most of the interesting questions—it defines the relationship backward, so to speak, by stressing its arguably vexed conclusion. In a 1984 essay, in fact, Wilson had argued that newly discovered Melville letters belied the estrangement theory because they seem to show cordial interactions between the two men after the alleged breach occurred.[19] Either way—estranged or not—the effect is to ignore the complexity of feeling between the two men, especially on Hawthorne's side where the letters are missing. If no estrangement occurred, the argument seems to be, it is unlikely that a homoerotic dimension existed. If the estrangement did occur, the effect is still to "cover" Hawthorne. What we now call homophobia and homosexual panic keep Hawthorne straight, resistant to Melville's advances. Whereas Melville's letters and review testify (for some scholarly jurors) to his homoerotic attraction to Hawthorne, Hawthorne's missing letters create a space where scholarly desire can preempt the possibility of reciprocal feeling. And Melville's feelings can be questioned, too, of course.

If this discussion is vexing, part of the reason is the historical moment of the encounter itself and of each interpretive act that succeeds it. Intimate male friendships were common in the nineteenth century, and it has been tempting for scholars to consider the precriminalization period a proto-gay utopia in which emotionally and physically intense relationships between men (and between women) bore none of the stigma we associate with most of the twentieth century.[20] On the verge of modern sexuality, Melville and Hawthorne had to find ways to give expression to their desires, in their lives as in their texts. As we confront similar problems, which we try to resolve as "queer," it is easy to see that earlier, more rigid paradigms are no longer very useful. The encounter of Hawthorne and Melville is an important site for the recognition of an evolving, or fluid, sexuality.

With the notable exception of Hershel Parker, recent biographers have not focused much attention on the Hawthorne-Melville friendship. Parker more than makes up for their reticence, devoting 150 pages in volume 1 of his Melville biography to the period when the two writers lived near one another. Parker certainly acknowledges the erotic feelings that Hawthorne aroused in Melville, although he goes to some length to displace those feelings from Hawthorne to other, more conventional love objects. He calls Melville's review of *Mosses* a "passionate private message to his new friend," and he speculates that "writing so intimately about Hawthorne's power to arouse his literary aspirations had left him more than a little febrile—excited intellectually, emotionally, and sexually—sexual arousal being for Melville an integral part of such intensely creative phases."[21] Parker concludes in fact by noting that in "this state of intense and undirected arousal Melville acted out an extraordinary display of deflected sexuality" (1:760). There follows a remarkable description of a kidnapping: "Lacking someone more appropriate to lavish

an excess of esteem upon, Melville abducted a younger man's bride"—
Mary Butler, wife of William A. Butler, whom Melville "whisked" into
his buggy and "whirled" away to the ancestral Melvill house. Melville left
Mary's husband to play catch up in a carriage with Evert Duyckinck, "all
the while imagining his wife somewhere ahead, in the hands of 'Typee,'
the American writer most notorious for his sexual conquests" (1:760).
Parker's language reveals a lot about the scholarly desire he brings to the
Melville-Hawthorne relationship—he acknowledges Melville's sexual
"arousal" but then displaces it onto a heterosexual encounter. This is a
perfect illustration of the triangulation of male-male relationships and
the homosexual panic that Eve Kosofsky Sedgwick has studied in *Between Men* and *Epistemology of the Closet.* But it could be Parker rather
than Melville who panics and attributes to Mary Butler's husband a different kind of panic that backhandedly compliments Melville's heterosexual prowess.

The evening of the same day as the incident with Butler's bride, Parker's Melville dressed up or perhaps allowed the women of his household
to dress him up as a Turk, a "figure society saw as sexually vigorous
and threatening" (1:761). Parker stops just short in these pages of analyzing the connection between Melville's arousal and his relationship with
Hawthorne. The "threatening" figure of unbridled sexuality that Melville makes as a Turk seems indiscriminately dangerous, even though
the energy for this display originated in his homoerotic response to
Hawthorne. The society Parker mentions might have found a homosex-
ually "vigorous" Turk even more threatening. If nothing else, this "extraordinary display of deflected sexuality" deserves more analysis for the
tensions it must have aroused in Melville. The sort of "deflection" that
Parker notes—a sublimation of desire in the review and a displacement
of desire onto a woman and into a carnivalesque disguise—makes sense
in the politics of nineteenth-century experience, but Parker's account
of events sheds no light on the internal struggle Melville must have experienced, even as it suggests delightfully ambivalent terms in which to
discuss (or not discuss) that struggle.

Laurie Robertson-Lorant devotes little space to the friendship in her
1996 Melville biography. She asserts that Edwin Haviland Miller's claims
"cannot be proved one way or another" and finds "no evidence" to support the "notion" that Melville made a sexual advance.[22] Her analysis
of the friendship seems governed by the assumption that the "behavior

of intimates, in any relationship, or combination of relationships, will always remain essentially mysterious to outsiders" (647n56). Resistance to imagining a less "mundane" relationship (645n45) may limit her ability to explore some of the potential literary consequences of this intense relationship. For example, citing the two men's August 2 visit with Julian Hawthorne and Evert Duyckinck to the Shaker Village in Hancock, she notes Hawthorne's revulsion at the way Shaker men slept in the same beds (270). "Melville certainly did not share Hawthorne's squeamishness," she recognizes, "as the opening chapters of *Moby-Dick* include hilarious descriptions of Ishmael and Queequeg sharing a honeymoon bed" (276). There is an important question here that Robertson-Lorant does not pursue—a question rooted in Melville's language. Telling Hawthorne "your heart beat in my ribs and mine in yours" as he reads the other's response to *Moby-Dick* recalls the marriage-bed scene between Ishmael and Queequeg (*WHM*, 14:212). The question is not just whether such language points to a sexual relationship between the two men but also how Melville's "astonishingly sexual" response to Hawthorne helped him represent a same-sex relationship in his novel and perhaps even revise the novel to make that relationship (not to mention the similar feelings expressed in "The Squeeze of the Hand") such an important counterpoint to Ahab's monomaniacal quest for Moby Dick. There is no doubt that Melville reacted to Hawthorne in an intense, erotically charged manner. The terms in which Hawthorne responded to Melville and the ways he may have translated that response into his own writing remain much more ambiguous.

Monika Mueller's *"This Infinite Fraternity of Feeling"* (1996) represents the most provocative scholarly attempt in the late twentieth century to explore the immediate literary effect of the Hawthorne-Melville relationship. Mueller pays little attention to the historical and cultural context of the friendship and offers no new insights as to what it might have meant for each man to feel desire for the other. Taking the homoerotic current between Hawthorne and Melville for granted, she applies it to *The Blithedale Romance* and *Pierre,* both of which read as "stories of male friendships doomed to fail because one of the two men involved could not tolerate the possibility of an erotic dimension in a male friendship."[23] The crux for Mueller, as for several earlier biographical scholars, is that Hawthorne felt "dismayed and confused by Melville's sexual interest in him" because it made him feel "feminized" (14). Gender anxiety then "caused" him to produce a text (*Blithedale*) dramatizing a "confu-

Queequeg and Ishmael at the Spouter-Inn. Rockwell Kent's illustration in *Moby-Dick; or, The Whale,* by Herman Melville (New York Random House, 1930), 36. By permission of the Plattsburgh State Art Museum, Plattsburgh College Foundation. Rockwell Kent Collection, bequest of Sally Kent Gorton.

sion of gender and genre," *Blithedale* being more feminine sentimental novel than masculine historical romance (15). The key moment in *Blithedale,* therefore, is Hollingsworth's attempted "homosexual rape" of Coverdale. "Afraid of being penetrated by Hollingsworth's phallic, rigid philanthropic idea," Coverdale "rebuffs his friend," reacting so violently against the "object" position in which this attempted rape places him that he determines to prove his manhood by differentiating himself from women (22). Similarly, Mueller argues that in *Pierre* "Melville reacts to Hawthorne's rebuff by dramatizing a failed male friendship that has dire consequences for everybody involved" (44).

The most recent biographies of the two writers—Brenda Wineapple's of Hawthorne and Andrew Delbanco's of Melville—give relatively few pages to the friendship. Like Robertson-Lorant and Wilson, Delbanco repeats the conventional wisdom that we "shall never know the details of their talks, the jokes they swapped, the judgments they discussed late into the night."[24] Citing the passage in which Melville asks "by what right" Hawthorne drinks from his "flagon of life," Delbanco does acknowledge the physicality of Melville's imagery—"it was as if their minds and hearts were linked by a common network of nerves and veins"—and he rec-

Hollingsworth to Coverdale: "There is not the man in this wide world whom I can love as I could you." From *The Blithedale Romance,* by Nathaniel Hawthorne (London: Service and Paton, 1899), illustration facing 158; quotation from 159.

ognizes that Melville was "drawn to the mysteries and contradictions in Hawthorne as if to plumb their depths would be to solve the riddle of existence itself" (137). Wineapple writes more suggestively, as if to keep possibilities open. She notes the "unmistakable" eroticism of the "germinous seeds" passage in Melville's review of *Mosses*.[25] And she summarizes the friendship in lyrical, sensual, emotionally rich terms that, in the limited space of a summary, honor a range of possible feelings and configurations:

> The two men enjoyed a friendship that echoes in the halls of American literature, where it's been probed, sexualized, and moralized, Hawthorne cast as a repressed and withholding father-figure, ungenerous to a fault, and Melville, needy son, rebuffed by the elder writer. Whenever Melville effused, Hawthorne shrank, or so it seems.
>
> Melville loved Hawthorne, of this there can be no doubt. And Hawthorne loved his male friends; he didn't need to categorize or condemn his feelings, or to fear them. He also cared for Melville. But Hawthorne did not love Melville, not the way—whatever way that was—that Melville needed love. (227)

"Whatever way that was"—the expression captures the ambiguity of nineteenth-century thinking about desire and sex, friendship, brotherhood, and love. Even though Wineapple evokes the conventionally understood dynamic of the relationship—Melville effused, Hawthorne shrank—her shifting the question from sex to love represents a useful revision of the terms in which we think of possibilities.

The Scholarly Chase: Present Days

Some biographical critics might protest that, in the absence of concrete new discoveries about how Hawthorne and Melville figured personally in each other's lives—especially during the sixteen-month period of their friendship's greatest intensity—there is not much more to say, but the essayists of the present venture prove that idea wrong from richly different points of view, in some cases spotlighting the biographical dimension and in others concentrating on common ground in the writing. Exploration of this deceptively narrow moment in literary history, they variously argue—and persuasively demonstrate—continues to give us fresh insights in such areas as mutual literary influence, political and social ideology, literary professionalism and marketplace analysis, psychoanalytical and philosophical applications to literature, gender issues, queer theory, and critical studies of race. While the collection has something to add to our understanding of American national narrative in the nineteenth century, it also extends across both temporal and geographical boundaries (from Roman pantheism to Renaissance notions of authorship to Italian revolutionary politics)—entering into the globalist conversation that is newly urgent for scholars today.

As the table of contents indicates, five of the essays move in largely biographical directions, while the other seven address themselves more strongly to literary connections between specific writings. In the cluster of biographically centered essays, we feature a recent Melville biographer, Laurie Robertson-Lorant—who introduces the collection by recounting the vivid episodes of friendship, those relatively few times when the two met in flesh or letter—and the most recent Hawthorne biographer, Brenda Wineapple—who traces the subtle literary politics that shaped their views of each other, finding in Melville an iconoclastic father figure whom Hawthorne both loved and feared. The next brace of essays, by Robert Milder and Gale Temple, extensively treats the Hawthorne-Melville affiliation in light of contemporary sexual and gender theory: Milder pursues the question of what Melville's "affection" for Hawthorne would have signified "within the context of mid-nineteenth-century male friendships as they were understood by the participants themselves and as they have variously come to be characterized by modern interpreters" (72); Temple takes this question into the thicketed border between economic being and gender identity, placing in tension, on the one hand, a capitalist (masculine) consumerism that perpetuates itself by keeping consummation always just beyond reach and, on the other, "an intimate bond with another man at some psychic, spiritual, or physical level" that might fill voids the marketplace works to maintain (114). And the section finale by Dennis Berthold crosses the Atlantic to track, through England and Italy, underexplored political trajectories in the latter days of the evolving, and perhaps waning, friendship between these two men.

In the more strictly literary essays, we have tried to ensure balanced coverage of the major works both writers produced after they first met. Robert Sattelmeyer, and to some extent Wyn Kelley, emphasize Hawthorne's influence on *Moby-Dick*—Sattelmeyer in the course of a detailed analysis of the novel's transformation during its complicated two-year gestation and Kelley in tandem with her primary attention to "Agatha"—the "most remarkable story Melville and Hawthorne never wrote *together*"— and the "dream" of Renaissance-style collaboration (174). Robert Levine explores intersections between *The House of the Seven Gables* and *Pierre*, steering away from an "overly biographical focus" on the fictionalization of mutual "feelings" to discover "a literary conversation between these great writers on questions of racial and national identity" (228). Finding the stubborn shade of Melville in both *The House of the Seven Gables* and *The Blithedale Romance*, Thomas Mitchell inverts the usual critical diagram of influence and emphasizes the challenge that the younger man posed for Hawthorne as an author—in complement to biographer Wineapple's reading of the friendship. Richard Hardack considers the writers' responses to Italy, bringing the "transcendental American pantheism" (269) dramatized in Melville's novels, from *Mardi* to *Pierre*, into contact with *The Marble Faun* and its complex critique of Catholicism. Pairing two critically neglected stories, Hawthorne's "Feathertop" and Melville's "Apple-Tree Table," Ellen Weinauer shows that fruitful mutualities run through the smaller as through the larger fictional efforts: these tales register the vexed power that spiritualism holds for both authors, which partly lies, Weinauer argues, in the movement's "challenge to the models of (sovereign, male) individualism at work in antebellum culture" (299)—a challenge "made more urgent" and personal by its resonance with the absorbed relationship between the two, which Melville repeatedly figures as "identic transposition" (311). And Chris Castiglia, in productive counterpoint to Berthold's transnational narrative, concludes the volume by contesting the common view that the bond of friendship came undone: "Melville and Hawthorne moved through and beyond national metaphors" for affective ties "to explore the possibilities of imperialism, universalism, and . . . *trans-intimacy*" (321–22)—an intimacy that doesn't depend on permanence or proximity, a state of relation made healthy and lively in proportion to the ways it values vagabond desire, as this essay's reading of Melville's monumental poem *Clarel* attests.

Most of the treatments we have labeled biographical nonetheless pay considerable attention to the literary works. Wineapple draws surprising relational insights from *The House of the Seven Gables, The Blithedale Romance,* and the "Agatha" story manqué. Milder treats virtually all of the important writings after 1850, including *Clarel,* and Berthold weaves a range of literary reference into his political commentary. Temple examines *The Blithedale Romance* as well as *Moby-Dick* and *Pierre*, after uncovering in *The Scarlet Letter* an uncanny prolepsis of the Hawthorne-Melville relationship. And Melville's anonymous review of *Mosses from an Old Manse* is, of course, never far from sight. Those essays labeled literary are likewise averse to strict categorical discipline. Our two-part organization, in fact, to some provocative degree undoes itself, pointing to an overarching concern of the collection: all the contributions are in a fundamental way about the boundary that the biographical and literary subheadings provisionally set up and the fictional "Letters on Foolscap" manifestly straddles—variously pushing at it, puzzling over it, disavowing its presence for purposes of criticism, or resisting crossover.

Epilogue

At the very end of volume 1 of his Melville biography, Hershel Parker stages a scene between Hawthorne and Melville that sends chills up the spine and reveals the hot lines of scholarly desire that this mysterious relationship inspires. Parker reasons that the only way Hawthorne could have read *Moby-Dick* in time to write his (missing) letter of praise to Melville was if Melville handed him a copy of the book prior to his departure from Lenox (1:882). *Moby-Dick* was officially published on November 14, 1851, and Melville invited Hawthorne to join him at Curtis's hotel in Lenox for a formal farewell dinner, perhaps on that very day. "At some well-chosen moment Melville took out the book whose publication they had both been awaiting and handed his friend an inscribed copy of *Moby-Dick,* the first presentation copy," Parker writes (1:882). Melville might have been robbed of this moment if the book had been delayed, of course, and thus of "the time when his friend held in his hand his farewell gift, the printed and bound book, a tangible token of Melville's admiration for his genius. Take it all in all," Parker concludes, "this was the happiest day of Melville's life" (1:878–79, 1:883). If this scene too neatly sublimates desire in art, substituting a book for the hand that Melville might have wished to squeeze, it positively drips with emotion and emotional release—Parker's at least as much as Melville's.

As for Hawthorne's response to Melville's gift and dedication of *Moby-Dick* in "admiration for his genius"? Hawthorne's letter is missing, and whether he took Melville's injunction not to "write a word about the book" to heart or simply did not choose to write more than he had in that missing letter, he did not review the novel (*WHM*, 14:213). He surely had Melville in mind when he wrote *The Blithedale Romance* about six months later. Melville's ecstatic reaction to Hawthorne's epistolary notice—"your heart beat in my ribs and mine in yours"—recalls the melting Ishmael experiences after sleeping with Queequeg and again in "The Squeeze of the Hand," and it anticipates Coverdale's unguarded response to Hollingsworth's "more than brotherly" nursing: "There never was any blaze of a fireside that warmed and cheered me, in the down-sinkings and shiverings of my spirit, so effectually as did the light out of those eyes, which lay so deep and dark under his shaggy brows" (*CE*, 3:41, 3:42). Melville's readerly desire would have been quick to flame, but our own desire suggests that Hawthorne's words encouraged his heart to beat. In his December 1, 1851, letter to their mutual friend Evert Duyckinck, Hawthorne would exclaim: "What a book Melville has written! It gives me an idea of much greater power than his preceding ones." Hawthorne had written Horatio Bridge two days after meeting Melville for the first time that he "liked him so much" he had invited him to visit for a few days (*CE*, 16:335, 16:508). Sixteen months later he was still singing Melville's praises. Melville was still causing his heart to beat.

Notes

1. Arvin uses the term "astonishingly sexual image" to describe the "germinous seeds" passage in Melville's review; see *Herman Melville*, 138. For the passage itself, see *WHM*, 9:250.

2. James C. Wilson provides a comprehensive and balanced survey of early studies, both critical and biographical, in *Hawthorne and Melville Friendship*. His annotated bibliography is especially valuable for its summaries.

3. Martin, *Hero, Captain, and Stranger*, 63.

4. Werth, *Scarlet Professor*, 37.

5. Arvin, *Hawthorne*, 6; hereafter cited parenthetically.

6. Arvin, *Herman Melville*, 128; hereafter cited parenthetically. In "Newton Arvin: Literary Critic and Lewd Person," Robert K. Martin notes Arvin's "reliance upon a largely Freudian model, and in particular the assumption of a connection between male homosexuality and excessive affection between mother and son" (309).

7. Werth, *Scarlet Professor*, 35.

8. See, for example, Bergman, "F. O. Matthiessen," in *Gaiety Transfigured*; Grossman, "Canon in the Closet"; and Foster, "Matthiessen's Public Privates."

9. Bergman, *Gaiety Transfigured*, 94, 96. Through such covert strategies, in Bergman's view, Matthiessen erected "virtually a gay canon of American literature" (96).

10. Matthiessen, *American Renaissance*, 186–87; hereafter cited parenthetically.

11. Weaver, *Herman Melville*, 15; hereafter cited parenthetically. Also see *WHM*, 14:191–92.

12. Mumford, *Herman Melville*, 139; hereafter cited parenthetically.

13. Stewart, *Nathaniel Hawthorne*, 101; hereafter cited parenthetically.

14. Howard, *Herman Melville*, 168; hereafter cited parenthetically.

15. Miller, *Melville*, 249–50, 36. Also see Watson, "Estrangement." Hawthorne, Watson concludes, "became increasingly aware that Melville [needed] an extraordinary degree of personal intimacy. While the yearnings of the spirit could be tolerated, any suggestion that those yearnings were also of the flesh—however latently—would surely have been sufficient to alarm Hawthorne to the point of flight" (402).

16. Miller, *Salem Is My Dwelling Place*, 311. Also see *CE*, 16:355.

17. Mellow, *Nathaniel Hawthorne*, 335.

18. Wilson, "An Essay in Bibliography," 19–39.

19. Wilson, "Melville at Arrowhead," 233; repr. in *Hawthorne and Melville Friendship*, 202.

20. See Katz, *Love Stories*.

21. Parker, *Herman Melville*, 1:760; hereafter cited parenthetically.

22. Robertson-Lorant, *Melville*, 645n41; hereafter cited parenthetically.

23. Mueller, *"This Infinite Fraternity of Feeling,"* 14; hereafter cited parenthetically.

24. Delbanco, *Melville*, 137; hereafter cited parenthetically.

25. Wineapple, *Hawthorne*, 224; hereafter cited parenthetically.

Toward the Biographical

Mr. Omoo and the Hawthornes

The Biographical Background

Laurie Robertson-Lorant

IN THE SUMMER of 1850, Melville reviewed Nathaniel Hawthorne's *Mosses from an Old Manse* for the *Literary World*. "I feel that this Hawthorne has dropped germinous seeds into my soul," Melville wrote. "He expands and deepens down, the more I contemplate him; and further, and further, shoots his strong New-England roots into the hot soil of my Southern soul" (*WHM*, 9:250). This eroticized rendering of the conventional trope for seminal artistic influence rivals some of the sexiest passages in literature—not least among them the scene where Hester Prynne and Arthur Dimmesdale meet in the forest after seven years of penitential separation and express their passion in taut, nearly wordless breaths.

Hawthorne, the older New England author of *Twice-Told Tales*, *Mosses from an Old Manse*, and *The Scarlet Letter*, had reviewed Melville's first book. The young New Yorker whose forebears were patrician Melvilles and Gansevoorts had gone whaling in 1841 and returned from the South Seas to write, in 1846, the alluring and scandalous *Typee: A Peep at Polynesian Life*. *Typee* appealed to readers who liked travel narratives about picturesque places and exotic natives far removed from themselves, and at the same time it echoed the social and economic idealism that inspired Fourierist communities like Brook Farm. Bronson Alcott, Margaret Fuller, Henry Wadsworth Longfellow, George Ripley, Henry David Thoreau, and Walt Whitman all praised *Typee* for its sympathetic portrayal of Marquesan life and its attacks on colonialism. Evert Duyckinck, editor of the *Literary World*, recommended *Typee* as "a lively and pleasant book, not over philosophical, perhaps" (*Log,* 206), and sent a copy to Nathaniel Hawthorne, who reviewed it for the *Salem Advertiser.* A disillusioned sojourner at Brook Farm, Hawthorne wrote that "no work . . . gives a freer and more effective picture of barbarian life" but scolded Melville for tolerating "codes of morals" quite different from those of his own culture (*Log,* 207–8). Four years later, the two men would finally meet.

In May 1850, Nathaniel Hawthorne moved his wife Sophia (Peabody) and their two children, Julian and Una, from Salem to a guest cottage on the Lenox estate of William Aspinwall Tappan. There, with a spectacular view of Lake Mahkeenac and Monument Mountain, the devoted husband and father and reclusive author of *The Scarlet Letter* worked on his next book, *The House of the Seven Gables.*

Herman Melville, who had written four more books in quick succession based on his voyages to Liverpool and the South Seas, was now toiling over a book about the sperm-whale fishery. Finding it almost impossible to concentrate during a heat wave in the three-story Manhattan brownstone he shared with his wife Elizabeth, younger brother Allan and Allan's wife Sophia Thurston Melville, plus their mother and four sisters and two teething toddlers, Melville decided to take Lizzie, Sophia, and the little boys to the old Melvill house in Pittsfield.

As a boy, Herman had spent several happy summers on the Berkshire farm helping his eccentric uncle Thomas Melvill with the chores and discovering nature with his bright, inquisitive cousin Julia Maria. In August 1848, when Lizzie was pregnant with their first child and Herman was exhausted from working on *Mardi,* he had taken Lizzie to Pittsfield to rusticate at the old Melvill house, which his aunt Mary Melvill and her son Robert and wife ran as an inn, welcoming such guests as Henry Wadsworth Longfellow and Massachusetts senator Charles Sumner.

Soon after Herman and Lizzie arrived at the inn in July 1850, Aunt Mary gave her nephew a copy of *Mosses from an Old Manse,* but he barely had time to glance at the book before his cousin Robert invited him on the agricultural tour of South County Robert was required to make as chairman of the Viewing Committee of the Berkshire County Agricultural Society. While the two men were rambling through the hills inspecting farms, Robert managed to talk his cousin into ghostwriting his report. Melville wrote the report with tongue in cheek, then went back to the city to rescue his mother and sisters from the heat and tropical diseases that took the lives of men, women, and children every summer.

Melville probably read *Mosses from an Old Manse* on the train bound for New York. In any case, he was charmed by this "rare, quiet book" (*WHM*, 9:240). Sensing that its author was "a man of a deep and noble nature" (*WHM*, 9:239) who veiled his face and did not invite his readers to go wandering hand in hand with him through the inner passages of his being, as "The Old Manse" phrased it, Melville was enchanted by Hawthorne's witchery—the dappled sunshine and shadow of his sinuous, muted prose, his sudden shifts from shade to light and back again, his strange alterations of languid reverie with violence told matter-of-factly, his ambivalent references to American Indians and his digs at Puritan divines, and his anxieties about his literary vocation. Melville was eager to meet a fellow writer who shared his obsession with history, guilt, and spiritual death.

While in Manhattan, Melville invited Evert Duyckinck, who had arranged the reissue of Hawthorne's *Mosses from an Old Manse* in Wiley and Putnam's Library of America in 1846 (the same year *Typee* appeared in that series), and Cornelius Mathews to join him in the Berkshires for the weekend. Mathews, former editor of *Yankee Doodle* magazine, was the author of two novels, *Little Abel and the Big Manhattan* and *Behemoth: A Legend of the Mound-Builders.* On the train they met attorney David Dudley Field, who invited Duyckinck, Mathews, and Melville to meet Hawthorne at a picnic on Monument Mountain followed by dinner at his summer home in Stockbridge. The following day, neighbor Sarah Morewood arrived to take the Melvilles and their New York writer friends on an afternoon excursion to Pontoosuc Lake. The irrepressible Mrs. Morewood arrived suitably garbed "in linen sack" and "armed with a bait box and fishing rod for the finny sport," while Lizzie Melville, who was not yet outfitted for rusticity, appeared in "a great flopping straw hat tied under the chin, floating about with the zephyrs in blue, pink or lilac" (*Log*, 383).

Between the Melvilles' third wedding anniversary on August 4 and the departure of Duyckinck and Mathews on August 12, Melville, his family, and his guests enjoyed a constant round of parties, picnics, dinners, rambles, hikes, and even a masquerade ball. On a misty August 5, small birds singing "sweeter than the Sunday newsboys or the demented milk man" awakened Duyckinck, Mathews, and Melville, who dressed

and went to the railway station to catch the train.[1] At the station in Pittsfield, they met Dr. Oliver Wendell Holmes, professor of anatomy at Harvard and dean of the medical school as well as a novelist, a poet, and the
Atlantic Monthly's "Autocrat of the Breakfast Table." Dudley Field met his
guests at the Stockbridge station and drove them to Eden Hill, the country estate Frederick Law Olmsted had designed for him. The four men
were hardly out of the carriage when Melville, followed by the New Yorkers, charged up a nearby hill to rehearse the great climb up Monument
Mountain, while they waited for Nathaniel Hawthorne to arrive with
James and Eliza Fields. When Hawthorne came on the scene, it was in
a "sumptuous" carriage driven by Fields. (Sophia had apparently stayed
behind in Lenox, as she and Nathaniel took turns minding the children
so that at least one of them could attend social functions.) Minutes later,
Harry Sedgwick, novelist Catharine Maria Sedgwick's nephew, showed
up on horseback to pilot three wagons over the rutted roads to the base
of the mountain.

For a piece called "Several Days in Berkshire," which appeared in the
Literary World on August 24, 1850, Cornelius Mathews would dub Evert
Duyckinck "Silver Pen," Melville "New Neptune," Hawthorne "Mr. Noble
Melancholy," and Dr. Holmes "Mr. Town Wit." James Fields and his wife
Eliza, who came dressed for Boston's boulevards, not the Berkshire Hills,
became "Mr. Greenfield" and "The Violet of the Season." Young Sedg-
wick became "Harry Gallant, a twig of a celebrated Stockbridge tree," and
David Dudley Field became "Our Stately Inviter" (*Log,* 384).

As the climbers trooped up the mountain, "a black thunder cloud
from the south dragged its ragged skirts towards [them]—the thunder
rolling in the distance," and a sudden shower drove them under an over-
hanging rock. The portly Dr. Holmes playfully "cut three branches for an
umbrella" to protect the ladies, and then amid a fair amount of ribbing
for toting his "glazed India-rubber bag" up the mountain (*Log,* 383–84),
he opened the bag to reveal several bottles of chilled champagne, which
he dispensed in silver mugs.

Melville and Hawthorne established a champagne-lubricated rap-
port that melted Hawthorne's customary reserve. By the time the rain
stopped, Melville was slightly tipsy and eager to reach the top of the
mountain, so he sprinted ahead in his typical fashion, while the others
puffed their way up the last steep hundred yards, clambering over ledges
of rock. From the mountain's masthead, sixteen-hundred feet above sea

level, Melville could see the Housatonic Valley to the south and Greylock breaching like a whale on the horizon.

Melville, "the boldest of all," dashed onto a peaked rock that jutted out like the bowsprit of a ship, and legs braced, the former sailor hauled "imaginary ropes" for the "delectation" of his companions, as Fields reported in *Yesterdays with Authors*. Meanwhile, Hawthorne pretended to be looking "mildly around for the great Carbuncle." Finally they "assembled in a shady spot," and out of deference to the New Englanders in the party, Cornelius Mathews toasted Longfellow, wishing "'long life to the dear old poet'" (*Log,* 384). Then he read William Cullen Bryant's "Monument Mountain," a poetic retelling of the legend of the Indian maiden who jumped to her death to escape punishment for loving a young brave from a rival tribe. When the poor girl landed in a tree, her angry tribesmen set the mountain on fire to bring her down, and her grieving family erected a cairn of stones as her monument.

After the climb, the merrymakers rode back to Dudley Field's house for an enormous midday dinner of "turkeys and beeves" (*Log,* 383), well fortified with appropriate wines, brandies, and champagnes and finished off sweetly with huge dollops of homemade ice cream. Hawthorne's publisher was surprised that the normally shy author "rayed out in a sparkling and unwonted manner." He had never seen "Hawthorne in better spirits" and pronounced it "a happy day throughout" (*Log,* 384).

During the three-hour-long repast, the men fell to discussing Melville's observation in *White-Jacket* that British sailors were physically stronger than American seamen. Before long, they found themselves in a heated debate about American and British authors. Holmes laid down "several propositions of the superiority of Englishmen," and Melville "attacked him vigorously" while Hawthorne just "looked on" (*Log,* 384).

After they had devoured as much food and drink as they could in one sitting, the intoxicated revelers roared through nearby Ice Glen, scrambling over gigantic boulders and sliding through tunnels between the huge, moss-covered rocks. Keeping pace with the rambunctious Melville, Hawthorne proved "among the most enterprising of the merrymakers," according to Fields (*Log,* 384). Proclaiming that Ice Glen looked "as if the Devil had torn his way through a rock & left it all jagged behind" (*Log,* 923), Hawthorne playfully boomed warnings that "certain destruction" awaited anyone who took another step (*Log,* 384). Heading back to the house, someone noticed that Hawthorne and Melville were nowhere to be seen, and fearing an accident, the group backtracked and found the two men deep in conversation.

Fortunately, they arrived at Eden Hill in time to have tea with the first lady of American letters, Catharine Maria Sedgwick, a regular summer visitor at the home of her brother Charles and his wife, Elizabeth, head of a school in Lenox for young ladies, one of whom was Melville's sister Helen. Miss Sedgwick had published a number of novels that paved the way for the historical fiction of James Fenimore Cooper and Nathaniel Hawthorne, among them *A New England Tale* (1822); the popular *Hope Leslie* (1827), an exploration of relationships between Indians and settlers; and *The Linwoods* (1835), a romance of the Revolutionary War that Helen Melville recommended to her sister Augusta as Sedgwick's best novel so far.

When Miss Sedgwick asked Melville what he was working on, he told her he had "a new book mostly done—a romantic, fanciful & literal & most enjoyable presentment of the Whale Fishery—something quite new" (*Log*, 385). She then subjected Duyckinck to "a cross examination on Hope Leslie and Magawisca" that revealed how woefully ignorant the editor of the *Literary World* was about her work (*Log*, 384). Although we have no direct evidence that Melville read any of Sedgwick's novels, hearing Miss Sedgwick grill Duyckinck about *Hope Leslie* may have made him curious to read that iconoclastic book.

Several of Melville's writings reflect Sedgwick's influence. The "bosom" friendship of Ishmael and Queequeg, for example, owes at least as much of a literary debt to the blood sisterhood of Hope Leslie and the proud, heroic Magawisca as it does to Cooper's stilted relationships between Indians and settlers. The opening chapters of *Pierre* evoke Sedgwick's historicized landscapes ironically, and "Poor Man's Pudding and Rich Man's Crumbs" appears to be Melville's pessimistic response to Sedgwick's *The Poor Rich Man and the Rich Poor Man* (1836).

On August 7, Melville and his guests, still in high spirits, rode over to call on Hawthorne at the "red shanty" where the couple had entertained such distinguished visitors as English novelist G. P. R. James; poet-critic James Russell Lowell, a future editor of the *Atlantic Monthly*; and Swedish novelist Frederika Bremer, who liked to seclude herself in the morning lest she risk "being sent to a mad-house by American hospitality."[2] Hawthorne greeted his visitors by opening a bottle of Heidsieck and, "popping the corks in his nervous way" (*Log*, 386), told them an aspiring poet named Mansfield had provided it for toasting the "next genius" he met. Both Nathaniel and Sophia seem to have realized that Herman Melville was that genius. Sophia Hawthorne studied Melville intently and later wrote her sister Elizabeth: "Mr Typee is interesting in his aspect—quite. I see Fayaway in his face" (*Log,* 923). Although Hawthorne tended to be shy and defensive with new people, he had liked *Typee* "uncommonly well" and Melville so much that he invited him to return for a longer visit (*Log,* 211, 389).

Friday, August 9, dawned rainy and overcast, giving Melville the whole morning to write—or continue writing—his review of *Mosses from an Old Manse* for the *Literary World.* Sitting in "a papered chamber" in the "fine old farm-house—a mile from any other dwelling and dipped to the eaves in foliage—surrounded by mountains, old woods, and Indian ponds," he poured out his admiration of "the Man of Mosses" (*WHM,* 9:239–40). Meanwhile Lizzie and the women "ransacked" the house, gathering "green goggles, yellow stuff for breeches, antique hats, long-tail coats, brought down from garrets; heavy boots, of a past fashion, fished up from cellars" for Sarah Morewood's masquerade ball (*Log,* 386), to which Melville went disguised as a Turk.

August 10 was overcast, giving the revelers an excuse to sleep a little later than usual and Melville a chance to finish the review so Duyckinck could take it back to New York in time for the next issue of the *Literary World.* By Sunday afternoon, Melville may have been able to show Duyckinck his finished article on Hawthorne before giving it to Lizzie to make the fair copy (*WHM,* 14:168).

Reading *Mosses from an Old Manse* was a catalytic event for Melville, comparable to John Keats's discovery of Chapman's Homer, and the review he would write was a tour de force of self-discovery and self-disclosure. He had sensed from the stories that Hawthorne was a kindred spirit, and meeting and talking with him had confirmed his intuition. In this writer whose sunlight masked "the blackness of darkness beyond," Melville recognized a universal genius "immeasurably deeper than the plummet of the mere critic" (*WHM,* 9:243–44). Melville's portrait of Hawthorne as a writer whose fictions conceal dark, subversive truths is clearly as much a projection of his own complex relationship to his texts, his family, and the reading public as a portrait of "the Man of Mosses."

Writing pseudonymously as "a Virginian Spending July in Vermont," Melville challenged the Boston critics who, he said, saw Hawthorne as "a pleasant writer, with a pleasant style,—a sequestered, harmless man, from whom any deep and weighty thing would hardly be anticipated:—a man who means no meanings" (*WHM*, 9:242). The "Virginian" challenged the New York critics, too, by dismissing Washington Irving as "a very popular and amiable writer" but one who, despite being "good, and self-reliant in many things, perhaps owes his chief reputation to the self-acknowledged imitation of a foreign model, and to the studied avoidance of all topics but smooth ones" (*WHM*, 9:247). A great writer, opined the "Virginian," should not have to bend to fit into a literary circle or swim in a particular "school." He should eschew both the innocuous pleasantries of New York's Knickerbocker school and the "literary flunkeyism" of Boston's Anglophiles.

For Melville, Hawthorne was a genius whose soul was "Indian-summer sunlight," on one side, "shrouded in blackness, ten times black," on the other (*WHM*, 9:243). Of all American writers, he had "the largest brain with the largest heart" (*WHM*, 9:253). Citing Shakespeare's popularity in American towns from the eastern seaboard to the western frontier as evidence that "lofty" literature could be popular with democratic audiences, Melville proclaimed Hawthorne the American Shakespeare or, at the very least, the precursor of an American Bard of bards who was destined to emerge as a result of Hawthorne's inspiration and example.

By exploring the dark side of the American experience, Hawthorne's tales of Puritan guilt, self-righteousness, and gloom paved the way for Melville to expose the deeper, darker truths that lay behind the myths on which America was founded. To the modern reader, Melville seems more Shakespearean than Hawthorne because his range of subjects is so much wider and his characters are so much more diverse; furthermore, he is capable of broader comedy than Hawthorne. Melville relished Shakespeare's bawdy, ribald humor as much as he savored the high tragedy, but he felt Hawthorne was the one American writer endowed with the tragic sense the country needed to reach cultural maturity. In *Moby-Dick* and most of his subsequent work, Melville would do what he imagined Hawthorne was trying to do: he would "write the *other* way" (*WHM*, 14:191).

After Lizzie Melville finished making the fair copy of "Hawthorne and His Mosses" for the printer from her husband's inky manuscript, he added the punctuation and gave it to Evert Duyckinck. By the time

Duyckinck and Mathews reached New York, Melville was ready to chase his "Whale" again. Rummaging around in the corn loft of the carriage house, he found an old desk whitened with the guano of pigeons who had laid their eggs in the pocky wood, and, hauling it to the "*garret-way*" of the house, he placed it at a "little embrasure of a window . . . which command[ed] so noble a view of Saddleback" (*WHM*, 14:167) and dove back into the book we know as *Moby-Dick*.

When Melville's essay "Hawthorne and his Mosses" appeared in two successive installments in the *Literary World* on August 17 and August 24, 1850, it revealed as much about Melville's own aspirations as it revealed about Hawthorne's achievements. When Melville exhorted readers to "confess" Hawthorne as though he were a personal savior and "[em]brace the whole brotherhood" of literary men—"for genius, all over the world, stands hand in hand, and one shock of recognition runs the whole circle round" (*WHM*, 9:249)—he was consciously, or unconsciously, voicing his hope that readers would embrace him as well.

When Sophia Hawthorne read the review, she was so moved that she wrote an appreciative letter to Evert Duyckinck, calling the marvelous Virginian the "first person who has ever in *print* apprehended Mr Hawthorne," a critic of "generous, noble enthusiasm" who "surrounds himself with a glory" while "bringing out the glory of his subject" (*CE*, 16:361). Whoever the author of these "inspired utterances" was (*CE*, 16:361), he had spoken her "secret mind," Sophia marveled in a separate letter that urged sister Elizabeth to read the review immediately. Sophia felt the reviewer rightly compared her husband to "the Swan of Avon," discovering in him "the Great Heart & the Grand Intellect combined" (*Log*, 924); and she begged Duyckinck to reveal the Virginian's identity: "The freshness of primeval nature is in that man, & the true Promethean fire is in him. Who can he be, so fearless, so rich in heart, of such fine intuition? Is his name altogether hidden?" (*CE*, 16:361).

When Melville arrived at the red house for several days' visit at the beginning of September in response to Hawthorne's invitation, neither Nathaniel nor Sophia knew he was the author of "Hawthorne and His Mosses." Sophia described Melville to her mother at length, as "a man with a true warm heart & a soul & an intellect—with life to his finger-tips—earnest, sincere & reverent, very tender & *modest*" (*Log*, 393). Mesmerized by his languid, seductive eyes, she went on:

> I am not quite sure that I *do not think him* a very great man. . . . He has
> very keen perceptive power, but what astonishes me is, that his eyes are
> not large & deep—He seems to see every thing very accurately, & how he
> can do so with his small eyes, I cannot tell. They are not keen eyes, either,
> but quite undistinguished in any way. His nose is straight & rather hand-
> some, his mouth expressive of sensibility & emotion—He is tall & erect
> with an air free, brave, & manly. When conversing, he is full of gesture &
> force, & loses himself in his subject—There is no grace nor polish—once
> in a while, his animation gives place to a singularly quiet expression
> out of those eyes, to which I have objected—an indrawn, dim look, but
> which at the same time makes you feel—that he is at that instant taking
> deepest note of what is before him—It is a strange, lazy glance, but with
> a power in it quite unique—It does not seem to penetrate through you,
> but to take you into himself. (*Log*, 393–94)

Melville could not keep his secret for long because they talked about
the article constantly. Finally he confessed that he was "the Virginian,"
and he and Sophia had "some delightful conversations . . . about the
'sweetest Man of Mosses'" (*Log*, 924). Sitting out on the verandah of the
red house "in the golden light of evening twilight, when the lake was
like glass of a rose tint," Melville told Sophia that "Hawthorne was the
first person whose physical being appeared to him wholly in harmony
with the intellectual & spiritual" and that the "sunny hair & the pen-
siveness, the symmetry of his face, the depth of eyes, 'the gleam—the
shadow—& the peace supreme' all were in exact response to the high
calm intellect, the glowing, deep heart—the purity of actual & spiritual
life" (*Log*, 924).

Mutual adoration of Hawthorne became their bond, and Melville's
endearing combination of boyish enthusiasm and manly sensuality appealed to Sophia as much as her charm and intellect appealed to Melville.
"Mr. Melville," she wrote, "is a person of great ardor & simplicity" and
"all on fire with the subject that interests him. It rings through his frame
like a cathedral bell. His truth & honesty shine out at every point. At the
same time he sees things artistically, as you perceive in his books. I have
just read again Typee. It is a *true history*, yet how poetically told—the
divine beauty of the scene, the lovely faces & forms—the peace & good
will—& all this golden splendor & enchantment glowing before the dark
refrain constantly brought as a background—the fear of being killed &

eaten—the cannibalism in the olive tinted Apollos around him—the unfathomable mystery of their treatment of him" (*Log,* 924–25). If Melville and Hawthorne had never met, we would not have Sophia's keen impressions of Melville.

Melville's writing was going so well that he hated to break his stride by leaving the Berkshires, and besides, he was enjoying himself immensely, so he decided to stay. In mid-September, with a three-thousand-dollar loan from Lizzie's father, Lemuel Shaw, the chief justice of the Massachusetts Supreme Judicial Court, Melville bought a 160-acre farm abutting the old Melvill property from Dr. John Brewster, who moved to East Street, nearer town. Situated about two and a half miles from Pittsfield, the farm included a "quaint old house, built in the early days of the settlement of the town, by Capt. David Bush," according to the *Pittsfield Sun.* Although Melville told the Hawthornes he intended to build a "real towered house" on the property (*Log,* 925), in the thirteen years he lived in Pittsfield, he never had enough money to do so.

In early October, the *Pittsfield Sun* reported that Sarah and John Rowland Morewood had decided to become permanent residents of Pittsfield and that Herman Melville had bought a farm not far from the summer residence of Dr. Oliver Wendell Holmes. Soon after, the *Boston Daily Times* announced, "Herman Melville, the popular young author, has purchased a farm in Berkshire county, Mass., about thirty miles from Albany, where he intends to raise poultry, turnips, babies, and other vegetables" (*Log,* 926). Melville did indeed raise corn, turnips, potatoes, pumpkins, and four children on the farm.

The record is spotty until January 1851, when Melville impulsively set off to visit the Hawthornes in Lenox, where he found the red cottage buried in snow and Hawthorne hard at work finishing *The House of the Seven Gables.* Hawthorne did not like impromptu visits and was not in the mood for company, but Sophia gave Melville the "warmest of welcomes" and served him a supper of cold chicken. She also gave him a copy of *Grandfather's Chair* for son Malcolm, and when Hawthorne joined them for supper, he presented Melville with a copy of *Twice-Told Tales.* Melville, who had read only "A Rill from the Town Pump," considered these stories even more subtle than the "Mosses," although they were "an earlier vintage from his vine" (*WHM,* 14:179–81).

Melville invited the Hawthornes, whom he described to his sister Augusta as "the loveliest family he ever met with, or anyone can imagine,"[3]

Melville's drawing of Arrowhead, his farm near Pittsfield, Massachusetts, 1860.
From *Herman Melville: Mystic and Mariner,* by Raymond Weaver (New York: Doran, 1921), facing 368.

to come for a few days' visit at Arrowhead within the next fortnight, and when Sophia agreed, he was pleased, as he was looking forward to "getting [Hawthorne] up in my snug room here, & discussing the Universe with a bottle of brandy & cigars" (*WHM,* 14:180). When Augusta heard Hawthorne was coming, she was so nervous at the prospect of meeting him face-to-face that she urged Helen to come home immediately and lend her superior "powers of entertainment" to the occasion (MFP, January 24, 1851).

Several days later, Sophia Hawthorne sent word that they would only be able to visit for a day, not a whole week, as Hawthorne couldn't tear himself away from his new book for long. Disappointed, Melville wrote Hawthorne a mock protest against this "side-blow," accusing Sophia of keeping him home by means of her "syrenisims" and reissuing his invitation: "Your bed is already made, & the wood marked for your fire." Two fowls, moreover, were "destined" as "victims for the table." "I keep the word 'Welcome' all the time in my mouth," Melville declared, "so as to be ready on the instant when you cross the threshold. . . . Do not think you are coming to any prim nonsensical house—that is nonsensical in the ordinary way. You won't be much bored with punctilios. You may do what you please—say or say *not* what you please" (*WHM*, 14:176).

Much to the disappointment of Melville and his family, when the day for the Hawthornes' visit to Arrowhead finally came, Hawthorne sent his regrets, "owing to sickness in his family . . . or else, he's up to the lips in the *Universe* again," Melville joked, offering to "send Constables" to fetch him. Despite Melville's promise to serve "excellent Montado [sic] sherry" and a "most potent Port," to season "mulled wine with wisdom, & buttered toast with story-telling," and to "crack jokes & bottles from morning till night," Hawthorne postponed his visit (*WHM*, 14:180, 14:176).

Although natural allies and friends, Melville and Hawthorne were fifteen years apart in age and temperamentally quite different. Hawthorne often found Melville's manic intensity exhausting, and Melville was frequently disappointed by Hawthorne's reticence and reserve. Much as Melville admired Hawthorne's ability to say "NO! in thunder" (*WHM*, 14:186), he also longed to remedy Hawthorne's lack of "plump sphericity" with a serving of "roast-beef, done rare" (*WHM*, 14:181).

Two days after the aborted visit, Melville rode over to the red cottage at dusk, and Sophia served a light supper of champagne foam with buttered bread and cheese. After supper, Melville regaled the family with exaggerated stories of the South Seas adventures described in *Typee* and *Omoo* ("the Rover"). He acted his stories out so dramatically that Julian Hawthorne reported that, when his mother was tidying the parlor, she looked in the corner for the club "Mr. Omoo" had used to fend off the hordes of cannibals.[4] Before he left that evening, Melville urged Hawthorne to come for a visit as soon as possible, and Hawthorne surprised him by driving over to Arrowhead with Una the next day through the deep spring snow. Hawthorne's handsome features and clear blue eyes made quite an impression on the Melville women, especially Augusta, who was so enamored that her friend Mary Blatchford referred to Hawthorne as "Gus's beau ideal" (MFP, April 21, 1851), which was not surprising. According to Sophia's sister Elizabeth, he was "handsomer than Lord Byron!"[5]

The two men spent most of that day in Melville's great barn "smoking and talking metaphysics" (*Log*, 407), with Hawthorne lounging on the carpenter's bench and Melville sprawled out on the hay. Their "ontological heroics" (*WHM*, 14:196), lubricated by liberal doses of gin and champagne, afforded Melville the kind of intense intellectual stimulation he needed, and Hawthorne proposed publishing their conversations as "A Week on a Work-Bench in a Barn"—a takeoff on Thoreau's *A Week on the Concord and Merrimack Rivers*—in which they would make fun of what Hawthorne called the mooncalf idealism of the transcendentalists.

Hawthorne aroused in Melville an intellectual and spiritual passion that paralleled his intense involvement with his art. In this gentle older man who was also a fatherless orphan, Melville found a soul mate, a father, a brother, and a friend. Theirs was a friendship based on shared tragedy as well as artistic affinity; both of them had experienced bereavement. Hawthorne's father was lost at sea when he was four years old, and only a year before he met Melville, his mother had died after a painful illness during which the grief-stricken Nathaniel had remained at her bedside so obsessively that Sophia feared for his health. As a friend, Hawthorne was both a comfort and a challenge: a comfort because he acknowledged the interpenetration of worlds, the seen and the unseen, the earthly nature and the inner man; a challenge because he was reserved, elusive, and mysterious. Soul mates in some ways, the two were opposites in others. Melville was Dionysian, passionate, impulsive. He stripped himself of all defenses and reached out to others in hopes of changing their hearts and minds. Hawthorne, by contrast, was Apollonian, cool, controlled. Hawthorne was Daedalus, artfully constructing a labyrinth to protect his inner secrets; Melville was Icarus, soaring recklessly toward the sun.

On August 1, 1851, his thirty-second birthday, Melville, sporting a broad-brimmed hat, rode over to Lenox to pay a surprise visit to the red cottage, and on the way, he met Hawthorne sitting in Love Grove reading his mail after having taken a walk to the post office with Julian. Melville greeted them in Spanish, and as soon as Hawthorne realized the "cavalier on horseback" was Melville, he invited him home. Melville lifted Julian onto his horse, and the boy rode back to the red cottage "with the freedom and fearlessness of an old equestrian," while the two men "walked alongside and chatted" (*CE*, 8:447–48). Later, Julian told his father "that he loved Mr. Melville" as much as he loved his papa, his mamma, and Una (*CE*, 8:468).

Sophia had taken Una and baby Rose to visit her sister in West Newton, so after Hawthorne put Julian to bed, he and Melville "had a talk about time and eternity, things of this world and of the next, and books, and publishers, and all possible and impossible matters, that lasted pretty deep into the night; and if the truth must be told, we smoked cigars even within the sacred precincts of the sitting-room" (*CE,* 8:448).

The following week, Hawthorne and Julian came to Arrowhead while George and Evert Duyckinck were visiting, and for the next few days, they were whirled around by that "maelstrom of Hospitality," Sarah Morewood (*Log,* 425), who arranged several excursions. The first event was a picnic at Berry Pond in Pittsfield's State Forest, and as a surprise, Mrs. Morewood had hidden a music box beneath the Balance Rock. As she led Melville and the others to the picnic spot, they could hear "sweet and mysterious music."[6] Melville named the stone "Memnon" after the Egyptian statue that sang by the Nile each dawn, and he toasted the ancient mysteries with champagne (the stone would later play a dramatic role in *Pierre; or, The Ambiguities*).

The day after, Melville, the Duyckincks, and Hawthorne visited the Hancock Shakers. Evert Duyckinck thought that the "glass eyed preacher" looked "like an escaped maniac" and that the religious services were "ghastly" (*Log,* 423), and Hawthorne was so discomfited by the way the women and girls scrutinized him and so disturbed to learn that men slept together in the narrow wooden beds that in his notebook he denounced the Shakers as a "filthy set" (*CE,* 8:465). Melville did not share Hawthorne's prudishness, as readers of *Moby-Dick* can attest.

In the fall, Melville went to New York to supervise the publication of his book, writing the conclusion as the early chapters were going through the press. *Moby-Dick; or, The Whale* was officially published on November 1, 1851, with this inscription:

IN TOKEN

OF MY ADMIRATION FOR HIS GENIUS

THIS BOOK IS INSCRIBED

TO

NATHANIEL HAWTHORNE

The book was a triumph of mixed form and metaphysics skillfully blended with spellbinding narrative, but Evert Duyckinck leaned toward the conservative side on matters of literary form; thus, the first installment of his two-part review of *Moby-Dick* was guarded. Hawthorne's epistolary response heartened Melville, who must have hoped Hawthorne would write a review.

Thanking Hawthorne for his "joy-giving and exultation-breeding" letter, Melville called it "the good goddess's bonus over and above what was stipulated" for the "ditcher's work" he had done on *Moby-Dick*. He apologized for responding to Hawthorne's "plain, bluff letter" with such "gibberish," but he could not stop himself from pouring out his gratitude and imagined himself with a paper mill at one end of the house and an "endless riband of foolscap rolling in upon [his] desk": "Upon that endless riband I should write a thousand—a million—billion thoughts, all under the form of a letter to you. The divine magnet is in you, and my magnet responds. Which is the biggest? A foolish question—they are *One*" (*WHM*, 14:212–13).

Hawthorne's letter made Melville feel "pantheistic," and he declared: "A sense of unspeakable security is in me this moment, on account of your having understood the book. I have written a wicked book, and feel spotless as the lamb." "Whence come you, Hawthorne? By what right do you drink from my flagon of life? And when I put it to my lips—lo, they are yours and not mine. I feel that the Godhead is broken up like the bread at the Supper, and that we are the pieces. Hence this infinite fraternity of feeling" (*WHM*, 14:212). Fearing that Hawthorne would think him mad to write such a long emotional letter, Melville explained that the "truth is ever incoherent, and when the big hearts strike together, the concussion is a little stunning." In closing, he said he would understand Hawthorne's not answering such a long letter, and in any case, if he addressed a reply to "Herman Melville," he would "missend it—for the very fingers that now guide this pen are not precisely the same that just took it up and put it on this paper" (*WHM*, 14:213).

It would have been natural for Melville to assume Hawthorne would write a review of *Moby-Dick*, but when none was forthcoming, Melville hinted at it backhandedly. Saying "Hawthorne and His Mosses" had been a "paltry" piece for which he did not expect Hawthorne to reciprocate, he wrote: "Don't write a word about the book. That would be robbing me of my miserly delight" (*WHM*, 14:213). Hawthorne took him at his word, which was unfortunate, because a laudatory review from Hawthorne might have increased sales of *Moby-Dick* considerably and given a much-deserved boost to the younger writer's career. After Melville's

"Hawthorne and His Mosses" appeared in the *Literary World,* advance orders for *Mosses from an Old Manse* poured in, but Hawthorne never wrote a public word about *Moby-Dick,* which must have hurt Melville deeply.

Hawthorne, in the midst of preparing to move his family to West Newton, was too preoccupied with his own affairs to focus on his friend Melville. He had always detested the Berkshire climate, and he could not face another winter cooped up in tight quarters so far from the center of town. The red cottage had no room for guests or live-in help, which meant that he and Sophia could never go out together, and with three growing children, Sophia was finding it difficult to cope. The coup de grâce came when their landlady Caroline Sturgis Tappan accused the Hawthornes' hired girl of conspiring with Mrs. Peters, their black cook, to plunder the estate's orchard of apples for pies. Hawthorne was furious. He asserted his family's right to enjoy the fruits of nature, and Mrs. Tappan asserted her sovereignty over the trees. The argument ended in a stalemate, and for Hawthorne, this was the last straw. One snowy, sleety day in late November, the Hawthornes fled their blighted Berkshire Eden, leaving five cats behind.

Hawthorne left the Berkshires before he and Melville had climbed Greylock and explored New York together as they had planned. The loss of the one man to whom Melville could open his deepest heart and mind stirred up grief for the loss of his father long buried in his soul. Although Hawthorne was neither a surrogate father nor a bear-hugging Queequeg, Melville had grown to rely on the intellectual and spiritual sustenance he drew from their relationship, and his friend's departure left an enormous void.

The second installment of the *Literary World's* review of *Moby-Dick* started out more favorably than the first. Duyckinck called the book "a most remarkable sea-dish—an intellectual chowder of romance, philosophy, natural history, fine writing, good feeling, bad sayings . . . exhibited in vivid narration," but then he added the unaccountable comment that all this had occurred in spite of the author, not because of him.[7] These and other barbs thrust by the *Literary World* cut deep, especially the implication that *Moby-Dick* was sacrilegious. Melville was wounded by such treatment from a friend who ought to have known him well enough to understand that it was not religion he hated but hypocrisy and narrow-minded fanaticism. In fact, Melville's book affirms the power of spiritual ideas. Hawthorne wrote Duyckinck directly to complain about the *Literary World*'s poor treatment of *Moby-Dick*. "What a book Melville has written!" he exclaimed. "It gives me an idea of much greater power than his preceding ones. It hardly seemed to me that the review of it, in the Literary World, did justice to its best points" (*CE*, 16:508). Yet, Hawthorne still did not publish a word about his friend's amazing book.

Sadly, Melville may never have known that Hawthorne had objected to Duyckinck's bad review. He was too busy wrestling with his own feelings. Despite his inner conviction that he was destined to achieve greatness, once again he had been dashed against the lee by critics. With *Moby-Dick*, he had succeeded in writing the great epic of America; yet, it had made no difference to either his reputation or his bank account. He must have winced when he thought of the letters he had written to Hawthorne claiming not to care about literary recognition when, in fact, he cherished the hope that he would someday be regarded as one of America's greatest literary men.

By December, Melville had buried himself so deeply in his work that Sarah Morewood worried openly about him. "[F]requently," she observed "[he does not] leave his room till quite dark in the evening—when he for the first time during the whole day partakes of solid food—he must therefore write under a state of morbid excitement which will soon injure his health" (*Log*, 441). To lure him out and cheer him up, Morewood concocted an old-fashioned English Christmas party with holly and mistletoe and apple bobbing, but Melville wasn't his usual convivial self when he arrived. He was clearly preoccupied, even obsessed with the book he was working on, and when Mrs. Morewood remarked that his reclusive life caused his city friends to think he was insane, Melville replied gloomily that he had long ago reached the same conclusion himself. After several holiday potations, his sociability returned, and he pranced around the room with a balsam wreath on his head.

Shortly before New Year's 1852, Melville received a letter from Sophia Hawthorne praising *Moby-Dick*, especially the bewitching "Spirit-Spout." Having wrongly assumed that "women have small taste for the sea," Melville was "really amazed" by her insight into "the part-&-parcel allegoricalness of the whole" (*WHM*, 14:218–19). Although he knew "some *men*" liked the book, the "only *woman*" who liked it, as far as he knew, was Sophia. Claiming that he hadn't realized *Moby-Dick* was "susceptible of an allegoric construction" before reading her letter, he complimented her discernment: "You, with your spiritualizing nature, see more things than other people," but even so: "My dear Lady, I shall not again send you a bowl of salt water. The next chalice I shall commend, will be a rural bowl of milk" (*WHM*, 14:219).

Pierre is anything but a "rural bowl of milk." It is a self-flagellating psychological novel and melodramatic family romance that ends disastrously. At the time of its gestation, Hawthorne was writing *The Blithedale Romance*, a novel inspired by his 1841 sojourn at Brook Farm, the transcendentalist utopian community founded by George Ripley. In this novel, Hawthorne endows the feminine with erotic power and explores sexual relationships. Like the Pierre-Lucy-Isabel triangle, the Coverdale-Hollingsworth-Priscilla triangle in *The Blithedale Romance* stands the Hester-Dimmesdale-Chillingworth triangle on its head.

When Melville overheard a woman in Boston telling her husband that she had brought him "*Hawthorne's* new book," he wrote Hawthorne the good news. Hawthorne then invited him to Concord, but Melville declined the invitation because he had just "returned from a two weeks' absence": "For the last three months & more I have been an utter idler and a savage—out of doors all the time. . . . The hour has come for me to sit down again" (*WHM*, 14:231). Besides, he was eager to read *The Blithedale Romance*.

Before finishing Hawthorne's new book, Melville read a story sent him by Judge John Clifford of New Bedford, whom he had met on the way to Nantucket with his father-in-law in 1852. It was the tragic history of a woman named Agatha whose sailor husband left her stranded in pregnancy and (unknown to her) took another wife. Thinking the story better suited to Hawthorne's genius than his own, Melville sent the transcript to his friend with an inscribed copy of *Pierre*—hoping, perhaps, to reestablish their former intimacy—but Hawthorne was not interested. In the end, Agatha's story may have inspired Melville's portrait of Hunilla, the long-suffering Chola woman in "The Encantadas."[8]

Melville and Hawthorne did not meet again until 1856, when Melville arrived in Liverpool en route to the Holy Land, a trip his family hoped would forestall a nervous breakdown. Hawthorne, who had been appointed U.S. consul in Liverpool by his old college friend Franklin Pierce (whose presidential campaign biography Hawthorne authored), left us a vivid picture of Melville's desperate mental and spiritual state. "Herman Melville," he wrote, "came to see me at the Consulate, looking much as he used to do (a little paler, and perhaps a little sadder), in a rough outside coat, and with his characteristic gravity and reserve of manner." Hawthorne found Melville's condition disturbing: "Melville has not been well, of late; he has been affected with neuralgic complaints in his head and limbs, and no doubt has suffered from too constant literary occupation, pursued without much success, latterly; and his writings, for a long while past, have indicated a morbid state of mind" (*CE*, 22:162).

Perhaps feeling a little uncomfortable because of his "ineffectual attempt to get [Melville] a consular appointment," Hawthorne invited him to Southport, a seaside village "20 miles distant on the sea-shore, a watering place" (*CE*, 22:162), where they found "Mrs. Hawthorne & the rest awaiting tea" for them (*WHM*, 15:51). Melville brought only "the least little bit of a bundle, which . . . contained a night-shirt and a tooth-brush," but Hawthorne reported, "He is a person of very gentlemanly instincts in every respect, save that he is a little heterodox in the matter of clean linen" (*CE*, 22:163).

The two men conversed "on pretty much [their] former terms of sociability and confidence," and Hawthorne took the next day off so he could spend it with his old friend. They shared a long walk on the beach and sat down "in a hollow among the sand hills (sheltering [them]selves from the high, cool wind) and smoked a cigar" (*CE*, 22:162–63). In his notebook, Hawthorne described Melville's spiritual state:

> Melville, as he always does, began to reason of Providence and futurity, and of everything that lies beyond human ken, and informed me that he had "pretty much made up his mind to be annihilated"; but still he does not seem to rest in that anticipation; and, I think, will never rest until he gets hold of a definite belief. It is strange how he persists—and has persisted ever since I knew him, and probably long before—in wandering to and fro over these deserts, as dismal and monotonous as the sand hills amid which we were sitting. He can neither believe, nor be comfortable in his unbelief; and he is too honest and courageous not to try to do one or the other. If he were a religious man, he would be one of the most truly religious and reverential; he has a very high and noble nature, and better worth immortality that most of us. (*CE*, 22:163)

By comparison, Melville's journal entry is terse: "An agreeable day. Took a long walk by the sea. Sands & grass. Wild & desolate. A strong wind. Good talk" (*WHM*, 15:51). That evening the two enjoyed the pleasures of "hearth and home," drinking stout and playing fox and geese with the Hawthorne children. A few days later, Melville secured a visa from the Turkish consulate, and Hawthorne certified that his passport was "[g]ood for Constantinople (via Malta & Gibraltar) Egypt & a tour about the Continent" (*WHM*, 15:389).

On Saturday, the two men made an excursion to Chester, and on Sunday, Melville attended services. By Monday, he told Hawthorne "he already felt much better than in America; but observed that he did not anticipate much pleasure in his rambles, for that the spirit of adventure is gone out of him" (*CE*, 22:169–70). Before Melville left, he assigned Hawthorne his power of attorney to sign the agreement for British publication of *The Confidence-Man,* and Hawthorne noted, "He is certainly much overshadowed since I saw him last; but I hope he will brighten as he goes onward" (*CE*, 22:170). On November 18, Melville boarded the screw-steamer *Egyptian* with only "a carpet-bag to hold all his travelling-gear," which struck Hawthorne as "the next best thing to going naked." In his notebook he wrote: "[Melville] needs no dressing-case—nothing but a tooth-brush—I do not know a more independent personage. He learned his travelling-habits by drifting about, all over the South Sea, with no other clothes or equipage than a red flannel shirt and a pair of duck trowzers. Yet we seldom see men of less criticizable manners than he [sic]" (*CE*, 22:170).

In his 1856 journal and in his eighteen-thousand-line *Clarel: A Poem and Pilgrimage in the Holy Land,* published with a subvention from his uncle Peter Gansevoort in 1876, Melville left a substantial record of his travel experiences, reflections, and ideas, and in the character of Vine, the silent pilgrim who fascinates the poem's young protagonist, he appears to have left us his impressions of the enigmatic Hawthorne, who was too busy to spend time with Melville when he called at the consulate on the return leg of his pilgrimage.

In May 1864, Melville "was much shocked" to hear of Hawthorne's death. He had not seen Nathaniel since the Hawthornes had returned from Rome and settled into the Wayside in Concord, Massachusetts, but Hawthorne's death severed a link to the old dreams of literary greatness that had burned in him during the writing of *Moby-Dick*. The books both men wrote after 1851, especially *Pierre, The Blithedale Romance, The Marble Faun,* and *Clarel,* reflect their intensely complicated relationship. "Herman was much attached to him & will mourn his loss," his mother Maria wrote her brother, Peter Gansevoort (*Log,* 669).

After Hawthorne's death, Melville reread *Mosses from an Old Manse* in an attempt to commune with the spirit of his departed friend, perhaps hoping to catch from those dark stories a wind as strong as the one that had filled his sails during the composition of *Moby-Dick*. In Hawthorne's sketch "Monsieur du Miroir," Melville marked the sentence "He will pass to the dark realm of Nothingness, but will not find me there" and next to it wrote, "This trenches upon the uncertain and the terrible" (*Log,* 674).

Rare as their later meetings were, Hawthorne had become for Melville a symbol of the gifted but unfulfilled literary man. No match for the prolific Melville, Hawthorne left several manuscripts unfinished when he died. Melville, by contrast, wrote steadily for twenty-seven years after Hawthorne's death, producing a volume of Civil War poetry, an epic poem about his trip to the Holy Land, three privately published books of poetry, and the manuscript of *Billy Budd, Sailor: An Inside Narrative,* published posthumously in 1924.

The relationship with Hawthorne had a profound effect on Melville. His reading of *Mosses from an Old Manse* and his heady philosophical conversations with Hawthorne inspired him with ambition and confidence during the writing of *Moby-Dick,* turning what might have been a conventional sea story into an epic with political, social, and religious overtones. The letters Melville penned to Hawthorne while composing *Moby-Dick* reveal his energy and passion for his "Whale" as well as his thoughts about authorship, obscurity, and fame.

Melville's relationship with Sophia and Nathaniel Hawthorne was intense, and their letters and journals shed light on Melville's state of mind at crucial moments in his life. Sophia's letters provide tantalizing descriptions of Melville as she saw him, and Hawthorne's notes on Melville's visit in Liverpool give a vivid picture of the spiritual crisis Melville suffered in the mid-1850s. Despite the comparatively small amount of time they actually spent with Melville during his seventy-two year lifespan, Sophia and Nathaniel Hawthorne have provided us with our most vivid physical descriptions of Melville as well as the most insightful glimpses into Mr. Omoo's restless, unsatisfied soul.

Notes

1. Duyckinck Collection, August 6, 1850, New York Public Library.

2. Sedgwick, *Life and Letters,* 315.

3. Melville Family Papers, January 24, 1951, New York Public Library; hereafter cited parenthetically as MFP.

4. Julian Hawthorne, *Hawthorne and His Wife,* 1:407.

5. Elizabeth Palmer Peabody, quoted in Norman Holmes Pearson, "Elizabeth Peabody on Hawthorne," *Essex Historical Collections,* July 1958, 264.

6. Smith, "Herman Melville," 147.

7. Parker and Hayford, eds., *"Moby-Dick" as Doubloon,* 49–52.

8. See Wyn Kelley's account of this episode in the present volume (173–95).

Hawthorne and Melville

Or, The Ambiguities

Brenda Wineapple

READERS CLAIMING LITTLE knowledge of *The Scarlet Letter* and less of *Moby-Dick* nonetheless picture their authors bound together like Ahab to the whale—at least for a short, intense time. For since its inception, the friendship between Hawthorne and Melville has been good copy. Cornelius Mathews transformed their first encounter in western Massachusetts into an American *Déjeuner sur l'herbe,* depicting Hawthorne in the *Literary World* as Mr. Noble Melancholy in pursuit of the Great Carbuncle and Melville, retired Sea-Dog—New Neptune by name—in rapturous pursuit of Hawthorne.[1] For his part, Hawthorne liked Melville so much he asked the younger author to spend a few days with him and his family at the small red cottage in Lenox, where they then lived.

Thus a snare was set for future biographers, literary critics, and sleuths, myself among them. But since I begin every enterprise with more dim doubts than divine intuitions, I admit to harboring an initial skepticism about any received wisdom, particularly the journalistic sort that links these two writers at the literary hip. Literary gossip—even when it hails from the nineteenth century—hardens too quickly into fact, especially if fueled by wish and the companion of wish, negligent research. On the other hand, the erotic does cling to Hawthorne (with or without Melville), as well it should—and not just because he was a handsome devil, his deep gray eyes shaded by long dark lashes, his physique strong, his deportment shy, his wit coruscating, and his spirit elusive. No, of all the canonical American authors of the mid–nineteenth century, only Hawthorne created memorable women characters, sexy, smart, and complex;

and of them, his supreme achievement is the amazing adulteress, Hester Prynne. In fact, this was one of the attractions for me, who spent seven years researching and writing a biography of Hester's author.[2]

From Hester Prynne to the androgynous minister with the creepy veil, from Zenobia to the childlike Donatello, from Hepzibah Pyncheon to Septimius Felton's hybrid Aunt Nashoba, Hawthorne, in the words of Emily Dickinson, "appalls, entices—."[3] His vision is tragic, subtly so, as well as coolly passionate and haunting, and whatever one makes of his spectral eroticism, beautifully parsed, it's the foundation of Hawthorne's allure, whether to women, such as myself, or to men, now and in the nineteenth century. And certainly it's what Melville discerned in Hawthorne; he considered Hawthorne a fellow traveler determined to stamp American literature with something Shakespearean and original, like himself. Plus, Melville is one of Hawthorne's most perceptive readers, grasping the tragic vision beneath Hawthorne's elegant, well-turned prose; "deep as Dante," Melville characterized Hawthorne, alluding to his sense of a fallible human nature in which our motives are always and painfully mixed.

But Melville's beguiling insights into Hawthorne's work titillate us, as only Melville can. In his euphoric review of Hawthorne's *Mosses from an Old Manse,* which appeared just weeks after the two men met, Melville donned the alliterative disguise of a Virginian spending July in Vermont, celebrating Hawthorne as the American writer par excellence who "shoots his strong New-England roots into the hot soil of my Southern soul."[4] This erotic performance of literary coupling bore a relationship so rich, so ripe, so available for the plucking it became, thenceforward, not a twosome but a threesome, a triangle of two men in the western hills of Massachusetts and the rest of us—Cornelius Mathews, James T. Fields, Sophia Hawthorne, critics, readers, you and me—who have, for better and worse, watered the germinous seeds of Melville's subsequent correspondence until they have bloomed into speculations about a friendship that, at its acutest, lasted only a year.[5]

For instance, biographer Edwin Haviland Miller rightly calls Melville's review a "love letter" to Hawthorne but then, with flat-footed certainty, alleges Hawthorne precipitously fled the Berkshires in the fall of 1851 because of Melville's so-called sexual "advance," which Miller dates as occurring "in the middle of September probably while the two men strolled in the woods near Stockbridge Bowl."[6] No evidence exists for any such advance, unless, of course, we assume, a priori, that Melville anguished over Hawthorne's departure and then reason backward to invent a cause to account for the anguish and the departure alike—and one that, coincidentally, ignores other grounds for Hawthorne's removal: discordant neighbors, financial stress, his wife's feelings, opportunities elsewhere, and his own dogged loneliness. However, the evidence, such as it is, swings at least two ways. Hershel Parker, in his recent biography of Melville, characterizes the last Berkshire supper of the two friends as "the happiest day of Melville's life," suggesting not that Melville's putative advances had been welcome or reciprocal but that his overture of friendship had been received and returned in good faith—assuming, of course, Melville's happiness depended on reciprocity.[7]

In either case, these biographical glosses rightly presume that, whatever its ending, the meeting of Hawthorne and Melville was, as Newton Arvin more circumspectly observed, a "cardinal moment, intellectually and emotionally," in Melville's life.[8] In Hawthorne's work and person Melville discovered what he called a power of blackness "ten times black," a commitment to the unsmiling, unscripted aspects of life that would help him chart the course of *Moby-Dick* and that would ripple through much of his subsequent work.[9] Hawthorne's "Fire-Worship" reverberates in "I and My Chimney," his "Chipping with a Chisel" in "The Chapel" chapter of *Moby-Dick*; *The House of the Seven Gables* finds its inversion in *Pierre*, "My Kinsman, Major Molineux" echoes in "Benito Cereno," and the phantom of Hawthorne himself trails *Clarel*.[10]

In fact, by dedicating *Moby-Dick* to his Berkshire neighbor, "in token of my admiration for his genius," Melville not only hints that the whale was cooked, to use his phrase, partly at Hawthorne's fire, but he also deliberately invites us into their literary pantry, asking us, voyeur public, to sample his variation on the Hawthorne diet of a "spicy and slowly-oozing heart" ("Hawthorne and His Mosses," 106). Nor should this surprise us. The dedicatory ritual suggests gratitude, to be sure, but something more as well. Mozart dedicates six quartets to Haydn, paying conventional homage to a revered and older composer, but as son and heir to Haydn's legacy, he also places himself within the musical tradition he intends both to preserve and to surpass. Comments Maynard Solomon, one of Mozart's recent biographers: "The dedicatory letter published in the first edition of the six 'Haydn' String Quartets . . . is by itself sufficient to indicate the extent of Mozart's veneration of Haydn as well as his desire to take his place squarely alongside him, for by the salutation 'Al mio caro Amico Haydn' Mozart put himself on an equal plane with the much admired older composer."[11]

Deference with a touch of condescension: humility is part of a protocol that frequently conceals unacknowledged aggression. Dedications look forward as well as backward. That is, respect for the past is not simply a conservative device for preserving the status quo but a tribute and a leave-taking; we praise the past in order to make it new. "No poet, no artist of any art, has his complete meaning alone," T. S. Eliot reminds us, dedicating *The Waste Land* to Pound. But as he also observes, "what happens when a new work of art is created is something that happens simultaneously to all the works of art which preceded it."[12] Captain Ahab is the fulfillment of "Ethan Brand," and "Ethan Brand" will never more exist without Captain Ahab.

Without doubt, Melville idolized Hawthorne, a darling of the New England literary clique and his senior by fifteen years. Poe may have called Hawthorne "*the* example, *par excellence,* in this country, of the privately-admired and publicly-unappreciated man of genius," but the entrance of publisher James T. Fields into Hawthorne's life and the appearance of *The Scarlet Letter* in March 1850 had begun to change all that.[13] True, Hawthorne had published fewer books than Melville, but his prestige was unassailable, and as for his person, Hawthorne was no insentient monument, stiff and self-regarding. Rather, as Hawthorne's wife Sophia reported, Melville said, "Mr. Hawthorne was the first person whose physical being appeared to him wholly in harmony with the intellectual & spiritual" (*Log,* 924).

Smitten, Melville doubtless began his lusty review of Hawthorne's *Mosses* after their now-famous meeting, as if to seal the friendship with a concrete pledge of admiration. This was Melville's gift to Hawthorne, intended to delight them both with its directive that "America be heedful of the increasing greatness among her writers" ("Hawthorne and His Mosses," 110). Of such stuff are American romances made. But like any family romance, this fantasy of Berkshire brotherhood ignores the more complex psychological and even commercial side of the relationship. Dedicating *Moby-Dick* to Hawthorne allied the two authors ever after, American writers breathing life into a new literature, comrades on an otherwise arid plain. Several early reviews of *Moby-Dick* took up the cry: "Edgar Poe, Nathaniel Hawthorne, Herman Melville are assuredly no British offshoots," the London *Leader* approves.[14] However, once Hawthorne and Melville were linked together, comparisons became inevitable, and for many years, not to Melville's advantage. "There were strange, dark, mysterious elements in his nature, as there were in Hawthorne's," wrote Richard Henry Stoddard in Melville's obituary, "but he never learned to control them, as Hawthorne did from the beginning, and never turned their possibilities into actualities."[15]

Mainstream Stoddard notwithstanding, new art reconfigures what came before, and the artist knows it. If Eliot's *Waste Land* salutes Pound as it replaces him, so too does Melville rewrite Hawthorne with his eye on a prize Hawthorne seems already to possess. Did Melville believe, or hope, or fantasize that he could surpass his Berkshire neighbor as profound truth-teller, afire with humanity? Just as surely as Melville's dedication broadcasts the debt of a younger writer to an older, more established one, the admiring inscription betrays his subtle competition with Hawthorne, alerting us to the friendship's vexed undertone. For like his review of *Mosses*, the dedication is Melville's generous yet ingenuously green-eyed effort to devour his neighbor whole and then serve him as the American zeitgeist "shared by a plurality," as Melville put it, "of men of genius"("Hawthorne and His Mosses," 114). The secret sharer is of course Melville himself.

"Whence come you, Hawthorne? By what right do you drink from my flagon of life?" Melville asks in the well-known letter of November 1851, rightly interpreted in ecstatic terms (*WHM*, 14:212). (Melville has just read Hawthorne's now-lost letter about *Moby-Dick* and reacts with joy and wonder.) But as we survey this and Melville's other passionate outbursts, we might consider that Melville has, as Hawthorne would say, "several voices . . . as well as two complexions" (*CE*, 11:226).

To be sure, Hawthorne's response to *Moby-Dick* exhilarates Melville. But much as he longs for a connection—"And when I put it to my lips—lo, they are yours and not mine"—Melville is ever anxious lest his identity be submerged by one larger or stronger. "I feel that the Godhead is broken up like the bread at the Supper, and that we are the pieces. Hence this infinite fraternity of feeling" (*WHM*, 14:212). As Melville well knows, this "infinite fraternity of feeling"—whether the pantheistic oneness described in the "Mast-Head" chapter of *Moby-Dick* or the spermy sexual baptism of "A Squeeze of the Hand"—this collaboration, an "*all* feeling" (*WHM*, 4:194) and sense of fraternal love, is inevitably accompanied by a chillness at the bone: detumescence and a sense of utter, abject loss.

And despite all his lavish praise of Hawthorne's *Mosses from an Old Manse*, Melville confided to Evert Duyckinck that *Mosses* was actually inferior to *Twice-Told Tales*. "[T]here is something lacking—a good deal lacking—to the plump sphericity of the man," Melville told Duyckinck, collapsing the distinction between Hawthorne and his work to denigrate—or emasculate—both. "He does'nt [sic] patronise the butcher—he needs roast-beef, done rare" (*WHM*, 14:181). Similarly, if more covertly, after the publication of *The House of the Seven Gables* Melville exclaimed to Hawthorne: "I say to myself, this N. H. is in the ascendant. My dear Sir, they begin to patronize. All Fame is patronage. Let *me* be infamous: there is no patronage in *that*" (*WHM*, 14:193; my emphasis).

The point is simple: Melville cast Hawthorne as soul mate, bobbing like him on the troubled seas of publishing, recognition, and posterity. But if Melville found in Hawthorne another writer attempting to shake and tremor "the tribe of 'general readers'" (*WHM*, 14:192), he also envied Hawthorne's skill, his standing, *and* his circumspection. Himself hoping to master and surpass Hawthorne, Henry James observed in his brilliant, begrudging 1879 tribute that Hawthorne had a "cat-like faculty of seeing in the dark."[16] Melville responded in much the same way. "There is a certain tragic phase of humanity which, in our opinion, was never more powerfully embodied than by Hawthorne," he wrote after reading *The House of the Seven Gables*. "We mean the tragicalness of human thought in its own unbiased, native, and profounder workings. We think that into no recorded mind has the intense feeling of the visable [sic] truth ever entered more deeply than into this man's. By visable truth, we mean the apprehension of the absolute condition of present things as they strike the eye of the man who fears them not, though they do their worst to him" (*WHM*, 14:186).

To Melville, Clifford Pyncheon incarnates this "awful truth" as he stands poised to jump from the arched window and take "the great final remedy" (*WHM*, 14:186, 14:185; *CE*, 2:166). But Hawthorne, as Melville shrewdly observed, was a man, like Solomon, who also "*managed* the truth" (*WHM*, 14:193). That is, Clifford does not jump. Hawthorne will not let him. At the conclusion of *The House of the Seven Gables,* Hawthorne spares Clifford any final confrontation with his decrepitude, appeased as he is by the book's happily contrived denouement. Melville could not do this. His characters do jump, to "take a deep, deep plunge into the ocean of human life," in Hawthorne's words, "and to sink down and be covered by its profoundness" (*CE,* 2:166)—only they, the Pips and Bartlebys, seldom emerge refreshed or restored. "What I feel most moved to write, that is banned,—it will not pay," Melville tells Hawthorne, implicitly comparing himself to his friend. "Yet, altogether, write the *other* way I cannot. So the product is a final hash, and all my books are botches" (*WHM,* 14:191). Of Hawthorne's *Seven Gables,* however, he notes in the same letter that he's "seen and heard many flattering (in a publisher's point of view) allusions" (*WHM,* 14:193). Hawthorne was doing well, suggests Melville, but not he: "Though I wrote the Gospels in this century," he presciently predicts, "I should die in the gutter" (*WHM,* 14:192).

Idealizing Hawthorne, Melville denigrated himself and not without, one supposes, the resentment that inevitably attends such outsize hero worship or the outsize disappointment that comes when the hero reveals feet of clay. In this sense, it's not unreasonable to suggest that Melville must have borne some unwitting hand in their relationship's failure insofar as it failed. The year after Hawthorne left Lenox, Melville urged him to write a story from some of the material he, Melville, had gathered during a trip to Nantucket in the summer of 1852 about Agatha Hatch Robertson, a woman who marries a shipwrecked sailor and nurses him back to health. The sailor deserts her, and the woman, bearing a child, waits for his return, patient as Griselda; she is unaware her husband has married another.

"I think that in this matter you would make a better hand at it than I would.—Besides the thing seems naturally to gravitate towards you" (*WHM,* 14:234), Melville declared. Recalling "Wakefield," Melville informed Hawthorne, "this thing lies very much in a vein, with which you are peculiarly familiar" (*WHM,* 14:234). Why "peculiarly familiar"? The Agatha story doesn't really resemble Hawthorne's Wakefield, a husband committed more to the fantasy of absence than its fact. And though Melville's sailor undergoes a moral transformation of sorts, at least in Melville's telling, Wakefield does not.[17] Actually, the story of Agatha Hatch

Robertson has little to do with Hawthorne or his work, as Hawthorne likely surmised. Rather, the story is Melville's story of abandonment, taken from a chapter in his own psychic history and written from the vantage point of the one left behind at Hawthorne's headlong flight from the Berkshires in the fall of 1851.

That is, in Melville's account, Agatha daily walks to check the mail at a little wooden postbox where the postboy drops his letters; daily, she hopes for a letter; daily, she returns home empty-handed. "For seventeen years she goes thither daily" (*WHM,* 14:236), Melville writes, imagining the scene for Hawthorne. Eventually, the postbox decays, the grass growing rank about it, and a bird nests there. If we cast Melville as Agatha, then he too awaits word from an absent companion, hungrily hoping for a sign of Hawthorne's return. But Melville is more impatient than Agatha. He sends a gift, not a laudatory review as before but the story that, as he portentously claims, restores to Hawthorne "your own property—which you would quickly enough have identified for yourself—had you been on the spot as I happened to be" (*WHM,* 14:237).

The spot is seaward-looking Nantucket, for Melville suspected, it seems, that Hawthorne craved a sea story. Indeed, Hawthorne doubtless told Melville, as he had told so many others, that he yearned for the "cut-throat East-wind" that blew by the shore.[18] He wanted to quit the Berkshires, in other words, for the very reason he found Melville attractive: Melville smelled of the surf.

Melville's overture suggests that he may have grasped something significant about Hawthorne's psyche that has become less comprehensible to us. For though the relationship between these two looming writers has been probed, sexualized, and moralized over the years, in its frequent telling, Hawthorne rarely appears. Instead, he is cast as a repressed and withholding father figure, ungenerous to a fault, and set against a Melville, poor castaway, spurned by the elder writer. This oft-told tale places Melville at the relationship's (sentimentally broken) heart, representing Hawthorne as a passive recipient of Melville's friendship, desire, and remorse. "[I]f anybody is lacking in the [Melville-Hawthorne] friendship, it's Hawthorne," claimed a Hawthorne scholar during a symposium in the late 1990s on Melville biography. "I don't think there's a Hawthornian that will not say that."[19]

That Hawthorne's letters to Melville do not survive is partly responsible for such serene confidence, and partly it does seem that whenever

Melville effused, Hawthorne shrank. But whatever Melville symbolized for Hawthorne—that, like the whiteness of the whale, as yet remains unsaid.

Melville, at least the way Hawthorne saw him, was the kind of lad Hawthorne probably dreamed of being: afloat on one craft or another, battling typhoons and doldrums, dropping anchor in exotic, distant lands. Born in a New England port awash with cod princes and briny yarns, at least until Jefferson's embargo, Hawthorne in his early tales summoned watery graves and the sound of the sea, ocean birds and gulls and quiet coves. For the sea represented to Hawthorne, as to any young man in his time, raw adventure and a test of manhood, on the one hand, with fortune and pleasure perfectly balanced by death, certain and uncertain, on the other. Plus, Hawthorne was the son and grandson of ships' captains, men respected for grit and sand—and, in the case of his own father, even beatified by Salem's elite, for having navigated around Cape Horn.

When Captain Hathorne died in 1808, he left behind a four-year-old son who insisted, in adulthood, that had he not turned to scribbling, he should have been a sailor. In 1820, his anxious mother sighed with relief when she first heard her sixteen-year-old son had given up his plan to go to sea.[20] Yet, Hawthorne's earliest compositions probably involved sea stories about tawny pirates and hardy privateers, or so said his sister, and two surviving early poems quiver over the sea's fearsome strength: "The billowy Ocean rolls its wave, / Above the shipwreck'd Sailor's Grave," Hawthorne droned at sixteen. Not long afterward, he again versified the fate of those mariners, like his father, "for whom we weep, / The young, the bright, the fair" (*CE*, 23:44, 23:6).

Such lyric stuff might be standard for a boy hoisted seaside, but the ocean retained its aura of destruction, secrecy, and solace, of male adventure, bonding, and terror even for the adult Hawthorne. "Of what mysteries is it telling?" he asks in "Foot-prints on the Sea-shore": "Of sunken ships, and whereabouts they lie? Of islands afar and undiscovered, whose tawny children are unconscious of other islands and of continents, and deem the stars of heaven their nearest neighbours? Nothing of all this. What then? Has it talked for so many ages, and meant nothing all the while? No; for those ages find utterance in the sea's unchanging voice, and warn the listener to withdraw his interest from moral vicissitudes, and let the infinite idea of eternity pervade his soul" (*CE*, 9:459–60). "Grief, not Joy, is a moralizer," as Melville points out in *Pierre*, and Hawthorne thinly coats his grief with a warning he never quite heeds (*WHM*, 7:36).

How could the young Hawthorne, mourning a father he hardly knew, not have imagined thousands of times that last voyage of Captain Hathorne as he left the Salem harbor on the brig *Nabby*, in the raw damp of December 1807, never to return? And hadn't Melville sailed this same scary, seductive sea? Yet here was Melville, seaman-rover come back to tell all, a young sailor, bearded and bronzed, who mixed with the old salts at wharfside, a real man—not a dry-docked customhouse inspector like Hawthorne—who strode off the gangplank into a garret, took out a pen, and became, of all things, a best-selling writer. "We landsmen have no variety in our lives," said Hawthorne of himself (*CE*, 16:195); Melville was no landsman.

Favorably reviewing *Typee* in 1846, Hawthorne described Melville as a "young and adventurous sailor" (*CE*, 23:235–36) and, after meeting the daring younger man, invited Melville to spend a few days in the Hawthornes' small red cottage in Lenox. This spasm of hospitality has seemed out of character to those observers, then and later, who imagined Hawthorne running out the back door when company came to call. But Melville was neither Brahmin author nor orphic chatterbox, two of the types of callers Hawthorne did elude. (After Hawthorne's death, Emerson admitted he had never been able to "conquer a friendship" with him.)[21] As for the rest, friends like John O'Sullivan, Horatio Bridge, and Franklin Pierce were welcomed in the Hawthorne home, wherever that home may have been. And Melville's appeal, like theirs, lay in his resistance to the cultured palaver of Boston Whigs, whom Hawthorne likened to clergy; it lay in his rough and ready willingness to "swim for his life," as Hawthorne said after first reading *Mardi* (*CE*, 16:362).

Unfortunately, Hawthorne committed no detailed impressions of Melville to his journals or to his friends, although we may suppose that he agreed in at least some points with the portrait sketched by his wife, Sophia, when she described their new acquaintance. Standing sentinel over Hawthorne's reputation as fiercely as Alice Toklas guarded Gertrude Stein's, Sophia Hawthorne easily admitted Melville into the family circle, especially after learning Mr. Typee, as she called him, was the author of the *Literary World*'s encomium to her husband.

The red cottage in Lenox, Massachusetts, residence of the Hawthornes in 1850–51. From *Lenox and the Berkshire Highlands,* by R. DeWitt Mallary (New York: G. P. Putnam's Sons, 1902), facing 146.

We find him . . . a man with a true warm heart & a soul & an in-tellect—with life to his finger-tips—earnest, sincere & reverent, very tender & *modest*—And I am not sure that he is not a very great man—but I have not quite decided upon my opinion—. . . . He has very keen perceptive power, but what astonishes me is, that his eyes are not large & deep—He seems to see every thing very accurately, & how he can do so with his small eyes, I cannot tell. . . . His nose is straight & rather hand-some, his mouth expressive of sensibility & emotion—He is tall & erect with an air free, brave, & manly. When conversing, he is full of gesture & force, & loses himself in his subject—There is no grace nor polish—once in a while his animation gives place to a singularly quiet expression out of those eyes, to which I have objected—an indrawn, dim look, but which at the same time makes you feel that he is at that instant taking deepest note of what is before him—It is a strange, lazy glance, but with a power in it quite unique—It does not seem to penetrate through you, but to take you into himself. (*Log,* 393–94)

With gesture and force, without grace or polish or affectation, Mel-ville struck Sophia and perhaps her husband as "free, brave, & manly"—one of the roughs, as it were, before Whitman claimed the title five years later with sea tales to prove it. Yet, adventuresome Melville also had a pedigree: "He is married to a daughter of Judge Shaw—Judge Lemuel Shaw," Sophia Hawthorne bragged, "& has a child of a year & half—Malcolm. He is of Scotch descent—of noble lineage—of the Lords of Melville & Leven, & Malcolm is a family name" (*Log*, 925).

Nostalgic family pride also links Hawthorne to Melville, for Hawthorne had yearned after those ancestors he derisively revered. Diminished by them, at least in his own mind, he had just published the mordantly humorous "Custom-House" essay, which depicts his forefathers as his own stern conscience, scorning him: "'What is he?'" Hawthorne imagines them snorting. "'A writer of story-books!'" (*CE*, 1:10). Simultaneously proud and ashamed of his profession, which he considered effete and unmanly, Hawthorne peered at Melville, of Scotch descent, the emotional and sensitive and brave and untrammeled writer nonetheless pursued, as was Hawthorne, by lost fathers and "the Blue Devils" (*WHM*, 14:200). There are "certain crotchetty and over doleful chimaeras," Melville assured Hawthorne, "the like of which men like you and me and some others, forming a chain of God's posts round the world, must be content to encounter now and then, and fight them the best we can" (*WHM*, 14:195).

Hawthorne met Melville at a cardinal moment in his own life, while he still reeled from the success of *The Scarlet Letter*. Just the summer before its publication, Hawthorne had buried his mother, to whom he was deeply attached, and lost his post at the Salem customhouse, where he had been employed for more than three years. Self-exiled, he withdrew from political life, at least for the period of the next administration, and like a nomad left his birthplace, vowing never to return. But he could not find a suitable spot near the sea, where he wanted to live, so moved his family to the Berkshires and squatted in the little red cottage loaned by a friend.

Moody under the best of circumstances, Hawthorne had left behind friends, position, and family in a wake of embarrassment and penury. The publication of *The Scarlet Letter* salvaged his pride and helped fill his purse, but he felt dull and displaced, having endured what his wife called the most trying year of his life. And now he had a new book to write, barely begun, that worried him. Small wonder: up until this time, he had not been a prolific author, quite the reverse, and he feared, as he confided to Duyckinck in 1845, that he had "reached that point in an author's life, when he ceases to effervesce" (*CE*, 16:136). From the Berkshires, the customhouse debacle and the success of *The Scarlet Letter* behind him, he felt in low moments that nothing had happened or changed. "How slowly I have made my way in life!" he lamented to Horatio Bridge. "How much is still to be done!" (*CE*, 16:407).

Enter Herman Melville, a willing acolyte hungry for literary companionship and eager to project onto Hawthorne the preoccupations assailing him while writing *Moby-Dick*. Hawthorne was an eager listener, flattered and lonely, generally suspicious of the highfalutin types and bereft of his cigar-puffing male cronies at the Salem wharves—those father figures unavailable in the snug Berkshires. In Melville, he found a perfect solution: a young salt and fellow foundling, a male writer called a loafer by the busy idlers of the world, an established author with four books under his belt, a man of far-flung reputation, and a neighbor willing to drink a bottle of brandy and "talk ontological heroics together" (*WHM*, 14:196). To Hawthorne, Melville appeared unashamed, sexual, tender, manly, a spendthrift stylist and prolific author promiscuously "tolerant of codes of morals that may be little in accordance with our own" (*CE*, 23:235).

When characterizing Holgrave, the daguerreotypist in *The House of the Seven Gables,* Hawthorne drew on his neighbor Melville: scantily educated and left early to his own guidance, a former country schoolmaster, a man who "had never lost his identity," writes Hawthorne, "[h]omeless as he had been—continually changing his whereabout" (*CE*, 2:177). Of course, Melville figures much more importantly in the later *Blithedale Romance,* which folds Melville's letters into its third chapter, infusing his tenderness and childlike egotism into the brawny character of Hollingsworth: "there was something of the woman moulded into the great, stalwart frame of Hollingsworth," Hawthorne writes; "nor was he ashamed of it, as men often are of what is best in them" (*CE*, 3:42). Hollingsworth converts himself into a nurse to care for the novel's narrator, Miles Coverdale, the Prufrock-like poet come to share in the common life and common good of a socialist community modeled on Brook Farm and Hawthorne's short-lived experience there. From their first meeting, Coverdale is drawn to the burly philanthropist. "[T]here was a tenderness in his voice, eyes, mouth, in his gesture, and in every indescribable manifestation, which few men could resist, and no woman," he expostulates before dissolving, the next day, into a lovesick fever. So gently does Hollingsworth minister at his bedside that Coverdale seeks no other nurse. "There never was any blaze of a fireside that warmed and cheered me, in the down-sinkings and shiverings of my spirit, so effectually as did the light out of those eyes, which lay so deep and dark under his shaggy brows" (*CE*, 3:28, 3:42).

But Coverdale learns, to his great frustration, that Hollingsworth "had taught his benevolence to pour its warm tide exclusively through one channel; so that there was nothing to spare for other great manifestations of love to man, nor scarcely for the nutriment of individual attachments." "Father Hollingsworth," as Coverdale calls the older man half in admiration and half in contempt, has promised much and delivered little. In retaliation, Coverdale firmly rejects Hollingsworth's invitation to "[s]trike hands" with him, join his philanthropic pursuits, and "never again feel the languor and vague wretchedness of an indolent or half-occupied man!" (*CE*, 3:55, 3:129, 3:133).

Despite a temptation to interpret Hollingsworth as a spurned and impassioned Melville, we can just as easily read Coverdale's rejection of Hollingsworth as the petulant reaction of a surrogate son to a powerful father whom he adores and resents, loves and fears, and whom he believes neglects and deceives him. Following Frederick Crews, Gloria Erlich indicates that Hollingsworth is a father figure spawned by Hawthorne's background and psychological constitution.[22] This interpretation also ushers Melville into Hawthorne's psychic life—where chronology is subjective and unaging fathers, forever young, haunt their full-grown, aging sons. As if acknowledging this complex aspect of their tangled friendship, Hawthorne gave Melville his copy of Archibald Duncan's *Mariner's Chronicle,* a four-volume compendium of shipwrecks, fires, famines, and "other calamities incident to a life of maritime enterprise."[23] The volume had been owned by Hawthorne's uncle Richard Manning, another figure of paternal compass, and given to Hawthorne shortly after Manning's premature death.

Sons often fear their fathers. Perhaps Hawthorne feared the publication of *Moby-Dick,* a book bigger in scope, vision, and manliness than his own, a book broiled in hellfire with a gigantic conception, as Hawthorne referred to it in *A Wonder Book for Girls and Boys,* a storybook for the children with whom Hawthorne partly identified and whom he wanted to protect. At the same time, Melville told Hawthorne, "I have written a wicked book," after finishing *Moby-Dick,* "and feel spotless as the lamb" (*WHM,* 14:212).

Unlike Melville, Hawthorne vacillated between the bourgeois conventions represented by the Phoebes and Priscillas and Coverdales in his gabled, well-turned fiction and the disobedient, downright sexual excitement of his Hesters and Zenobias and Hollingsworths. Uncomfortable with both, he was a regional expatriate longing for the security of an idealized home and community, be it among Brook Farm idealists or Concord literati, yet he compulsively moved from house to house seeking the sea and the rugged men of the sea, as if real domesticity (and its association with women) would smother him.

At the same time, Hawthorne wanted and needed to sell books; his livelihood, financial and emotional, depended on it. So did Melville's, but Melville willingly took risks Hawthorne avoided. Trying to pour a little sunshine over the conclusion of *The House of the Seven Gables,* Hawthorne had hoped to win a larger audience than he had theretofore enjoyed, and in this enterprise James T. Fields acted as impresario, encouraging the writer to stay at his desk while Fields whetted the public's appetite for more Hawthorne. "We intend to push your books a-la-Steam Engine, and do better for you than any other house," Fields declared, rallying Hawthorne's spirits; after the publication of *The House of the Seven Gables,* he planned to reissue *Twice-Told Tales* with a new author's preface, also proposing yet another collection (*The Snow-Image*) to appear after *A Wonder Book.*[24]

But in the summer of 1851, the summer Melville completed *Moby-Dick,* Hawthorne was restless, homesick, ill, and fretful. He longed for the sea and the men of the sea, his pals in Salem, and the income from a steady job, which would spare him the indignity of living as a kind of indentured servant at the behest of rich friends. All this Melville must have guessed if he hadn't already been told during one of those visits when the two men discussed, according to Hawthorne, "time and eternity, things of this world and of the next, and books, and publishers, and all possible and impossible matters, that lasted pretty deep into the night" (*CE,* 8:448). Unable to shake his malaise, Hawthorne dispatched friends like Bridge to look for houses to let along the shore. "Oh that Providence would build me the merest little shanty," he hoped, "and mark me out a rood or two of garden-ground, near the sea-coast" (*CE,* 16:486). Hawthorne eventually anchored himself in genteel Concord, where Melville visited him in the winter of 1852, still enthusiastic about the Agatha story as if aware that Hawthorne's thirst for the sea remained unslaked. Hawthorne refused the material. He may have craved sea stories, but he did not write of the sea, as Melville surely knew, and he definitely wouldn't write this one. Having recently produced a campaign biography for his friend Franklin Pierce, he awaited the fruits of friendship to deliver him, once again, into government employ.[25]

Melville may have assumed, then, not only that Hawthorne would decline his gift, but that the Agatha story would further divide the friends, alienating and possibly wounding the landlocked Hawthorne, with its tale of a sailor who, like Hawthorne's own father—at least from a bereft son's point of view—abandons his family. Even more, Agatha bears her fate with the quiet, depressed pride of Hawthorne's deceased mother—and of Hawthorne himself. For Melville had to know that stories of deserted women living seaside, like Hawthorne's mother and sisters, cut too close to the bone. Worse yet, in July of that same year, Hawthorne's younger sister Louisa had been killed when the steamer *Henry Clay* ran aground on the Hudson River.

Nonetheless, Melville persisted. Perhaps Hawthorne allowed him to think he might try his hand at the story, or perhaps Melville refused to hear Hawthorne's demurral. For he may have been angry, albeit unawares, at Hawthorne's multiple defections: his departure from the Berkshires, his not having written a review of *Moby-Dick* in answer to the ovation for *Mosses,* and most recently, his decided move toward, quite literally, the world of patronage. Hawthorne's long-trusted friend Franklin Pierce, whom he had known since their youth at Bowdoin College, was intending to run for president of the United States in November, and if Pierce won, Hawthorne could count on another stint on the government payroll that would let him feed his growing family.

From this vantage point, Melville's overture seems less an offering than a taunt, a challenge thrown down by the younger man who fathomed the psychic demons stalking Hawthorne's solitude. "The divine magnet is in you," wrote Melville, "and my magnet responds" (*WHM,* 14:213). Perhaps, too, Melville knew precisely how to elicit Hawthorne's rebuff, and Hawthorne knew how to grasp the meaning of Melville's story. Unable to plunge into foreign waters, Hawthorne was the timid bride abandoned by the sailor, and the tale itself was Melville's whispered farewell.

"Truth is ever incoherent, and when the big hearts strike together, the concussion is a little stunning" (*WHM,* 14:213), Melville had written Hawthorne in a phrase Hawthorne would work into *Blithedale* (*CE*, 3:21), knowing Melville would find other magnets to direct his compass, as would he. Competition between the two men, alike in as many ways as they differed, had stunned Hawthorne, it seems, into a belated confrontation with Melville's sublime egotism, similar to his own, and to Melville's appropriation of the tenderer parts of his own life. Sensitive to any slight, painfully proud, and a man beset by ghosts remarkably like Melville's, Hawthorne allowed distance and time to sap the friendship of its verve. He did try to help Melville secure a post in the Pierce administration after he secured his own position as U. S. consul in Liverpool, but it seems he acted in the half-hearted manner he would later recall, guiltily, with a certain remorse.

As for the Agatha story, neither man could manage it the same way or write it—or anything else—for the same public, a fact they tacitly acknowledged. Hawthorne returned to Melville his account of Agatha, Melville began to work on Agatha alone, and the friendship never recovered its white heat. Unbound, the two friends drifted, as Melville ruefully wrote after Hawthorne's death, "estranged in life, / And neither in the wrong" (*WHM*, 12:893).

Notes

1. See [Mathews], "Several Days in Berkshire," 145–47, 166, 185–86.

2. See Wineapple, *Hawthorne*.

3. Dickinson to T. W. Higginson, December 1879, in *Letters of Emily Dickinson*, 2:649.

4. [Melville], "Hawthorne and His Mosses, by a Virginian spending July in Vermont," 112; hereafter cited parenthetically.

5. See Wineapple, "Nathaniel Hawthorne, Writer; or, The Fleeing of the Biographied," in Bell, ed., *Hawthorne and the Real*. See also, for a bibliographic introduction to the literature devoted to this relationship, Wilson, "An Essay in Bibliography," and for a cogent introduction to the literary dimensions of the relationship, see Hayford, "Melville and Hawthorne: A Biographical and Critical Study"; Jones, "Some 'Mosses' from the *Literary World*"; and Vincent, ed., *Melville and Hawthorne in the Berkshires*. On psychological and sexual aspects, see Turner, *Nathaniel Hawthorne*; Levin, *Power of Blackness*; Chase, *Herman Melville*; Watson, "Estrangement"; Seelye, "'Ungraspable Phantom'"; Leuders, "Melville-Hawthorne Relationship," 323–44; and Murray, introduction to *Pierre*, lxxvii–lxxix. For a discussion of Hawthorne's link to romantic and postromantic

writing in relation to Melville, deduced in large part from biographical assumptions, see Davis, "Hawthorne's Shyness"; and for a fine treatment of the two writers' correspondence and their investment in the "democratic poetics" implied by such communication, see Hewitt, "Scarlet Letters, Dead Letters."

6. Miller, *Melville*, 36, 250; Miller, *Salem Is My Dwelling Place*, 363.

7. Parker, *Herman Melville*, 1:883.

8. Arvin, *Herman Melville*, 136.

9. For a cogent discussion of the racial implications of this metaphor, see Simon, "Race for Hawthorne."

10. For an overview of Hawthorne's influence on Melville, see Matthiessen, *American Renaissance*, 179–91, 282–92; and more recently, Brodhead, *School of Hawthorne*, 25–31. For an example of a more specific study, see Kelley, "*Pierre's* Domestic Ambiguities."

11. Solomon, *Mozart*, 315.

12. Eliot, "Tradition and the Individual Talent," 38.

13. Poe, "Tale-Writing—Nathaniel Hawthorne," 98.

14. Review of *The Whale*, by Herman Melville, *Leader* (London), November 5, 1851; repr. in Parker and Hayford, eds., *"Moby-Dick" as Doubloon*, 25.

15. Richard Henry Stoddard, obituary of Melville, *New York Critic*, November 14, 1891, repr. in Parker and Hayford, eds., *"Moby-Dick" as Doubloon*, 111–12. A significant exception is John Macy's 1913 *Spirit of American Literature*, quoted in *"Moby-Dick" as Doubloon*, 124.

16. James, *Literary Criticism*, 1:394.

17. Notes Melville: "In his previous sailor life Robinson [sic] had found a wife (for a night) in every port. The sense of the obligation of the marriage-vow to Agatha had little weight with him at first. *It* was only when some years of life ashore had passed that his moral sense on that point became developed" (*WHM*, 14:240).

18. Sophia Hawthorne to Elizabeth Palmer Peabody, October 21, 1851, in Sophia Hawthorne, Letters, Berg Collection.

19. Quoted in Garner et al., "Biographers on Biography," in Bryant and Milder, eds., *Melville's Evermoving Dawn*, 247. During this discussion, Hershel Parker noted that he thought "the friendship ha[d] been overemphasized" (242), particularly in relation to the composition of *Moby-Dick*.

20. Elizabeth Manning Hawthorne to Robert Manning, January [26], 1820, Hawthorne/Manning Family Letters.

21. Porte, ed., *Emerson in His Journals*, 522.

22. See Erlich, *Family Themes and Hawthorne's Fiction*, 128–32. Although I agree with Erlich's assertion that designating Melville as Hollingsworth's model ignores much about the Hawthorne and Melville relationship, I find surpris-

ing her contention that a difference in age disqualifies Melville from serving as Hawthorne's "father." Regardless, she rightly suggests that someone else lies behind the characterization of Hollingsworth. Indeed, there is more than one someone else (Erlich nominates Hawthorne's uncle Robert Manning) melded into his character.

23. Sealts, *Melville's Reading,* 174.

24. James T. Fields to Nathaniel Hawthorne, January 14, 1851, in Sophia Hawthorne, Letters, Berg Collection.

25. For a more extended discussion of this and related issues, see Wineapple, *Hawthorne,* esp. chs. 17, 19, and 21.

"The Ugly Socrates"

Melville, Hawthorne, and the Varieties of Homoerotic Experience

ROBERT MILDER

Man is an animal organism with (like others) an unmistakably bisexual disposition. The individual corresponds to a fusion of two symmetrical halves, of which, according to some investigators, one is purely male and the other female. It is equally possible that each half was originally hermaphroditic.
—FREUD, *Civilization and Its Discontents*

What Cosmic jest or Anarch blunder
The human integral clove asunder.
—MELVILLE, "After the Pleasure Party"

Homosocial, Homoerotic, Homosexual, Homotextual

"The Ugly Socrates," an echo of Alcibiades' words in Plato's *Symposium,* is drawn from a letter Melville wrote to Hawthorne on or around November 17, 1851, in response to Hawthorne's "joy-giving and exultation-breeding letter" of praise for *Moby-Dick* (*WHM*, 14:212).[1] What we know of Melville's feelings toward Hawthorne is largely contained in such letters, along with "Hawthorne and His Mosses," which Edwin Haviland Miller called "a love letter" in the guise of a book review.[2] Hawthorne's letters to Melville do not survive, and his journal entries on Melville, while respectful, even admiring, tend to hide rather than reveal his private feelings and to hint very little about Melville's.

"Our intellectual and active powers increase with our affection," Emerson observed in "Friendship": "the scholar sits down to write, and all his years of meditation do not furnish him with one good thought or happy expression; but it is necessary to write a letter to a friend,—and, forthwith, troops of gentle thoughts invest themselves, on every hand, with chosen words."[3] Emerson was speaking generally, but the content and language of his essay borrow from his sometimes ardent letters of the period to twenty-one-year-old Caroline Sturgis. What was Emerson, married and in his later thirties, thinking when he told Sturgis he "could spend 'the remainder of [his] days' in her 'holy society'" or when he wrote erotically in "Friendship" of those "jets of affection which make a young world for me again?" (114).[4] What is the spectrum of relationship between sexuality and textuality, or genital desire and an overheated rhetoric that may be anything from metaphor to fantasy to a form of emotional masturbation? How may we determine where on that spectrum a particular textual utterance lies? Could Emerson himself have said what he thought, felt, fantasized, and intended vis-à-vis Sturgis? And with what confidence and on what evidential grounds may interpreters write of these things? When so much is suggested but so little determinably known—the meaning of a text, the relationship of text to consciousness, the relationship of consciousness to subconsciousness, the ambiguity of marginally erotic feelings generally—questions and provisional speculations seem the most proper discursive mode. To claim more is to mythologize or ideologize.

Melville's letters to Hawthorne of 1850–51 show him at his happiest and most fertile. With what sort of affection—fraternal, filial, homoerotic; all of these in some combination?—did Melville write to Hawthorne? How conscious was he of the nature of his affection? What did this affection signify within the context of mid-nineteenth-century male friendships as they were understood by the participants themselves and as they have variously come to be characterized by modern interpreters? And how did this affection figure in his writing, especially in *Pierre*, written immediately after the height of their relationship?

These are difficult questions to answer, not only for want of biographical evidence but because cultural changes have created a chasm of idiom and ideology between Melville's time and the present while politicizing the issue in ways that occlude discussion of the singular relationship at hand. To say flatly that Melville was homosexual, latently homosexual, or not homosexual is not simply to overread the evidence; it is to neglect the problematizing work of recent cultural historians which suggests, in Eve Kosofsky Sedgwick's words, "that the differences between the homosexuality 'we know today' and previous arrangements of same-sex relations may be so profound and so integrally rooted in other cultural differences that there may be no continuous, defining essence of 'homosexuality' to *be* known."[5] If styles of sexuality have changed, so have categories for thinking about sex, often because of the changes in styles, and with radical consequences for interpreting past behaviors. Before the later nineteenth century, a gradational notion of sexuality prevailed, in which shades of homosociality and homosexuality ranged themselves along a spectrum. The twentieth century replaced this idea of gradational sexuality with what Carroll Smith-Rosenberg calls a "dichotomized universe of deviance and normality, genitality and platonic love," a universe we continue to inhabit and can only with difficulty extricate ourselves from as we try to understand creatures from a very different universe.[6]

The challenge in thinking historically about homosexuality, as David M. Halperin said, "is, first of all, how to recover the terms in which the experiences of individuals belonging to past societies were actually constituted and, second, how to measure and assess the differences between those terms and the ones we currently employ."[7] What languages did historical actors have or not have available to them, and how did that (un)availability affect their understanding of themselves? In her autobiographical essay "A Sketch of the Past" (1940) Virginia Woolf speaks of reading Freud "only the other day" and "for the first time . . . discover[ing] that [her] violently disturbing conflict of love and hate [toward her father] is a common feeling; and is called ambivalence."[8] Thirteen years after she published *To the Lighthouse,* one of the subtlest treatments of filial love/hate in the English novel, Woolf finds that simply having the word "ambivalence" has brought together a constellation of feelings in a sudden epiphany. For most of her life Woolf did not have the word "lesbian" available to her; as late as 1925 she writes (of Vita Sackville-West) as if observing a new phenomenon, "These Sapphists *love* women; friendship is never untinged with amorosity."[9] It seems only dawningly to occur to Woolf at age forty-three that she herself may be a "Sapphist," though for years she has been aware of her strong emotional and imaginative preference for women, and soon she would sexually experiment with Vita.

The word and concept "homosexual" was not current in England and America until Melville was past fifty, when his active sexual life was long behind him; he certainly had no term or idea analogous to the modern "sexual orientation." "Homosexuality" for him would have meant certain acts people performed. It might have extended to a class of people who enjoyed or preferred those acts. It did not constitute a psychosexual identity, if only because few nineteenth-century Americans defined themselves in terms of "psychosexual identity." In the absence of primary materials like letters and journals, it is difficult to determine how people before Freud's or Havelock Ellis's time understood their feelings and intentions. Perhaps they would have been naively unsuspicious of them, in many cases with good reason—the "strict interdiction against full genital sexuality" permitting, as Robert K. Martin has suggested, "a much fuller expression of male friendship" precisely because it "in no way threatened to spill over into genitality."[10] If present-day distinctions such "as an absolute split between homo- and heterosexual based on genital behavior . . . were nascent and fluid" in mid-nineteenth-century America, as Martin contends, then it is highly probable that the rise of the term "homosexual" later in the century came to preclude "many spontaneous forms of open affection that had previously seemed normal" and that seem "abnormal" to us largely because we live on the hither side of the threshold of suspicion (14).[11] The same is true for language. It was one thing for Melville as "Virginian" to speak of Hawthorne "shoot[ing] his strong New-England roots into the hot soil of my Southern soul" in the decorous *Literary World* in 1850 (*WHM*, 9:250); it would be quite another for him to publish the words in the *New York Times Book Review* in 2008.

As a matter of vocabulary, I will be using "homosexuality" to refer to same-sex relationships that demonstrably involve genitality or at least a pronounced and persistent pattern of genital fantasy, "homosociality" to refer to same-sex friendship, and "homoeroticism" to suggest the broad middle range from intermittent sexual desire unaccompanied by characteristic adult behavior, on one side, to feelings of extraordinary warmth, delight, and personal intimacy, on the other.[12] To these terms, I would add a neologism of my own in response to Martin's 1986 differentiation between statements about books and statements about authors—"homo*text*uality": a pattern of same-sex eroticism in a work or body of work that has no necessary implications for the author's life.[13]

I mention this idea chiefly to discount it; I am not concerned with "Melville" simply as a canon.

In sifting these terms, the alienness and frequent inscrutability of mid-nineteenth-century psychoerotic experience should always be kept in mind. In a world of gradation, ambiguity, and cultural otherness, signs and behaviors that today would be taken as proclamations or hints of homoeroticism could seem sufficiently innocuous to pass muster even among the conventional. Melville admired busts of Antinous, the emperor Hadrian's lover, and late in life he owned one himself; but so did Sophia Hawthorne, who furnished the red cottage in Lenox with a bust of Antinous, "a favorite nineteenth-century subject, considered an emblem of ideal friendship," James R. Mellow notes—and of whatever other complex of feelings we can only surmise.[14] *Pierre* devotes several pages to its hero's youthful friendship with Glen Stanly, but while reviewers censured the book's many offenses against religion and morality, none seem to have objected to its florid celebration of "boy-love" (*WHM*, 7:216).[15] Was this embarrassment? Obtuseness? A journalistic conspiracy of silence? Or was the mock-heroic overtness of the eroticism a signal to contemporary readers that it was not transgressively sexual at all but a form of giddy preadolescent masculine chivalry, benign because soon to be transferred to heterosexual love? We don't know.

"Platonic Love"

Within the spectrum of cultural possibilities, problematic in itself, Melville occupies an anomalous position thanks to his youthful experience aboard ship, where homosexual practices were not uncommon even among otherwise heterosexual men, and in Polynesia, whose sexual customs may have bred in him an erotic latitudinarianism that John Bryant calls "'pansexual'"[16] and that Freud would likely have viewed as polymorphously perverse. Even within Melville's "sexual orientation" (if so homogenizing a term can be applied to his relationships to individuals), his feeling for Hawthorne would have been a special case of his attraction to male beauty and male character, just as his feeling for Jack Chase of the frigate *United States*—"that great heart" to whom he dedicated *Billy Budd, Sailor* nearly half a century later—was a special case of a different sort.[17] With Hawthorne, the legacy of South Seas eroticism was less important for Melville than the masculine rituals of feasting, drinking, smoking, and genial conversation, which Melville enjoyed even in their lighter forms and which, when combined with heady speculation, were among his greatest pleasures. The difference between talking "ontological heroics" with Hawthorne (*WHM*, 14:196) and "high German metaphysics" with George J. Adler (*WHM*, 15:19), his companion during part of his 1849–50 journey to England and the Continent, was that Hawthorne was darkly handsome with a spellbinding air of mystery almost universally remarked on by contemporaries. In Hawthorne Melville found an unmatched union of the four things that most attracted him to men: physical beauty, an air of natural aristocracy, a taste for (modest) festivity and frank conversation, and a brooding melancholy suggestive of deep sorrow. Hawthorne was also a fellow writer.

Possibly no other man, through a combination of these qualities, could have affected Melville as Hawthorne did. Could a woman? Probably not any woman of his acquaintance. If "there was . . . something in Herman Melville's life that caused him to dissociate woman from his account of man's deepest experience," as Lewis Mumford observed, that "something" may have been his want of opportunities for knowing an intellectual yet distinctively feminine woman.[18] When Melville finally did come upon such a woman in his reading of Mme. de Staël's *Germany* in 1862, it was with a sense of wonder that "such penetration of understanding" could coexist with "so feminine & emotional a nature."[19] The lines that prompted Melville's admiration were those remarking on Goethe's *"profound"* but *"discouraging knowledge"* of the "human heart,"[20] an echo of "that Calvinistic sense of Innate Depravity and Original Sin" which Melville had found in Hawthorne and ascribed to all "deeply thinking mind[s]" (*WHM*, 9:243) but seems surprised to have encountered in a woman.

This was not misogyny on Melville's part, nor was he alone in first discovering an intellectual woman abroad. Reading George Sand through the lens of her own cultural acquaintance with gender differences, Margaret Fuller professed "astonishment" at Sand's "insight into the life of thought," which Fuller believed must have come to her "through some man." "Women, under any circumstances, can scarce do more than dip the foot in this broad and deep river," Fuller noted, adding that "they have not strength to contend with the current. . . . It is easy for women to be heroic in action, but when it comes to interrogating God, the universe, the soul, and, above all, trying to live above their own hearts, they dart down to their nests like so many larks."[21] The Melvill(e), Gansevoort, and Shaw women, though intelligent and sometimes gifted, were conventionally religious; there was no Mary Moody Emerson in Melville's life; Pittsfield neighbor Sarah Morewood, lively and acute, was of a social rather than an intellectual disposition; even Sophia Hawthorne, with her artistic tastes and "spiritualizing nature" (*WHM*, 14:219), was sunny-minded and Christocentric. One wonders how Melville might have reacted to a woman with the intellect of Mme. de Staël and the vibrant sexuality of, say, Hawthorne's Zenobia. But Melville never met such a woman—the Duyckinck circle he frequented in New York was a masculine one—and looking for a soul mate, or a recipient for the superabundance he felt in himself, it was both serendipitous and biographically appropriate that he should have discovered one in Zenobia's creator.[22]

"Superabundance" seems the right word for the prodigal outpouring of self that distinguishes Melville's letters to Hawthorne through the fall of 1851. Their conversations during visits seem to have been largely one-sided, with Melville (in Sophia Hawthorne's words) "dash[ing] his tumultuous waves of thought against Mr. Hawthorne's great, genial, comprehending silences," broken occasionally by "a wonderful smile or one powerful word" that would change Melville's "foam and fury into a peaceful booming calm" or "murmuring expostulation."[23] As his letters bound forward from subject to subject—nearly all of them connected to *his* book-in-progress, *his* career, *his* opinions on God, man, and truth—Melville senses that his grandiose self-display may tax Hawthorne's patience or demand a requital Hawthorne is unwilling to give. "Don't trouble yourself, though, about writing; and don't trouble yourself about visiting; and when you *do* visit, don't trouble yourself about talking. I will do all the writing and visiting and talking myself" (*WHM*, 14:192).

There is an aptness to Melville's offer of unilateral egotism, for what is of greatest interest to him is not Hawthorne but himself as he emerges in his relation to Hawthorne. His performance, as he says, is done "incidentally and without premeditation" (*WHM*, 14:195–96), like that of a jazz musician improvising on a tune, intoxicated by his own virtuosity yet conscious of a special listener whose approval would be the measure and vindication of his enterprise. "You did not care a penny for the book [*Moby-Dick*]," he wrote Hawthorne in November 1851 in response to just such a vindication: "But, now and then as you read, you understood the pervading thought that impelled the book—and that you praised. Was it not so? You were archangel enough to despise the imperfect body, and embrace the soul. Once you hugged the ugly Socrates because you saw the flame in his mouth, and heard the rushing of the demon,—the familiar,—and recognized the sound; for you heard it in your own solitudes" (*WHM*, 14:212–13).

Melville alludes naturally to Plato's *Symposium* because the dialogue is "fresh in his mind in November of 1851."[24] In book 1 of *Pierre*, composed close to this time, he invokes the *Symposium* when he cites Aristophanes' myth of the parts of the divided self "roaming in quest of each other" as they seek completion.[25] Aristophanes' purpose is to explain the origin and significance of Eros, or the desire "implanted in us" of "reuniting our original nature, making one of two, and healing the state of man" (32). Originally there were three sexes, Aristophanes explains, each with a pair of genitals: one (the noblest) was doubly male, another doubly female, and the third male and female. Cut in two by the gods for their assault upon heaven, the severed halves searched for their complement, whether of the same or of the opposite sex; and so, ever since, human beings have been driven by "the desire and pursuit of the whole [which] is called love" (33). When aboriginal selves meet, "the pair are lost in an amazement of love and friendship and intimacy" and overwhelmed with an "intense yearning which . . . does not appear to be the desire of lover's intercourse, but of something else which the soul of either evidently desires and cannot tell, and of which she has only a dark and doubtful presentiment" (33). The elusiveness of this "something else" survives in the ambiguous contemporary definition of "Platonic love": "a close relationship between two persons in which sexual desire is *nonexistent* or has been *suppressed* or *sublimated*," a definition that implies nothing about the erotic character of such a relationship except that it is not overt.[26]

In mid-nineteenth-century America "Platonic love" functioned as a screen behind which a complex and virtually indecipherable set of emotions might lurk. "It is so true that a woman may be in love with a woman and a man with a man," Margaret Fuller wrote, adding immediately, as if to deny the erotic, that "undoubtedly it is the same love we shall feel when we are angels." Quoting Goethe—"'Sie fragen nicht nach Mann und Weib'" [It is not a question of man and woman]—Fuller described such love as "purely intellectual and spiritual, unprofaned by any mixture of lower instincts," and motivated by "the desire of the spirit to realize a whole, which makes it seek in another being what it finds not in itself."[27] It would be naive to take such words at face value yet unwarranted to assume they necessarily mask conscious or unconscious sexual desire. Speakers like Fuller were often themselves confused about their impulses, and the idiom of Platonic soul-completion provided a language in which ardent feelings could be expressed without having to be examined or acted upon. Whether or not these feelings were truly asexual in the most literal sense of nongenital, the invocation of Platonism could allow the speakers to think they were.

What Melville *was* conscious of finding in and through Hawthorne was the figurative "other" who drew forth and completed his fragmented self as dark characters in Melville's fiction had given promise of doing for his heroes since *Typee*. "Whence come you, Hawthorne?" the "ugly Socrates" passage begins: "By what right do you drink from my flagon of life? And when I put it to my lips—lo, they are yours and not mine. I feel that the Godhead is broken up like the bread of the Supper, and that we are the pieces. Hence this infinite fraternity of feeling" (*WHM*, 14:212). Freud appeals to a similar idea in *Beyond the Pleasure Principle* when he alludes to Aristophanes' myth as a metaphor for psychic reintegration: "Shall we follow the hint given us by the poet-philosopher, and venture upon the hypothesis that living substance at the time of its coming to life was torn apart into small particles, which have ever since endeavoured to reunite through the sexual instinct?"[28] Through one vocabulary or another, Christian mystery or Platonic myth, Melville is laboring to express his wonder at finding his ideal self-image reflected back to him from the pages of his letters to Hawthorne, then ratified by an appreciation of *Moby-Dick* so penetrating and sympathetic it might almost have been written by the author himself. "If our loves were perfectly accomplished, and each one returning to his primeval nature had his original true love," Aristophanes says, "then our race would be happy," by which he means rescued from the urgencies of seeking and harmoniously at rest (34). Melville implies just such a harmony when he refers to the "sense of unspeakable security . . . in me this moment, on account of your having understood the book." "It is a strange feeling," he adds: "no hopefulness is in it, no despair. Content—that is it; and irresponsibility; but without licentious inclination" (*WHM*, 14:212). Eros in this context is not a desire for sexual consummation but an impulse toward integration of being that drives Aristophanes' lovers and that Melville makes an attraction of preappointed souls: "The divine magnet is in you, and my magnet responds. Which is the biggest? A foolish question—they are *One*" (*WHM*, 14:213).

Jonathan Lear sees Aristophanes' myth as directing psychic energies away "from any tendency to strive for the transcendent" toward a search for "human completion" in "the socio-political realm."[29] This is how Eros functions for Ishmael in "A Squeeze of the Hand" as he "lower[s], or at least shift[s], his conceit of attainable felicity" from "the intellect or the fancy" to the satisfactions (sexual and otherwise) of the human community (*WHM*, 6:416). In Melville's letters to Hawthorne, the intellect and the fancy—the spirit's quest for truth—comprise the very basis for community, or at least for an elite kind of male bonding. Rather than a social counterforce to aspiration, the (homo)erotic becomes its affective stimulus and reinforcing accompaniment. For once in Melville's life, the twin foci of his nature—"land" and "sea," senses and intellect, the ethico-political realm and the realm of metaphysics—are in full harmony as he fronts the present and imagines the spiritual journey ahead. "Ah! it's a long stage, and no inn in sight, and night coming, and the body cold," Melville writes Hawthorne: "But with you for a passenger, I am content and can be happy" (*WHM*, 14:213).

In the bower scene by the Jordan in *Clarel* that Edwin Haviland Miller and others have read as an emotional projection of the Melville-Hawthorne relationship, Clarel silently implores Vine, "Give me thyself!" (*WHM*, 12:225). What Melville implicitly asked of the actual Hawthorne seems rather to have been, "Give me *myself!*" Having enlisted Hawthorne as a comrade in an adventure à deux, Melville transforms the prospective colloquy into an epistolary soliloquy, with Hawthorne as catalyst for and recipient of Melville's boundless self-enthusiasm: "I'll tell you what I should do. I should have a paper-mill established at one end of the house, and so have an endless riband of foolscap rolling in upon my desk; and upon that endless riband I should write a thousand—a million—billion thoughts, all under the form of a letter to you" (*WHM*, 14:213).[30]

It was Melville's narcissistic delight in himself that gave his relationship to Hawthorne its special ardor and, with Hawthorne's departure from the Berkshires in late November 1851, its special devastation. There is no evidentiary basis for Edwin Haviland Miller's conjecture that Melville overstepped the bounds and at some point made what was intended or received as a homoerotic "'advance,'" a word even Miller chooses to render in quotation marks (250).[31] Given Hawthorne's reserve and almost abnormal fastidiousness on matters of touch, together with his uneasiness about sexuality of any sort other than heterosexual monogamy, Melville would have known better than to try. If he did transgress by word or deed, it is extremely unlikely that Hawthorne would have invited him to visit Concord in 1852 or found himself "on pretty much our former terms of sociability and confidence" when Melville stayed with him in Liverpool four years later (*CE,* 22:162). Even in *Clarel* the intimacy Vine rejects in the bower scene is not a homosexual but a homosocial one— "the *soul's* caress," for which "[t]he negatives of flesh" imply "*analogies of non-cordialness / in spirit*" (*WHM,* 12:227; my emphasis). Hawthorne had more than enough reasons to leave the Berkshires—he disliked the isolation and the climate; he missed the ocean; the little red cottage was too small for his family, soon to receive a third child; he quarreled with his landlords[32]—and when the opportunity to rent his sister-in-law's house in West Newton presented itself, he seized it quickly, with no apparent change in his relationship to Melville. The probable truth of the friendship during their months together in the Berkshires, as Walter Bezanson suggests in his "Historical and Critical Note" on *Clarel,* is that "Hawthorne responded" to "Melville's reckless emotional attachment" with as much openness and "warmth" as his native reserve allowed but with considerably less than could satisfy Melville's accumulated need (*WHM,* 12:596, 12:597). If an "estrangement" did occur—and like Bezanson and others, I read "Monody" as an elegy for Hawthorne ("To have known him, to have loved him / After loneness long; / And then to be estranged in life, / And neither in the wrong. . . .")—it was almost certainly one of gradual attenuation, undramatic and, as "Monody" suggests, with no fault on either side.[33]

Mourning and Melancholia in *Pierre*

To the degree that Hawthorne had become essential to Melville's ideal of himself as well as to his emotional life, his removal was felt as a profound deprivation second only to the loss of Melville's father years before, an event whose feeling of abandonment it rekindled. There is a ring of truth to Newton Arvin's conjecture that "a sense of having been somehow rejected, unreasonable and egoistic though it was, festered in Melville's consciousness."[34] Hawthorne's withdrawal (so it would have seemed to Melville) was like a defection or a death. And taking place amidst a Berkshire landscape haunted with familial associations, it would have linked itself with the emotions and reversal of fortune consequent upon Allan Melvill's death in 1832. Already susceptible to remembrances of his father, Melville all but came upon him in spirit on July 7, 1851, when he "first detected [Allan's] pencil signature" in an edition of Robert Burton's *Anatomy of Melancholy* he had chanced to purchase in a New York book store four years earlier. "Strange!" he mused; strange, too, that of all Allan Melvill's books, probably "sold at auction, at least twenty-five years ago" (*Log*, 416), Melville should have found the inscription in Burton's *Anatomy*, a work he had cherished since his teenage years and whose title evoked feelings of "enduring grief and melancholy" left in him by Allan's death.[35] "Never again can such blights be made good," Melville has Redburn say of his own father's bankruptcy and death: "they strike in too deep, and leave such a scar that the air of paradise might not erase it" (*WHM*, 4:11). Melville would return to the subject of father-loss in *Pierre*, close to the time Hawthorne left Lenox. "Tranced grief" he would call such "coffined" but still vital suffering, capable of reawakening at any moment in response to a prompting situation (*WHM*, 7:286).

Long before Freud's classic essay "Mourning and Melancholia," Melville seems to have grasped the affinity and relational etiology between the mourner's chronic, unresolved grief and the depression of the melancholic with his sense, in Freud's words, of "being slighted, neglected or disappointed" by a loved object he cannot abandon.[36] In his memoir of depression, *Darkness Visible*, William Styron remarks that "loss in all of its manifestations is the touchstone of depression" (Styron traces the "probable genesis" of his own suicidal crisis to the death of his mother when he was thirteen).[37] British psychologist John Bowlby argued the point exhaustively, stressing the importance of "childhood experiences" in "predispos[ing] an individual towards a pathological response to loss."[38] Developing Freud's notion of ambivalence toward the lost object, Bowlby finds that a child "at risk of developing chronic mourning" will "almost always" have, on one side, "a model of his parents as above criticism and a complementary one of himself as a more or less worthless person," and, on the other side, a view of his parents "as grudging in their affection and attention and too often unavailable" and of himself as neglected, underappreciated, and justified in his resentments of them

(234)—the Ishmael/Abraham syndrome. As the third of eight children, Melville had reason to feel neglected, particularly as he was outshone by his older, more aggressive, and outwardly more brilliant brother, Gansevoort, the favorite of both parents and the bearer of family ambitions as well as of the maternal surname. Herman was "an uncommon good Boy" but "more sedate" and "less bouyant [sic] in mind" than Gansevoort, Allan wrote in one of several such judgments.[39] It is a measure of the tenacity of Allan's undervaluation that even the achievements of his second son, such as proving "the best Speaker in the introductory Department of the High School," came as a surprise to him.[40] Nothing seems to have occurred in later years to revise the father's opinion, so that when Allan died in 1832 Herman was left not only with vastly reduced expectations but with no possibility of ever vindicating himself in his father's eyes.

The mourning theories of Freud and Bowlby help explain Melville's lifelong preoccupation with the quest for the father, both human and divine. Still more directly pertinent may be Heinz Kohut's account of narcissistic personality disorders. According to Kohut, a child responds to "the unavoidable shortcomings of maternal care . . . (a) by establishing a grandiose and exhibitionistic image of the self: the *grandiose self*; and (b) by giving over the previous perfection to an admired, omnipotent (transitional) self-object: *the idealized parent imago*," to be replaced in time by the child's consolidating superego.[41] "Under optimal circumstances," Kohut says, this process occurs gradually as the child discovers the idealized parent's imperfections and is able to wean him- or herself from the need for parental approval and develop an autonomous sense of self-worth (45). If, however, "the child suffers the traumatic loss of the idealized object . . . or a traumatic . . . disappointment in it," the "psyche remains fixated on the archaic self-object" and will experience "throughout life . . . an intense form of object hunger" (45) leading it to seek "a union with the idealized object" as represented by various "present-day . . . replicas" (55).

In their different idioms, Freud, Bowlby, and Kohut are describing versions of the process by which adult crises of self-esteem build on and reenact childhood traumas, as investments of the self are shattered by the loss of or rejection by a subsequent loved object. In Kohut's terms, the psychodynamic visibly at work in Melville's letters to Hawthorne through November 1851 is that of the grandiose self performing for and seeking the approval of an idealized parent imago. At once father, brother, and Platonic second self, Hawthorne gave Melville the assurance of being known and valued for what he took himself to be at his best. Correspondingly, the effect of his departure was to deflate Melville and plunge him into a state that might now be diagnosed as depression but for which the older term melancholia, with its literary resonance and link with mourning, seems more appropriate. The melancholic, Freud speculated, has also lost a loved object (not necessarily by death), but unlike the mourner, whose grief is focused and readily comprehensible, the melancholic "knows *whom* he has lost but not *what* he has lost in him" (245). Essentially, what he has lost is himself. The melancholic shares the mourner's profound dejection and reduced energy and affect but differs from the mourner in "an extraordinary diminution in his self-regard. . . . In mourning it is the world which has become poor and empty; in melancholia it is the ego itself" (246).

Freud is wary of assigning a single explanation to a phenomenon so various and so rudimentarily understood; Bowlby, however, finds the experience of "feeling abandoned, unwanted and unlovable" to stem "in most forms of depressive disorder" from the sufferer's incapacity "to make and maintain affectional relationships" (246–48), a failing he traces to the family history, which more often than with other children includes the loss of a parent. The sufferer is likely to feel he has disappointed his parents' expectations of him despite his efforts to please, and he is prone "to interpret any loss he may later suffer as yet another of his failures" to relate successfully to others (247). Adults vulnerable to this kind of narcissistic injury, according to Kohut, frequently experienced in childhood a "sudden, unexpected, intolerable disappointment" in or loss of an idealized parent prior to their development of stable structures of identity and value (55). It is significant in this regard that Hershel Parker should begin his two-volume biography of Melville with a chapter titled "The Flight of the Patrician Wastrel and His Second Son," which opens with the eleven-year-old Herman helping his father pack up their house and slip away from his creditors at night.[42] Melville intimately witnessed the humiliation of his father; less than sixteen months later he would witness his father's death.

Hawthorne's departure from the Berkshires reawakened the trauma of Allan Melvill's death, not because Melville doubted Hawthorne's regard but because thriving in its felt presence, even through the substantial gaps in their letters and visits, he had become dependent on it for his *self*-regard. Two characteristics of Freudian melancholia are particularly relevant here: first, the proneness of the melancholic to blame himself for "the loss of the loved object" (251) and to join in the other's real or imagined humiliation of him and, second, the "remarkable . . . tendency [of melancholia] to change round into mania," its affective opposite (253). The portrait of Melville in late 1851 given by granddaughter Eleanor Melville Metcalf shows a "sick man" of "driven and flagging energies" who struck neighbor Sarah Morewood as "'more quiet than usual,'" given to "'irreverent language,'" and writing "'under a state of morbid excitement which will soon injure his health.'"[43] The chronology of late 1851 is uncertain. When did Melville learn of Hawthorne's decision to leave the Berkshires? When did he begin *Pierre*? Mid-to-late October is a likely date for both events—but the febrile, half-diabolical tone of the opening books of *Pierre,* which Brian Higgins and Hershel Parker take for buoyant confidence, seems rather the splenetic counterfeit of confidence, "a mixed state, in which," as psychiatrist Kay Redfield Jamison describes the phenomenon, "manic and depressive symptoms exist together."[44]

Desolated by Hawthorne's removal, Melville felt himself a monumental fool for having nourished illusions of intimacy. Freud notes that the melancholic, in responding to present loss, "extends his self-criticism back over the past" and "declares that he was never any better" (246). So Melville may have believed when he looked back upon the development of mind on which he had progressively come to stake his life since *Mardi.* The long journey with "no inn in sight, and night coming, and the body cold" (*WHM,* 14:213) seemed infinitely less alluring without Hawthorne beside him as companion and witness. It was one thing to boast of stepping from *Moby-Dick* to bigger fish, to "Krakens" (*WHM,* 14:213), with a godlike listener empathetically at hand, and quite another when the listener turned Deus absconditus, and one's words echoed mockingly in an empty room. *Pierre* is Melville's ironic deconstruction of the quest, embodied in a hero who at once invites identification with the author and serves as an object for the author's relentless unmasking of self-infatuated idealism. Like the Freudian melancholic, who, far from feeling shame about his imagined failures, displays an "insistent communicativeness which finds satisfaction in self-exposure" (247), Melville turned against himself early in *Pierre* through the mocking self-reference of the Glendinning/Gansevoort parallels and the giddy delight his narrator takes in promising to topple Pierre from his "noble pedestal" (*WHM,* 7:12) and strip him of all inward and outward complacencies.

In directing his formidable powers of analysis against a parodic fictionalization of his younger self, Melville was systematically uprooting his own familial, personal, intellectual, and vocational identity, apparently in response to a profound psychological shock. Was the shock that of discovering that Allan Melvill had an illegitimate daughter? This was the conjecture of Amy Puett Emmers and later of Henry A. Murray and two collaborators working from a letter from Thomas Melvill (Allan's brother) about a claim made against Allan's estate after his death. Judiciously weighing the evidence, Hershel Parker finds it inconclusive even apart from the related problems of how and when Melville might have heard such a story and how it might have affected him twenty years after Allan's death.[45] "A well-constituted individual refrains from blazoning aught amiss or calamitous in his family" (55), Melville would write in *Billy Budd*. If Allan did have an illegitimate daughter, why did Melville choose to flaunt it in print? If not, why was he insinuatingly blackening Allan's name and "horrifying his mother and other close relatives"?[46] Perhaps Melville in the fall of 1851 was not "a well-constituted individual." In a letter to Sarah Morewood of mid-September he wrote of "certain silly thoughts and wayward speculations" that "the Fates have plunged me into" (*WHM*, 14:206). Within several weeks these wayward speculations or others would evolve into *Pierre*, in F. O. Matthiessen's words "about the most desperate [book] in our literature."[47]

Matthiessen ascribes *Pierre* to the "surg[ing] up into Melville's mind" of material that "remains unconscious for most authors" and that tapped "Melville's pained awareness of an Oedipus-relation" (with which parent Matthiessen does not say) and of "the latent homosexuality" he projected into the Pierre–Glen Stanly friendship (480). Was the putative shock that catalyzed *Pierre* the shock of homoerotic self-recognition? In *Closet Writing/Gay Reading* James Creech contends it was when he takes Pierre's "I will write it, I will write it!" (*WHM*, 7:273)—Pierre's enthusiast response to the discovery of incest-desire—as the author's own veiled declaration of coming out. Creech's argument owes much to two sources, Newton Arvin's theory of father-son incest ("Pierre's unconscious wish is to escape from Lucy and to preserve the incestuous bond with his father by uniting himself" to the father's self-proclaimed illegitimate daughter [224]) and John Seelye's suggestion that the Pierre-Isabel relationship draws on Melville's "passionate feelings for Hawthorne," substituting one form of proscribed sexuality (incest) for another (homoeroticism).[48]

Creech joins these threads in a "camp reading" of *Pierre* as the "trans-vested" story "of a man who forswears his fiancé [sic] and runs away to the city with his homosexual lover."[49]

Arvin and Creech are right to see the initial action of *Pierre* as the rejection of domesticity for an alliance with a darkly erotic being associated with the father, though it is important to note that Pierre is fascinated by Isabel *before* she tells him she is his father's child. Are Arvin and Creech also right to infer a fantasy of homosexual incest? And if so, what can this mean? Was Melville implying literal, genital incest or some form of emotional incest such as Phyllis Chesler suggests when she asks apropos of the final plate of William Blake's *Jerusalem*: "Do sons wish to mate with their fathers? Is the shame of their abandonment by fathers so great that the 'Oedipal dilemma' can only be 'resolved' through prohibited erotic means—and then only in a 'spiritual' sense which excludes woman entirely?"[50] Was it sexual consummation with the father or father substitute that Melville sought with Hawthorne or was it the loving acknowledgment of worth withheld by the earthly father (Allan) and by the spiritual Father (God)? Was it both at once—the former as a means to and token of the latter, the exiled son reuniting with the exiling F/father through the vehicle of sexual consummation?

In *The Analysis of the Self* Kohut discusses the case of a Mr. A., whose history and condition bear notable resemblances to Melville's. Though intelligent and professionally accomplished, Mr. A. was "forever in search of guidance and approval" from his "elders or superiors," whose praise was crucial to his self-esteem. The immediate cause of his entering analysis was anxiety over homosexual fantasies extending back to his adolescence. These fantasies, Kohut came to believe, were only subordinately related to a wider tendency to depression that surfaced whenever Mr. A. felt his seniors' indifference to him. Mr. A.'s father, like Melville's, had been a successful businessman whose financial collapse was accompanied by "emotional and physical deterioration" and "hypochrondriacal complaints" witnessed intimately by his son at an impressionable age (58, 59). His mother, also like Melville's, had been an erratic caregiver whose fluctuations of attention and empathy caused him to overidealize the father imago and thereby expose himself to later traumatic injury in response to the father's humiliation.[51] Mr. A.'s homosexual fantasies, in Kohut's view, were "sexualizations" of his father imago—that is, by-products and "means for the discharge of intense narcissistic tensions" rather than symptoms of genuine incestuous desire or deep-seated ho-mosexuality. As the analysis proceeded, Kohut reports, these fantasies and their associated fears "disappeared almost completely" (70, 72, 70).

Was Melville like or unlike Mr. A.? Did he harbor incestuous feelings for his father that were displaced onto Hawthorne, as Arvin and Creech maintain, or did his feelings for Hawthorne involve the sexualization or quasi sexualization of a narcissistic trauma asexual in itself? With respect to Melville the man, we can only speculate; with respect to *Pierre* as a literary text and the fictive site containing, as Matthiesen puts it, "the most evident traces of the interaction of Hawthorne and Melville" (468), the weakness of Creech's argument is all that it leaves out: virtually the entire philosophical content of the book, which Creech dismisses as an "alibi" on Pierre's part and an obfuscation on Melville's (167). Arvin had also foundered on the difficulty of reconciling the book's sexual inter-est and presumptive roots in "the accumulation of emotional strains" (202) dating back to Melville's childhood with its dominant concern with the "ambiguity of idealistic absolutism" (219). Arvin's response was the Freudian one of separating manifest content (intellectual and conscious) from latent content (sexual and unconscious), a division Creech repli-cates when he argues that "a literary text can wink at us about its homo-erotic content without, as it were, knowing what it is doing" (113).

The indications are, however, that through book 14 at least ("The Journey and the Pamphlet") *Pierre* knows perfectly well what it is doing and that the distinction between manifest and latent, intellectual and erotic, is precisely what it sets out to contest: this is the terra incog-nita to which Melville's relationship with Hawthorne has led him. The "spiritual" in *Pierre* is not a mere superstructure of illusions reared up from the desires of the unconscious; spiritual drives in the form of im-pulses toward an enigmatic wonder world in the self and the universe are *part* of the unconscious, entangled with other drives (the sexual in-cluded) but by no means reducible to them. For Pierre, who has "never known" grief or been deeply "initiated into that darker, though truer aspect of things" (*WHM*, 7:41, 7:69), the mournfulness of Isabel's face unlocks depths in himself and discloses "one infinite, dumb, beseech-ing countenance of mystery, underlying all surfaces of visible time and space" (*WHM*, 7:51–52), which previously "had seemed but too common and prosaic to him" (*WHM*, 7:128). Incantatory words like "mournful," "mystical," "melancholy," "sadness," "anguish," and "grief," smokescreens within Creech's reading, invest Isabel with a transcendent woefulness reminiscent of *Mardi*'s heaven, an "extraordinary atmospheric spell" so interpenetratingly "physical and spiritual" (*WHM*, 7:151) that one quality is barely distinguishable from the other. In *Moby-Dick* Ishmael's pursuit of "the ungraspable phantom of life" had been associated with the sea, the whale, and "one grand hooded phantom, like a snow hill in the air" (*WHM*, 6:5, 6:7). In *Pierre* Isabel assumes the function of spiritual magnet as Pierre, seized by "the divine beauty and imploring sufferings of [her] face," feels his sense of "the solid land of veritable reality . . . audaciously encroached upon by bannered armies of *hooded phantoms,* disembarking in his soul, as from flotillas of specter-boats" (*WHM*, 7:49; my emphasis). Melville's "phantoms" have been relocated from the outer world to the mind of the hero and have taken on an aspect of compulsion. It is as though Melville suddenly realized the meaning and psychic origin of the dark Other he had been creating in book after book. What fascinates Pierre is not so much "the mournful person of the olive girl" as what she evokes in "his own soul": "*There,* lurked the subtler secret" (*WHM*, 7:51). Isabel is the epitome of what Milton R. Stern called the "lure" in Melville's writings, a figure or idea that directs the hero "toward God's ideal realm of other-world" but that at bottom is "an external objectification of the quester's own predisposition."[52] As Henry A. Murray put it, "the 'ungraspable phantom of life' is not in Isabel but in [Pierre]. He is Narcissus plunging to embrace his own image."[53]

I am not trying to explain away the eroticism and cryptic homoeroticism of *Pierre* but to understand it in its own fictive and psychobiographical context. Since Murray's 1949 introduction to *Pierre*, it has been common to see Isabel as "the personification of Pierre's unconscious" (lii), particularly of his "aroused soul-image, or [Jungian] anima" (xliv), which Murray goes on to give an atypically Freudian character. On the Jungian side, Isabel points ahead to a fuller self to be realized through the ego's integration with "the as-yet-unformulated components" of the personality usually projected by a male upon a female but sometimes (as in Aristophanes' myth) upon another male; on the Freudian side, Isabel leads Pierre backward to "the child in him who felt unloved" and to "the grief and the self-pity which have been bottled up" (lii). Though Murray draws on two conflicting notions of the unconscious—as a reservoir of mature intellectual and creative possibilities (Jung); as a labyrinth of repressed childhood desires (Freud)—his eclecticism is apt, for the object of Melville's investigation in *Pierre* is precisely this relationship between the developmental and the fixational, the intellectual quest and its buried psychic determinants.

What does Melville mean by intertwining the drive toward individuation with the regressive pull of the archaic and by representing both of these things in the alluring Janus-faced melancholy of Isabel? To pursue this question is to dive into the Melvillean self and speculate on "subtile causations" that "defy all analytical insight" (*WHM*, 7:67). Through some process that can only be fitfully reconstructed, the sadness of father-loss to which *Redburn* testifies was transmuted beginning in Melville's teens into a protometaphysical stance at once defiant of God, hungry for God, and enamored of melancholy as an affective surrogate for the emotions of filial and religious devotion. Allusions to *Childe Harold's Pilgrimage* and Burton's *Anatomy of Melancholy* in "Fragments from a Writing Desk" suggest a literary acquaintance with melancholy that helped Melville cope with depression and blight by elevating sadness into a noble malaise. As Murray argued, the life and writings of Byron as mediated through Thomas Moore's *Life of Byron* were instrumental in shaping the adolescent Melville who was father of the man (xli). From the similarities between Byron's situation and his own—a dead father, a "supremely bossy" mother,[54] a Calvinist heritage they could neither accept nor wholly discard, economic privation and social slights, sexual ambiguity—and from the glorious way in which Byron turned suffering and exile into dark heroism, Melville came to assimilate, on some level of consciousness, a nexus involving p/Paternal abandonment, intellectual aspiration, pervasive Weltschmerz, an alternating sense of grandiosity and worthlessness, an open or insinuated eroticism (including homoeroticism), and a fixation on metaphysics as the idiom in which these combined things were played out. Through the medium of Byron, Melville converted narcissistic father-loss and father-hunger into God-loss and God-hunger, which later as a writer he came to embody in a series of mournfully dark anima figures through whom his hero affirms his identity as a noble sufferer and spiritual son of God.

One might term this process the homoeroticization of father-loss into quasi religion. It was not unique to Melville. In his early journal written in college, Emerson, who himself lost his father in youth and was an ardent admirer of Byron, confides his fascination with a dark, brooding classmate aptly named Martin Gay. Emerson never spoke to

Gay or seems to have attempted to; they only exchanged what Emerson described as piercing glances, as Clarel would with his imagined soul brother, the dark Celio. Gay was not a distinct individual for Emerson so much as an externalization of the mysterious, romantic self Emerson wished himself to be but knew he was not. In fact, Emerson's idea of "Gay" preceded the actual encounter. "Before I ever saw him, I wished my *friend* to be different from any individual I had seen. I invested him with a solemn cast of mind, full of poetic feeling, . . . & possessing a vein of rich sober thought. When I saw ———'s pale but expressive face & large eye, I instantly invested him with the complete character which fancy had formed."[55] As a same-sex anima figure, Gay is an idealizing mirror for Emerson as he contemplates and imaginatively reaches out toward a fantasized self.

In homoerotic relationships like Emerson's with Gay or, more profoundly, Melville's with Hawthorne, the sexual element is part of a larger constellation of factors—psychological, intellectual, spiritual—of almost unanalyzable intricacy: the love that defies being named. In *Pierre* Isabel becomes the object of that love. Darkly mournful, Isabel takes her place with earlier figures in Melville's writings as the representative of a larger, more exhilarating, God-infused world of suffering and knowledge, with the difference that Isabel is female, which allows the libidinal attraction of melancholy to surface as an explicit theme (brother/sister incest was a staple of gothic and Byronic romance as well as a fact of Byron's actual life). John Seelye is right, I think, in associating Isabel with Hawthorne as a figure pointing away from the ordinariness of domesticity toward "the darkness and suffering of Truth" (438). If Pierre's early behavior reveals, as Arvin suggests, "a man whose unconscious is lying in wait for the first plausible opportunity to desert" (223) (Isabel providing the opportunity), a similar lurking receptivity might be ascribed to Melville on the eve of meeting Hawthorne—"Mr. Noble Melancholy," as Cornelius Mathews called him in his literary account of the Monument Mountain expedition that brought the two men together (*Log,* 383). Though Melville sometimes "took comfort (and perhaps even inspiration) from domesticity,"[56] he could also, when writing, feel himself besieged by it. Ensconced now in a Berkshire farmhouse with his wife, two children, his mother, and three unmarried sisters, Melville must have felt, as Arvin says, "the smothering network of family relations and family responsibilities [pulled] tighter than ever about his head" (203). His visits, even his epistolary visits, to Hawthorne were a deliverance from this life and a reimmersion in the world of intellect and frank, genial conversation that was his greatest pleasure but that found no satisfying outlet in his life at Arrowhead. Other feelings may have surfaced as well: nostalgia for his bachelor days with their youthful sexual opportunities aboard ship and in Polynesia; responsiveness to male beauty; the narcissist's yearning for an approving father and soul brother; his fascination with dark, mysterious introverts; his effort to know, articulate, and ratify himself through dedication to his journey of mind. All of these things combined to draw him powerfully toward Hawthorne and away from the confining, if supportive, domesticity of his household.[57] Like his fictive heroes, Melville impulsively fled the land for the sea and, in a kind of emotional adultery, made his relationship with Hawthorne the identic center of his life even as the Pittsfield farmhouse remained its practical center.

Pierre's spiritual fortunes turn in the moment of "terrible self-revelation" (WHM, 7:192) in which he realizes the erotic underpinnings of his devotion to Isabel. A comparably shattering self-revelation overtook Melville, I would suggest, as his feeling of bereftness at Hawthorne's departure made him aware that in some fashion, for reasons buried deeply in his life history, he had been "in love" with another man. Intimations of the crisis go back several months, as if Melville's emotions had already begun to make for uneasiness even as his intimacy with Hawthorne was at its height. Early in June 1851 he confided to Hawthorne that strange premonition of decay so crucial to an understanding of his self-conception and so prophetic of Pierre. Adapting the romantic metaphor of growth as the unfolding of a plant from a principle contained in the seed, he characterized himself, not yet thirty-two and at the height of his imaginative powers, as having "come to the inmost leaf of the bulb" and "shortly" to "fall to the mould" (WHM, 14:193). Perhaps Melville was simply exhausted by the imaginative strain of writing Moby-Dick, yet even as he "cooked" the "tail" of his book (WHM, 14:196) he may already have been looking beyond or beneath Ahab to the psychic underpinnings of the quest that his heroic purposes required him to suppress. In Pierre he would write that no man ever arrives at "the Ultimate of Human Speculative Knowledge," there to "abide": "Sudden onsets of new truth will assail him, and overturn him as the Tartars did China; for there is no China Wall that man can build in his soul, which shall permanently stay the irruptions of those barbarous hordes which Truth ever nourishes in the loins of her frozen, yet teeming North" (*WHM*, 7:167). The image joins two literary sources: Emerson's phrase "a Chinese wall that any nimble Tartar can leap over" and Milton's description of the throng of fallen angels in *Paradise Lost* ("a multitude, like which the populous North / Pour'd never from her frozen loins").[58] The implication is that truth, formerly the hunted, has now become the hunter and turned upon the quester in the unwelcome revelation of something primitive, chaotic, and deeply subversive of the structures of the self.

The truth that overturned Melville I take to be his realization that the quest for a knowledge associated with otherworldly sadness and divinity was fueled by a F/father-hunger rooted in the child's need for love and approbation. Writing of Ahab's drive to "make converse" led Melville to investigate his own need for converse and to glimpse how his attachment to Hawthorne was somehow connected to it. It was not, however, until the euphoria of writing *Moby-Dick* waned and Melville, like Pierre after his Enceladus dream, "woke from that ideal horror to all his actual grief" that he turned inward "to penetrate into [his] heart, and memory, and inmost life, and nature" and began to excavate the foundations of his personality (*WHM*, 7:346, 7:67). In a letter to Sarah Morewood from mid-September 1851 he spoke of "certain silly thoughts and wayward speculations" that "the Fates have plunged me into" (*WHM* 14:206). By late October or early November, the time he most likely began *Pierre*, Melville knew of Hawthorne's impending departure from the Berkshires, and the shock of an abrupt termination to a relationship he had come to live in caused a heartsickness that, in the mind's analysis of its nature and sources, led to a "terrible self-revelation."[59]

"Why this strife of the chase?" Ahab asks toward the end of *Moby-Dick*, thinking of the ordinary comforts of the land he forsook for the transcendent (*WHM*, 6:544). In the fall of 1851 Melville was asking that question of himself. Reacting to the new wound of Hawthorne's departure as it reopened and compounded the old wound of his father's humiliation and death, he began to drop "his angle into the well of his childhood, to find what fish might be there" (*WHM*, 7:284). Instead of a selfless aspiration toward God and truth, the quest now seemed obscurely grounded in his feelings toward his father and father surrogates—the male love-objects that drew him toward an eroticized otherworld of "Gloom and Grief" (*WHM*, 7:169) associated with the divine Father who had replaced the earthly one as his idealized parent imago. In his earlier writings Melville had taken this attraction to melancholy unquestioningly as the mark of intellectual depth and spiritual heroism; in *Pierre* he anatomizes it virtually as a narcissistic personality disorder. In his new mood, the values and commitments to which he had mortgaged his domestic life seemed tainted by unconscious compulsion. The "infinite fraternity of feeling" he had felt in Hawthorne's presence (*WHM*, 14:212) now appeared to him a symptom of psychic dependence; even the quest itself, so far as he imagined it occurring under the gaze of an approving Parent, seemed to derive from a baffled father-love and father-resentment—the child's ambivalence writ large in the adult's mythopoesis. Reacting to the discovery of incest-desire, Pierre cries, "I will write it, I will write it!" (*WHM*, 7:273); reacting to the uncovered tangle of feelings for which incest-desire was a literary symbol, Melville did write it:

> There is a dark, mad mystery in some human hearts, which, sometimes, during the tyranny of a usurper mood, leads them to be all eagerness to cast off the most intense beloved bond, as a hindrance to the attainment of whatever transcendental object that usurper mood so tyrannically suggests. . . .
>
> Weary with the invariable earth, the restless sailor breaks from every enfolding arm, and puts to sea in height of tempest that blows off shore. But in long night-watches at the antipodes, how heavily that ocean gloom lies in vast bales upon the deck; thinking that that very moment in his deserted hamlet-home the household sun is high, and many a sun-eyed maiden meridian as the sun. He curses Fate; himself he curses; his senseless madness, which is himself. For whoso once has known this sweet knowledge, and then fled it; in absence, to him the avenging dream will come. (*WHM*, 7:180–81)

The "avenging dream" is to *Pierre* what "The Lee Shore" is to *Moby-Dick* but with a complete reversal of mood and idea. With the recognition of the trauma-based origins of his spiritual life—symbolized in Isabel, whose lineaments of grief seem to beckon Pierre onward to God, truth, and his own deepest self but whose fascination is sourced in her transgendered resemblance to the father—Melville recoiled against himself and his family with proselytic zeal. Allan Melvill was the special focus of his anger as undervaluing father, as stand-in for the current father image, Hawthorne, who just deserted him, and as source or scapegoat for his present crisis of self-esteem. Bowlby notes that when a child has been divided in his attitude toward a lost parent—on the dominant side admiring the parent and blaming himself for failures in the relationship, on the subordinate side blaming the parent and feeling himself misunderstood or wronged—a "change of cognitive balance" may occur some time in later life in which "the individual's latent resentment breaks through and . . . he rebels" (236). Whether or not Allan Melvill had, to Herman's knowledge, an illegitimate child, the significant fact is that Melville chose to found his plot on the discrediting insinuation that he did. "I will no more have a father" (*WHM*, 7:87), Pierre exclaims as he replaces fidelity to an earthly father with allegiance to a divine one, symbolized in his devotion to Isabel. In some wordless subterranean fashion, Melville seems to have recognized that he himself had done the same years earlier when he came to terms with Allan's bankruptcy and death by supplanting him with the image of an idealized father surrogate/quasi-lover/divinity, now crowningly realized in Hawthorne. To lose Hawthorne was to lose what had become the emotional prop of his self-definition and of his justification vis-à-vis his family for the domestic derelictions of his life. It was as if instead of being one of "God's posts" (*WHM*, 14:195), Melville suddenly found himself to be what he would make Pierre—God's fool. The "hardest" lesson Pierre is brought to confront is the one Melville seems to have confronted as he set out to write his book: that the quester who has renounced common happiness for truth finds himself not only spurned by the social world, the mother (and Melville's own mother was always harshly critical of his failure to make a living as a writer), but "likewise despise[d]" by the gods, the father, who "own him not of their clan" (*WHM*, 7:296).

From its own time through the present, *Pierre* has been called a morbid book. It may also be morbid in the clinical sense of arising from and illustrating what Kohut describes as the regressive phases of a narcissistic personality disorder, shown in the diagram from *The Analysis of the Self*. In their exhibitionism and drive toward an intimacy bordering on psychic merger, Melville's letters to Hawthorne through November 1851 belong to Kohut's phase (2). The opening books of *Pierre*, from the hero's first glimpse of Isabel's face to his utter bewitchment by her dark mystery, exemplify phase (3) with its "hypochrondria" and "disjointed mystical religious feelings," its "vague awe." The narrative tone of *Pierre's* early books (manic melancholy) suggests authorial morbidity as well, though in a form that heightens rather than impairs Melville's capacity for analysis. Originating in the melancholia of object-loss, *Pierre* is not a mad book but a keenly insightful book about madness that projects a catastrophic version of the author's situation in the downward course of its hero toward dissolution. In its closing sections *Pierre* oscillates wildly between belligerent grandiosity and masochistic self-abasement ("there was nothing he more spurned, than his own aspirations; nothing he more abhorred than the loftiest part of himself" [*WHM*, 7:339]), accompanied by paranoid feelings of persecution by society and the fates. This is Kohut's phase (4), irreversible psychosis: Melville's prophecy of his own fate, perhaps, should he succumb to the feelings of anger, betrayal, and self-betrayal roiling within him, which the act of writing allows him to objectify and control. His affinities of background, character, and condition with Pierre allow him to psychoanalyze himself under the cover of fiction, while his differences of knowledge and self-knowledge enable him to transfer his self-castigation onto his naive hero and stage a purgational melodrama of overreaction, excess, and self-destruction.

Do the sexual themes of *Pierre* pertain only to the melodrama of the character Pierre or to the self-analysis of the author as well? To both, it seems to me, but with a perplexity on Melville's part that leaves their erotic significance unclear. Kohut observes that "the regressive psychic structures, the patient's perception of them, and his relationship to them, may become sexualized both in the psychoses [Pierre's condition] and in the narcissistic personality disorders [Melville's]. In the psychoses the sexualization may involve *not only the archaic grandiose self and the idealized parent imago . . . , but also the restitutively built-up delusional replicas of these structures which form the content of the overt psychosis*" (9–10; my emphasis). In some respect Melville may have arrived at a comparable distinction between "psychotic" and "narcissist" in ascribing to Pierre a sexualization of Isabel as "delusional replica" that may only have problematically applied to himself in his relationship to Hawthorne. The child's desire for the father and, with his loss, for the father surrogate is profound and compelling, Melville realized, but he seems genuinely unsure whether the feelings attached to the father and transferred to the father surrogate are literally sexual (as in Creech's supposition of the young Melville's homosexual incest fantasy) or transformational and metaphoric—the eroticization years later of emotions that were not sexual in the original relationship and *may* not in any genital sense be

Development and regression in the realm of the grandiose self		*Development and regression in the realm of the omnipotent object*	
(1) Mature form of positive self-esteem; self-confidence.		(1) Mature form of admiration for others; ability for enthusiasm.	Normalcy
(2) Solipsistic claims for attention: stage of the grandiose self.		(2) Compelling need for merger with powerful object: stage of the idealized parent imago.	Narcissistic Personality Disorders
(3) Nuclei (fragments) of the grandiose self: hypochondria.		(3) Nuclei (fragments) of the idealized omnipotent object: disjointed mystical religious feelings; vague awe.	
(4) Delusional reconstitution of the grandiose self: cold paranoid grandiosity.		(4) Delusional reconstitution of the omnipotent object: the powerful persecutor, the influencing machine.	Psychosis

The solid arrow indicates the oscillations of the narcissistic configurations in the course of the psychoanalytic treatment of the narcissistic personality disorders (see Diagram 2 in Chapter 4); the dotted arrow indicates the direction of the process of cure in the analysis of these disorders. The alternatingly dotted and interrupted part of the long arrow indicates the still reversible depth of the regression toward psychosis; the interrupted part signifies that depth of the regression toward psychosis at which the psychotic regression has become irreversible.

Diagram from *The Analysis of the Self: A Systematic Approach to the Psychoanalytic Treatment of Narcissistic Personality Disorders,* by Heinz Kohut (New York: International Universities Press, 1971), 9.

sexual in the present relationship enlisted to replace it. Melville knew that Hawthorne had touched his center of being, or helped him to touch it, as no other person had, and he sensed that his feeling of completion and self-worth under Hawthorne's eye was obscurely linked to a complex of emotional and spiritual needs rooted in his father's underappreciation of him and solidified by his father's premature death. Beyond that, and in the face of the fundamental mysteriousness of "the strongest and fieriest emotions of life" (*WHM*, 7:67), everything was dim and uncertain. The terrible insight behind *Pierre* was not Melville's suspicion of homoeroticism, which could remain only a suspicion and seems not in any case to have been either a spur for self-redefinition or a ground for shame, but his recognition of the incontrovertible truth (so he saw it) that the entire enterprise of his intellectual and spiritual life was connected in ways he could hardly begin to measure with the unmet needs of the child. Written in the wake of Hawthorne's departure and with what Freud calls the "self-reproaches and self-revilings" of the melancholic (244), *Pierre* was Melville's act of autopsychoanalyis, of self-exposure, of self-laceration, and, he may have hoped, of therapeutic cure.

After Great Pain

That *Pierre* was, in the end, an exorcism and partial cure owed largely to the circumstance of Melville bottoming out and arriving at a center of indifference beyond love and devastation alike. Depression has its life cycle—this is its "only grudging favor," William Styron remarked (73)—and as with Emerson in "Experience" or Whitman in "As I Ebb'd with the Ocean of Life," the very act of self-humiliation, of shedding illusion and taking one's stand on the bedrock of a diminished self, can become a source of strength and potential renewal. For the melancholic, even the gesture of self-punishment—joining with the world or the wounding love-object in heaping scorn upon oneself—may be cathartic. Pelted by "Hate the censor," the speaker in "Shelley's Vision" (from *Timoleon*) decides that he "too would pelt the pelted one." He casts a stone at his shadow,

> When lo, upon that sun-lit ground
> I saw the quivering phantom take
> The likeness of St. Stephen crowned:
> Then did self-reverence awake. (*Poems*, 323)

In anatomizing his F/father-dependence, Melville may also have acted as his own psychotherapist. The conditions for resolving a narcissistic personality disorder, according to Kohut, are, first, "analytic penetration of the defensive structures" of the self resulting in "cognitive and affective mastery" of its "*primary defect*" and, second, the creation of reliable "compensatory structures" that allow for successful functioning.[60] In *Pierre* Melville was both analyst and analysand. By probing Pierre's unconscious and being "more frank with [him] than the best men are with themselves" (*WHM,* 7:108), Melville was able, through the displacements of plot and stylized characterization, to be frank with himself and explore the "defensive structures"—rationalizations, denials, metonymic substitutions, fictions of the self—that masked his affective dependencies and motivating needs. The "compensatory structures" emerged later, after the impulses that incited the book expended themselves and left him in the narrative and tonal slackwater evidenced by most of the early New York sections (*WHM,* vol. 7, books 15 and 17–20). As he began to describe Pierre as a truth-telling author beset by the "Imbecility, Ignorance, Blockheadedness, Self-Complacency, and the universal Bleardness and Besottedness around him" (*WHM,* 7:338–39), his aggression turned outward from himself and his family to the social world (including the reviewers of *Moby-Dick*) and, in bitter opposition to it, he came to rehabilitate himself on new grounds. For a man who had inscribed a fantasy of converse with the divine, it was humbling to acknowledge that, in addition to bearing society's contempt, he must allow that the heavens were indifferent to his trials. Yet unlike the "little soul-toddler Pierre" (*WHM,* 7:296), Melville was able to negotiate his exile by "wrest[ing] some final comfort" from the myth of Enceladus (*WHM,* 7:346)—namely, however tainted by clay the seeker's drive toward the transcendent might be, it still raised him above the creatures of clay who lived only for clay. When narrator Melville commends the thwarted, aspiring Enceladus ("Wherefore whoso storms the sky gives best proof he came from thither!" [*WHM,* 7:347]), he is assuming the emptied role of vindicating father surrogate and royally commending himself.

Years later Melville would return to this theme in "Timoleon," whose hero, "estranged" from the citizenry of Corinth through the "transcendent deed" of slaying his tyrant-brother Timophanes, finds himself ignored by the silent gods and left "fatherless" (*Poems,* 308, 309). With time, Timoleon comes to discover his justification in himself, independent of the acclaim of Corinth (his mother and the social world) and the approval of the gods. By the end of *Pierre* Melville had only a tentative grasp of this idea, but it was enough to serve as the foundation for a new "compensatory structure" on which to build an identity and further a career. The measure of Melville's new stability is the character of his work after *Pierre,* which, though "wary of the naked attack upon unspeakable truths,"[61] shows him objectifying emotions and points of view that were formerly part of his psychological and ideational constitution. Instead of writing *from* melancholia, Melville can now, in tales like "The Fiddler," "Bartleby, the Scrivener," "Cock-A-Doodle-Doo!" and "I and My Chimney," write seriocomically *about* it. The contrast between "dark" and "bright" views of life, a matter of dire personal importance in *Pierre,* has become part of the writer's free exploration of the relationship between temperament, life history, and philosophical worldview as he works to consolidate his own renascent sense of how to live.

This is not to say that Melville put Hawthorne and homoeroticism behind him. If the tone of his 1852 letters can be trusted, Melville bore himself with the dejection of an abandoned lover resigned to his condition, adopting a stoic reserve but not above subtly parading his injury when occasion allowed. Hawthorne had not merely deserted him; he had bartered friendship for celebrity and advanced to better, or at least worldlier, things. Melville's letter declining Hawthorne's invitation to visit Concord during the summer of 1852 is notable for its tacit acknowledgment of the personal and professional distance between them. Hawthorne is now the triumphant author of *The Blithedale Romance,* and borrowing a hint from the stationery on which he wrote (embossed with a crown and two garlands), Melville offers Hawthorne a crown: "Significant this. Pray, allow me to place it on your head in victorious token of your 'Blithedale' success" (*WHM,* 14:230). Crowning Hawthorne meant one thing in "Hawthorne and His Mosses" when Melville himself was bestowing the acclaim, and his own career seemed meteorically on the rise, and quite another when Hawthorne was reveling in praise and *Pierre* had just been deposited for publication, its prospects dubious. (Melville knew what his audience could abide; he could not have been in his senses if he anticipated success.) The vanquished's sigh of acquiescence breathes through Melville's final words on the subject: "Well, the Hawthorne is a sweet flower; may it flourish in every hedge" (*WHM,* 14:230). The letter is signed "H Melville," in contrast to the "Herman" of nine months earlier (*WHM,* 14:231, 14:213). Melville will no longer presume on intimacy.

When Melville wrote Hawthorne again the following month it was to call attention to the story of Agatha Hatch Robertson, which he had recently heard in Nantucket while traveling with his father-in-law, Judge Shaw. Melville probably did feel that the "great patience, & endurance, & resignedness" (*WHM*, 14:232) of women like Agatha, herself an abandoned lover, was more naturally suited to Hawthorne's talent than to his own, but in hinting that the appeal of the story for him came from "very different considerations" than literary ones (*WHM*, 14:234) he was inviting Hawthorne to look beyond the emotional reserve of his letter to the writer's unspoken feelings. "Perhaps this great interest of mine," he resumes, as if unwilling to let the subject drop, "may have been largely helped by some accidental circumstances or other; so that, possibly, to you the story may not seem to possess so much of pathos, & so much of depth" (*WHM*, 14:234). In effect Melville is telling Hawthorne that he himself has private reason to be moved by a story of desertion and patient waiting as Hawthorne does not. In embellishing the account of Agatha, which he later received from its teller (lawyer John H. Clifford) and which he now forwards to Hawthorne, Melville adds the picture of Agatha "feverishly expecting a letter" from Robertson, of her daily trek to the mail-post, and of the post eventually rotting away (*WHM*, 14:236; for Clifford's narrative of Agatha, see *WHM*, 14:621–24). Like the Freudian melancholic, Melville is obliquely "taking revenge" on the love-object by "tormenting" him with a display of his pain (251).

A like impulse may underlie Melville's otherwise gratuitous postscript to the Agatha letter of October 25, 1852: "If you find any *sand* in this letter, regard it as so many sands of my life, which run out as I was writing it" (*WHM*, 14:240). Kohut sees "pervasive feelings of emptiness and depression" as "indicative of the ego's depletion because it has to wall itself off against the unrealistic claims of an archaic grandiose self, or against the intense hunger for a powerful external supplier of self-esteem" (16–17). Both conditions apply to Melville in 1852. Having formerly imagined himself filling "an endless riband of foolscap" with thoughts addressed to Hawthorne (*WHM*, 14:213)—the grandiose self performing for the idealized self-object—Melville now feels on the brink of exhaustion and, with the melancholic's accusatory self-humiliation, he wants Hawthorne to know it. The two men met again in Concord on December 2, a visit Melville "greatly enjoyed," he wrote in acknowledgment, and from which he hoped, in an oddly formal phrasing, Hawthorne had "reaped some corresponding pleasure" (*WHM*, 14:242). The effusive, self-dramatizing persona of the 1851 letters has become laconic and guarded, not because his affection has diminished but because, wounded by casual neglect, he has learned to armor himself against further hurt.

The armor would be lifelong. "Monody" expresses no bitterness toward Hawthorne, only sadness and regret, and *Clarel*, though keenly analytic, even critical, in its treatment of Vine, is tonally remote. Nonetheless, when Julian Hawthorne visited him in 1883 to inquire about letters from his father, Melville replied "with agitation" that "if any such letters had existed, he had scrupulously destroyed them," and when Julian pressed further for "memories in him of the red-cottage days—red-letter days too for him—he merely shook his head," as if the entire subject were still too painful to recall (*Log*, 783). As time, distance, and Hawthorne's death in 1864 made their relationship seem almost to belong to another life, Melville achieved a measure of emotive control, but only in art, not in life, and even in art he remained uncertain of the character of his feelings for Hawthorne.

In *Clarel*, where, as Bezanson notes, Melville "brood[s] privately and at length over the man who had meant most in his own life" (*WHM*, 12:596), the question is not whether the title character is homoerotic (he is) but what his homoeroticism signifies as an ambiguous middle ground between homosociality and homosexuality and to what extent his feelings are a projection of what Melville's had been. "Possessing Ruth," Clarel is "still, in deeper part / Unsatisfied" (*WHM*, 12:377), and he imagines an intimacy, like David's with Jonathan, "[p]assing the love of woman fond" (*WHM*, 12:377).[62] What Clarel seems to want, consciously at least, is a "solacement of mate" (*WHM*, 12:8) founded in the other's spiritual and intellectual strength, such as he might have with Vine or Celio but not, he feels, with the domestic Ruth and her mother, Agar, his models for womanhood. Moreover, virginal in temper as well as in body, Clarel requires a love free of the earthliness of sexuality, which woman, whose very appeal he regards as sexual, cannot provide:

> Can Eve be riven
> From sex, and disengaged retain
> Its charm? Think this—then may ye feign
> The perfumed rose shall keep its bloom,
> Cut off from sustenance of loam.

But if Eve's charm be not supernal,
Enduring not divine transplanting—
Love kindled thence, is that eternal?
Here, here's the hollow—here the haunting!
Ah, love, ah wherefore thus unsure?
Linked art thou—locked, with Self impure? (*WHM,* 12:379)

Young and sexually squeamish with the hypersensitivity of the innocent, Clarel is not Melville as he was in 1851–52, much less at the time
he wrote the poem, yet the issue remains of whether a manly love would
also be entwined with fleshliness, Clarel's "Self impure." Here Melville returns to the central ambiguity of Platonic homoeroticism and of his own
relationship to Hawthorne: is "Uranian" or "heavenly" love, as idealized
male friendship is called by Pausanias in the *Symposium* (22–23), higher
than heterosexual love because exempt from carnality, or is the language
of heavenliness a (self-)deception meant to gild homosexual passion or,
at the other extreme, to deny passion altogether owing to a Manichaean
repugnance to the flesh?

Melville's answer in the poem is inconclusive: Clarel may be a Platonic idealist; he may be a latent homosexual; he may be a naïf or a
fastidious ascetic; or in some proportion he may be and probably is all
of these things, as when he responds to Derwent's enthusiasm for the
"warm / Soft outline" of the Lyonese Jew with a "stare / Of incredu-
lity" that may suggest prudish shock, unwelcome self-recognition, or
both at once (*WHM,* 12:477). The sexuality of *Clarel* exists in such la-
cunae, which readers fill as they like. In Clarel's dream in "The Prodigal" (*WHM,* 12:468–77), the Lyonese is set against the Franciscan monk
Salvaterra, one symbolizing the fleshpots of the East, the other a desert
asceticism, yet neither is as unambiguous as he seems. The attraction of
the Lyonese may be homoerotic—the Russian, his cell mate for a night,
calls him "a juicy little fellow" (*WHM,* 12:480)—or, as a sensualist indifferent to Judea, he may be a stand-in for Ruth and the "Fruit of the tree
of life" (*WHM,* 12:484), which supplant him in Clarel's thoughts as a
counterforce to the transcendent—or is it as heterosexual displacement
of the homosexual? On the other side, the St. Francis–like Salvaterra,
"slender . . . and young, / With curls that ringed [his] shaven crown" and
"under quietude . . . Excitable" (*WHM,* 12:424, 12:425), may have erotic
leanings of his own as well as distinct homoerotic appeal. The boundary

between the sexual and the spiritual in *Clarel* is bewilderingly indefinite and permeable. The blithesome Cypriote is a beguiling figure of "homoerotic fantasy," according to Edwin Haviland Miller (331), but so in an opposing way is the hair-shirted Syrian monk, whose otherworldliness radiates a kind of tumescence of the spirit that enthralls his listeners, the Melvillean Rolfe in particular, more completely than any physical magnetism could.

Melville was not alone in struggling with the indeterminacies of Uranian love. Under the aegis of Platonist Benjamin Jowett, as Linda Dowling has shown, students at Victorian Oxford developed a "counter-discourse of spiritual procreancy" that celebrated an "innocent or asexual" homoeroticism as "superior to the blind urgencies" of both heterosexual reproduction and homosexual sodomy. For students of Jowett like John Addington Symonds, however, the sublimations of Uranian love proved an unsatisfying, hypocritical compromise that denied the claims of the body in favor of a rarefied mysticism. Looking back thirty years, Symonds berated Jowett for revealing, then morally curbing, the truth which men like himself "'had been blindly groping after'"—that homosexuality was "once an admitted possibility" within a high civilization and a stimulus to its "great achievements and . . . arduous pursuit of truth."[63]

If Melville himself never reached such a conclusion, it was partly because his "characteristic gravity and reserve of manner," as Hawthorne called it (*CE*, 22:162), was accompanied by a strong inner check on behavior and, progressively, on attitude and emotion as well. In his poem "After the Pleasure Party" (from *Timoleon*) the astronomer-heroine Urania, lured by love from study of the heavens and subsequently betrayed, complains bitterly against the power of sex to usurp allegiances of mind and spirit. Urania, too, cites Aristophanes' myth of the divided self, but her words are in protest against the urgencies of Eros rather than in praise:

> For, Nature, in no shallow surge
> Against thee either sex may urge,
> Why hast thou made us but in halves—
> Co-relatives? This makes us slaves.
> If these co-relatives never meet
> Self-hood itself seems incomplete.

And such the dicing of blind fate
Few matching halves here meet and mate.
What Cosmic jest or Anarch blunder
The human integral clove asunder
And shied the fractions through life's gate? (*Poems,* 312–13)

Urania's tragedy is that she *has* met her other half but has been deserted by him, tasting completion, then losing it. Since her lover is male, the line "against thee either sex may urge" is oddly inapplicable to her situation, but it does apply to Melville's if one reads the poem with Robert K. Martin as Melville's projection of his relationship with Hawthorne.[64] Urania is the muse of astronomy, but the name also recalls the distinction Pausanias makes in the *Symposium* between the "'heavenly'" Aphrodite, daughter of Uranus and patron of an ennobling love between "intelligent" males (22), and the "'common'" Aphrodite, daughter of Zeus and goddess of those who seek the love "of the body rather than of the soul" (23). Urania's example confounds the supposed split, along with the illusory notion that the "intelligent" are lifted above physical passion. "One's sex asserts itself," Urania says ambiguously, referring either to one's sexual nature or to the sexual claims of one's own gender. Martin views the poem as "a defense of homosexuality" and a "warning against the consequences of repression" (100), but the thrust of the poem is in quite the opposite direction. Urania's monologue is an outcry against the disturbances wrought by *any* form of sexuality, which "clogs the aspirant life" (*Poems,* 314) and overwhelms self-conceived "heavenly" commitment to intellect and art.

To read "After the Pleasure Party" as figurative autobiography is not to imply that Melville lusted after and was rejected by Hawthorne, but to suggest that in the wake of Hawthorne's departure from the Berkshires he was overcome by feelings of emptiness and self-accusation that obliged him to ask what Hawthorne had meant to him and that left him questioning the erotic underpinnings of spiritual life for the next forty years. At first, like Urania, he felt angry and ashamed at the power of his emotions to overthrow him ("And kept I long heaven's watch for this . . . ?" [(*Poems,* 311]) and bitter at life for so constituting human nature. However, as Hawthorne retreated as a presence in his life, with no remotely comparable figure to replace him, the subject of homoeroticism increasingly became one for remembrance and, in *Clarel* and later in

Billy Budd, Sailor, for absorbed and largely (though not entirely) disinterested exploration.

The speaker of "After the Pleasure Party" claims not to know if Urania ever forgot the party or "lived down the strain / Of turbulent heart and rebel brain" (*Poems,* 313). Did Melville live down the turbulence? It is fitting that "After the Pleasure Party" immediately follows the title poem in *Timoleon,* for the two narratives are complementary recastings of *Pierre.* The first is concerned with transcendent virtue and the indifference of the remote father-gods, the second with psychosexual impulses that avenge themselves on the aspiring spirit for its slighting of the flesh. Melville has not forgotten the pleasure party, if so his months of intimacy with Hawthorne can be called, but neither does he seem to agonize over its legacy. Hawthorne is long dead and the question of "sexual orientation" was not a critical one for the older Melville; wanting opportunity, incentive, boldness, and probably even desire to act upon his homoerotic feelings, he was content to relegate them to the closed episode of "Hawthorne" and channel his natural sensuousness into aesthetic appreciation and creation. Given his interest in art, history, and a refined Epicureanism, it is surprising that the late Melville seems not to have read Walter Pater's *The Renaissance,* which grew out of Oxford Platonism and whose synthesis of the intellectual, the spiritual, the aesthetic, and the ambiguously erotic might have spoken to matters that remained a tangle in him till the last.

Notes

1. Merton M. Sealts Jr. calls the words "an unmistakable allusion" to Plato (*Pursuing Melville,* 299).

2. Miller, *Melville,* 36; hereafter cited parenthetically.

3. Emerson, "Friendship," in *Collected Works,* 2:113; hereafter cited parenthetically.

4. Emerson, letter to Caroline Sturgis, quoted in Smith, *My Friend, My Friend,* 49.

5. Sedgwick, *Epistemology of the Closet,* 44.

6. Smith-Rosenberg, *Disorderly Conduct,* 58–59. See Sedgwick, *Between Men,* 1–2. Like Sedgwick, Smith-Rosenberg argues that "rather than seeing a gulf between the normal and the abnormal, we [should] view sexual and emotional impulses as part of a continuum or spectrum of affect gradations strongly affected by cultural norms and arrangements," which in the nineteenth century

"permit[ted] individuals a great deal of freedom in moving across this spectrum" (*Disorderly Conduct*, 75–76).

7. Halperin, *One Hundred Years of Homosexuality*, 28–29.

8. Woolf, *Moments of Being*, 108.

9. Woolf, *Diary of Virginia Woolf*, 3:51.

10. Martin, "Knights-Errant and Gothic Seducers," 180; hereafter cited parenthetically.

11. See also Martin, *Hero, Captain, and Stranger*, 12.

12. I emphasize "characteristic" along with overt because I do not think that participating in widespread shipboard sexual practices (if so he did) is sufficient to categorize Melville as "homosexual" in a continuing identic sense of the term. Martin seems to agree: men in confined all-male institutions like prisons "remain heterosexual or homosexual, according to their principal sexual orientation, regardless of the sexual activity they may engage in while in a homosocial environment." As to the larger point, I think Martin obfuscates things when he chooses to apply "homosexual" to "feelings" that refer "to desires and not practices" (*Hero, Captain, and Stranger*, 13). The virtue of "homoerotic" is that it covers cases like this without discounting strong same-sex feelings but also without locating those who have them in the very different class of practicing homosexuals. Given the current status of the term, the claim that Melville was "homosexual" is not justified by anything that scholarship has been able to discover about him.

13. In *Hero, Captain, and Stranger*, Martin emphasizes that his "approach is in no way biographical and that what Melville actually 'did' is of absolutely no literary significance" (14).

14. Mellow, *Nathaniel Hawthorne in His Times*, 312.

15. Elizabeth Hardwick notes, apropos of *Redburn*, that "the readers of [Melville's] own time, the publishers and booksellers do not seem to have paused before the enthusiastic and relishing adjectives surrounding male beauty" ("Melville in Love," 18).

16. Bryant, introduction to *Typee: A Peep at Polynesian Life*, xx.

17. Melville, *Billy Budd, Sailor (An Inside Narrative)*, 42; hereafter cited parenthetically.

18. Mumford, *Herman Melville*, 201. Hershel Parker speaks of Melville's "inexperience with intellectual women" (*Herman Melville*, 2:2).

19. Melville in Cowen, *Melville's Marginalia*, 2:650.

20. Melville in Cowen, *Melville's Marginalia*, 2:650.

21. Fuller, *Memoirs of Margaret Fuller Ossoli*, 1:247.

22. I am not at all suggesting that Hawthorne was a substitute for Zenobia or, as Robert K. Martin and Leland S. Person mistook me to imply in an earlier version of this essay, that men with an interest in other men "simply have not met

the right woman." My point is that Melville responded most deeply to a mixture of beauty, fearless intelligence, and noble grief, and that given what women were trained and allowed to be in his nineteenth-century New York/New England middle-class culture he was not likely to meet such a woman there. Melville might well have been drawn to both Hawthorne and Zenobia. As it happened, he never met a Zenobia; he did meet Hawthorne. (See Martin and Person, "Missing Letters," 115.)

23. Sophia Hawthorne, quoted in Mellow, *Nathaniel Hawthorne in His Times*, 344.

24. Sealts, *Pursuing Melville*, 319.

25. Plato, *Symposium*, 27; hereafter cited parenthetically. See Sealts, *Pursuing Melville*, 320.

26. *Langenscheidt New College Merriam-Webster*, 892; my emphasis.

27. Fuller to Anna Barker, in Chevigny, ed., *Woman and the Myth*, 112–13.

28. Freud, *Beyond the Pleasure Principle*, 52.

29. Lear, *Open Minded*, 152.

30. Even "Hawthorne and His Mosses" is driven largely by Melville's exhilaration about his own personality and prospective career as he comes to envision them while meditating on his outward subject. Melville marvels at Hawthorne for having "dropped germinous seeds" into his soul (*WHM*, 9:250), yet so far as Hawthorne is a distinct "other" Melville can almost wish him away ("Would that all excellent books were foundlings," so that one might "glorify them, without including their ostensible authors" [*WHM*, 9:239]). If on one side Melville scans Hawthorne's tales for signs of the author's mind and sensibility, on the other he generalizes the qualities he finds into common endowments of genius he himself might share.

31. In "Missing Letters" Martin and Person object to my objection to Miller's notion that Melville made a homosexual advance toward Hawthorne "for lack of biographical evidence" ("Missing Letters," 114), yet Martin himself is dismissive of Miller: "Recent biographical criticism of Melville, notably the biography by Edwin Haviland Miller, is so offensive as to make almost anyone doubt the method" (*Hero, Captain, and Stranger*, 14).

32. See Stebbins, "Berkshire Quartet."

33. Melville, *The Poems of Herman Melville*, 319; hereafter cited parenthetically as *Poems*. In his introduction to the Hendricks House edition of *Clarel*, reprinted as the "Historical and Critical Note" to the Northwestern-Newberry edition, Bezanson argued persuasively that "Monody" was Melville's "tribute" to Hawthorne (*WHM*, 12:602). Surveying the evidence in a tough-minded, if sometimes literalistic, fashion, Harrison Hayford took a more skeptical attitude in his pamphlet *Melville's 'Monody': Really for Hawthorne?* reprinted in

abridged form in the Northwestern-Newberry *Clarel* as "Melville's 'Monody':
For Hawthorne?" (*WHM*, 12:883–93). For a discussion of Hayford's reasoning,
see Milder, "Editing Melville's Afterlife," 400–403.

34. Arvin, *Herman Melville*, 206; hereafter cited parenthetically.

35. Gilman, *Melville's Early Life and "Redburn,"* 60. Paul McCarthy similarly feels that "the loss of his father left Herman with a sense of rejection and
loneliness he would never get over" (*Twisted Mind*, 7). For Neal L. Tolchin,
the failure of the Melvill(e) family and the culture at large to provide adequate
outlets for grief left Melville with a "lifelong inability to finish mourning for
his father" (*Mourning, Gender, and Creativity*, xii). Melville alludes to Burton's
Anatomy in the opening sentence of his 1839 "Fragments from a Writing Desk"
(*WHM*, 9:191).

36. Freud, "Mourning and Melancholia," 251; hereafter cited parenthetically.

37. Styron, *Darkness Visible*, 56; hereafter cited parenthetically.

38. Bowlby, *Loss*, 217; hereafter cited parenthetically.

39. Quoted in Metcalf, *Herman Melville*, 8–9. See Parker, *Herman Melville*,
1:34–39.

40. Quoted in Metcalf, *Herman Melville*, 9.

41. Kohut, *Analysis of the Self*, 25; hereafter cited parenthetically. Joseph
Adamson has applied Kohut's theories to Melville in *Melville, Shame, and the
Evil Eye*.

42. Parker, *Herman Melville*, 1:1.

43. Metcalf, *Herman Melville*, 135, 133.

44. Higgins and Parker, introduction to *Critical Essays*, 2; Jamison, *Touched
with Fire*, 19. Newton Arvin had a similar mood in mind when he spoke of
"something . . . wrong psychologically with the distance between Melville and
his material" (*Herman Melville*, 226–27), an opinion shared by several of *Pierre*'s
contemporary reviewers who sensed (without Arvin's sympathy) that the literary problems of the book stemmed somehow from the psychological problems
of its author. The "pervading" spirit of *Pierre* was "intolerably unhealthy," the
critic for *Graham's Magazine* reported, or as the *New York Day Book* extrava-
gantly put it, in block letters: "HERMAN MELVILLE CRAZY" (in Higgins and
Parker, introduction to *Critical Essays*, 55).

45. See Emmers, "Melville's Closet Skeleton," 339–43; and Murray, Myerson,
and Taylor, "Allan Melvill's By-Blow," 1–6. Parker concludes that "there is, as of
now, no way of knowing" whether Allan Melvill had an illegitimate daughter or,
if so, who the daughter might have been (*Herman Melville*, 1:65).

46. Higgins and Parker, "Reading *Pierre*," 223.

47. Matthiessen, *American Renaissance*, 471; hereafter cited parenthetically.

48. Seelye, "'Ungraspable Phantom,'" 438; hereafter cited parenthetically.

49. Creech, *Closet Writing/Gay Reading*, 118, 119, 118; hereafter cited parenthetically.

50. Chesler, *About Men*, 22. See also Patterson-Black, "On Herman Melville," 107–42. I would like to thank both Chesler and Patterson-Black for helping me think about this elusive subject.

51. Janet Duckham in "Melville and the M(Other)" revises the established views of Maria Melvill(e) as either a monstrous parent (as early biographers Raymond Weaver and Lewis Mumford saw her) or a nurturing Dutch-American matriarch (as for William H. Gilman and Alice Kenney). Working with family letters and carefully sifting the evidence, Duckham shows that Maria's attentiveness to and empathy with her second son were seriously compromised by her regular pregnancies and recoveries, her extended absences to visit her family, her illnesses, her fretfulness (which preceded Allan's financial difficulties), and her periods of depression. However affectionately she may have regarded Herman, she was simply not there for him, physically and/or emotionally, during a good part of his childhood.

52. Stern, *Fine Hammered Steel of Herman Melville*, 16.

53. Murray, introduction to *Pierre*, lxxxiii; hereafter cited parenthetically.

54. Parker, *Herman Melville*, 1:795.

55. Emerson, *Journals and Miscellaneous Notebooks*, 1:52–53.

56. Parker, *Herman Melville*, 1:793.

57. To a degree, Melville's feeling was replicated in Hawthorne but with greater ambivalence and native reserve. Hawthorne would not have been unreceptive to Melville's enthusiasm. The idyll of his first years of domesticity at the Old Manse had faded with the responsibilities of fatherhood, and by 1851–52, as Thomas Mitchell argues, he may well have been suffering "middle-aged discontent with his life and his work" (*Hawthorne's Fuller Mystery*, 175). Hawthorne had reviewed *Typee* in 1846 with a paterfamilias's wistfulness at the life of adventure, geographical and erotic. Telling stories in his parlor, Melville was a surrogate self for Hawthorne and also, as Chillingworth the freethinker was for Dimmesdale, a breath of intellectual fresh air to a mind that characteristically shrank before the metaphysically subversive.

58. Emerson, "Spiritual Laws," in *Collected Works*, 2:80; Milton, *Paradise Lost*, 1.351–52.

59. On November 3, Melville received an invitation to a farewell party to be given for the Hawthornes (Parker, *Herman Melville*, 1:876); it is unlikely that the invitation was the first Melville heard of Hawthorne's plans.

60. Kohut, *Restoration of the Self*, 4–5.

61. Berthoff, *Example of Melville*, 57.

62. In adapting 2 Samuel 1:26 ("passing the love of *women*") Melville makes females an entire gender ("woman") rather than a group of individuals, and he appends the adjective "fond": foolishly tender; weakly indulgent; doting.

63. Dowling, *Hellenism and Homosexuality in Victorian Oxford*, 115, 128, 129.

64. Martin, *Hero, Captain, and Stranger*, 99–100; hereafter cited parenthetically.

Ishmael at the masthead. Woodcut by Raymond Bishop, from *Moby-Dick* (A. and C. Boni, 1935), 140.

"Ineffable Socialities"

Melville, Hawthorne, and Masculine Ambivalence in the Antebellum Marketplace

GALE TEMPLE

WHEN NATHANIEL HAWTHORNE wrote to Herman Melville in November 1851, he apparently told him that he liked *Moby-Dick,* which had just been released in America. Hawthorne's letter no longer exists, but we do have Melville's reply—a lengthy, passionate, effusive paean to the possibility of a triumphant, transcendent same-sex bond, one that would flow with the distilled essence of solace and sympathy in the midst of an increasingly competitive and alienating world. Melville's exultation over Hawthorne's praise is palpable. That another man could so thoroughly understand and appreciate his work brings new optimism, even ecstasy, to the journey of life. "Ineffable socialities," he writes, "are in me. . . . It is a strange feeling—no hopefulness is in it, no despair. Content—that is it." The ardent connection Melville feels to Hawthorne's intellect, his spirit, his body ("your heart," he writes, "beat[s] in my ribs and mine in yours, and both in God's") is "ineffable," for existing structures of language and desire offer no precise way of conceptualizing what he feels (*WHM,* 14:212).[1] That Melville should describe his feeling as "content[ment]" is significant, for the notion of self-completion runs directly counter to the ideal of the competitive, questing middle-class male that was rapidly ossifying in the United States during Melville's lifetime.[2]

The bond Melville imagines is also noteworthy for what it says about the relationship between art and audience, for he senses in this moment that he needs no other reader than Hawthorne. He imagines a paper mill in his house that generates "an endless riband of foolscap," on which he will write "a thousand—a million—billion thoughts, all under the form of a letter to you." "The divine magnet is in you," he says, "and my magnet responds. Which is the biggest? A foolish question—they are *One*" (*WHM,* 14:213). Dollars may damn him, his works may be commercial botches compared to nineteenth-century blockbusters such as *The Lamplighter* and *The Wide, Wide World,* but if his thoughts can find a spiritual conduit to a comprehending reader, life will be worthwhile in the end. To create art, in this sense, is to carve from the granite of the antebellum commercial world a space for privacy, isolation, and intimacy. Melville will write—now, at last—not for popular success or to support his growing family but instead to achieve a metaphysical union with a kindred soul.[3]

From a modern-day vantage point one cannot help feeling that Melville overshot the mark just a bit. Despite his temporary ebullience, he continued throughout his artistic career to struggle in various ways against the caprices of the literary marketplace, against a seemingly ungrateful, even deliberately misunderstanding, readership, and against what often appeared to be a hypocritical, groveling, and paltry terrestrial existence. More importantly, perhaps, the relationship between Melville and Hawthorne seems never again to have matched the intensity of this moment. One finds, in fact, that Hawthorne, not long after he had moved away from the Berkshires, declined Melville's enthusiastic wooings to "cowrite" a novel about a scorned sailor's wife named Agatha (Melville decided to write the book by himself; it was never published) and that after several more pedestrian visits and exchanges, the next time the two met was when Melville visited Hawthorne—at that time serving in a staid, lucrative, ruminative post at the American consulate in Liverpool—five years later on a European tour undertaken to restore his sanity.[4] From a historical, pragmatic standpoint, then, the consummation Melville envisions in his November 1851 letter is at best imaginary, at worst the overenthusiastic response of a man whose desire bubbled up and overran his psychic glass.[5]

This famous epistolary moment serves as a useful starting point from which to explore the ways Melville and Hawthorne responded to an emergent form of marketplace-oriented masculinity. In Melville's letter, and repeatedly in the fiction of both Hawthorne and Melville, the ability to break free from the codes and constraints of mainstream American life is linked to an opportunity to consummate an intimate bond with another man at some psychic, spiritual, or physical level.

As Melville indicates in his letter, such a consummation would allow for the circumvention of many of the most vexing and limiting aspects of life as a man burdened with the onus of economic productivity in antebellum America.

For Hawthorne, conversely, to have reciprocated Melville's passion would seem to have been all but impossible, for Hawthorne acknowledges and accepts in his fiction, and ruefully in his life, something that Melville persistently fights against: the self-protective, self-defining forms of capitulation at which citizens arrive in response to social institutions. Put differently, Melville and Hawthorne have radically different levels of faith in ideological transcendence. For Hawthorne, the very fiber of the social contract is woven through the self-protective fabric—sexual, economic, religious—that human beings put between themselves. To probe beneath those forms of mediation is less an act of soul-liberating jouissance than it is a violation, a form of vertiginous self-annihilation. Like the voyeuristic Coverdale, Hawthorne both longs for and repudiates prolonged plunges into territories that threaten the sovereignty of the middle-class masculine self, an identity with which he associates only ambivalently but that is no less restrictive and paralyzing for that ambivalence.[6] Melville, conversely, offers characters who fight heroically, often quixotically, against their own seeming impotence in the face of what Marx refers to as capitalism's "restless, never-ending pursuit of profit-making."[7]

Fundamental to my argument is the notion that capitalism depends on a view of the masculine subject as competitive, as well as perpetually in process, forever striving for a form of isolated, privatized self-completion that must by nature exist in the always mystified future. Citizens must feel that their current selves are inadequate and that healthy processes of self-completion can only be accomplished through what Joel Kovel refers to as "restless reconsumption."[8] In other words, the market is never so healthy as when its subjects view themselves as incomplete yet also as somehow moving toward an ever-receding form of ideal selfhood. To achieve a sense of sheltered contentment through an infinitely pure commingling of sympathetic male souls, as Melville imagines he has done with Hawthorne, is therefore to reject a vision of the true self as always on the horizon, which is tantamount to rejecting the validity of the market itself. Melville's 1851 letter also suggests a resignification of the ideal of antebellum domesticity, which depended on a rigidly structured yet always slippery distinction between proper roles and behaviors for men and women. Melville's idealized social relationships could not be contained by the strictures of the bourgeois nuclear family, and in his letters and fiction one sees him continually exploring new forms of intimate attachments with other men. Hawthorne, conversely, seems to have believed that illicit, or "queer," desire is better kept veiled, a process that allowed Hawthorne to thrive for a time along an accepted axis but that also generated for him a great deal of anxiety and anguish.

I begin with a reading of *The Scarlet Letter*, a novel that is especially significant for understanding Hawthorne's ambivalence about gender roles and their relationship to the developing commercial society of antebellum America. Hawthorne's 1850 novel dramatizes the difficult choice he faced between an allegiance to an economically and systemically sanctioned form of masculine selfhood and a countervailing desire to align himself with a form of being and writing that would challenge readers to think differently about their individual and collective histories. The resolutions about antebellum masculinity to which the novel ultimately comes, are, to borrow a phrase from *Pierre*, "ambiguous still" (*WHM*, 7:360), suggesting that Hawthorne saw himself, or at least saw the figure of the male "romance" writer, as a culturally liminal figure. Hawthorne's response to Melville's friendship is thus uncannily prefigured by his portrayal of Dimmesdale, a character ridden with conflicted desires. Once I have established a foundation for my argument in *The Scarlet Letter*, I will turn to *Moby-Dick, The Blithedale Romance,* and *Pierre,* three works that were profoundly influenced by the relationship between these two writers and that trace the different ideological and pragmatic paths they followed in their lives.

Masculine Ambivalence in *The Scarlet Letter*

Near the end of *The Scarlet Letter*, Dimmesdale is faced with a choice. He can either make good on the plan he has made with Hester to form a "proper" family in a distant land, or he can remain in Puritan Boston, write and deliver his election-day sermon, and confess publicly his involvement with Hester and Pearl. He chooses the latter, of course, and in so doing becomes a martyr for the well-being of the status quo.[9] His subject matter, which creates in his auditors uproarious excitement and admiration ("never had man spoken in so wise, so high, and so holy a spirit, as he that spake this day"), is rather vague, in the narrator's account, but it concerns the "high and glorious destiny for the newly gathered people of the Lord" in New England—a nonspecific yet wholly affirmative message (*CE,* 1:249). It is appropriate that Dimmesdale should deliver such a sermon in the marketplace, for his election-day speech symbolizes a particularly saleable ideal, one that renounces self-doubt, internal angst, and shame over historical precedent (both individual and collective) and urges citizen-consumers to forge ahead with hope and innocence into the always promising future.[10]

As several recent critical takes on the novel have suggested, Dimmesdale's choice is consistent with his panicked flight from the probing intimacy of Roger Chillingworth, who makes it his life's work to "[dig] into the poor clergyman's heart, like a miner searching for gold" (*CE,* 1:129). Scott Derrick argues that the "central effort" of Hawthorne's novel is "the homophobic control of the disruptive eroticism of Dimmesdale's relation to Chillingworth," whom Derrick views as a sort of "(pre)homosexual."[11] Lora Romero similarly argues that the Dimmesdale/Chillingworth subplot indexes "the structural conditions of male-male relationships in the homophobic culture which we share with Hawthorne."[12] By fleeing the threat of Chillingworth's altogether too ardent interest in his own mind and body, delivering an inspiring speech about the glorious hope and promise of America's future, and then publicly announcing an obviously heterosexual, albeit unsanctioned, "sin" with Hester, Dimmesdale secures for himself what he feels is a safer, more socially acceptable identity form.[13]

Dimmesdale's decision is a predictable one given Hawthorne's conceptualization of the civic sphere, which is predicated on citizens tacitly acknowledging various forms of illicit desire in themselves and others but leaving the throbbing actualities of sin tactfully where they belong—closeted away in the private home or in the dark recesses of the psychic interior. Dimmesdale's popularity as a minister is a case in point, for it owes less to his superior piety than to his particular talent for revealing just enough inner suffering to create sympathetic bonds with other community members.

Dimmesdale's flight from Chillingworth situates the young cleric firmly within a sanctioned space of ostensibly normal, albeit withered, masculine desire. And significantly, Dimmesdale's decision to renounce Chillingworth links him with what might be considered a more market-friendly philosophical worldview, for his election-day speech is consistent with the rhetoric of hope, optimism, and civic re-formation that has defined characterizations of the "New World" since the time of the Puritans. What is more, Dimmesdale's message is reminiscent in a general way of the self-affirming plots of the popular fiction that saturated the literary marketplace in Hawthorne's day. From the perspective of the novel, then, "normal," domestically oriented, heterosexual bonds are inextricably linked with normative forms of writing and oratory.

Chillingworth, conversely, represents a far darker and more disturbing view of the writer figure, a type that recurs throughout Hawthorne's fiction. He is the character who goes altogether too far in unearthing and uprooting the secrets of nature and of the private demons that invest and constitute the stuff of subjectivity for Hawthorne. Ethan Brand, Aylmer, Rappaccini, Westervelt and Coverdale, Holgrave, and Chillingworth, to name a few, all symbolize one vision of the task of the writer, which is to probe subtly beneath the surfaces and illusions of the social contract in order to dredge up and expose to light something more profound and even troubling about the human psyche. Rather than embrace the philosophical inquisitiveness and psychic/metaphysical probings embodied by the Chillingworth within, Dimmesdale chooses to exorcise this anti-systemic element of himself, purging the Roger in his soul so that he can disseminate a message of hope and self-affirmation for the always deferred future of America.

In the ambivalent, conflict-ridden bond between Chillingworth and Dimmesdale, we can see at work a struggle that is particularly significant and meaningful for Hawthorne at this time: the conflict between a desire to make money through his writing, and as such to become a proper middle-class masculine subject, and an opposing desire to write meaningful fiction that would complicate the affirmational solace offered through the productions of the "scribbling women" that Hawthorne and Melville persistently vilified.[14] Both conceptions of the role of the writer lead to psychic impasses, for to reject the imperatives of the market is to fail as a bourgeois paterfamilias and to embrace masculine economic productivity is tantamount to an agonizing and paralyzing form of self-suspension, one that negatively affects the capacity for agency and equality for both men and women.

Something similar might be said about Hawthorne's view of his relationship with Melville. Melville imagines in his 1851 letter a friendship based not on competition, power, or relative sexual and economic potency but on a sort of commingling of souls. Such a bond, Melville suggests, would render the market in many ways obsolete. He will write, he says, for Nathaniel alone. For Hawthorne, however, the very definition of heterosexual masculinity is based on proprietary self-denial and the continual deferral of all meaningful forms of consummation between men. To form an intimate bond with another man would be tantamount to rejecting a vision of himself as a marketplace-oriented provider, a man on a quest for a self-made self forever receding into the horizon. This is the dilemma, then, facing Hawthorne as he begins his relationship with Melville in the Berkshires, a friendship that would catalyze a series of artistic and personal choices in both men's lives. Hawthorne's career seems to have followed a path very similar to the one charted in *The Scarlet Letter,* for his life became increasingly more domestically mainstream, but in his art he continued to hint at the various desires and psychoses that forever shadow the body of normative ideology.

Consummation in *Moby-Dick*

Melville's ardor for intimate same-sex friendships is powerfully registered in *Moby-Dick,* which he completed while living near Hawthorne in the Berkshires. In *Moby-Dick* and the letter with which I began this essay one sees similar themes: the desire, for example, for a shared bond with another man that would transcend the strictures and prejudices of the mainstream world; the desire to eschew a relentless pursuit of conclusions in favor of both textual and metaphysical meandering; a rejection of the alienating imperatives of the marketplace in favor of what Marx referred to as "human sensuous activity," which savors and embraces the minutia of vocation rather than viewing labor (in this case, the labor of writing and/or whaling) as merely a means to an end.[15] But the broader thematic that unifies the myriad narrative strains of *Moby-Dick* and that connects Melville's 1851 novel with his most passionate letter to Hawthorne is the quest for a form of subjective, vocational, and interpersonal consummation.

In one sense, the plot of *Moby-Dick* revolves around the kinds of personal fulfillment one derives from one's vocation. Each of the novel's primary characters embodies a different perspective about the relationship between labor and identity. Even Ahab, whose quixotic pursuit of a single whale runs directly counter to the capitalist goal of accumulating surplus value, can still be viewed as wedded to the logic of the market, for he is competitive rather than cooperative, individuated rather than communal, and monomaniacally driven to achieve a form of self-sovereignty that would be answerable only to the private ego.[16] But as the novel suggests, the "spirit spout" of definitive self-completion is an ever-receding illusion, one that is crucially necessary for the pursuits that drive the *Pequod,* just as the ideal of the imperially dominant, perpetually ascendant masculine self is an illusion necessary for the individual pursuits that, collectively, drive the economic market in antebellum America.[17]

The various perspectives about the labor of whaling held by the *Pequod's* officers contrast with Ishmael's more communally oriented ethic. Ishmael desires a sort of soul-commingling consummation with his fellow sailors and readers, one that would renounce the never-ending pursuit of ideal masculine selfhood in favor of a present-oriented form of textual, metaphysical, and homoerotic basking.[18] *Moby-Dick* implies that any form of meaningful self-actualization must not be based on the drive to impose a single, unilateral view of life and subjecthood on all others. Instead, it must be fluid, queer, open to the subtle nuances of a love that cannot be contained by normative definitions of sexual or familial identity.

Ishmael's ethical stance is powerfully symbolized through his ability to regard his labor as a fulfilling and satiating end in itself rather than as an odious chore that he must complete in order "really" to live his life. In the 1844 "Economic and Philosophical Manuscripts," Marx suggests that one of the effects of "alienation of labour" is that the worker "feels himself outside his work, and in his work feels outside himself."[19] Ishmael's ability to revel in his vocation represents a subversive antidote to the forms of alienation theorized by Marx, for he is able to steer virtually all his tasks aboard the *Pequod* into profound ethical and philosophical meditations. For example, in the "Squeeze of the Hand" chapter, Ishmael's "job" is to sit before a vat of warm spermacetti, squeezing with his fellow sailors congealed globules of cooling whale oil into a consistent fluid. As Ishmael happily squeezes away with his fellow sailors, the sperm "richly" discharges its "opulence," and he floats into a realm of pure soul-commingling joy. The sperm "washes" him clean and helps him to forget the oath he swore with the rest of the crew to pursue the white whale to the death. "[W]hile bathing in that bath," Ishmael says, "I felt divinely free from all ill-will, or petulance, or malice, of any sort whatsoever." The bath of sperm, a sort of ambrosial ejaculate from Ishmael's metaphysical consummation with the other men on the ship, cleanses him of his competitive drive, allowing him to eschew the pursuit of dominion in favor of reveling ecstatically in the orgiastic present. "Come," he says, "let us squeeze hands all round; nay, let us all squeeze ourselves into each other; let us squeeze ourselves universally into the very milk and sperm of kindness" (*WHM*, 6:415, 6:416).

While it is certainly true that squeezing case is a vital part of the process of converting live whales into marketable oil, Ishmael never allows such menial tasks to objectify him, to turn him into yet another cog in the wheel of the machine. As such, his desire to merge with his fellow sailors, which is precipitated by their collective immersion in sperm, runs directly counter to the ideal of the atomized, competitive, ever-questing masculine subject. This desire is epitomized in Ishmael's resignification of the sperm itself. Reformers and social scientists commonly viewed masturbation as a sort of gateway vice, and as such it represented the most lascivious and counterproductive of all the various addictive psychoses they sought to eradicate. "Wasted" semen would have been viewed as the shameful aftereffect of an effeminate loss of vitality and self-control.[20] For Ishmael, conversely, the sperm is a glorious elixir. His ability to revel in what otherwise might be viewed as a mundane step in a lengthy economic process is consistent with the entire narrative trajectory of *Moby-Dick*, which emphatically eschews the drive for final conclusions in favor of reveling in the minutia of philosophical and sexual meandering.[21]

Moby-Dick ends with the *Pequod* and its crew destroyed by the otherness they seek to conquer and with the lone survivor Ishmael floating in a seemingly limitless sea, saved at last by the coffin of his altruistic soul mate, Queequeg. This ending parallels Melville's own psychic state after writing his novel. He is poised to embrace a new way of living in the world, for he feels fully self-possessed as an author and as a man and believes that he can now reach out to a fellow seeker of alternative and more liberating truths. What he finds, however, is that such epiphanies in the midst of capitalist America can only ever be short lived, for the "malicious Devil" of economic necessity forever "[grins] in upon [him], holding the door ajar" (*WHM*, 14:191). Melville's angst regarding the dependency of his writing on the market was exacerbated by Hawthorne's pragmatically driven exodus from the Berkshires, for the choices Hawthorne made regarding his life and career associated him in Melville's mind with a way of being he had desperately hoped to reject.[22]

The Blithedale Romance: Coverdale Says NO!

Just as Melville's writings reflect his response to how he saw himself in his relationship with Hawthorne, so too do we see in Hawthorne's writings Melville's influence at various levels. In a letter written to Hawthorne in April 1851, Melville waxes poetic about Hawthorne's recently published *House of the Seven Gables*. This is a book, Melville says, that is more subversively profound and cryptically symbolic than Hawthorne's previous works. Despite its ostensibly happy ending, in Melville's view, the darker truths of the novel still confront the reader with one stark and stern message: "There is the grand truth about Nathaniel Hawthorne. He says NO! in thunder; but the Devil himself cannot make him say *yes*. For all men who say *yes*, lie; and all men who say *no*,—why, they are in the happy condition of judicious, unincumbered [sic] travellers in Europe; they cross the frontiers into Eternity with nothing but a carpet-bag,—that is to say, the Ego. Whereas those *yes*-gentry, they travel with heaps of baggage, and, damn them! they will never get through the Custom House" (*WHM*, 14:186). One cannot help feeling that Melville's desire to conscript Hawthorne into a shared sense of willful and happily disdainful poverty would only have repelled the older writer at this stage in his life.[23]

But in *The Blithedale Romance*, the novel Hawthorne penned just after *The House of the Seven Gables*, one sees a writer figure in mourning for the loss of the sort of intimacy Melville offered Hawthorne. That sense of mourning is conveyed through Coverdale's anguished inability to commit himself to the idealism and soul-sharing friendship of the charismatic and manly Hollingsworth, who as numerous critics have noted bears a striking resemblance, both physically and behaviorally, to Melville.[24] Hollingsworth's eyes "fill with tears," as he offers Coverdale the chance to join him in efforts at prison reform. "[T]here is not the man in this wide world, whom I can love as I could you," he intones. "Do not forsake me!" Coverdale's refusal fills him with anguish, causing him a "heart pang" that is "not merely figurative, but an absolute torture of the breast" (*CE,* 3:133, 3:135). Once he has explicitly refused Hollingsworth, all interest Coverdale has felt to this point in the Blithedale experiment withers, and he leaves soon after for a sojourn in the city that effectively ends his participation at the commune.

As Thomas R. Mitchell notes, Coverdale's "No!" looks strikingly similar to the one Melville imagines Hawthorne idealistically shouting out to the world in *The House of the Seven Gables,* but it comes from an entirely different perspective.[25] Instead of refusing the easy solace of the status quo as Melville imagines Hawthorne doing in "Mosses," Coverdale turns away from the idealistic intimacy offered by Hollingsworth. His "No!" springs not from a desire to disavow the mainstream but from his devotion to the cultivation of his individuality, a process inextricably wedded to the ideology of capitalist America. His refusal allows him to keep his options open surrounding his future life, to keep alive his potential to consummate sexually his relationship with Priscilla or, less desirably, Zenobia, and his imaginary plans to become one day a sort of hero—"Uncle Coverdale"—to the reformed generations that will follow. But as the novel makes clear, Coverdale is only ever interested in the anticipation that such potentialities inspire in him. He never effectively consummates his relationship with any of his fellow socialists, male or female, and it is this form of subjective paralysis that defines Coverdale as the quintessential masculine subject of market capitalism.

Coverdale's inability to commit himself genuinely to any form of interpersonal intimacy is effectively symbolized by his "hermitage," the place at Blithedale where he goes to reacquaint himself with his always threatened individuality. Secreted away in the midst of a high white pine, the hermitage is shaped through the agency of a "wild grape-vine," which "had twined and twisted itself up into the tree, and, after wreathing the entanglement of its tendrils around almost every bough, had caught hold of three or four neighboring trees, and married the whole clump with a perfectly inextricable knot of polygamy." Like the commune itself, which Coverdale continually identifies with a pandirectional erotic energy, the hermitage is formed by the unification of separate trees and branches into a federated "polygamous" whole. The space within is erotically charged, says Coverdale, an ideal place for a "honey-moon," although the one specific person with whom he thinks of sharing his retreat is a man. "I brought thither no guest," he says, "because, after Hollingsworth failed me, there was no longer the man alive with whom I could think of sharing all" (*CE*, 3:98–99).[26]

The hermitage is a pathetic outlet for Coverdale, an anguish-ridden compensation for his fears about getting too close to others. When he experiences any sort of vulnerability-prompting desire, he flees to his tree-closet where he can both hide from the painful "socialities" of the world and privately indulge in the sexual fantasies that same world has inspired in him. But perhaps most significantly, Coverdale describes the hermitage as "an admirable place to make verses," an ideal place for him to generate material for his poetry, fiction, and essays (*CE*, 3:99). This is a process that, given his characterization of the hermitage, explicitly parallels a nonproductive, shameful, and painfully lonely form of autoeroticism. Rather than "really" engaging in a form of sexual or soul-sharing consummation with Hollingsworth, Coverdale instead retreats to the safety and comfort of his private nest, where his repressed sexual frustration finds an outlet through writing.

Coverdale's productions arise out of an anguished psychosexual paralysis. He cannot ever effectively open himself up to an intimate plunge with Hollingsworth or, less significantly, with Priscilla or Zenobia, because of his reliance on the self-protective cocoon that his middle-class masculinity has woven around his psyche. By the time his experiences at Blithedale end, virtually nothing has changed in his life, at least outwardly. He remains a bachelor, well-to-do, living with a modest degree of happiness in his well-appointed home. Yet behind the walls of Coverdale's bachelor apartments, and within his demure, sometimes petty, seemingly self-controlled exterior, one senses an immensity of frustration and caged desire. He is not particularly happy, or particularly successful as a writer, and he has developed no significant relationships in his life. All of these failures stem from Coverdale's allegiance to a form of masculinity that shields and protects the ostensibly sacrosanct interiors of the bourgeois self, views other males not as potential intimates but as competitors, and conceptualizes women as commodified objects rather than as reciprocally interactive equals.

Coverdale's neuroses surrounding his sexual virility and the power of his writing index Hawthorne's own anxiety about his status as a middle-class male author. As T. Walter Herbert argues, Hawthorne was tormented by his desire to reject the mind-numbing routine of mainstream workaday professional jobs because of the apparent divergence from "normal" masculinity that being a writer entailed. "His poetic identity—centered on cultivating emotional sensitivities in seclusion from the world—was feminine. As a civil servant, he was a man among men."[27] Scott Derrick similarly argues that nineteenth-century American "male writers found themselves famously alienated from what might be called the masculinity of commerce, and they had to negotiate a treacherous relation to masculine authority that could not be attained by simple appeal to the cultural position of literature."[28] On one hand, men were encouraged to become productive members of the public world of commerce and capitalism, and if one was a writer, this productivity would be evidenced through book sales. On the other hand, the popularity of what was often portrayed as a flabbily self-affirming "feminine" writing made commercial success the mark of masculine lack. This sense of the male writer as embodying a bifurcated identity is epitomized in Coverdale, whose psychosexual paralysis precludes his entering into the thrilling, soul-sharing intimacies that genuine relationships can produce.[29]

Pierre: Death in the Marketplace

Melville's *Pierre* expresses a frenetic, self-destructive, willfully iconoclastic impulse, perhaps resulting from the relatively negative reviews that were at that time coming out about *Moby-Dick,* and from what Melville felt as his physical and philosophical abandonment by Hawthorne.[30] Much like *The Blithedale Romance, Pierre* dramatizes the untenability of nonnormative intimacies in a society increasingly organized around the imperatives of the marketplace, the viability of which depends on citizen consumers forever keeping consummation at bay. Consummation, the novel suggests, is radically antithetical to the affective house of cards that constitutes mainstream bourgeois domesticity in the nineteenth century.

Pierre's relationships to his mother, to his betrothed, Lucy Tartan, and particularly to his ancestral estate are sustained in all their piquant intrigue by a desire that forever teeters on the anticipatory cusp of consummation. Pierre's relationship to his mother, for example, is characterized by "[t]hat nameless and infinitely delicate aroma of inexpressible tenderness and attentiveness which, in every refined and honorable attachment, is cotemporary with the courtship, and precedes the final banns and the rite." His relationship with Lucy also perpetuates itself in the yearning ache of deferred sexual intimacy. As he enters her bedroom in order to retrieve her sketch pad for her, he spies a sort of mysterious "ruffled thing"—her underwear?—rolled up on her bed, and he freezes in a suspended, lingering erotic paralysis: "Never trembling scholar longed more to unroll the mystic vellum, than Pierre longed to unroll the sacred secrets of that snow-white, ruffled thing. But his hands touched not any object in that chamber, except the one he had gone thither for" (*WHM*, 7:16, 7:39).

This portrayal of life's particular deliciousness, a deliciousness crucially informed by the deferral of all forms of consummation, is consistent with the rhetorical tropes of sentimental fiction.[31] Pierre's initial happiness, then, as numerous critics have suggested, is sustained through sentimental affect, which is precisely why he is so particularly skilled and even famous as a writer of marketable fiction. His intellectual and economic complacency, his blithe inability to acknowledge the various forms of oppression and injustice that have gone into his own privileged genealogy, and his sense of the future as a welcome page on which he will write his own storied chapter in the Glendinning saga—all parallel Pierre's role as a popular writer of sentimental verse. The system that supports him, as well as the various forms of writing that he initially produces, are of a piece with the moral and economic status quo, at least from the perspective of the novel.

But when Pierre comes to believe that his historical forbears are irrevocably fallen, he is hurled into a metaphysical void. In a way that seems to combine Ahab's monomaniacal drive with Ishmael's desire for a form of soul-sharing intimacy, Pierre attempts to rectify the historical record by entering into a secretive, conspiratorial, sexually charged bond with a forbidden being.[32] The novel ultimately suggests, however, that such a rectification is not possible, at least not within the terms of the existing social contract. From the time Pierre learns of Isabel and makes his vow—"From all idols, I tear all veils; henceforth I will see the hidden things; and live right out in my own hidden life!" (*WHM*, 7:66)—he attempts to live in a metaphysically pure, ideal realm that moves beyond anticipatory sexual self-suspension and actually engages in various forms of consummation that are tantamount to outright ideological rupture.

Slavoj Žižek's work on ideology is helpful for making sense of what happens to Pierre as he attempts to correct the injustices of history. According to Žižek, ideology is always formulated in opposition to a tabooed, obscene otherness that serves as the obverse of moral law: "The moral Law is obscene in so far as it is its form itself which functions as a motivating force driving us to obey its command—that is, in so far as we obey moral Law because it is law and not because of a set of positive reasons: the obscenity of moral Law is the obverse of its formal character."[33] In other words, normative morality is enacted in response to its ostensibly "obscene" other, which in the world of sentimental fiction might be defined as incest, miscegenation, pedophilia, and so on. When Pierre believes that his historical idols have fallen, he attempts first to violate and then ultimately to rectify the moral Law, but what he does instead is effectively occupy the space of the obscene "other" that serves as the moral negative of sentimental domesticity.[34]

If we accept that at some level Pierre's attraction for Isabel mirrors Melville's attraction for Hawthorne, then Pierre's tragic plight suggests that Melville came to view such intimacies as at best quixotic, at worst a form of psychological death.[35] Unlike Melville, whose writerly optimism leaps off the page in his 1851 letter to Hawthorne as he describes a rhapsodic ideal of writing on an "endless riband of foolscap" for the sympathetic and comprehending eyes of Hawthorne only, Pierre has no sympathetic soul with whom to share his profound yet commercially untenable insights. Instead, he writes only for himself, for the "elementalizing of the strange stuff, which . . . has upheaved and upgushed in his soul" (*WHM,* 7:304). In contrast to *Moby-Dick,* the philosophical idealism of which is suffused with a divine and magnanimous selflessness, *Pierre* is about the melancholic inward trajectory of such ideals. The joyous intermasculine unity imagined by Ishmael has become a consummation with death itself, for the novel suggests that the cost of ideological nonconformity in a society driven by economic productivity is nothing short of subjective erasure. Viewed in this way, *Pierre* represents a trenchant critique of the bizarre and binding nature of traditional domestic relationships.[36] It is also a eulogy for the loss of Hawthorne, whose intimacy and affection symbolized the ideal of writing not for commercial gain but for the shared exploration of a more ethically and spiritually enriching way of life.

Melville's Carpetbag

In his account of Melville's visit to England in 1856, Hawthorne describes Melville as a kind of melancholy Ishmael, "wandering to-and-fro" over various "dismal and monotonous" philosophical and metaphysical "deserts" (*WHM*, 15:628). His characterization of Melville as a wanderer is not merely metaphorical. In an almost clinical way, Hawthorne describes Melville's method of travel:

> He sailed from Liverpool in a steamer on Tuesday, leaving his trunk behind him at my consulate, and taking only a carpet-bag to hold all his travelling-gear. This is the next best thing to going naked; and as he wears his beard and moustache, and so needs no dressing-case—nothing but a tooth-brush—I do not know a more independent personage. He learned his travelling habits by drifting about, all over the South Sea, with no other clothes or equipage than a red flannel shirt and a pair of duck trowsers. Yet we seldom see men of less criticizable manners than he. (*WHM*, 15:633)

Hawthorne's tone in this passage seems deliberately distanced. Melville is a "personage," linked with his early and notorious career as a South Sea traveler. Unlike a proper nuclear family, which would need to travel with a full equipage of bags and domestic paraphernalia, Melville travels only with his carpetbag, an island unto himself. Hawthorne's description of Melville's traveling gear hearkens back to Melville's earlier praise of *The House of the Seven Gables,* where he describes Hawthorne heroically and persistently saying "NO!" to the easy solace of the status quo, a stand that allies him not with the "*yes*-gentry" but with those deep-diving seekers of truth who will "cross the frontiers into Eternity with nothing, but a carpet-bag" (*WHM*, 14:186). Hawthorne tacitly disavows such an identification, and in the end Melville is forced to carry his carpetbag alone, for his antisystemic desire is out of touch with Hawthorne's newfound bourgeois complacency.[37]

That Hawthorne would remark on Melville's "mannerly" deportment is also noteworthy, for it suggests in Hawthorne a reluctance to read or share in Melville's barely restrained yearning after some form of ideological transcendence, a yearning tinged with mourning for the ineffable intimacies made increasingly inaccessible due to the ossifying norms of nineteenth-century American culture. It seems ironic that late in his life Hawthorne would have found comfort in mainstream domestic life, for like his fictional character Dimmesdale, he purchased that sense of belonging through the foreclosure of a myriad of life-affirming, nonnormative intimacies, and with very little life remaining to enjoy such a sanctioned form of selfhood.

Notes

I thank Rebecca Bach, Alison Chapman, Ann Hoff, Sue Kim, Danny Siegel, and Cheryl Temple for their incisive feedback and helpful suggestions on this essay.

1. It has become a critical commonplace that precise definitions of homo- and heterosexuality didn't exist as such until late in the nineteenth century. See vol. 1 of Foucault, *History of Sexuality.*

2. For more on the competitive nature of ideal male subjectivity under capitalism, a good starting point is Macpherson, *Political Theory of Possessive Individualism.* See also Sellers, *Market Revolution*; and Gilmore, *American Romanticism and the Marketplace.*

3. For more on capitalism's influence on the development of gender identity and the role of the author in nineteenth-century America, see Charvat, *Literary Publishing in America, 1790–1850*; Gilmore, *American Romanticism and the Marketplace*; Newbury, *Figuring Authorship in Antebellum America*; Ryan, *Cradle of the Middle Class*; and Whalen, *Edgar Allan Poe and the Masses.*

4. For a complete account of Melville's "story of Agatha," see Melville's August 13, 1852, letter to Hawthorne (*WHM*, 14:232–37). Hawthorne's position in the consulate was given to him by his Bowdoin classmate and friend Franklin Pierce as a sort of reward for writing a biography about his life, one that contributed to his successful run for the presidency.

5. Edwin Haviland Miller argues that Melville probably made an overt sexual "advance" to Hawthorne that precipitated Hawthorne's exodus from the Berkshires. See Miller, *Melville,* 234–50.

6. On Hawthorne's ambivalent relationship to middle-class masculinity, see Herbert, *Dearest Beloved*; Gilmore, "Hawthorne and the Making of the Middle Class"; and Derrick, *Monumental Anxieties.*

7. Marx, *Capital,* 170.

8. Kovel, *Age of Desire,* 82.

9. On Hawthorne's fiction as staging moments of capitulatory compromise, see Bercovitch, *Office of "The Scarlet Letter."*

10. The historical context for *The Scarlet Letter* is, of course, seventeenth-century Boston. As Gilmore notes, however, the plot of the novel is also fundamentally about how nineteenth-century American life was structuring itself in relation to the onset of market capitalism. See Gilmore, "Hawthorne and the Making of the Middle Class."

11. Derrick, *Monumental Anxieties,* 36.

12. Romero, *Home Fronts,* 91. See also Herbert, "Pornographic Manhood and *The Scarlet Letter.*"

13. This formula of triangulated desire has famously been theorized by such gender and sexuality critics as Gail Rubin and Eve Sedgwick. See Rubin, "The Traffic in Women"; and Sedgwick, *Between Men.* For a Sedgwick/Rubin-inspired

reading of *The Blithedale Romance* and *Pierre*, see Mueller, "This Infinite Fraternity of Feeling."

14. On Hawthorne's struggles with the feminized position of the writer, see Leverenz, *Manhood and the American Renaissance*; Romero, *Home Fronts*; Herbert, *Dearest Beloved*; Derrick, *Monumental Anxieties*; and Gilmore, "Hawthorne and the Making of the Middle Class."

15. Marx, "Theses on Feuerbach," 143.

16. For a different view of Ahab's masculinity, see Leverenz, "Ahab's Queenly Personality: A Man Is Being Beaten," chap. 10 of *Manhood and the American Renaissance*, 279–306.

17. For several more thorough interpretations of *Moby-Dick* as economic critique, see Dimock, *Empire for Liberty*; Rogin, *Subversive Genealogy*; Karcher, *Shadow over the Promised Land*; and Gilmore, *American Romanticism and the Marketplace*.

18. My reading of *Moby-Dick* is indebted to Martin, *Hero, Captain, and Stranger*. See especially 81–82.

19. Marx, "Economic and Philosophic Manuscripts of 1844," 74.

20. For more on nineteenth-century American fears surrounding the social repercussions of wanton venereal indulgence, particularly "self-pollution," see Walters, *Primers for Prudery*.

21. For more on the masturbatory connotations of this chapter, see Martin, *Hero, Captain, and Stranger*. Martin refers to the sailors' squeezing case as "group masturbation" (82).

22. For an in-depth treatment of Melville's feelings of abandonment, see Milder, "'Ugly Socrates.'"

23. As Mitchell suggests, Hawthorne's novel may well have been intended to inspire sentiments exactly opposite to those toward which Melville here gestures. In his letters to his publisher, for example, Hawthorne repeatedly promises a novel more blithe and saleable than his previous work, and although the writing itself may have been less inspired than that of *The Scarlet Letter*, in the end it seemed to fulfill this ideal of a more popularly oriented production. See Mitchell, "In the Whale's Wake."

24. See, for example, Miller, *Melville*, 242.

25. Mitchell, "In the Whale's Wake," 69.

26. For alternative takes on the implications of Coverdale's attraction to Hollingsworth, see Grossberg, "'The Tender Passion Was Very Rife among Us'"; Berlant, "Fantasies of Utopia in *The Blithedale Romance*"; Miller, "Eros and Ideology"; and Gable, "Inappeasable Longings."

27. Herbert, *Dearest Beloved*, 6.

28. Derrick, *Monumental Anxieties*, 2.

29. On the oppressive nature of normative heterosexuality, see Berlant and Warner, "Sex in Public."

30. See, for example, Milder, "'Ugly Socrates'"; and Otter, *Melville's Anatomies*.

31. For more on the thematic and formal significance of sentiment in *Pierre*, see Silverman, "Textual Sentimentalism." See also Otter, *Melville's Anatomies*.

32. For an interesting take on the homosexual implications of Pierre's bond with Isabel, see Creech, *Closet Writing/Gay Reading*.

33. Žižek, *The Sublime Object of Ideology*, 81.

34. Creech suggests that the bizarreness of Melville's portrayal of the relationship between Pierre and Isabel results from its transgression of normative heterosexuality rather than from its dalliance with incest; see *Closet Writing/Gay Reading*, 115–18.

35. On parallels between Isabel and Hawthorne, see Seelye, "'Ungraspable Phantom,'" 438–39.

36. For a more comprehensive reading of *Pierre* as a critique of the conventions of antebellum domesticity, see Kelley, "Pierre's Domestic Ambiguities."

37. This domestic complacency is well illustrated in Hawthorne's letter to Longfellow in October 1852. "I am beginning to take root here, and feel myself, for the first time in my life, really at home," he writes. "As all great landed proprietors have a name for their residences, I call mine 'The Wayside'" (*CE*, 16:602).

Italy, the Civil War, and the Politics of Friendship

Dennis Berthold

LIKE MANY AMERICANS, Hawthorne and Melville dreamed of visiting Italy. In an 1851 letter to Grace Greenwood, Hawthorne said that a visit to Italy was a "long-cherished idea," and in 1849 Melville put Evert Duyckinck "all in a flutter" by proposing to him "a cheap adventurous flying tour of eight months, compassing Rome!" (*Log,* 313). Hawthorne had to wait until he completed his four-year tour of duty as consul in Liverpool before finally being able to spend a lavish sixteen months with his family in Rome and Florence in 1858–59. Melville, who ran out of cash in England in 1849, managed to include a more Spartan two months in Italy as part of his eight-month tour of Europe and the Levant in 1856–57. Traveling alone, with only a carpetbag for luggage, he saw far more of the country than Hawthorne, landing first at Messina, Sicily, and continuing up the peninsula from Naples and Rome to Florence, Venice, Milan, and Turin (*WHM,* 15:380–83). Although both authors took standard itineraries and exhibited conventional responses to Italian art, architecture, and scenery, they reacted differently to the country's complex politics, a contrast that exposes a dimension of their friendship seldom discussed yet important in understanding their distance after 1857. Their Italian tours occurred at a crucial moment during the Risorgimento (1815–70), Italy's long struggle to break the chains of French, Austrian, and Bourbon domination and create an independent, unified nation. The most famous and persistent nationalist movement of the era, the Risorgimento—literally, "resurgence," with connotations of resurrection and rebirth—exposes Hawthorne's and Melville's varying attitudes toward revolution, democracy, authority, American identity, and nationhood itself, ideological differences that contributed significantly to their estrangement during the Civil War. John McWilliams has productively mined these issues on native grounds and shown how the conflict between Calvinism and Young American individualism frustrated both writers in their quest for a coherent "American character." I seek to place their politics on a transnational playing field, the common ground of Italy and consular appointment-seeking that they shared during the seven years they maintained contact after the year-and-a-half Berkshire idyll—an orientation that expands the grounds for assessing their ideologies against the norms of their times, not vaguely worded essentialisms. The Risorgimento and the Civil War challenged antebellum definitions of revolution, democracy, Federalism, freedom, and other American shibboleths and revealed their cultural contingency and philosophical vacuity. In an internationally comparatist context, as Larry Reynolds has taught us, ideologies that today seem reactionary may have been more genuinely attuned to contemporary needs and broadly humane values, while the headlong rush toward a new politics—one thinks of the postbellum Radical Republicans—may have undermined the very freedoms that progressives sought to extend.[1]

A series of unsuccessful revolts in Italy during the 1820s and 1830s culminated in the rise and fall of the Roman Republic in 1849, a dramatic event that awakened Americans to Italy's desire for independence and galvanized support for the Risorgimento.[2] Hawthorne's friend Margaret Fuller wrote trenchant letters to the *New-York Daily Tribune* explaining the intricacies of Italian politics to a sympathetic American public and made heroes of Giuseppe Mazzini and Giuseppe Garibaldi, the movement's most famous leaders.[3] In 1850–51 Garibaldi found political asylum in New York, where he mingled with sympathizers such as Henry Theodore Tuckerman, a friend of Melville's and one of the country's most ardent supporters of Italian nationalism.[4] The *Democratic Review, Putnam's Monthly,* the *Literary World,* the *North American Review,* and *Harper's Weekly,* periodicals Hawthorne and Melville either published in or read, vociferously supported the Italian cause and monitored its progress. In two well-known allusions to the European revolutions of 1848, the authors reveal their knowledge of these events and their emerging political differences. In *The Blithedale Romance* Miles Coverdale famously refuses to join Louis Kossuth's fight for Hungarian freedom unless the battle is held nearby on "a mild, sunny morning, after breakfast" (*CE,* 3:247), while Melville's narrator opens "Cock-A-Doodle-Doo!" by observing that "many high-spirited revolts from rascally despotisms had of late been knocked on the head" (*WHM,* 9:268). Coverdale avoids moral judgment and belittles the revolutionists' sincerity, implying that many of their supporters are, like himself, sunshine soldiers, good only "for one brave rush upon the levelled bayonets" (*CE,* 3:247). Melville's narrator, while not any more committed to action than Coverdale, admires the revolutionists' idealism and condemns the "rascally" tyrants they temporarily dethroned. Over the next decade these shaded opinions assumed a starker contrast that signaled an important ideological shift: Hawthorne clung to "primordial nationalism," a national identity based on common racial, religious, geographic, and linguistic characteristics, and rejected "civic nationalism," one constructed out of shared principles and values.[5] Melville, the more cosmopolitan of the two men, took just the opposite tack, a difference that eventually opened a political gulf between them that yawned wider than any peculiarities of temperament.

History refused Coverdale's condescending formula for avoiding transnational conflict. Redoubled oppression in every Italian state throughout the 1850s kept revolution simmering like an active volcano. From exile in London Mazzini inspired several abortive insurrections, ending with Carlo Pisacane's failed invasion of Naples only four months after Melville's visit there.[6] Ada Shepard, the Hawthornes' governess, recognized the continuing danger that the Italian revolutionaries posed in a letter of November 23, 1857 (*CE,* 22:726n), a fear that materialized when Felice Orsini attempted to assassinate Louis Napoleon in Paris only two days after the Hawthornes left the city (*CE,* 14:729n). Shaken by Orsini's act, Napoleon embraced the constitutional monarchists of Piedmont-Sardinia led by her foreign minister Camillo Benso di Cavour, and the two countries declared war on Austria on April 27, 1859. Cavour enlisted Garibaldi in the war, a canny move that inspired Italian patriots across the political spectrum. The red-shirted general won a series of dashing, hit-and-run battles that made his name famous around the world. Within a few months Piedmont annexed Lombardy, Tuscany, Modena, and Parma, leaving only the Kingdom of Two Sicilies and the Papal States outside the expanded Kingdom of Italy. Garibaldi, dissatisfied with the partial victory, organized an irregular militia of one thousand soldiers ("The Thousand," or *Il Mille*) and drove Francis II from

This dramatic cover for *Harper's Weekly* of September 9, 1871, celebrates the combined efforts of Garibaldi and Victor Emmanuel II that led to the complete unification of Italy with Rome as its capital.

Sicily and Naples in September 1860. He presented his conquest to Victor Emmanuel, unifying North and South for the first time since the fall of the Roman Empire.

Hawthorne's and Melville's journals reveal distinct attitudes toward these events. Hawthorne's response to Orsini's assassination attempt indicates his cavalier view of European politics: "I rather think the good people of Marseilles were glad of the attempt, as an item of news and gossip, and did not very greatly care whether it were successful or no; it seemed to have roused their vivacity, rather than their interest" (*CE*, 14:42). What proved to be a transformative agent in French-Italian relations excited neither Hawthorne's vivacity nor interest. In all the pages of *The French and Italian Notebooks* for 1858–59, with revolution suffusing the atmosphere, Hawthorne barely mentions the political turmoil. His only overt comment comes at Leghorn on May 29, 1859, where he observes that "the French are concentrating a considerable number of troops at this point" (*CE*, 14:527). Given his political experience and his friendships with Robert and Elizabeth Browning, William Cullen Bryant, and other proponents of the Italian cause, not to mention Ada Shepard's trepidations, Hawthorne certainly knew of Italy's unrest. Yet as he had avoided confronting the issue of slavery in his campaign biography of Franklin Pierce (*CE*, 23:352), so he avoided touching the tightly wound springs of Roman and Florentine society. He describes seeing French soldiers at various sites, but rather than considering the political implications of foreign armies defending papal authority he identifies more closely with them than with the Italians whose land they patrol: "I have no quarrel with the French soldiers; they are fresh, healthy, smart, honest-looking young fellows enough, in blue coats and red trowsers; it seems as if they were nearer akin to me than these dingy and dusky Romans; and at all events, they serve as an efficient police, making Rome as safe as London, whereas, without them, it would very likely be a den of banditti" (*CE*, 14:64). Hawthorne aligns himself with those Americans who considered the typical Italian too superstitious, ignorant, and emotional for republican autonomy, one of the swarthy races who required the firm hand of Anglo-Saxon or Gallic patriarchs to maintain order.[7] In declaring kinship with the French, Hawthorne declares his kinship with tyranny, the "rascally despotisms" Melville condemned.

Traveling en famille, Hawthorne prizes the personal comfort and security of the bourgeois tourist, happily accepting authoritarian regimes as long as they make the trains run on time. After an easy passage through the city gates of Florence, with no fees or baggage inspections, he exclaims, "Thank Heaven, and the Grand Duke, or the Emperor of Austria, or whoever it may be that has the government of this country!" (*CE*, 14:278). Hawthorne's lame attempt at humor reveals both his knowledge of and indifference to Italy's foreign despots. Everyone knew that Leopold II, a Hapsburg, ruled as Grand Duke of Tuscany as he had since 1824. He was renowned as one of Italy's most enlightened and popular monarchs, but after the revolutions of 1848 he grew fearful of his own populace and relied on Austrian troops to maintain order. His regime became more repressive and reactionary, and by 1858, when Hawthorne entered Florence, Leopold was little more than an Austrian puppet. Hawthorne's jest is on the mark: it doesn't matter who runs the country, the grand duke or the Austrian emperor. But Hawthorne fails to appreciate that both rulers are foreign oppressors, resistant to change and personal freedom, the antithesis of what Americans supposedly value. Hawthorne's levity bespeaks his apathy toward Italy's national aspirations and his approval of a seemingly benevolent dictatorship. "It is funny enough," he later wrote in Geneva, "that a stranger generally profits by all that is worst for the inhabitants of the country where he himself is merely a visitor. Despotism makes things all the pleasanter for the stranger" (*CE*, 14:552). Such statements dovetail with his defense of Pierce, where preserving national order and states' rights justifies compromising with slavery and opposing abolition, "the mistiness of a philanthropic theory" (*CE*, 23:292).

Melville, on the other hand, brought to Italy a more sympathetic awareness of transnational politics and a keener ear for the people's cri de coeur. *Mardi* allegorizes the European revolutions of 1848 (*WHM*, 3:497–500), and *Moby-Dick* employs a revolutionary iconography derived from the French revolution of 1848.[8] Italian politics figure in both novels, whether in *Mardi*'s attack on the pope as the reactionary Hivohitee MDCCCXLVIII, a cognomen recognizing Pius IX's opposition to the revolutions of 1848, or in *Moby-Dick*'s brusque reference to Napoleon III as "Louis the Devil" (*WHM*, 3:332–34, 6:155). Melville calls Austrians treaty-breakers in *The Confidence-Man* and finds them ominous figures in his travel journal of 1856–57, as when they spy on the New York rabble-rouser Mike Walsh or turn the Foscari Palace into a barracks (*WHM*, 10:146, 15:97, 15:119). Just riding in an Austrian coach from Florence to Venice gives Melville an eerie feeling: "Old fashioned vehicle.

Mysterious window & face. Secret recesses. Hide. Old fashioned feeling"
(*WHM*, 15:117). Traveling alone, Melville strikes up conversations with
ordinary Italians who register the popular discontent that Hawthorne
ignored. The Risorgimento opposed the pope's temporal authority over
Rome and the Papal States because it prevented national unity, a sentiment Melville hears from an Italian merchant who grumbles "Estates of
the Church—Estates of de Debel!" even as an "Austrian man-of-war"
hovers in the background (*WHM*, 15:98). Melville's collocation of voice
and image portrays a hypocritically materialistic papal regime supported
by foreign military power, a conclusion Hawthorne assiduously avoids.
Yet Melville recognizes Italy's political complexity and understands that
some Austrians have good intentions. Touring Venice with his guide An-
tonio, who "lost his money in 1848 Revolution & by travelling," Melville
thinks he spies the Austrian governor Archduke Ferdinand Maximilian:
"Anxious to settle it; & in my favor, for I consider that some of the feirce
[sic] democracy would not look with disrespect upon the man who had
&c &c &c" (*WHM*, 15:120). Maximilian, brother of the Austrian emperor
Franz Joseph and later the ill-fated emperor of Mexico, advocated an independent Italian federation under the pope but failed to win the trust
of Venetian liberals, "the feirce democracy" who sought independence
on their own terms.[9] Nowhere does Melville share Hawthorne's pleasure in despotism; rather, his journal infuses conventional touristic descriptions with a brooding sense of political oppression in understated,
cryptic images that vividly portray Italy's plight: "The forts of Messina
command the town, not the sea. Large tract of town demolished, so as to
have rest at command from fort" (*WHM*, 15:100). This passage, Melville's
first description of Sicily, recalls the vicious bombardment of Messina in
1848 that gave Ferdinand II (ruled 1830–59) the opprobrious nickname
"King Bomba," a brutal oppressor whose kingdom was known around
the world as, in William Gladstone's indelible words, "the negation of
God erected into a system of government."[10] Melville knew state violence
when he saw it.

When Hawthorne and Melville met in Liverpool in 1856, they had
developed more nuanced political attitudes than they possessed during their Berkshire days. Both had been good Democrats, men who
supported the party of Andrew Jackson and its compromises over slavery that maintained the Union. Like many American writers, they had
sought government appointments under the spoils system, Hawthorne

successfully in the Boston and Salem customhouses and in the remunerative Liverpool consulship, and Melville unsuccessfully in 1847 and 1853.[11] Hawthorne, as he explained in his "Custom-House" preface to *The Scarlet Letter,* knew the gritty world of party politics firsthand. Although he was out of office when he met Melville in 1850, he remained politically connected through a network of old college friends and Salem politicos. Shortly after leaving the Berkshires he agreed to write the fateful campaign biography for his Bowdoin classmate Pierce. The book cost Hawthorne "hundreds of friends" (*CE,* 16:605), he told another old college chum, Horatio Bridge, but it gained him the consulship as well as considerable political influence. As he wrote Richard Henry Stoddard in March 1853, "I have had as many office-seekers knocking at my door, for three months past, as if I were a prime minister" (*CE,* 16:649). Although Melville seems never to have asked for Hawthorne's favor, his brother Allan and his father-in-law Lemuel Shaw directly enlisted Hawthorne's support as they energetically promoted Melville for a consular post. Hawthorne came through in fine fashion, delivering letters of recommendation to President Pierce and meeting with both Pierce and Secretary of State William Marcy (*Log,* 471). Nevertheless, Melville failed to win an office—not through any lack of effort on Hawthorne's part but probably because of his own procrastination, as Hershel Parker thinks.[12] Hawthorne didn't know this. When Melville walked into the Liverpool consulate in November 1856, Hawthorne felt an initial surge of guilt over events three years earlier: "I felt rather awkward at first; because this is the first time I have met him since my ineffectual attempt to get him a consular appointment from General Pierce. However, I failed only from real lack of power to serve him; so there was no reason to be ashamed, and we soon found ourselves on pretty much our former terms of sociability and confidence" (*CE,* 22:162). Anxiety over politics, not homosexual panic, strained Hawthorne's later relationship with Melville, and only when it was resolved could he invite Melville to stay two nights in the family's Southport residence, meditate with him among the sandhills, take a day trip to Chester, and share stout and cigars in a local snuggery, arguably the most intimate and extended contact the two men ever enjoyed (*CE,* 22:162–70). They had only one more brief encounter at the Liverpool docks on Melville's return trip in 1857 and then never saw or wrote each other again.

Even as their personal lives diverged, their literary efforts overlapped, as both began writing on the same subject—Italy. Hawthorne started mining his travel notebooks for *The Marble Faun* in July 1858 in Florence (*CE*, 14:375). Melville had already delivered at least sixteen lectures on "Statues in Rome" the previous winter in America (*WHM*, 9:723) and was beginning to compile a volume of poems that may have included "Fruits of Travel Long Ago," lyric and meditative pieces about Venice, Naples, Sicily, Florence, Rome, and other sites from his Italian tour.[13] Their differing attitudes toward the Risorgimento emerged in these imaginative writings and shaped their reactions to America's own battle for nationhood, the Civil War. As Melville engaged the terrors of the political present ever more directly, Hawthorne fled from them in the United States as he had in Italy, creating an ideological gulf that no cigar-induced conviviality could bridge.

By the time Hawthorne wrote his preface to *The Marble Faun* in England in December 1859, he had accepted his inability to portray "Italian manners and character":

> He has lived too long abroad, not to be aware that a foreigner seldom acquires that knowledge of a country, at once flexible and profound, which may justify him in endeavouring to idealize its traits.
>
> Italy, as the site of his Romance, was chiefly valuable to him as affording a sort of poetic or fairy precinct, where actualities would not be so terribly insisted upon, as they are, and must needs be, in America. (*CE*, 4:3)

If we read this famous demurrer for its politics, not just its aesthetics, it shows Hawthorne's understanding that Americans might demand books that portray "actualities" not only within their native land but also in a foreign locale. Actualities do not matter to Italians, but they do to Americans, especially in a book about Italy written in 1859. Both Hawthorne and his American audience knew that Italy's "traits" at this time were aggressively revolutionary, with troops gathering for war. They knew that Napoleon betrayed the nationalist cause by forcing Victor Emmanuel to sue for peace at Villafranca in July 1859, they knew of Cavour's patient determination to unite the peninsula, and they knew of Garibaldi's campaign to gather a million rifles to continue fighting in the south. Hawthorne's indifference to Italian political and social life had left him with too little material in his notebooks and too little sympathy for the Risorgimento to flesh out Italy's "actualities," and instead of describing the Italy of the day, a revolutionary land rushing toward national liberation, he fell back on the Arcadian formulas popular since the seventeenth century, combining art, travel, theology, history, morality, and psychology in a dreamy, symbolic narrative that presents a timeless and exotic Italy more like his "long-cherished idea" than the land he visited.[14] Perhaps this is why, as he wrote Fields, he objected to an "Italian name" for the novel (*CE*, 18:196); it would be too politicized, like Edward Bulwer-Lytton's historical romance about a medieval Italian revolutionary, *Rienzi, the Last of the Roman Tribunes* (1835).

To be sure, as Robert S. Levine has argued, conspiratorial priests and ubiquitous French soldiers serve as motifs of political unrest and substantiate a political allegory that identifies Miriam with revolutionary assassins and the Roman Carnival with the revolutions of 1848. Such turmoil leads Hawthorne reluctantly to accept papal authority and prefigures his uneasiness with Abraham Lincoln, another figure of strong central authority, as Levine acutely proposes.[15] In the immediate context of 1859 rather than 1848, however, the novel's papal politics more closely resemble Jacksonian anti-Federalism than Republican Unionism. Archduke Maximilian's ill-fated idea of an Italian confederation under papal rule was closer to Pierce's position on states' rights than Lincoln's insistence on union; the anti-Catholic Garibaldi, not the pope, represented national unity; and Cavour's motto "A Free Church in a Free State" alienated American Irish Catholics, a key constituency of Northern Democrats, while galvanizing support from anti-Catholic northern Protestants.[16] Committees to support Italian unity and raise funds for Garibaldi sprang up all over the United States, linking the two countries' fates as never before, and even included some who had questioned Italian nationalism, such as Hawthorne's old friend George Stillman Hillard, author of the most popular American travel book on Italy.[17] Insofar as *The Marble Faun* valorizes Catholic authority and ritual, it is a profoundly reactionary and antirepublican novel that is hopelessly out of touch with Italian life. By 1859 no republicans, American or Italian, believed the pope could unify Italy. Hawthorne could voice his religious sentiments and preserve Democratic Party orthodoxy only by eliding the Risorgimento in his narrative. *The Marble Faun*, as Mark A. R. Kemp argues, "dehistoricizes Italy" as it "resists the allegory of national liberation . . .

and strives, especially in the final chapters, to substitute its own familiar allegory of fall from grace and Protestant redemption."[18] For Hawthorne, in other words, art collaborates with political power to suppress revolt.

While Melville hardly waves the red flag of revolution in his Italy-inspired writings, his work strives to understand the relationships among history, art, and politics that Hawthorne deflects. Although *The Marble Faun* finds moral significance in Roman art, from its eponymous statue to the lost seven-branched candlestick and the newly recovered statue of Venus, Hawthorne avoids drawing moral parallels to contemporary politics and indulges in misty metonymies worthy of a transcendentalist. The faun represents humanity's mixed spiritual and animal nature, the candlestick inspires Hilda to vague allegories "full of poetry, art, philosophy, and religion," and the narrator finds in Venus the Victorian ideal of divine "Womanhood" (*CE*, 4:9–10, 4:371, 4:424). In contrast, Melville's lecture "Statues in Rome" intermingles contemporary politics and timeless aesthetics, praising Roman legal innovations and deprecating social change in favor of artistic permanence:

> As the Roman arch enters into and sustains our best architecture, does not the Roman spirit still animate and support whatever is soundest in societies and states? Or shall the scheme of Fourier supplant the code of Justinian? Only when the novels of Dickens shall silence the satires of Juvenal. The ancients of the ideal description, instead of trying to turn their impracticable chimeras, as does the modern dreamer, into social and political prodigies, deposited them in great works of art, which still live while states and constitutions have perished, bequeathing to posterity not shameful defects but triumphant successes. (*WHM*, 9:408–9)

Robert Milder finds in these words an uncharacteristic and temporary "aesthetic withdrawal" into artistic idealism: "On some level Melville understood that his ancient 'Rome' was an idealization, but the ideal, he had come to feel, was always preferable to the actual."[19] Yet when read against American sympathy for the Risorgimento, the lecture posits ancient Rome as a model for national unity peculiarly valuable in a country beset by sectionalism. Melville moves beyond Hawthornean allegory to identify "whatever is soundest in societies and states" with Roman practice. He embeds Roman art in its culture and favorably compares Rome's legal and literary achievements to Fourier's socialism and Dickens's realism, a political movement and aesthetic development he condemns despite their popularity. Such present fads ignore the lessons of the Roman past, a position compatible with Risorgimento nationalist theory. Mazzini, for example, denounced socialism for its irreligiosity and authoritarianism and considered Fourier and other French socialists politically maladroit.[20] He venerated Roman history, as evident in his declaration of the second Roman republic in 1849 and his demand that Rome be the new nation's capital, a symbolic move that Victor Emmanuel completed in 1871. Similarly the most inspirational novel of the Risorgimento, Alessandro Manzoni's *I Promessi Sposi* (1827), or *The Betrothed,* combines the scope and verisimilitude of a Dickens novel with the historical romance tradition of Sir Walter Scott by plunging two centuries into the past to discover the genesis of Italy's indomitable spirit of nationalism. Epic narrative on the scale of *Moby-Dick* was the best vehicle to express Italian and American aspirations, Melville believed, and both countries' zealots gained credibility insofar as they eschewed visionary ideologies and built on the foundations of ancient glory. Americans also had long fashioned their republic as a latter-day Rome, a convention reinvigorated by Constantino Brumidi's frescoes in the rotunda of the Capitol (1855–59) and the new iron dome on the Capitol, modeled on Rome's Pantheon, which became for Melville a powerful symbol of national authority in a time of rebellion.[21] Melville's lecture roots Italian and American patriotism in a common Roman past that aspires to a stable, coherent, and unified national identity.

When the Italian war heated up in June 1859, Melville turned to poetry to express his support for the Risorgimento. In a letter to a neighbor he penned his short poem "Epistle to Daniel Shepherd," a dream vision allegorizing the French-Italian alliance against Austria and questioning Napoleon's motives for helping Victor Emmanuel expand his "laurel grove" of trees:

> Such a weight of friendship pure
> The grateful trees could not endure.
> This dream, it still disturbeth me:
> Seer, foreshows it Italy? (*WHM*, 14:337–38)

Perhaps around the end of the year, after Garibaldi's Thousand conquered southern Italy, Melville began "At the Hostelry," an overtly political piece whose first hundred lines celebrate Garibaldi's conquest of Naples and Cavour's statesmanship. He continued working on this poem and its companion piece, "Naples in the Time of Bomba," at least until Garibaldi's death in 1882, an event "Bomba" commemorates in its closing lines. Melville eventually wove the poems into his Burgundy Club project, a mixture of prose and poetry whose subjects include the Risorgimento and the American Civil War, a conflation that forces transnational comparisons. "At the Hostelry" shows strong sympathy for the Italian revolutions of 1859–60 and celebrates both Garibaldi's battlefield exploits and Cavour's diplomatic skills. Naples lay in chains "Till Savoy's red-shirt Perseus flew / And cut that fair Andromeda free," the poem opens, while at the same time, "Few deeds of arms, in fruitful end, / The statecraft of Cavour transcend."[22] Later passages, some written after Rome's incorporation into Italy in 1870, praise the liberation of Venice, the freedom of the press in Rome, the demise of "Popedom" (*CP*, 322), and the public works envisioned by the new central government. Unlike the anarchic French, Italian liberals recognized that national unity depends on a strong central authority, and rather than insist on a democratic republic they settled for a constitutional monarchy under Victor Emmanuel II. This compromise infuriated Mazzini, whose omission from the two poems reveals Melville's sympathy for Cavour's political pragmatism and foreshadows Melville's position on the Civil War.

Transnationalism does not stop at the water's edge. Rather, like literary intertexts, it merges disparate countries' interests and practices in selective ways that sometimes defy rationality. It can create, as Don H. Doyle has observed in his comparatist study of the Civil War and the Risorgimento, a cosmopolitan, liberal, and humanitarian "International Nationalism," as in Mazzini's identification of abolitionism with Italian nationalism.[23] In November 1860 Garibaldi formally conveyed Naples to the Kingdom of Italy; a month later, South Carolina seceded from the United States. Reversing their historical destinies, the fractured and ungovernable Italian peninsula was uniting while expansionist America was dividing. A monarchy was proving more durable than a republic, and the European revolutions Americans had watched with glee now seemed imminent on their own soil. Prewar anxiety may have driven increased media fascination with Garibaldi. His face appeared on the cover of *Harper's Weekly* for June 18, 1859, newspapers charted his every move, and his ardent nationalism earned him the sobriquet "the Washington of Italy."[24] A decade of fruitless compromise ending with a four-way race for the presidency and a minority president left the United States with few heroes, and the country now looked abroad for decisive leadership. In January 1861 Melville's friend Henry Tuckerman published an article arguing for "the moral necessity of such a leader as Garibaldi" and presented him as a courageous, daring, and chivalrous military champion whose moderate political principles and fealty to the king demonstrated his loyalty to the nation.[25] Without mentioning secession, Tuckerman speaks to dissident Southerners by quoting one of Garibaldi's proclamations: "It is time that Sicily, as well as the rest, should see that the only remedy is in the union and co-operation of all."[26] Tuckerman deftly positions Garibaldi as a peacemaker between North and South, not only in Italy but in the United States. Little wonder that in the grim summer of 1861, after the disastrous Union defeat at Bull Run, Lincoln made an astonishing offer: he asked Garibaldi to become a major-general in the Union army.[27] Although Garibaldi refused because Lincoln would not immediately emancipate the slaves, the offer and the enthusiasm it generated among Americans cemented the ideological linkage between the Union and the Risorgimento: national unity had to be preserved, even if it meant war, and strong leaders had to be followed, whether Victor Emmanuel of Piedmont or Abraham Lincoln of Illinois.[28] As New Yorkers organized for war, one of their proudest legions marched under the banner of the "Garibaldi Guard."[29]

Hawthorne and Melville's friendship had survived time, geographical separation, and political misunderstandings. They still enjoyed each other's company and conversation, by their own accounts of 1856, whether in Melville's journal record of "Good talk" (*WHM*, 15:51) or Hawthorne's fuller account of discussing "Providence and futurity, and of everything that lies beyond human ken" (*CE*, 22:163). No record exists to show any personal conflicts that diminished their mutual regard between 1857 and December 1860, when they were finally within visiting distance of each other for only the second time in eight years. Hawthorne had returned to Concord in June while Melville was sailing around the world on his brother's ship and reading *The Marble Faun*, a book he included in his shipboard library.[30] Given Melville's earlier raptures over *Mosses from an Old Manse*, *The House of the Seven Gables*, and *The Blithedale Romance*, and Hawthorne's proxy signature on the contract for *The Confidence-Man* in London, one would expect further literary discussions between the two, especially concerning their mutual writings on Italy. Yet while Melville had accepted a rare invitation from Hawthorne and visited the Wayside in December 1852 (*WHM*, 14:241–42), no such invitation arrived in December 1860 or anytime thereafter. "Considering that in Liverpool [Melville] had simply appeared at Hawthorne's door, why did he not now simply appear at the Wayside?" Stanton Garner rightly asks. "The lapse in their friendship is a perplexing mystery, the solution to which is complex and, in all likelihood, ultimately unknowable."[31] One part of that solution lies in the political differences that germinated in Italy and now blossomed during the Civil War. The Risorgimento, previously so distant from Hawthorne's concerns, was now identified with the Union cause. Melville grasped the significance of this connection and welcomed the historical foundation it gave to America's national aspirations, essentially posing Italy and the United States, twin inheritors of Roman civilization, against the slavocracy of the South. Hawthorne, however, recoiling in his New England provincialism, sought security in artistic isolation and political orthodoxy. For the first time, the two men stood on different sides of the political fence.

The blurred party lines of the 1850s now sharpened into Republicans, Northern Democrats, Southern Democrats, and Constitutional Unionists, the four parties that won electoral votes in 1860. Although Hawthorne's party—the Northern Democrats—finished second in the popular vote, it won by far the fewest electoral votes.[32] The party of Franklin Pierce was in disarray, baffled by sectionalism, secession, and slavery, leaving Hawthorne bitter, disillusioned, and politically confused: "Hawthorne loved his country, he hated it, and he wanted to flee," says Brenda Wineapple.[33] His indifference toward Italian unity spilled over into his views of American unity, and well before the election he was ready to let the South secede: "I go for a dissolution of the Union," he wrote on February 10, 1860, in an oft-quoted letter to William D. Ticknor (*CE*, 18:227). The letter's less-studied closing paragraph connects Hawthorne's anti-Unionism with his willful disregard for the Risorgimento and indicates his growing distaste for politics:

> All the advantages of residing in England are concentrated in London. Leave out that, and I would rather be in America—that is to say, if Presidential elections and all other political turmoil could be done away with—and if I could but be deprived of my political rights, and left

to my individual freedom. The sweetest thing connected with a foreign residence is, that you have no rights and no duties, and can live your own life without interference of any kind. I shall never again be so free as I have been in England and Italy. (*CE*, 18:227)

Ironically, Hawthorne's disjunction of "individual freedom" from "political rights," along with the word "sweetest," echoes the criticism some Americans leveled at apolitical Italians. They were content, so the argument went, to follow the motto *dolce far niente*, or "sweet to do nothing," a phrase Hawthorne knew and used (*CE*, 18:164).[34] Again and again Hawthorne's letters, the surest guide to his beliefs, express strong anti-Union sentiments (letters to Henry Bright and Horatio Bridge, *CE*, 18:355, 18:381, 18:412, 18:428). He knew he was skirting treason and even disagreed with Pierce, who wanted to "fight it out" for the Union (*CE*, 18:543, 18:428). Skeptical of the regional, racial, and cultural diversity that union implied, he identified ever more closely with New England and his home state of Massachusetts and went so far as to advocate making New England "a separate nation" (*CE*, 18:363). He refused to join his Saturday Club colleagues, including Ralph Waldo Emerson, in publishing a prowar document and told Elizabeth Peabody that he placed his hopes in the Peace Democrats and despised "the present administration with all [his] heart" (*CE*, 18:544, 18:591–92). Both his controversial antiwar essay "Chiefly about War Matters" and his dedication of *Our Old Home* to Pierce profoundly alienated him from many in his circle and deprived him of political influence, leaving him unable to help Bayard Taylor gain a diplomatic post (*CE*, 18:496–97).[35] He died in 1864, a deeply disaffected man.

Melville left no record as clear as Hawthorne's on his views of the Civil War. He arrived home after the 1860 election and made few partisan political comments. But his actions reveal his comparative ease with the most liberal elements in the new Republican administration. Urged by his brother Allan he again sought a consular appointment, this time specifically naming Florence as his choice, a locale that would have placed him at the heart of the new Italy (*WHM*, 14:359).[36] Although family members remained largely Democratic, they were also pragmatists, and they gathered letters of support from prominent Republicans such as Thurlow Weed, Julius Rockwell, and Richard Henry Dana (*WHM*, 14:359–70).[37] Especially helpful was Melville's Republican brother-in-law

John C. Hoadley, who not only served in the 1858 Massachusetts legislature but also chaired one of the many committees formed in early
1861 to congratulate Italy upon its unification, events that were widely
publicized and well attended.[38] Bolstered by his Republican supporters,
Melville managed to arrange a meeting with Charles S. Sumner, the abolitionist Republican senator from Massachusetts and another advocate
for Italian freedom and unity.[39] Although Sumner had supported Hawthorne for the Salem surveyorship in 1846 and congratulated him on his
Liverpool consulship in 1853, no one in Melville's family, least of all Melville himself, requested Hawthorne's recommendation this time.[40] They
recognized that Hawthorne's indifference to Italian nationalism, dogged
loyalty to traditional Democratic politics, and emergent antiunionism
had isolated him politically and rendered his support worthless. By the
time Melville met with Sumner the Florence post was filled, and when
Lemuel Shaw died on March 29, Melville abandoned all thoughts of
travel abroad and returned to Pittsfield (*WHM*, 14:370).

While Hawthorne satirized Lincoln and advocated disunion, Melville
remained firmly in the Union camp. He let his brother Thomas know
that "the war goes bravely on. . . . We beat the rascals in almost every
feild [sic], & take all their ports &c, but they dont cry 'Enough!'—It looks
like a long lane, with the turning quite out of sight" (*WHM*, 14:378).
He checked the war news daily and cheered on his cousins, Guert and
Henry Gansevoort, who were serving in the conflict (*WHM*, 14:376,
391–93). When he visited Guert in the Brooklyn Navy Yard in 1861, he
and Evert Duyckinck went aboard the *Iroquois,* a U.S. Navy sloop that
Garibaldi visited after it protected him during the siege of Palermo (*Log,*
641).[41] Melville's visit to Henry at the Virginia front in 1864, courtesy of
a note from Sumner, graphically revealed the horrors of war and further
ingratiated him to the pro-Union senator.[42] While Hawthorne turned
to nostalgic and descriptive essays of England in *Our Old Home,* Melville directly engaged the war in *Battle-Pieces,* perhaps the finest book
of poetry to emerge from any American conflict. As the war continued,
Melville developed sympathies for both sides and deplored the mutual
carnage, moving beyond ideology to humanitarianism. Whereas Hawthorne would have preferred to live in the country of "New England,"
Melville clearly hoped his poems would reunite North and South on an
equal basis that, like Italy's reunification, accepted a constitutional basis
for nationhood.

In the most overt political statement of his career, the "Supplement" to *Battle-Pieces* (1866), Melville poured balm on the wounds of war through a mediatory, ruminative discourse that measured the conflict against Italian history: "Were the Unionists and Secessionists but as Guelphs and Ghibellines? If not, then far be it from a great nation now to act in the spirit that animated a triumphant town-faction in the Middle Ages" (*CP*, 467). Reconstructionists must avoid revenge, a lesson that the Italian parties of the pope and the state only learned after centuries of feuding. The United States must model itself on contemporary Italy, a country that has (at least in American eyes) overcome such intransigent disputes and created "A unit and a telling State / Participant in the world's debate" ("At the Hostelry," in *CP*, 315).

Under the "iron dome" of the Capitol, North and South might achieve a similar reconciliation. Each country's factions could draw on their common heritage of Roman virtue to establish national unity, as evident in *Battle-Pieces*' frequent classical allusions: Stonewall Jackson's "Roman heart," comparison of Americans in "The House-Top" to "Nature's Roman, never to be scourged," Robert E. Lee's striding out of a capitol that looks "Like porches erst upon the Palatine," or comparisons between Pompey and Caesar's rivalry and the American Civil War (*CP*, 53, 57, 152, 90, 455). While these references cut in many directions, in general they invoke Roman law as a counterweight to the democratic excesses unleashed by the Risorgimento and the Civil War and validate both movements with the historical imprimatur of the world's most successful civilization.[43]

By identifying the Union cause with the Risorgimento, Melville distinguished himself from Hawthorne and revealed a political pragmatism that served him well in his final years. When he finally received a political appointment in 1866 to the New York customhouse, the federal government was split between a Republican Congress and a Democratic president, a balancing act that nicely imaged the nuanced politics of *Battle-Pieces*. If, as Carolyn L. Karcher thinks, Melville owed his appointment to the finely tuned logic of the "Supplement," it was a resilient logic, for he maintained his low-profile position for nineteen uninterrupted years, longer than all of Hawthorne's tumultuous appointments combined.[44] Evaluated simply in the practical terms of vocational durability, Melville was the more adept bureaucrat of the two, more like the patriarch at the Salem customhouse who kept his office "out of the whirlpool of political vicissitude" than he was like the loyal party man Hawthorne (*CE*, 1:12). Melville's comparative political success derives from a supple ideology that views democracy primarily as a means rather than an end, a method of empowering the common citizen and providing political choice but only within the larger economy of orderly governance and social necessity. Melville learned this at sea, where the good of the ship comes first and the rights of the crew second, the lesson Captain Vere expounds and the drumhead court, like many readers, reluctantly accepts in *Billy Budd.*[45] National consolidation aligned state interests with the immense energies of Henry Adams's Dynamo, the combination of governmental, industrial, and military power that characterizes modern nations, and paved the way for contemporary globalism, a phenomenon the world traveler Melville understood well even if he didn't always approve of it. Speakers such as Ungar in *Clarel,* for example, warn against the dangers of utilitarianism, material progress, and the leveling tendencies of modern societies, as do parts of the Burgundy Club manuscripts; yet nowhere does Melville advocate secession or express regret at the outcome of the Civil War. He remained in New York City as it evolved into the world's most multicultural metropolis and lived to see his hometown honor Garibaldi in 1888 with a statue in Washington Square, a fitting emblem of American affinity for the Risorgimento and Italy's new civic nationalism.

Melville's evolution toward a more pragmatic politics, one that like Garibaldi's accepted the necessity of strong leaders in order to attain national unity, contrasts sharply with Hawthorne's unreconstructed Jacksonianism. Jacksonian ideology reposed political power in the individual, the state, and the region rather than the national government, and its strict construction of the Constitution validated states' rights up to the point of nullifying federal law, making consistent national economic and civil policies difficult. Jacksonian anti-Federalism underpins Hawthorne's secessionist views and makes them, ironically, more ruthlessly democratic than Melville's pragmatic concessions to federal authority, for democracy advocates dispersing power as broadly as possible. One may even say that Hawthorne is ultimately more principled than Melville, unwilling to alter his political beliefs in order to save a nation that required force to maintain its unity. Hawthorne remained true to the Democratic Party's traditional emphasis on states' rights and resisted the shifting tides of circumstance that led to abolition and a stronger central government, two fundamental reorientations of American society that, however virtuous they may have been, were not without their problems, as Reconstruction and years of segregation have demonstrated.

The issue is not finally one of right and wrong, of course, but of recognizing the role that politics played in the later years of the Hawthorne-Melville relationship. Hawthorne's principled conservatism affirmed values of gradualism, individualism, and regionalism that many Americans cherish today, but it placed him at odds with Melville's pragmatic acceptance of a new American politics of national consolidation. Whatever the temperamental and psychological differences between Hawthorne and Melville, their political differences are readily observable and verifiable in their words and behavior and point to alternative ways of understanding both their relationship and their cultural role as registers of changing American values.

Notes

1. McWilliams, *Hawthorne, Melville, and the American Character*; Reynolds, *European Revolutions*.

2. See Marraro, *American Opinion*. Works that have extended Marraro's study are Buonomo, *Backward Glances*; and Vance, *America's Rome*.

3. Fuller's letters are collected and fully annotated in *"These Sad But Glorious Days,"* ed. Reynolds and Smith.

4. Marraro, "Garibaldi in New York." For the Tuckerman-Melville friendship, see Parker, *Herman Melville*, 1:572–73.

5. Doyle, *Nations Divided*, 11–16, uses these terms in his lucid summary and critique of such theorists of nationalism as Eric Hobsbawm, Ernest Gellner, and Benedict Anderson. Doyle begins his analysis with an 1867 essay by Charles S. Sumner, illustrating that this distinction grew out of concrete historical conditions, not just academic theorizing.

6. Woolf, *History of Italy, 1700–1860*, 432.

7. Gemme, *Domesticating Foreign Struggles*, explores these prejudices at length, especially in ch. 1 (15–56).

8. Reynolds, *European Revolutions*, ch. 6 (97–124).

9. King, *History of Italian Unity*, 2:52–53.

10. *Oxford Dictionary of Quotations*, 223.

11. Hayford and Davis, "Herman Melville as Office-Seeker."

12. Parker, *Herman Melville*, 1:151–56.

13. Parker, *Herman Melville,* 2:418–25.

14. Viewing Italy as a "fairy precinct" has roots in English travel narratives, and it continued through the nineteenth century. In the huge literature on this topic, the books that best present the romantic contexts of *The Marble Faun* are Brooks, *Dream of Arcadia;* Baker, *Fortunate Pilgrims;* Wright, *American Novelists in Italy;* Vance, *America's Rome;* and Buonomo, *Backward Glances.*

15. Levine, "'Antebellum Rome' in *The Marble Faun,"* 33.

16. Berthold, "Melville, Garibaldi, and the Medusa of Revolution," 431–36.

17. Marraro, *American Opinion,* 287–304. Marraro mentions Hillard on 289. Hillard's *Six Months in Italy* (1853) derives from the author's travels of 1847–48, before the Risorgimento made headlines, and consequently has little to say about politics.

18. Kemp, "The Marble Faun and American Postcolonial Ambivalence," 226, 230.

19. Milder, "'Connecting Link of Centuries,'" 222, 220.

20. Mack Smith, *Mazzini,* 87. See also the longer discussion of Mazzini's mature critique of socialism on 196–202.

21. Wolanin, "Constantino Brumidi's Frescoes." McWilliams, *Hawthorne, Melville, and the American Character,* 210, precedes the fuller treatment of the "iron dome" motif in Rogin, *Subversive Genealogy,* ch. 8 (259–87).

22. Melville, *Collected Poems,* 313–14; hereafter cited parenthetically as *CP.*

23. Doyle, *Nations Divided,* 22–23. Doyle quotes Mazzini's 1859 letter to Theodore Dwight Weld identifying abolitionism with Italian nationalism: "We are fighting the same sacred battle for freedom and the emancipation of the oppressed,—you, Sir, against negro, we against white, slavery. The cause is truly identical" (23).

24. Berthold, "Melville, Garibaldi, and the Medusa of Revolution," 433.

25. [Tuckerman], review of *Italy in Transition,* 15.

26. [Tuckerman], review of *Italy in Transition,* 52.

27. Marraro, "Lincoln's Offer of a Command to Garibaldi." Major-general was the highest rank held by any Union officer at the time, effectively giving Garibaldi a command equal to George C. McClellan's.

28. For a good discussion of slavery and the Risorgimento, including Frederick Douglass's outspoken support for Garibaldi, see Gemme, *Domesticating Foreign Struggles,* 124–30.

29. Moore, ed., *Rebellion Record,* 1:307.

30. Parker, *Herman Melville,* 2:433.

31. Garner, *Civil War World,* 59.

32. *World Almanac,* 108.

33. Wineapple, *Hawthorne,* 340.

34. Gemme, *Domesticating Foreign Struggles,* 35–52.

35. Wineapple, *Hawthorne,* 348–60, covers these controversies in detail.

36. Parker, *Herman Melville,* 2:456–66, updates Hayford and Davis, "Melville as Office-Seeker," 384–85. See also the editorial discussion of Melville's letter to his uncle Peter Gansevoort of March 15, 1861, requesting help in securing a consulship in Florence (*WHM,* 14:359).

37. Garner, *Civil War World,* 2–27, discusses the Melville family's Democratic traditions. For a compact narrative of Melville's final attempt at a consulship, see Parker, *Herman Melville,* 2:458–59.

38. Hoadley chaired the pro-Italy committee in Lawrence, Massachusetts (Parker, *Herman Melville,* 2:460).

39. See, for example, Sumner's letter of September 3, 1860, wishing for the overthrow of Francis II of Naples as well as the pope (*Selected Letters,* 2:34).

40. Sumner, *Selected Letters,* 1:161–62, 1:386.

41. For Garibaldi's visit to the *Iroquois,* see Mooney, *Dictionary of American Naval Fighting Ships,* 3:459.

42. Garner recounts the visit in detail; see *Civil War World,* ch. 7 (294–344).

43. For a balanced analysis of Melville's appeal to Roman tradition, see McWilliams, *Hawthorne, Melville, and the American Character,* 217–20, along with Melville's discussion of law in *Battle-Pieces,* 209–11.

44. Karcher, "The Moderate and the Radical," 232.

45. For an especially sensitive reading of Vere as a tragic figure who deals with "the inexorable state of things as they are," see Sten, "Vere's Use of the 'Forms'" (48).

Letters on Foolscap

Unable to support my growing family on what I earn by the labor of my pen, I began some years ago, never mind how long precisely, seeking summer employment to supplement my income. Drawn by my admiration of Hawthorne and Melville to the Berkshires and inspired by Thoreau's example to take the requisite courses, I sought and gained a position as a Surveyor in the area around Lenox and Pittsfield. Besides affording me healthful exercise in the open air, this occupation allowed me to explore the mossy meadows and umbrageous woods that Hawthorne and Melville loved.

One day, while eating a simple repast in the cornfield near Arrowhead, as my gaze drifted to the horizon and the monumental bulk of Mount Greylock, I noticed a glint—of metal?—in the grass at the margin of the field. Luckily equipped with the proper tools, I was able to dig for a mere two hours before uncovering a small but heavy sea chest with the initials "HM" executed on the top in fancifully arranged studs. Although a sturdy lock protected the contents, years of dank rust had corroded it so that I was able to break it off and pry open the mysterious vessel. Imagine my astonishment at finding within a collection of tissuey letters tied in a black ribbon with a paper marked "Secret" pinned to the top sheet. Opening this eagerly, I read the following words: "Being the correspondence between myself and Hawthorne from summer and fall of 1852. Some of the letters appear to be missing—could Augusta have gotten hold of them somehow?—but these remain—and remain cherished as tokens of what might have been." There was no signature: just a curious symbol resembling Queequeg's mark.

The state of the manuscripts being exceptionally fine, I had to do little more than copy them in my crimpy hand. I thank the editors of this volume for allowing me to present them here for the first time.

—WYN KELLEY

 Concord, Aug. 15, 1852

My dear Melville—I am in receipt of your letter and the enclosure supplied by your friend Mr. Clifford. They tell a wonderful tale indeed, if you can believe them; all the better if you cannot. The story of the resourceful Agatha, saving Robinson from drowning in the shipwreck—how minutely you sketch the broad cliff, the vast sea, the coming storm. Mr. Clifford's letter verifies the truth of the tale, yet your embroid'rings give the story its truer meanings—marking the aged father in his lofty lighthouse, the meditative Agatha looking out to sea under the calm eye of the equally meditative sheep on the cliff above—and then, after Robinson marries her and leaves her behind, her daily visits to the post box, rotting over the years on its wooden post until it falls to earth. How are our aspirations so inclined to corruption and decay. I am puzzled by Mr. Clifford's tale of Robinson's later life—his second and third wives, his visits to Agatha and the daughter he left so long ago, his gifts of shawls belonging to his dead spouse. And Agatha herself—what a figure of fortitude! You say you and Mr. Clifford discussed her as one of those marvelously patient women, like the wives of Nantucket sailors waiting long years for their departed husbands and lovers. How many, think you, would have shouldered their griefs as Agatha does hers—raising her daughter and educating her among the Quakers, nursing the sick for her bread, guiding her aging father's faltering footsteps to the grave? It is the story of a great woman's heart, left crushed and bleeding but heroically carrying on in the toils of love.

And yet, Melville, you say that you cannot write this story yourself, although you have sent me many closely-written sheets, and that I must do it! That it is in a vein with which I am peculiarly familiar, you say. How so? Why, the story is in *your* vein, concerning sailors and shipwrecks and the mysterious impulses of a class of men about whom I know only what one sees on the docks and wharves of Salem or Boston. I never saw such a Robinson in the Customs House. (By the by, your Mr. Clifford calls him Robertson, but since his account is only the factual one, I will dismiss it.) I am somewhat provoked, indeed, that you would suggest it.

Agatha is very fine, I agree, and I could happily recreate her life by the sea and weave around it all the fancy at my command. Perhaps you remember my little sketch of many years ago, "Footprints on the Seashore"? I am ever partial to scenes of women on the marges of the sea, and I remember in that sketch certain images of charming white feminine feet that might rival the brown ones of your island maidens. But that Robinson or Robertson or whatever you want to call him. Do you think it would give me pleasure to write about such a low character? You compare him to my "Wakefield," and yes, Wakefield did leave his wife, while lingering in the vicinity and observing her from the vantage of his new life only steps away from the old. But Wakefield, you remember, was a "London husband," not this brute of whom you speak. How to imagine the degraded temptations that called Robinson from the side of his virtuous spouse! You say the sin stole upon him insensibly, so that it would have been hard for him to settle on the exact day when he could say, "Now I have deserted my wife." My Wakefield was crafty and possibly as self-deluded as you say this Robinson was, but I cannot imagine him marrying two other women and then presenting their old clothes to his long-abandoned love!

But I have other more urgent reasons, alas, why I cannot accept your kind offer—and I do believe it is kindly meant, although since publishing my Blithedale Romance I have had little leisure for story-making. As you know, I am deep in the biography of General Pierce—anticipating, of course, soon being able to style him by a grander title. And tho' I expect no more recompense than the gratitude of our next president, I find myself somewhat pressed to write the very best account I can of his life, especially since this campaign has produced such scurrilous attacks on his character. You may well understand, then, my reasons for haste. I have worked harder to promote his name in the public eye than I ever did to advance my own. Thus, although I would look forward with pleasure to the prospect of some months spent in the company of the heroic Agatha, I must put aside romance for the present and stick to politics instead.

If you are willing, however, I would like to keep your papers just a while longer and contemplate the melancholy picture you have drawn of this Nantucket wife. Or no, indeed, she was from

Pembroke. Pray present my kindest compliments to your lady and boys. Have you enjoyed your Monument Mountain picnics this summer? Or are you too busy haying to partake of the usual Berkshire fetes?

Truly yours
Nathl Hawthorne

Pittsfield, Aug. 20, 1852

My Dear Hawthorne,

Your letter finds me in a season of labor like that of your Coverdale and Hollingsworth, except that my farming is not as transcendental as what you describe in your Blithedale Romance. I have in fact made negligible progress with your novel and its little knot of dreamers since you sent it in July, much as I look forward to its pleasures. I am struck, however, by your Zenobia and am more than ever convinced that you, not I, are the one to write the character of Agatha. I confess I am little given to domestic scenes (in fiction, at any rate) and have had little experience with female characters. My venture into that area, which you and your wife were so kindly disposed to encourage last winter, now gives me pain to contemplate. My *Pierre,* I fear, may sink as silently as the Whale did the year before. While I have corn to harvest, I can hardly afford to repine.

To repeat, however, I can think of no one better situated to write Agatha's story. Your biography of Pierce will soon be done, and a blessing will it be to its subject to have your wind in his sails! (Tho' I cannot admire his position on the slavery issue, and I wonder that you can write it calmly. But then, surely you have sounded this for yourself, and you know the man as few others can.) I am surprised that you recoil at the figure of Robinson, however—(and I shall persist in my error, Robinson not Robertson, in honor of your bold refusal to face the facts). He is a man like any other—swept up in a sudden passion, then as suddenly exhausted and seeking ever new stimulants for his restless and hungry spirit. We have spoken of such passions while drinking champagne in the hayloft. My Pierre is such a man, tho' a man of the land, not like Robinson, a waif of the sea. But surely you see the romance of Agatha's saving this man from death and nursing him back to life and to love. She is Zenobia in depth of heart and Priscilla in gentleness and humility. And after all, is Robinson so different from Coverdale, who cannot devote himself to the woman, or the women he loves? Or Hollingsworth, for that matter?

Now I must confess that I first wrote to you of this matter after opening your new book, realizing how exquisitely you have anatomized, once again, the hearts of women and men. You are right, I can write of seas and storms. But I fear that my study does not welcome such guests as yours—the gentle spirits of Phoebe and Priscilla and the dauntless ones of Hester and Zenobia. And surely you are not going to give yourself to politics forever! The world awaits your next romance, and you have promised another "sunny gleam." I am but the humble post man bringing you the sheets of your next story.

Awaiting me are not sunny gleams but a sudden shower, and I must go and put the buggy up in the barn, which in my haste to answer your letter I have neglected. May the little Rosebud, and Mistress Una and Master Julian wreath you and Mrs. Hawthorne with their summer smiles, even when the season has passed, as I fear it soon will.

H. Melville

Concord, Aug. 27, 1852

My Dear Melville—I write somewhat in haste, considerable exhaustion too, and it must be admitted, a severe headache. I have just this forenoon posted the ending of the biography to Ticknor with explicit instructions that he print the proofs by Monday so that I can take them to Brunswick that day and show them to Pierce. We are to celebrate the Bowdoin Semicentennial, and it gives me humble pleasure to participate in it at this glorious moment in the General's career. Otherwise, you may guess that I would not travel in my state of fatigue and distress. Your animadversions on his slavery views but too narrowly interpret the truth of the matter, but to be fair, you are not the first friend to have pressed me on that point. I have navigated some treacherous shoals in this latest literary endeavor, and if I did not love the man and admire his cause, I would not have risked my reputation so far. But I don't mind telling you that although I informed him from the outset I would accept the commission only if I did not benefit from it in any way, I am beginning to reconsider that position. Serving my government in some overseas port would suit me much better at the moment, and Mrs. Hawthorne seems to agree. In truth, when you urge upon me another romance, I want to fling the letter into the fire. I am sick of romance!

You appear, however, to have some appetite for it and to have read my Blithedale much more closely than your "negligible" progress would suggest. You have seen truths in it I little recognized. I am sympathetic with your view that Agatha might share traits of some of my other characters, especially if you are seeing her less as a patient Griselda and more as a brave champion. If only Robinson were worth the effort! But perhaps you are right about him too, and he is simply the sum of human passions. I suppose Arthur Dimmesdale might abandon Hester and Pearl if he had a mind to. Heavens! Are all my heroes so weak and sinful as that?

You spoke of the painful subject of your last novel. I have hesitated to write my own opinion, knowing how much you have suffered at the hands of the press. I cannot say that I see it the way I saw *Moby-Dick,* the book you honored with my name. You know how profoundly that book affected me. I said once of *Mardi* that it was a book to make a man swim for his life. *Moby-Dick* makes one long to drown. You wrote such a book as only a very reckless man can venture, and you won the wager. *Pierre* is in some ways an even braver book, putting Ahab into a parlor. It is a marvelous conception of youthful enthusiasm crashing its surf against an adamantine world. But Melville, the book spills the inmost You over the floor along with Pierre's brains! It commits suicide. And for what? *Pierre* is a book such as only a great man could have written, let there be no mistake about that. But you have even greater ones in you—have written them already—and I hope you will return to those.

I have taken to heart, though, your tender portrait of Agatha and her erring husband. After this gathering of the aging graduates at Bowdoin, I spirit myself off to the Isle of Shoals for a spell.

Pierce has recommended me to his friend's hotel and plans to join me there after a time, but I expect to have much leisure, the first in several months, for revery and writing. I cannot promise to compose this story, but I will bring it with me and see if I can conjure up a narrative from the materials you have so kindly provided. It seems to me, tho', that we should do this together over gin or rum punch. Now that I have written a purely practical work for the world, my pen is resigned to more pedestrian tasks than of yore. Perhaps you will make it take flight once again!

Ever truly yours,
Nath'l Hawthorne

❧ Pittsfield, Sept. 2, 1852

My Dear Hawthorne—I address this to you at your Enchanted Isles, in the fervent hope that this season of repose will restore to you health, well being, and a peaceful and satisfied mind. I am sure that Mrs. Hawthorne feels the most anxious wishes for your health as well and is pleased to surrender you to the company of those who venture to the islands this late in the summer. And to the companionable Pierce, of course, and his friends. Perhaps you are all rejoicing in the triumphant completion of your literary campaign and envisioning in its success the equally glorious victory of the political one. I am surprised to hear that you actually think of seeking a political post abroad, however. I had thought your years in the Custom House cured you of that fancy! But of course, your country owes you all honors for your crowning achievements, and would await with eager anticipation your correspondence from Rome or Leghorn or wherever you should alight.

Thank you for your acknowledgment of *Pierre*; I cannot call it, or hope for, praise. Its reception, I must admit, has caused me no little depression of spirits, and your honest, bluff words pretty much state the case. It has been a disaster. I remember telling you once that I feared breaking down like an old nutmeg-grater, worn out by the attrition of the wood. Well, I have written two books since then, books that have used up the best substance of my heart, brain, and soul, and what can I do more? I have no voyages left to write, and evidently I cannot write about the rural gentry either.

When a man has a growing family to feed and only one body with which to feed them, he becomes Prometheus chained to the rock, with vultures nightly consuming his liver and lights. But he grew back together again each night, and I do not. Would that I could join you at your Happy Isle and be whole once more!

I am wearying your patience, however, with this melancholy strain. Tell me of your walks and your thoughts. Perhaps I will catch some of your poetic fire and ignite my own flagging inspiration. With chopping wood for the winter and getting in the hay, I am fully employed for at least a few more weeks. May yours pass more pleasantly than mine!

Ever yours,
H. Melville

Isle of Shoals, Sept. 6, 1852

My Dear Melville—I write to you with great expansion of spirit since my last. I am staying at Laighton's hotel, a grand edifice with a charming veranda drawing the sea breezes and affording one perfect leisure and freedom from care. The food is good and abundant and the company acceptable. I am particularly companionable with mine host's son-in-law, Mr. Thaxter, with whom I have passed some very pleasant evenings. We have given ourselves over to the dissipations of whist, singing negro melodies, and apple-toddy, a particularly rich and spicy concoction for which I will have to obtain the secret.

As for the islands themselves, they have reminded me of the mysteries of sea and sky, which I thought I'd forgotten in my months of study and writing. I have had Agatha much in mind among these scenes, and my journal has consumed many hours of reflection on this island existence.

I have had before me the spectacle of an astonishing array of women. First there is Mrs. Thaxter herself, who sings like a bird and lives a honeymoon existence with her young husband, along with Miss Thaxter, their amiable companion and sister. But the women I have seen and heard of on the island would make you stare! The other day on Star Island, I saw a perfect witch with an enormous basket, creeping about gathering herbs or perchance

poisons. She seemed the female offspring of Chillingworth collecting rank weeds, and I mentioned her to Mr. Thaxter. He knew
just who she was: "Oh, that's the bearded woman," he said. I had
observed her venerable years but no beard, sad to say.

I was reminded of Agatha in a conversation I had with Mr.
Thaxter; well, truth to tell, I was speaking to him of what you had
learned about the women of Nantucket and their hardy tolerance
for their sailor husbands' long absences. He said that the women
hereabouts are very timid about the sea, never going forth on it
themselves, and frightened for their husbands, even though none
have died in accidents in recent years. Mr. Thaxter says the men
are generally strongly attached to their homes and seldom venture far from the coast, fishing for mackerel and only occasionally
shipping for the West Indies. Quite different from your intrepid
whalemen.

The story that curdled my blood was of Betty Moody. Pierce
arrived yesterday, and so we sought the services of the town clerk
of Gosport as a guide around the local cemetery, only he turned
out to be thoroughly inebriated and besought the General's aid
in building a sea-mole at the entrance to the harbor as soon as
he should become President. He took us to see the local attraction, Betty Moody's Hole. It is a kind of cave along the shore, with
several great rocks obscuring it so that one could conceal oneself
completely. I crept in myself and found it a long, low, strait passage into a small hiding-place. Apparently in the old times, the
Indians raided the island, and this Betty Moody ran to the cave
to hide herself and her children. That was all that Joe Caswell,
our drunken cicerone would say, but Mr. Thaxter later informed
me that one of the children began to cry; and afraid that it would
betray her place of concealment, Betty Moody murdered the child
"to save herself." You may imagine how our party, which included
Judge Upham and his brother and their wives, Pierce and his wife,
and three young ladies, would have received this intelligence!

Very different was the story Mr. Thaxter told of a schoolteacher
living on the island just a few years ago. She seems to have been
like our young Agatha, of a thoughtful disposition and given to
roaming the beach and sitting on the rocks to look abroad upon
the sweeping expanse of ocean. According to Mr. Thaxter a wave
carried her off the rock and out to sea, never to be seen again.

I have heard legends of island ghosts—including a little old woman who places herself at the hearthside unasked—and of digging for treasure and any number of other romantic tales, which is all to say that I begin to see the romance of Agatha as something that could really exist, not just as a febrile dream on your part. I have been gathering immense amounts of natural scenery in my journal and collecting lore like a miser—or like the bearded woman—and for the first time in many a day begin to feel the stirrings of fancy, rather than the dull proddings of fact. (Do not pass that last remark on to Pierce. To him his story is pure heroic epic, let me tell you.) I will tell you more in my next.

Yours truly
Nathl Hawthorne

Isle of Shoals, Sept. 9, 1852

My Dear Melville, I have just returned from White Island, where I saw the lighthouse and its strange and mysterious denizens. Mr. Thaxter rowed me over with great labor, I presume, since it was immensely hot and still. We landed on a rocky shore and walked up to a most unprepossessing house with an odd garden—just a patch of onions, which the lighthouse keeper was harvesting already, before the insects devour them, and some squashes and cabbages; hardly enough, you would think, to keep body and soul together, especially since I saw no evidence of cow or pig or even a hen. If Agatha's father lived like this—and come to think of it Agatha herself—it could hardly have been a very comfortable existence.

The lighthouse stands behind the house—a cottage, really, small and whitewashed—and is connected to it by a covered walkway. We ascended into the light itself, a great revolving lantern with copper reflectors and colored glasses. He had maps spread out of all the islands and bays, and we could see them for ourselves from that great height—at least eighty feet. The surf broke on his little shingle of a beach and the low rocks. I found him a suspicious character, and have heard rumors that since he came to the lighthouse he has lost two wives. One he used to leave alone out there and drove to such terror that she died. The other left *him* after seeing how much he drinks. We heard the voice of a woman in the house when we came down, but I did not see her.

It seems a romantic place enough. I could imagine Mr. and Mrs. Thaxter enjoying honeymoon bliss there for a year or so. They are the Ferdinand and Miranda of these isles. But apparently this man got so intoxicated one night that he rowed out alone into a head tide, and Mr. Thaxter had to rescue him. I can now heartily sympathize with Agatha's desire to have nothing to do with the sea. Did not you say that she had made a resolve never to live a maritime life? Or to marry a sailor? No honeymoon lighthouse for her.

In my rambles I have thought often of the margin between land and sea. One lives in this island world never far from the beach. It is the place where you, my ocean-going friend, and I, poor creature of the land, may meet. I have no other way to experience the sea than from the shore, that shore that you described in *Moby-Dick* as hostile to the ship. Someday perhaps I will cross the ocean myself, but for now I see it from the same kind of cliffs that Agatha ascended for her sea-views. I find myself strangely drawn to that figure of meditation and melancholy—but also defiance and grandeur. In your letter, you must realize, you described her most fully *before* Robinson comes into her life. Did you see something that Mr. Clifford, the lawyer, did not? He wept over her feminine patience and suffering. Yet you seem to have detected the masculine firmness and courage in her character. I begin to see it myself, now that I have lived this beachcomber life for a time.

Your friend
Nathl Hawthorne

❦ Concord, Oct. 27, 1852

Dear Melville—As yours of the 25th correctly surmises, I have given more thought to Agatha's story. It occupies exceedingly idle hours, for as I mentioned to Bridge in my last communication with him, my mind is gripped with Pierce's affairs, which of course will be resolved in a matter of days. I stand at the brink of a precipice, for I have the greatest anxiety about my future. Whatever it holds, I must make it profitable. I cannot be a devotee of the "Flesh Brush Philosophy," which you so delightfully exhibit in *Pierre*. No, my sights are set on a foreign legation, as yours, Melville, might be too, with your wide travels and knockings about the world. If something opens in the Sandwich Islands, you must get out your carpet bag at the first opportunity.

Nevertheless, I continue to imagine the new romance, which I informed Bridge would be more genial than Blithedale. For I have in mind a happier reunion than that which your last letter implied. You paint a picture of Robinson as incorrigible. You speak of the "peculiarly latitudinarian" habits of sailors, who take a wife for the night in every port. Such a character might find his place in a low comedy but not a romance. I am imagining him instead as burdened with a terrible secret, some indelible suffering that makes him an outcast from the world—hence *ashamed* to remain at Agatha's side. What could it be? What is this taint, this impurity that he bears? Whatever it is, I expect to reward Agatha's patience with the knowledge that her husband's heart, though errant, is true. But he will die in her arms before the end—I must find some plausible way to get her to Missouri.

You see, Melville, that I have little sympathy for this latitudinarian sailor of yours. You would give him a "moral sense," make him suffer remorse, only at some late stage of his career, after he has wronged his innocent wife. Such a man makes no sense to me as a literary character. He must have a moral sense from the beginning of the story but be so tinged with guilt that he flees his family in despair. His later prosperity in Missouri must signal the successful results of his penance. And we must never forget that Agatha's love for him confirms his salvation.

Now it is true that the story may not be not so genial as I have sketched it here, and perhaps, as with my others, a melancholy strain will seep into its fabric and darken its dyes. The father, for instance, may develop an incurable disease and utter some horrible dying prophecy that Robinson will bring to pass. The daughter may be carried away by an ocean tempest like the young schoolteacher Mr. Thaxter described to me. Agatha's suffering will indeed surpass that of Robinson, as does her heroism.

But I go on. It is all an attempt to pass the weary hours until Pierce's fate—and thus mine—be known. Perhaps by the time you arrive in Boston—you are visiting your wife's family as usual at Thanksgiving?—all these idle speculations will have hardened, either into a story or into a part of my life that I have left behind. If you can come out to Concord during your stay with the Shaws, I will be glad. Mrs. Hawthorne and the children will be visiting her sister in West Newton. The champagne and the gin, now safely stowed in their puncheons, await a piratical raid on their contents.

Your friend,
Nath'l Hawthorne

🌺 Pittsfield, Nov. 11, 1852

My dear Hawthorne—Your letter gives me an infinite variety of inducements to visit Concord. I will come at the earliest opportunity after the holiday feast. Beyond the chance of seeing you—and Mrs. Hawthorne and your beloved children?—, the pleasures you hold out for clinking glasses and hearts together exert a mesmeric hold on my soul. I have long restrained the ardent expressions of my admiration for your genius since you left the Berkshires. I have long languished in that drought of imagination, which your streams of inspiration once fed. Let us unite once again, Hawthorne, in that empyrean that seems to partake of the infinite, of the celestial, of the divine. I mean, of course, the fumes of punch and the *herba santa* of the ancients; I have a select store of especially fine cigars which I will bring along to flavor the vapors of inspiration.

What you say of Robinson, however, suggests that we must put our heads together on the matter of this story of Agatha. Clearly you know nothing of sailors if you think that Robinson can be such a guilt-ridden and sorry wight as you describe. Why, he is a confidence-man! You wish to load him up with a romantic past full of mystery and hidden significance. Give him a secret by all means, but let it be something that speaks to our times. Let him be a West Indian Creole anxiously scanning the visage of his smiling new-born babe for signs of his mulatto mother's blood. Or let him be plighted already to a bonny Scottish lass over the seas, or perhaps a belle of the Azores. Perchance he is some wealthy offshoot of a noble house traveling *incog*, or a buccaneering refugee from a pirate colony in the Enchanted Isles, or a traveling scrivener fleeing the nefarious dens of Wall Street. Anything but this poor flea-bitten remorse-gnawed guilt-devoured sinner of a Robinson.

But now, reading your letter more closely, I seem to see some other phantom pass between us, and it is not this woeful sailor. Your General has won the election, and you look toward new vistas of success, a new home where your pens will lie unmended near the untouched inkpot on your desk. Indeed, Hawthorne, an ocean rolls between us as I write, and I seem to see your ghostly form drifting over it in a ghostly ship. Now I will be the man of the shore and you the man of the sea. Let me not drop a tear into that ocean; 'twould salt it through and through, and you would never let me hear the end of it! Hey ho, for Thanksgiving and the noble roast and the frothing ale and an end to all low spirits.

Ever thine,
H. Melville

✻ Concord, Dec. 17, 1852

My dear Melville—Greetings on your safe return home, and thanks for your last. I too regret that we did not come to the conclusion you have just proposed when we were together after Thanksgiving. I could not bring myself to tell you in a letter before you came, and whilst in your company did not want to pass the time in advising you on a story you have always known how to write better than I. But I see that you understand all and have forgiven me for not writing it, for not writing at all at present.

Thank you too for not adverting too explicitly to my political future. You know better than anyone what it costs me to put aside my pen, and tho' I speak often of detesting it, we both know that my heart will be not in my professional labors but in the reveries I will not be able to afford. Perhaps I will turn over some tales for children to occupy my thoughts in the uncertain months ahead. But I have no spirit for a story as profound and ambiguous as that of Agatha.

As for the other matter to which you alluded, the presentiment of which you spoke—that we may never meet again in this world—I can only say that I share your sentiments. As the year approaches its end, I have felt like a man awaiting his execution.

The President has not yet made up his mind, but I prepare myself daily for the call. When it comes, I could wish that you might likewise be called, that we might meet in some European capital to exchange the greetings of those who have known each other long and well. I can only hope that you would retain your old friendship for me under those circumstances and not turn a cold shoulder on one who has lived in penury too long and has sought out the relative wealth a consulate provides.

There is more I have wished to say, but you of all my friends have always known what it was and have accepted my silences with a forgiving spirit. God bless you, Herman!—N.H.

❧ Pittsfield, July 10, 1853

Dear Duyckinck—I know you will not be expecting a letter from me, especially since my last of over a year ago, canceling my subscription to *The Literary World*. I write now in the spirit of old friendship, feeling bereft of friends in a season when I am used to great crowds of them migrating from the city. I have been much occupied with events in our household of late: the birth of my first daughter on May 22 and of her almost-twin, my *Isle of the Cross*. Sadly, the story, which absorbed my thoughts from last midwinter until the spring, lies still-born in my desk. The Harpers did not deign to publish it, and I have embarked on some new ones instead. Perhaps they found the *Isle of the Cross* not genial enough; it concerns storm and wreck, betrayal and loss. I may yet find a place for it. But it has left me heartsore and weary, and I have turned to more comical sketches: one of a man, for example, seeking a miraculous cock that he hears crowing in the woods; and one of a "Happy Failure" who gives up his foolish dreams of glory and happiness, and one of "The Fiddler" who chooses anonymity rather than fame. You may not find these comical, but I do.

Yours truly,
H. Melville

Toward the Literary

Hawthorne and Melville in the Shoals

"Agatha," the Trials of Authorship, and the Dream of Collaboration

WYN KELLEY

THE "AGATHA" STORY is the most fascinating text Melville never wrote.[1] From the little we know of it, scholars have speculated vigorously on what Melville *might* have made of material given him by lawyer John Henry Clifford in 1852. All that has emerged, however, are three letters to Hawthorne urging him to write the story, outlining scenes, supplying documentation, and suggesting approaches that Hawthorne decided not to take up—and that Melville possibly did. References in the Melville family correspondence to another narrative written in 1853—*The Isle of the Cross*—imply that he may have expanded "Agatha" and given it that title, but no manuscript evidence exists; details in his later works suggest that *The Isle of the Cross* could also have been an early version of some other narrative. Melville never published *The Isle of the Cross*—in an enigmatic letter to *Harper's* in November 1853, he speaks of "the work which I took to New York last Spring, but which I was prevented from printing at that time" (*WHM*, 14:250, November 24, 1853)—and no copy remains. Nevertheless the surviving text of "Agatha" has been understood as significant in Melville's career. His epistolary account of a woman abandoned by her shipwrecked sailor-husband, with its haunting evocation of the shore and sea, a decaying postbox to which no letters come, and a lone woman's courage, has been viewed as the germ of such later fictions as "Bartleby, the Scrivener" and "The Encantadas."[2]

Less attention has been paid to the fact that "Agatha" may be one of the most interesting stories that *Hawthorne* never wrote. Perhaps because his journals contain ideas for many sketches and tales, one more unwritten story has avoided notice. His side of the correspondence no longer survives, and the only known trace of his participation involves the title. In the last of his letters concerning "Agatha," Melville announces, "With your permission I shall make use of the 'Isle of Shoals,' as far as the name goes at least," and he proposes to "introduce the old Nantucket seaman, in the way I spoke to you about," thus implying Hawthorne's contribution to their discussions, if not to the writing (*WHM*, 14:242). It is possible, however, that Hawthorne had Melville's first letter of August 13, 1852, in mind when he went on September 6 to the Isles of Shoals, where he spent two weeks recovering from the summer's literary labors—finishing *The Blithedale Romance* in June and writing a campaign biography for Franklin Pierce. In the journal he kept during his vacation, Hawthorne responded to the islands in ways that imply he was thinking about future stories, including "Agatha," and in October he wrote his friend Horatio Bridge to say, "in a day or two, I intend to begin a new romance, which, if possible, I mean to make more genial than the last."[3] "Genial" is hardly the word one would use to describe "Agatha," if he is indeed referring to it, but Hawthorne had made similar such incongruous declarations in the past.[4]

Very little if anything, however, has been made of the fact that "Agatha" is the most remarkable story Melville and Hawthorne never wrote *together*. The project has been seen, certainly, as an outgrowth of their friendship, and "Agatha" has been taken to reflect the psychological, erotic, and literary dimensions of their mutual influence from the time they met in August 1850 in the Berkshires until whatever endpoint seems most significant: Hawthorne's move to West Newton in November 1851; his departure for Liverpool in the summer of 1853 to take up the consulship awarded him by President Franklin Pierce; the final meeting of Hawthorne and Melville in England in November 1856; the year 1864, when Hawthorne died and Melville may have written the poem "Monody" for him; or even as late as 1876, when Melville included his friend as a character in his long poem, *Clarel*.[5] But the "Agatha" story is also the closest Melville ever came to collaborating professionally with another author, even if all that remains of that collaboration resides in his letters and Hawthorne's journal. As a text, this residue evokes the issues of authorship, property, and the literary marketplace that occupied both men's attentions in a period when public concern over these issues ran high.[6] It also coincides with a shift in the way both authors were thinking about their work during the annus horribilis of 1852, when, after the completion of Melville's *Pierre* and Hawthorne's *The Blithedale Romance,* an election season converged with changes in their literary fortunes to make them both consider leaving authorship and taking political posts under the new administration. The fact that Hawthorne did leave off writing to assume the consulship at Liverpool, while Melville turned from full-length novels to magazine fiction after desultory attempts to win a consulship for himself, suggests the importance of the "Agatha" project as a turning point for both. It seems even more important as a text that resituates their literary work and reimagines the contours of literary collaboration itself.[7]

The Campaigns of 1852

1852 was a key year for Hawthorne and Melville. Both published books that signal internally the breakdown of their authors' commitment to romance, if not to literary art itself. Both looked to Franklin Pierce's administration for relief from personal dilemmas that were closely intertwined with national concerns during the election. As they struggled with questions over their futures, the "Agatha" story seemed to dramatize the personal, professional, and political crises that consumed them throughout the year.

At the time, August 13, 1852, when Melville first wrote to Hawthorne proposing that he compose the "Agatha" story, few outward signs of trouble loomed with respect to the authors' investments in the romance. Hawthorne's *The Blithedale Romance,* published in mid-July, received mixed reviews, particularly from antislavery writers, but nothing to indicate that he had reached an impasse in his literary career.[8] The reviews of Melville's *Pierre,* which would reach exactly that conclusion, were just beginning to come out.[9] Both books, however, give evidence of a collapse from which their authors struggled to recover.[10] As much as both authors seem to view their unsuccessful writer-protagonists with ironic detachment, they are deeply implicated in them too. The isolation, emasculation, and paralysis Coverdale and Pierre suffer reflect the exhaustion of their authors. In *Pierre* the narrator remarks that both character and author are moored in shallow waters: "[I]t may possibly be, that arrived at this quiet retrospective little episode in the career of my hero—this shallowly expansive embayed Tappan Zee of my otherwise deep-heady

Hudson—I too begin to loungingly expand, and wax harmlessly sad and sentimental" (*WHM*, 7:259). Such a "harmlessly sad and sentimental" character is Hawthorne's Coverdale, who likewise seeks a "shallow" retreat from the world, taking refuge in genteel poetry and bachelor reverie. Even in their attempts to break free of the romance and write of contemporary social issues, Hawthorne and Melville find themselves trapped in the solipsism of their protagonists.

Perhaps then it is no surprise that both turned to fantasies of alternative careers, though given the political moment, their choices seem rather desperate. Both saw the election of 1852 as an opportunity for professional advancement through the spoils system. But if it offered new vistas for two frustrated authors, to the nation the election presented a grim stalemate. As the first nationwide referendum on the Compromise of 1850, it inspired intense debate, but both parties were riven by sectional controversy, and neither offered an appealing candidate or a coherent policy on slavery. Whigs and Democrats sought a solution by choosing candidates who had served in the Mexican War: Winfield Scott and Franklin Pierce. Both candidates were compromise choices, aiming to appeal to patriotism and rise above local divisions over the extension of slavery into new territories. Both clung to the dubious Compromise of 1850 as a way to uphold the Constitution and Union at all costs.[11] This political drama—a spectacle of inaction and avoidance of the country's most pressing issues—seems a version of Hawthorne's and Melville's lives writ large.

Of the two, Hawthorne, as author of Pierce's campaign biography, was by far the more energetically involved in this political scene.[12] In spite of his usual pose of authorial mystification, Hawthorne was no stranger to writing for hire. His partnership with Horatio Bridge in the publication of Bridge's *Journal of an African Cruiser* (1845) demonstrated how successfully he could blend his voice with that of an alternate persona. The result reveals Hawthorne's ability to assume the attitudes and prejudices of another, including his racism.[13] At the same time, as Hawthorne showed in writing *The Life of Franklin Pierce,* he maintained a characteristic detachment, seeming to struggle with, while also engaging in, his political task.

The trajectory from *The Blithedale Romance* to the *Life* to the proposed "Agatha" story evinces Hawthorne's conflict between his role as writer and his obligations as citizen, and this internal struggle makes itself evident on every page of the *Life*. His preface exhibits his usual reluctance to come before the public, this time tinged with a sense of political unfitness: "... being so little of a politician that he scarcely feels entitled to call himself a member of any party" (*CE*, 23:273). With what seems like supremely poor judgment, Hawthorne emphasizes Pierce's weaknesses as a student and failures as a lawyer in an attempt, apparently, to make him seem just as ordinary as he really was. An appended note returns to the subject of Pierce's deficiencies, affirming that when he wanted to, the candidate could improve. The task was difficult, however: "His mind, having run wild for so long a period, could be reclaimed only by the severest efforts of an iron resolution." Hawthorne's final point seems directed as much at his own unsettled status as at Pierce's attempts to take himself in hand: "The moral of this little story lies in the stern and continued exercise of self-controlling will, which redeemed him from indolence, completely changed the aspect of his character, and made this the turning point of his life" (*CE*, 23:372). One can almost hear Hawthorne beating off his inner Coverdale in this ambivalent call to action and decisiveness. It is an unnerving confession of Hawthorne's own anxiety about his future.

He appears, however, to take refuge in Pierce's position on slavery, with its affirmation of party and national cohesion.[14] Hawthorne argues that Pierce has consistently upheld the Constitution and national Union as a "statesman of practical sagacity" must do: a national leader "must not narrow himself to adopt the cause of one section of his native country against another" (*CE*, 23:351–52). Hawthorne takes the long and pious view of slavery as "one of those evils, which Divine Providence does not leave to be remedied by human contrivances, but which, in its own good time, by some means impossible to be anticipated, but of the simplest and easiest operation, when all its uses shall have been fulfilled, it causes to vanish like a dream" (*CE*, 23:352). This statement is disturbing not only for what it reveals about Hawthorne's attitudes vis-à-vis abolition but also in terms of his own professional dilemma. The *Life*'s position on slavery suggests Hawthorne's own desire for a stable union, not only between the conflicted sections of the nation but also between the discordant sides of himself—dreamer and doer, writer and politician, poet and professional.

In many ways, Hawthorne and Melville did not appreciably differ in their positions on slavery; Melville appears to have been no more actively an abolitionist than Hawthorne.[15] Nor did Melville involve himself directly in election politics. But he did spend some of the spring and early summer of 1852 consorting with important Whigs. Melville's father-in-law, Lemuel Shaw, chief justice of the Massachusetts Supreme Court, has been viewed as a significant and controversial influence on Melville's politics, though there is considerable disagreement over the nature of that influence.[16] While they toured Nantucket together, Shaw introduced Melville to a close associate, John Henry Clifford, another Whig. This New Bedford lawyer had served as prosecuting attorney when Shaw judged the famous murder of George Parkman by William Webster—the so-called Harvard murder case.[17] Clifford was an aggressive and successful prosecutor—he won a conviction of Webster, against much public outcry and conflicting evidence—who went on to become governor of Massachusetts in 1853. At about the same time that Hawthorne was proposing himself to the Democrat Pierce as biographer, Melville was hobnobbing with some of the most powerful Whigs in Massachusetts.

In this legal and political context, it becomes clear that the "Agatha" story concerns issues of property and union, treated rather differently than in Hawthorne's *Life*. The story's center, for Clifford, was its consideration of a peculiar inheritance case involving an errant husband. In the papers Clifford supplied, John Robertson of England married Agatha Hatch of Pembroke, Massachusetts, in 1807 after she rescued him from shipwreck and restored him to health. Two years later, leaving her pregnant, he went to find work, moved to Alexandria, Virginia (or D.C., as the documents say), and married another woman. Seventeen years after his departure, he returned with money and gestures of affection, having prospered in his business. When his second wife died, he presented his original family—Agatha, her daughter Rebecca Gifford, and Rebecca's husband—with shawls and a gold watch that most likely belonged to the deceased woman. During one final visit, he invited them to move to Missouri with him, where he did indeed resettle, marry once again, and accumulate an estate of twenty-thousand dollars. On his death (sometime before 1842) his only heirs seemed to be his widow, the former Mrs. Irvin, and her children from a previous marriage. A letter from Rebecca Gifford, however, revealed the existence of legitimate heirs, and a Missouri lawyer, Mr. Janney, settled the case satisfactorily. In Clifford's terms, the story shows the importance of marriage in establishing legitimate transfers of property and keeping it within the family unit.

But the story also reflects Melville's political environment in mid-1852 and questions concerning the American Union and its threatened demise. Whereas Hawthorne's *Life* upholds the idea of union at all costs, the "Agatha" story shows a more fluid view of both national and connubial union. The rovings of Robertson (or Robinson, as Melville dubs him) from state to state and wife to wife reflect his "latitudinarian" character, which Melville explains as typical of sailors. A cosmopolitan—sailors find "a wife (for a night) in every port" (*WHM*, 14:240)—the transnational Robertson travels freely from one country to another. Thus he has no particular allegiance to America; nor is he bound by sectional loyalties. From Massachusetts he journeys to the boundary between north and south (D.C.) and then to Missouri. Whereas Pierce would not "narrow himself to adopt the cause of one section of his native country against another," Robertson, like Melville's early *omoo* and *taboo* men, samples the nation's different regions in turn.

Clifford suggested that such liberality of sympathies is immoral, but Melville objects: "I take exception to that passage from the Diary which says that *'he must have received a portion of his punishment in this life'*—thus hinting of a future supplemental castigation" (*WHM*, 14:234). Melville grants Robertson's weakness, but the story shows that he is a thriving American type, like Melville's own future Confidence-Man. His rapid accumulation of twenty-thousand dollars in Missouri even hints that he may have profited from the extension of slavery granted by the Missouri Compromise of 1820 and that he has made a successful transition from the kind of capital represented by gold watches and fine shawls to more liquid and possibly shady assets. Melville's caution to Hawthorne not to assign moral terms to Robertson's behavior suggests his tolerance of Robertson's equivocal relationship to national and familial unity. Clifford, on the other hand, would have returned the wandering husband to his wife, masking his proprietary concerns in the rhetoric of sentimental romance.

In contrast with Clifford's conservative framework, Melville's strong interest in the wandering husband speaks obliquely to the most noxious feature of the Compromise of 1850. The Fugitive Slave Act mandated that slaves be returned to their masters even if they fled to free states. It thus resisted "latitudinarian" challenges to property rights. Robertson's test of traditional property laws is not entirely heroic, of course. He is an opportunist who appropriates the property of his wives and seizes the main chance. His assumption of radical freedom threatens the union of husband and wife, parent and child, and his legacy, though substantial and generous, is a complicated one. But his transgressive behavior casts in stark relief the proprietary panic of lawyers like Clifford and Shaw, who sent Thomas Sims back to his master in 1852 in the way Clifford would have sent Robertson back to his wife.

Melville had dealt explicitly with issues of property and slavery in his "Fast-Fish and Loose-Fish" (chapter 89) of *Moby-Dick*. In those terms, Robertson is a Loose-Fish. But as Melville points out, not only "Republican slaves" but also, ultimately, all human beings are Fast-Fish as well: "what are you, reader, but a Loose-Fish and a Fast-Fish, too?" (*WHM*, 6:398). Although Robertson was a Loose-Fish in his life, his legacy gets caught in the toils of the law, and only the generosity and decency of his heirs make for a successful conclusion. The story ends happily, at least in the lawyers' estimations, as Robertson's property finds its way to the rightful owners. But this solution requires the formation of a new family, linked by amity between the northern Agatha Hatch, Rebecca Gifford, and her husband, and the southern former Mrs. Irvin and her children. Union comes to pass, not from above by national fiat but through the individual actions of compassionate human beings: "'I had no wish' said the wife [Agatha] 'to make either of them unhappy, notwithstanding all I had suffered on his account'" (*WHM*, 14:624). Union requires more, then, than restoring property to its "original" owners.

Indeed Melville's account of Agatha suggests a more expansive notion of America than the tense, self-enclosed nation described in Hawthorne's *Life*. Walking along the beach, seemingly awaiting the arrival of her sailor-lover, young Agatha looks out over a sea that reminds her that she lives within no essential boundaries: "There is no land over against this cliff short of Europe & the West Indies" (*WHM*, 14:235). Her America is not the seamless Union of Pierce's patriotic vision but an open border to the world. Similarly in *Moby-Dick* Melville speaks of the Nantucket whalemen as knowing no limits to their sovereignty: "thus have these naked Nantucketers, these sea hermits, issuing from their ant-hill in the sea, overrun and conquered the watery world like so many Alexanders" (*WHM*, 6:64). The cosmopolitan air Agatha breathes seems of the same substance as Robertson's latitudinarian views.

Melville's disposal of the "Agatha" manuscript to Hawthorne also takes up the story's property issues in ways that implicitly address and also to some extent anxiously enact Clifford's and Shaw's views on fugitive husbands and slaves in the political climate of 1852. In an extraordinary maneuver, Melville offers the story to Hawthorne to write, free of charge, then goes on to lay on him various charges as to how he should write it. In a curious transfer of property, the story comes from John Henry Clifford, who assumes Melville "purpose[s] making literary use of the story." Melville decides: "[T]hinking again, it has occurred to me that this thing lies very much in a vein, with which you [Hawthorne] are peculiarly familiar. To be plump, I think that in this matter you would make a better hand at it than I would."[18] Nevertheless Melville feels no hesitation in passing along "the following tributary items, collected by me," which, like Clifford's and Janney's testimonials, lend further meaning to the story. Although claiming "I but submit matter to you—I dont decide," Melville sketches an elaborate sequence of events, things that "seem legitimately to belong to the story" (*WHM*, 14:234–35), as if its right to own property were independent of the storyteller's. The story is beginning to behave like a free agent—or a fugitive.

Yet in an odd turn, Melville concludes by assigning away the rights to the story—to Hawthorne: "I do not therefore, My Dear Hawthorne, at all imagine that you will think that I am so silly as to flatter myself I am giving you anything of my own. I am but restoring to you your own property—which you would quickly enough have identified for yourself—had you but been on the spot as I happened to be" (*WHM*, 14:23). Melville's definition of property here seems as fluid and opportunistic as Robertson's. But his assumption that the story *can* be returned to its real owner seems to reflect national anxieties over such assertions of slaveholder rights. Melville's liberality with "Hawthorne's" tale begins to resemble, then, Robertson's openhandedness with his wife's goods, which he can give away—to his first wronged wife—because his second wronged wife has no rights over herself. The hand that gives—"you can construct a story of remarkable interest out of this material furnished by the New Bedford lawyer"—has already taken (from Clifford) and can take away from Hawthorne: "if I thought I could do it as well as you, why, I should not let you have it" (*WHM*, 14:237).

Melville's proprietary language suggests both generosity and guilt. As Ellen Weinauer argues for his earlier "Hawthorne and His Mosses," the "Agatha" letters betray the writer's anxiety over the ownership and boundaries of his own work. The gesture of generosity appears to relieve that anxiety by absolving the giver of guilty ownership, but it reveals its own self-serving mechanisms. That both authors struggled with questions of authorship within the framework of political debate over escaped slaves does not seem surprising. That they would consider joining forces in this enterprise does. Did they imagine that together they could break free of the rigid compromise that held the nation's different constituencies in suspension and that seemed to have frozen their writings too? Or, failing such utopian hopes, did they simply look for refuge in literature from the nation's political challenges? Would making the story common property in some way remove the onus of single proprietorship and responsibility? For Melville, at least, these issues had already presented themselves in earlier dreams of utopian collaboration. Part of what he was proposing to Hawthorne, it seems clear, was an arrangement along the lines of Renaissance playwriting—something like what Beaumont and Fletcher enjoyed in their time. In the dream of common property, one that might efface individual ownership, Melville sought to escape the burdens of literary mastery. Hawthorne, it seems, could dally in but not ultimately share this vision.

Renaissance Dreams

In *Moby-Dick* Melville suggests the erotic nature of collaboration in his extraordinary "A Squeeze of the Hand" (chapter 94): "Squeeze! squeeze! squeeze! all the morning long; I squeezed that sperm till I myself almost melted into it; I squeezed that sperm till a strange sort of insanity came over me; and I found myself unwittingly squeezing my co-laborers' hands in it, mistaking their hands for the gentle globules" (*WHM*, 6:416). Mistaking one hand for another co-laborer's or for the medium itself captures exactly the allure of Renaissance drama for many nineteenth-century readers, as scholars of Renaissance collaboration have shown.[19] Which hand wrote Shakespeare's plays? Or Beaumont's and Fletcher's? For Melville, the idea of merging singular authorial identities in a common text produced a characteristically conflicted range of responses.

Melville's earlier "Hawthorne and His Mosses" appears to be an ecstatic tribute to singular authorship. By comparing Hawthorne to Shakespeare and by speaking of them both as geniuses, as "masters of the great Art of Telling the Truth," Melville fervently reinscribes the romantic myth of "solitary genius."[20] Nevertheless, the essay also reveals his ambivalence about this picture of solitary authorship, as he struggles with the idea that, great as Shakespeare was, he shared the stage with other equally deserving men. The spirit that animates Shakespeare may be "shared" by "Marlow, Webster, Ford, Beaumont, Jonson," writers "between whom and Shakespeare the distance was by no means great" (*WHM*, 9:252). As Melville was aware, even smaller was the distance between the great collaborators of Renaissance drama: Beaumont and Fletcher, Fletcher and Shakespeare, Fletcher and Massinger. Even before the Melville-Hawthorne relationship has gotten off the ground, it seems, Melville is imagining a community of literary men whose creative commingling will produce a new American Renaissance.

As critics and historians of Renaissance collaboration have argued, the dream of literary coauthorship is powerfully erotic. To these critics the world of Renaissance drama represents a lost Eden, a precapitalist male subculture (not unlike the democratic, homoerotic universe Robert K. Martin describes in *Moby-Dick*) where author-ity rests not in the hands of a single genius but in the clasped hands of the many.[21] What for romantic and modern writers could be seen as a loss of the self—the intermingling of Beaumont's and Fletcher's authorial voices so that in the end one cannot distinguish between them—appeared to Renaissance authors as acceptable, even desirable. In this sense, then, the Renaissance provides an alternative to the dominant romantic concepts of authorship infusing Melville's culture.

Along with Shakespeare, Beaumont and Fletcher recur periodically in Melville's writing from 1849–54 as emblems of literary and bodily commingling. In *Mardi*, for example, he describes a grave that holds the remains of King Yoky of Hooloomooloo and his bosom friend, a chimpanzee named Rozoko: "[N]ot even in decay were these fast friends divided. So mingled every relic,—ilium and ulna, carpus and metacarpus;—and so similar the corresponding parts, that like the literary remains of Beaumont and of Fletcher, which was which, no spectacles could tell" (*WHM*, 3:572).[22] In *White-Jacket,* Melville speaks of "that literary Damon and Pythias, the magnificent, mellow old Beaumont and Fletcher, who have sent the long shadow of their reputation, side by side with Shakspeare's, far down the endless vale of posterity" (*WHM*, 5:168). In 1849, while in London, he had bought his own copy of Beaumont and Fletcher's plays and had marked them considerably. It is possible, too, that his reading of Montaigne and Emerson may have included their ambiguous essays on

"Friendship," both of which could have contributed to Melville's thinking about intimate (working) relationships between men.[23] As he was writing "Hawthorne and His Mosses," he may have imagined that the Fletcher to his Beaumont, the Pythias to his Damon, had arrived, ready to fit into a preexisting space. Indeed this thought develops almost visibly as the essay progresses.

One can speculate, too, that early in his friendship with Hawthorne, Melville was thinking about literary collaboration between them. Their apparently unprecedented intimacy in the Berkshires, in visits and letters, did not eventuate in a published literary work, but Melville's famous response to Hawthorne's letter praising *Moby-Dick* and his telling Hawthorne not to review the book may not have been quite as foolish or selfless a gesture as it might appear. If Melville substantially reworked his original text after meeting Hawthorne and finished it in the sunshine of Hawthorne's genius, he may have felt it in a sense a joint work: not, therefore, something Hawthorne could review. The corporeal metaphors in his letters—"your heart beat in my ribs and mine in yours, and both in God's" (*WHM*, 14:212)—may indicate what intellectual collaboration felt like to Melville.

Without further evidence it is difficult to do more than speculate on the possibility of *Moby-Dick* as an intellectual and emotional collaboration between Melville and Hawthorne. With the "Agatha" story, however, we have a glimpse of what Robert K. Martin and Leland S. Person identify as the ways "Hawthorne and Melville sought to express their desires textually, or sometimes to repress them" through their common labors: "In the absence of a complex discourse in which male-male relationships could be understood and expressed, both men must have struggled to find terms and forms."[24] But the examples of Shakespeare, Beaumont, Fletcher, and others offered precisely those terms, embedded in literary practice. In particular it is the *mutuality* of the "Agatha" project (although we have only one side of the correspondence to examine) that makes this case. Melville proposes the idea to Hawthorne; Hawthorne tries writing the story; for various reasons he stops and sends it back to Melville; Melville tries writing the story. Although Hershel Parker has argued for the idea that "Agatha" became a later finished story by a single author, Melville, what we see here is a working collaboration in letters between Melville and Hawthorne. It is one of few such collaborations in American literature that we know of before Emily Dickinson and Susan

Francis Beaumont

John Fletcher

Francis Beaumont and John Fletcher. Frontispiece to *The Plays of Beaumont and Fletcher: An Attempt to Determine Their Respective Shares and the Shares of Others,* by E. H. C. Oliphant (New Haven: Yale Univ. Press, 1927).

Gilbert Dickinson started writing letters and poems together in their "workshop."[25]

The details of Melville's letters point to such a practical working partnership between the men. Melville writes not as a spurned friend or lover but as a partner confident that his forceful suggestions will meet with an equally firm and frank response.[26] What Melville refers to as "strange impertinent officiousness" (*WHM,* 14:237) might also be read as familiarity—a familiarity that Hawthorne shrank from except in his closest friends. In the spirit of a literary partnership, Melville's comments seem no more officious than Hawthorne's correspondence with Pierce, whom he too instructs with businesslike terseness: "[I] should be glad if you will supply me with the whole, if in your possession, and supposing it to be reliable. . . . There will be ample stuff, I think, for this part of the work—which, though it should be made prominent, ought not to be much so as to overshadow you as a man of peaceful pursuits. 'Cedant arma togae.' A statesman in your proper life—a gallant soldier in the hour of your country's need—such, in the circumstances, is the best mode of presenting you" (*CE,* 16:561). Melville's advice to Hawthorne seems couched in similarly pragmatic terms: "Consider the mention of the *shawls*—& and the inference derived from it. Ponder the conduct of this Robinson throughout.—Mark his trepidation & suspicion when any one called upon him.—But why prate so—you will mark it all & mark it deeper than I would, perhaps" (*WHM,* 14:237). Melville's extended recital of the "tributary items" that make up the story and indeed advance considerably into its narration does not seem unusual when viewed in the context of Hawthorne's similarly assertive suggestions about the campaign biography.

The "Agatha" letters show, then, that Melville's dream of Renaissance collaboration came close to being a reality, if the free exchange of ideas between him and Hawthorne is any indication. The readiness with which Hawthorne seems to have taken up these ideas, as evinced in the notes he made during his sojourn at the Isles of Shoals, implies that Melville's confidence was not misplaced.

For Hawthorne too seems to have been wrapped in a kind of Renaissance dream during his idyll at Laighton's Hotel on Appledore, among the Isles of Shoals. He called his hostess, Celia Thaxter, a "Miranda" and seems to imagine himself somewhat as a Prospero cast ashore on Shakespeare's imaginary isle. His flirtation with Renaissance drama, however, appears to have ended with his turning his back on authorship for the time. He may have embarked on a new romance based on the "Agatha" story when he got home, but the seeds of its failure appear in his journal's pages. It would seem that his reluctance grew out of professional anxieties more than any shrinking from Melville's literary or homoerotic overtures. The journal suggests, on the contrary, considerable openness to the ideas Melville offered.

Melville encountered the "Agatha" story first while on vacation, and Hawthorne considered it while on vacation as well. His journal reads like one extended sigh of relief after what must have been an extraordinarily stressful summer. He paid attention to fellow travelers, to the weather, to island lore and legends, to local characters, to amusements, to the weather, to ghost stories, to landscapes and seascapes, and to the weather. The journal contains key hints, however, that Hawthorne did indeed keep Melville's August 13 letter in mind as he traveled about the islands. The most obvious connection is his strong interest in the family of his host, Thomas B. Laighton, which included Celia Thaxter, his sixteen-year-old daughter and future poet, artist, and chronicler of the Isles, and her husband Levi.[27] Although Laighton began as businessman, postmaster, editor, and New Hampshire state senator, in 1839 he became the lighthouse keeper on White Island. Living there with his wife and three children, he may have seemed to Hawthorne a figure like Agatha's seafaring father, who after an active career took up a life of quiet isolation. Although Thomas Laighton went on to build a thriving hotel on Appledore Island, his children remained secluded from the mainland, educated at home by their parents, and Celia, a precocious and thoughtful girl, might have seemed like a protected young Agatha.

Lending romantic overtones to the analogy was the story of the arrival of Levi Thaxter, who appears to have washed up on the island almost as accidentally as Robertson did at Pembroke. A victim of depression, a failed actor, well educated but apparently aimless, Thaxter quickly became Laighton's partner in the hotel business, then the children's tutor, and finally Celia's husband. He also appears to have made a fast friendship with Hawthorne, gladly offering his services as oarsman and guide to the islands. Hawthorne enjoyed a festive evening in their parlor, singing "glees and negro melodies" and drinking apple toddy; "Mrs. Thaxter sang like a bird . . . and all were very mirthful and jolly" (*CE*, 8:516–17).

As much as he was drawn to sociality, Hawthorne seemed equally attracted to the island's stories of isolatoes, ghosts, and shipwrecked sailors, possibly testing the "Agatha" story's gothic potentialities. Levi Thaxter rowed him out to see the lighthouse where the Laightons lived, and Hawthorne took careful note of its remote location, the new keeper attending his meager vegetables, and in particular the rumors that "he ha[d] lost two wives—the first a young creature, whom he used to leave alone upon this desolate rock; and the gloom and terror of the situation were probably the cause of her death. . . . The second wife, experiencing the same kind of treatment, ran away from him and returned to her friends." Alert to the lighthouse keeper's mysteries, Hawthorne recorded, "[W]hile we were standing in his garden-patch, I heard a woman's voice, inside the dwelling; but know not whose it was." Thinking of the newlywed Thaxters, he added, "A light-house, nine miles from shore, would be a delightful place for a new-married couple to spend their honeymoon, or their whole first year" (*CE,* 8:526). Levi Thaxter was shortly to lose patience with living on Appledore and to begin an extended period of roaming, although, unlike Robertson, he brought his family along with him until he and Celia separated in the 1860s. For the moment, however, he and Celia might have resembled the young Robertsons, especially since marriage with Celia seems in some sense to have restored Thaxter's health or at least to have masked his symptoms for a time.

Hawthorne noticed other details that possibly reflect his reading of Melville's letter. He appears to have paid particular attention to stories, again predominantly gothic, of the island's women, many of whom were legendary or spectral. He mentions several witches, including at Gosport "one old witch-looking woman, creeping about with a cane, and stooping down, seemingly to gather herbs" (*CE,* 8:515). He notes that "the women on Star Island are very timid as to venturing on the sea—more so than women of the main land—and that they are easily frightened about their husbands" (*CE,* 8:518)—a trait not found in Agatha, except perhaps in her anxious daily trips to the mailbox. He also records the story of Betty Moody, "a woman of the island, in old times." When "Indians came off on a depredating excursion," she ran with her children to hide in a cave along the shore; when they began to cry, she "murdered them, to save herself" (*CE,* 8:520). Another island woman, a schoolteacher "of a romantic turn" (*CE,* 8:520), became so enamored of sitting on the rocks contemplating the waves that one day she was carried away by the surf.

Agatha is neither so desperate as Betty Moody nor so silly as the school-teacher, but both supply unusual traits of women on the island whom he seems to have been trying to characterize.

At another moment, Hawthorne seems to be thinking of Agatha's meditative strolls along the beach, which he reenacted for himself on many occasions. Describing the surf that "swelled against the rocky shores of the island," he comments that the "sheep bleated loudly; and . . . according to Mr. Leighton, foreboded a storm to windward" (*CE,* 8:522–23), much as in Melville's description of a coming storm and the flocks of grazing sheep. As with Melville's note that Agatha sees "no land over against this cliff short of Europe & the West Indies" (*WHM,* 14:235), Hawthorne remarks, "Sometimes I have a dim sense of the continent beyond, but no more distinct than the thought of the other world to the unenlightened soul" (*CE,* 8:535). He also notes several stories of shipwreck, one with a comic ending—the sailors surviving comfortably—and another tragic—bodies found littered around the island months later.

Hawthorne responded most profoundly, it seems, to the fury of the elements, and in particular to one story, which he mentions several times, of a tempest a year or so before that flooded the entire island. In one telling, "a great wave passed entirely through this valley" directly in front of Laighton's hotel: "It roared and whitened through, from sea to sea, twenty feet abreast, rolling along huge rocks in its passage. . . . Would I had been here to see" (*CE,* 8:524). On another occasion, seeing the wind come up, he comments, "Judging by the pother which this 'half a gale' makes with the sea, it must have been a terrific time, indeed, when that great wave rushed and roared across the island" (*CE,* 8:535). Against this backdrop of threatening and tempestuous nature, it is little wonder that Hawthorne saw the Laightons and Thaxters as preserving a welcome and, as he put it, romantic refuge: "It is certainly a romantic incident to find such a young man on this lonely island; his marriage with this pretty little Miranda is true romance" (*CE,* 8:537). As Jane Vallier points out, the reference to Miranda may refer to Margaret Fuller's figure of the lonely woman educated by a demanding father figure, but Hawthorne seems to have had Shakespeare's *The Tempest* primarily in mind.[28] If Celia Thaxter represented for him both Agatha and Shakespeare's Miranda, his notes suggest that he might have seen the "Agatha" story as a romance with overtones of gothic horror implied by the foreboding tempest.

But if Celia is Miranda and Levi her Ferdinand, Thomas Laighton, the keeper of lighthouses and hotels, would seem an unlikely Prospero. It is more probable that as his island retreat came to a close—and Hawthorne mentions Miranda near the end of his visit—he saw himself as Prospero. Like that island king, he "lov'd [his] books" (1.2.166), wherein his powers seemed to lie. At the end of Shakespeare's play, however, Prospero answers the call to civic service and leaves to take up his political responsibilities. Turning from magic, the island's "sweet airs," he declares his intention to "break my staff / Bury it certain fathoms in the earth / And deeper than did ever plummet sound / I'll drown my book" (5.1.54–57). Hawthorne seems at several points of his sojourn to have been seized by a fear of drowning in the relentless sea encroaching on Appledore Island. To save himself from the crisis of his personal and professional paralysis, it may have seemed, as it did to Betty Moody, better to kill than be killed. Sacrificing his writing career, drowning his book instead of himself, Hawthorne returned to public life, biding his time until Franklin Pierce called him to service. The fact that he may have spent a few weeks or days trying to write the "Agatha" story after all suggests the strength of his regard for Melville, not a desire to avoid their friendship. But when Melville came to call in Concord in December, a month after the election, Hawthorne's course was clear to him, and he told Melville to try writing the story himself.

Crossing the Shoals

Whether or not Melville was disappointed by Hawthorne's response, he apparently took up the challenge, asking permission to use the title Hawthorne had contemplated, "Isle of Shoals." The name reflects the "shallowly expansive" waters Melville mentioned in *Pierre* and his own sense, shared with Hawthorne, that he, and elite literary authorship in general in America, had arrived in a secluded cove. Hawthorne was afraid of drowning in the shoals, but Melville seems to have crossed them to new literary waters—the navigable seas of magazine fiction. His first attempt was a failure—*The Isle of the Cross*—but he went on to produce sixteen short stories, the novella *Israel Potter*, a collection titled *The Piazza Tales*, and his novel *The Confidence-Man* before his and Hawthorne's final meeting in Liverpool. During that time, Hawthorne, who at first wrote in 1853, "the more I use a pen, the worse I hate it" (*CE*, 16:636), crossed the ocean to England, where he eventually came to long once again for the writing life. A few months after Melville's visit in 1856, he left the political arena—Franklin Pierce's fortunes had not prospered either—and returned to a period of frustrated authorship in which *The Marble Faun* (1860) was his major achievement.

If Melville continued writing the "Agatha" story in the winter of 1852–53, why did he give it the title *The Isle of the Cross,* as Hershel Parker has argued? Some readings suggest that Agatha's story represents Melville's own crucifixion on the crosses of debt, failure, and abandonment by Hawthorne or his readers.[29] Other critics have noted the "armorial cross" at the end of "Sketch Eighth," "Norfolk Isle and the Chola Widow," of *The Encantadas* (*WHM*, 9:162, 151). These interpretations depend on reading the "cross" as a biblical symbol and reflect Melville's elaborate uses of crosses and crucifixions in his later works, particularly *Clarel* and *Billy Budd.* Given that Melville did undergo severe trials before and during the writing of *The Isle of the Cross,* it seems an appropriate, if restricted, reading. But "cross" has many other meanings. It can denote a process of interblending or interbreeding, producing a hybrid result. Or it can mean a "crossing" or passage through or over. As text, the "Agatha" story represented in Melville's letters and Hawthorne's journal is a literary hybrid—neither letter nor journal nor tale either. And as a passage, the story signifies a traversing and an intersection both, a crossroads for two authors traveling ultimately in very different directions.

Greg Dening has identified further and richer meanings of "cross" in describing cultural contact as what happens when strangers "cross the beach."[30] In his anthropological description of Pacific Island beaches as a dense contact zone, he emphasizes that islands are seldom as remote, untouched, "primitive," or "innocent" as Euro-Americans would like to see them. Indeed, they are busy crossroads, like hotels, where travelers both move and rest and where narratives circulate within a seemingly free transnational space.[31] This concept of the beach and the island seems useful for describing the imaginative isle of shoals on which Melville and Hawthorne found themselves moored in 1852. The "Agatha" text is itself a meeting place for their dreams of new literary adventure, and their collaboration may have proved a pacific island in the shifting seas of their lives.

If so, then "The Encantadas" provides one bittersweet coda. The epigraph to "Sketch Sixth," "Barrington Isle and the Buccaneers," comes from Beaumont and Fletcher's *Wit without Money*, a satire of London rakes and tricksters.[32] Although a number of critics have connected the "Agatha" correspondence with Melville's figures of silence and forlorn abandonment in his short fiction, the Beaumont and Fletcher passage bespeaks a more carefree spirit: "How bravely now we live, how jocund, how near the first inheritance, without fears, how free from little troubles!" (*WHM*, 9:144). If the passage reminds us of Melville's favorite Renaissance literary couple, it does so in the context of pirates and freebooters who wielded daggers and plundered gold, crossing beaches and raiding islands. As a description of a male idyll, like, perhaps, the attempted collaboration between Melville and Hawthorne in 1852, it pays tribute to a season of liberation from "little troubles" among brave and jocund men. In 1854, at a time when Hawthorne and the promise of crossing wakes with him seemed entirely remote, Melville might have regretted the consolations of solitary genius and deeper waters.

Melville did have an opportunity to speak with Hawthorne again, when they met in Liverpool in late 1856 and again in 1857. Whether they discussed their aborted collaboration or considered a new one, two of their later works provide another coda to the "Agatha" story. In 1857 Melville's lecture "Statues in Rome" played with the idea of the ways marble figures of Demosthenes, Socrates, Julius Caesar, Seneca, and Plato resembled contemporary figures of "an Irish comedian," "the President of the New York and Erie Railroad," and "a Greek Grammont or Chesterfield" (*WHM*, 9:400). It is unlikely that Hawthorne read the newspaper accounts of this lecture. In the opening chapter of *The Marble Faun*, however, he mentions several of the statues that Melville noted—the Dying Gladiator, the Antinous—as he, too, toys with the concept of an ancient marble coming to life as a living human type. Did Hawthorne and Melville in Liverpool discuss their plans to visit Rome, a dream both had cherished for years? Over their stout and cigars, did they whimsically imagine the famous Roman statues coming to life?

Whether or not they did, Hawthorne's preface to *The Marble Faun*, an unusually emotional one for him, may speak to the memory of his most sympathetic reader, "that one congenial friend—more comprehensive of his [Hawthorne's] purposes, more appreciative of his success, more indulgent of his short-comings, and, in all respects, closer and kinder than a brother" (*CE*, 4:1). Hawthorne had deep friendships with men whom he plainly stated that he loved. But did any of them, Bridge or Pierce or Longfellow, mean to him what this preface upholds as an ideal—"that all-sympathizing critic, in short, whom an author never actually meets, but to whom he implicitly makes his appeal whenever he is conscious of having done his best" (*CE,* 4:1)? Melville was that "all-sympathizing critic" in "Hawthorne and His Mosses." The two authors did actually meet, but their relationship lives for us, as perhaps it did for them, most intensely when they did not meet, or rather when they met in letters and in the world of fiction that their letters created. In chapter 11 of *The Marble Faun,* Hawthorne articulated the sad wonder of this ultimately unsuccessful form of fiction-making: "In weaving these mystic utterances into a continuous scene, we undertake a task resembling, in its perplexity, that of gathering up and piecing together the fragments of a letter, which has been torn and scattered to the winds. Many words of deep significance—many entire sentences, and those possibly the most important ones—have flown too far, on the winged breeze, to be recovered" (*CE,* 4:92–93).

Notes

I am deeply grateful to Jana Argersinger, Mary K. Bercaw Edwards, Diana Henderson, Robert S. Levine, and Leland S. Person for their generous help with this essay. I dedicate it to Jay Fliegelman, with love and gratitude.

1. Hershel Parker has argued that Melville did write the "Agatha" story as *The Isle of the Cross;* see Parker, "Herman Melville's *Isle of the Cross*"; and Parker, *Herman Melville,* vol. 2. While drawing from his scholarship on many points, I wish to distinguish "Agatha," a text on which both Melville and Hawthorne may have worked, from *The Isle of the Cross,* a text we may assume was written solely by Melville. Until very recently, most critics have thought that the story never got written as a publishable work. For other general treatments of the "Agatha" correspondence, see Hayford, "Significance of Melville's 'Agatha' Letters"; Robertson-Lorant, *Melville;* Hewitt, "Scarlet Letters, Dead Letters"; Milder, "'Ugly Socrates'"; and Wineapple, "Hawthorne and Melville."

2. See Hayford, "Significance of Melville's 'Agatha' Letters"; Watson, "Melville's Agatha and Hunilla"; Sattelmeyer and Barbour, "Sources and Genesis"; Ra'ad, "'The Encantadas' and 'The Isle of the Cross'"; and Sealts, "Historical Note" (*WHM,* 9:457–533).

3. On Hawthorne's journey to the Isles of Shoals and the possibility that he was thinking about the "Agatha" story there, see Wineapple, "Hawthorne and Melville"; her *Hawthorne* does not address the connection. Mellow speaks

of Melville's fascination with the story and observes that "it was almost as if he were suggesting a collaboration," but does not indicate that Hawthorne responded to Melville's offer: "Despite the slow waltz of collaboration between the authors, . . . the Agatha story was never written" (*Nathaniel Hawthorne in His Times*, 417). Turner states that the Isles of Shoals was "an appropriate setting for a romance" and that Hawthorne and Melville "agreed on the Isles of Shoals" for the setting of "Agatha" but did not write it (*Nathaniel Hawthorne*, 249). Miller makes no mention of the link between "Agatha" and the Isles of Shoals journal and claims that Hawthorne "was giving no consideration to developing the story of Agatha" (*Salem Is My Dwelling Place*, 388). See also Parker, *Herman Melville*, 2:136–37.

4. See Mitchell, "In the Whale's Wake."

5. Hayford, "Melville's 'Monody'"; Bezanson, "Historical and Critical Note" (*WHM*, 12:505–637).

6. My argument for the "Agatha" letters and journal as text owes much to John Bryant's work: see *Fluid Text*. On the literary market in which Hawthorne and Melville worked, see Post-Lauria, *Correspondent Colorings*; Weinauer, "Plagiarism and the Proprietary Self"; and Evelev, *Tolerable Entertainment*.

7. On collaboration, see Koestenbaum, *Double Talk*; Weinauer, "Plagiarism and the Proprietary Self"; Carringer, "Collaboration and Concepts of Authorship"; Ede and Lunsford, "Collaboration and Concepts of Authorship"; Hirschfeld, "Early Modern Collaboration"; Inge, "Collaboration and Concepts of Authorship"; and Silverman, "Textual Sentimentalism."

8. Wineapple, *Hawthorne*, 254.

9. Higgins and Parker, eds., *Herman Melville: The Contemporary Reviews*, 417–52; Parker, *Herman Melville*, 2:129–30.

10. Mueller argues in *"This Infinite Fraternity of Feeling"* that this collapse arose from the failure of the relationship between Hawthorne and Melville. See also Miller, *Melville*.

11. See Cook, *Civil War America*; and Gara, *Presidency of Franklin Pierce*.

12. See Casper, "Two Lives of Franklin Pierce."

13. See Goddu, "Letters Turned to Gold."

14. Wineapple, *Hawthorne*, 262–64.

15. On Melville's attitudes on race and slavery, see Karcher, "The Moderate and the Radical"; Stauffer, "Melville, Slavery, and the American Dilemma"; Robertson-Lorant, *Melville*; and Wallace, *Douglass and Melville*.

16. On Melville's politics and Shaw's influence, see Karcher, *Shadow over the Promised Land*; Rogin, *Subversive Genealogy*; Garner, *Civil War World*; and Wallace, "Fugitive Justice."

17. Parker, *Herman Melville*, 2:113–16.

18. Melville was thinking of Hawthorne's "Wakefield," but as the preceding analysis suggests, he imagined Hawthorne's English marriage in a distinctly American idiom.

19. See especially Masten, *Textual Intercourse.*

20. Stillinger, *Multiple Authorship.*

21. Martin, *Hero, Captain, and Stranger,* and also "Melville and Sexuality."

22. On Melville and Beaumont and Fletcher, see Eddy, "Melville's Response to Beaumont and Fletcher"; Sealts, *Melville's Reading;* Bercaw, *Melville's Sources;* and Kelley, "Rozoko in the Pacific."

23. See Emerson, "Friendship," in *Complete Works,* 2:189–217; Cottrell, *Sexuality/Textuality;* and Greenblatt, "1563, 18 August."

24. See Martin and Person, "Missing Letters," 113.

25. See Smith, *Rowing in Eden.*

26. For an opposing view, see Wineapple, "Hawthorne and Melville."

27. On Celia Thaxter, see Thaxter, *Among the Isles of Shoals;* Vallier, *Poet on Demand;* and Fetterley, "Theorizing Regionalism."

28. Vallier, *Poet on Demand,* 5.

29. See Parker, *Herman Melville,* 2:146–47. For a view of the religious significance, see Ra'ad, "'The Encantadas' and 'The Isle of the Cross.'"

30. I am grateful to Mary K. Bercaw Edwards for her thoughts on this subject; see also Dening, *Islands and Beaches;* Dening, *Beach Crossings;* and Calder, "Pacific Paradises."

31. See Clifford, "Traveling Cultures"; and Gibian, "Cosmopolitanism and Traveling Culture."

32. See Eddy, "Melville's Response to Beaumont and Fletcher," 375.

"Shanties of Chapters and Essays"

Rewriting *Moby-Dick*

ROBERT SATTELMEYER

ONE OF THE MOST remarkable features of *Moby-Dick* is the provocative evidence it offers of major revision and reconception during the nearly two years Melville struggled to complete it. On August 7, 1850, Evert Duyckinck, Melville's friend and editor of the *Literary World*, wrote his brother George from Pittsfield, Massachusetts, where he was staying with Melville, that the novelist had "a new book mostly done—a romantic, fanciful & literal & most enjoyable presentment of the Whale Fishery—something quite new" (*WHM*, 6:622). Melville himself, in a June 27 letter to his British publisher, had pitched his new work as "a romance of adventure, founded upon certain wild legends in the Southern Sperm Whale Fisheries," and confirmed that the book was on schedule for publication in fall 1850 (*WHM*, 14:163). Both descriptions indicate that the novel in progress was primarily an adventure story amplified by descriptive and discursive passages, based on Melville's own experiences and fleshed out with secondary sources—the same formula he had employed in all his earlier novels. Although this is not to say that nothing serious, reflective, or symbolic appeared in the text at this point, neither description hints at the dark and portentous religious and philosophical themes embodied in Ahab's tragic quest for the white whale.[1]

Rather, Melville originally saw his principal aesthetic challenge in making the notoriously ugly and brutish business of whaling—its floating slaughterhouses manned by the dregs of the maritime world—into an appealing and salable book. In a letter to Richard Henry Dana on May 1, 1850, he put the problem in a jocular way: "It will be a strange sort of a book . . . I fear; blubber is blubber you know; tho' you may get oil out of it, the poetry runs as hard as sap from a frozen maple tree;—& to cook the thing up, one must needs throw in a little fancy, which from the nature of the thing, must be ungainly as the gambols of the whales themselves. Yet I mean to give the truth of the thing, spite of this" (*WHM*, 14:162).

Then, as had been the case with *Mardi* and would become the case with *Pierre* and much later *Billy Budd,* something happened to alter the trajectory of the work drastically and delay its appearance for a year beyond its projected publication date. Buoyed in the late summer of 1850 by his discovery of what he felt to be a kindred spirit in Hawthorne and his rereading of Shakespeare's tragedies, Melville began to grow more restive and ambitious, despite the fact that he needed money and his novel was "mostly done." In "Hawthorne and His Mosses," published in the *Literary World* in August, Melville clearly references his own ambitions and creative daring, invoking Hawthorne and Shakespeare as his models for "the great Art of Telling the Truth" (*WHM*, 9:244).

Melville did not finish *Moby-Dick* until almost a year later, in midsummer 1851, some time after an undetermined number of early chapters had already been typeset in New York in May.[2] His letter to Hawthorne on June 29 gives the first direct clue to its revised nature: "The 'Whale' is only half through the press," he writes, and "the tail is not yet cooked—though the hell-fire in which the whole book is broiled might not unreasonably have cooked it all ere this. This is the book's motto (the secret one),—Ego non baptiso te in nomine—but make out the rest yourself." As late as July 20, Melville wrote his British publisher that he was "now passing thro' the press, the closing sheets of [his] new work" (*WHM*, 14:195–96, 14:198).

The book's "secret motto" refers, of course, to Ahab's diabolic baptism of the harpoon intended for Moby Dick in chapter 113, "The Forge": "'Ego non baptizo te in nomine patris, sed in nomine diaboli!'" (*WHM*, 6:489). Both this thematic transformation and the book's extended gestation became evident to scholars when Melville's correspondence and other archival material began to come to light during the Melville revival in the 1930s, and the dimensions of the puzzle were first articulated by Leon Howard in a 1940 article, "Melville's Struggle with the Angel." Since that time, a considerable body of scholarship and speculation has devoted itself to the conundrum of the novel's genesis, and yet a number of questions posed by these circumstances are still unanswered. How did the novel evolve from a "most enjoyable presentment of the Whale Fishery" to a Lear-like tragedy steeped in "hell-fire"? If the novel was "mostly done" in the summer of 1850, what elements of the original story might Melville have retained in the final version? How did the roles assigned to the various characters evolve in the adumbration of new themes, and what new characters were introduced? Finally, since the novel's tragic climax clearly represents Melville's final design, what might originally have been the intended fate of the *Pequod* and its crew?

In this essay I attempt to answer these questions—at least conjecturally, given the tenuous nature of the evidence available. I believe that the most likely course of revision suggests a more startling and complete metamorphosis than previous critics have posited and also points to the pervasive presence of Hawthorne—to whom the book is dedicated—in Melville's reformulations of the novel: not only Hawthorne the author, who "says NO! in thunder" and whose influence on Ahab's tragic quest is well documented, but also, and even more powerfully, Hawthorne the man, for whom Melville felt and from whom he craved an intense friendship and affection during the critical months of revision (*WHM*, 9:186).

An interpretation that focuses on the way the novel is likely to have evolved—rather than on what it finally became—foregrounds the romantic dynamism not only of its growth but also of its author's aesthetic theory. For Melville, as for many another romantic writer, art was, in Emerson's phrase, "the path of the creator to his work" rather than the finished work itself.[3] Melville's aesthetics of failure ("the true test of greatness," as he phrased it in "Hawthorne and His Mosses" [*WHM*, 9:248]) grounded his hope that *Moby-Dick* might be a great book despite his recognition that the finished work was, as he confessed to Hawthorne, "a final hash" between his original and ultimate conceptions, between his need to make money and his lofty aspirations (*WHM*, 14:191). Rather than apologize for being a "jack-leg" novelist, as Mark Twain did in similar circumstances when *Those Extraordinary Twins* metamorphosed into *Pudd'nhead Wilson*,[4] Melville steps out from behind the persona of Ishmael and brags, at the end of his "Cetology" chapter (with one of his raunchiest phallic puns), that "small erections may be finished by their first architects; grand ones, true ones, ever leave the copestone to posterity. God keep me from ever completing anything. This whole book is but a draught—nay, but the draught of a draught" (*WHM*, 6:145).

That same valorization of imperfection and incompleteness might authorize the critical project, too (if authorization were needed), of undertaking the "reverse engineering" process of deliberately searching out the ligatures of Melville's novel for evidence of the original story—for, like the real whale, Melville's whale is not diminished by the inquiry. Although much of my argument rests on the minutiae of textual evidence, my intention is to consider and to emphasize *Moby-Dick,* in John Bryant's apt term, as "a fluid text," bearing in mind that the phases of any literary production are likely to include "initial inspirations, reflective moments of expansion and revision, periods of collaboration, and continual negotiations with family, editors, reviewers, and influential readers." As Bryant argues elsewhere, the point of this sort of criticism is not to recover the author's intentions but rather to acknowledge that textual fluidity provides "the material evidence of *shifting* intentions" and thus a vantage point from which to read both a text and the culture in which it is situated.[5]

In the speculations that follow I am, like Ishmael in his cetological system, both copiously drawing on the works of other scholars—especially Harrison Hayford—and leaving my own system unfinished.[6] The available evidence about the composition of *Moby-Dick* and the development of theories of its genesis based on that evidence are carefully documented and weighed in the nearly two-hundred-page "Historical Note" to the Northwestern-Newberry scholarly edition that appeared in 1988. Despite this extensive review, which sifts more than sixty years of scholarly attention to the puzzle, much remains unknown and, probably, unknowable. No direct manuscript evidence survives—as it does for *Billy Budd*—that would allow one to chart with confidence Melville's shifting ambitions and conceptions. Nor do Melville's letters from the period allude with any specificity to the revision process—only that it certainly took place, that he struggled with it, and that at the end he felt both elated (over Hawthorne's appreciation) and disappointed with the "final hash" of the printed text.

The sorts of evidence that exist do not permit conclusions to be drawn with rigor or with certainty. These include comments in letters by Melville and others, such as those already cited; textual changes presumably made by Melville between the first American and the first English edition (in which some vestigial plot elements were deleted);[7] Melville's employment of source material, which he acquired at different times and used in different chapters; internal anomalies and inconsistencies in the text that point to early conceptions of the plot and themes; jarring shifts in theme and diction; and, most important for my purposes, passages and chapters that can tentatively be designated what I term "shanty" passages—text written to reconcile or explain inconsistencies and changes of course that, when isolated, allows us to draw inferences about both the original elements of the novel and Melville's reasons for changing them.

The term "shanty" comes from Melville's June 29, 1851, letter to Hawthorne, in which he says, "I have been building some shanties of houses (connected with the old one) and likewise some shanties of chapters and essays," suggesting that as the book was already starting through the press he was still writing passages that helped tie it together (*WHM*, 14:195). (This text is analogous to what biblical scholars would identify as "R"—the work of a redactor—although less obvious, since Melville was doing his own redacting.) These passages offer crucial if tenuous evidence about both the earlier and the later stages of the book. Reading the novel with its compositional history in mind, one may venture to identify and analyze these passages, which point both forward to Melville's evolving aspirations for his novel and backward toward earlier material he wished to retain within his enlarged conception of the work.

The most prominent and well-known example of such a shanty passage is the whole of chapter 23, "The Lee Shore," devoted to the absence, in the ensuing narrative, of Bulkington, a character introduced early in the shore chapters and identified as one destined to play a major role as Ishmael's companion. But once the *Pequod* puts to sea, he never appears again. Rather than revise chapter 3, "The Spouter-Inn," to remove Bulkington, Melville chose instead to add a chapter apotheosizing him as a character who, though absent, represents his own artistic strivings for truth and independence of thought in the face of forces that would conspire to cast him "on the treacherous, slavish shore" (*WHM*, 6:107). In this case, Melville chose not to explain an inconsistency, but rather to highlight it (and his own willingness to risk failure), by inserting a chapter unconnected with the surrounding narrative that would amplify the overall drive of the novel toward romantic rebellion and the questioning of received wisdom.

Many other passages and some full chapters, however, do evince Melville's efforts to reconcile inconsistencies and, more importantly, to retain as much of his earlier work as possible (as in the case of Bulkington) while grafting on it his later conception. In combination with the other sorts of more traditional scholarly evidence already cited, such shanty passages and chapters—most of which are much less obviously inserted than Bulkington's "six-inch chapter" (*WHM*, 6:106)—play a major role in supporting my conjectures about the changes that took place in the course of *Moby-Dick*'s composition. My approach and my conclusions differ from most previous efforts to chart the novel's development in that I attempt to extend and complicate the notion of its having been written in different "phases" by keeping in mind the overall thrust of the revisions that Melville is likely to have made to accommodate earlier material to his later conception and final plot structure. There were doubtless many stages of revision, and, even if it were possible to determine clearly which chapters or groups of chapters were written in a certain order—by datable source material or topical references, for example—the fact would remain that Melville, like any author of any kind of text, certainly went back to his manuscript to add, delete, and revise elements to bring the entire novel as nearly as possible in line with his evolving aspirations for it. Thus, for example, some of the early or "shore" chapters contain accurate foreshadowings of the climax, while they simultaneously point to plot developments that never take place. The presence of both kinds of passages confirms one's sense not only that Melville lacked the "Time, Strength, Cash, and Patience," as he concludes the "Cetology" manifesto of incompleteness (*WHM*, 6:145), to polish his novel in a lapidary fashion, but also that he wrote with a kind of reckless bravura, confident that the novel's overarching intellectual and spiritual daring would outweigh its inconsistencies.

At the same time, and especially as he was trying to bring the novel to a close, Melville adopted a fatalistic attitude toward both his novel and his career. Interpreting Melville's early May 1851 letter to Hawthorne, the one in which he says, "all my books are botches," Hershel Parker sums up Melville's compositional habits and state of mind at this stage:

> His books were hashes partly because he habitually worked bits from other books into them, and they were botches not merely because they were bungled but because they were patched, never written sequentially, one chapter growing out of the previous chapter while determining the shape of the next, first to last, until the end. In the weeks just ahead, he

had to finish *The Whale* [as it was still titled at this point] somehow, but however competently he did the job, there seemed no point to his driving himself as hard as he knew he would do: "What's the use of elaborating what, in its very essence, is so short-lived as a modern book? Though I wrote the Gospels in this century, I should die in the gutter."[8]

Before I examine the individual elements of the novel that underwent significant revision, it will be useful to review the largest overall inconsistency that remains, one that all readers notice and that probably causes many of them to give up the chase. Ahab's declaration of his quest for Moby Dick and his subversion of the officers and crew to this end occur early in the voyage in chapter 36, "The Quarter-Deck." Nearly four hundred pages and almost a hundred chapters then come between the announcement of this quest and its being taken up in earnest, and much of the intervening material seems to have little to do with the stated purpose of the voyage. In aid of mapping the novel's revision, however, this inconsistency clearly reflects the way in which the quest for Moby Dick and the tragic character of Ahab were grafted onto the original material: Ahab's mysterious malady is presaged in a relatively few passages and chapters early in the text, he appears and announces his revenge quest after the *Pequod* sails, and then he figures only occasionally in the action and description until he begins to dominate once more in the last hundred pages or so. Much of the material in between consists of the "presentment of the Whale Fishery" that Melville had no doubt written before fixing on Ahab's diabolical quest as the "secret motto" of the book. Keenly aware of the difficulty and yet not wishing to abandon so much productive work, Melville undertook to account for this largest discrepancy with two shanty chapters explaining the intervening time and material, one geographical and temporal and the other psychological.

In chapter 44, "The Chart," which takes place shortly after the announcement of the quest for Moby Dick, Melville explains that the time and place for finally encountering Moby Dick is to be the equatorial season, the "Season-on-the-Line":

> Now, the Pequod had sailed from Nantucket at the very beginning of the Season-on-the-Line. No possible endeavor then could enable her commander to make the great passage southwards, double Cape Horn,

and then running down sixty degrees of latitude arrive in the equatorial Pacific in time to cruise there. Therefore, he must wait for the next ensuing season. Yet the premature hour of the Pequod's sailing had, perhaps, been covertly selected by Ahab, with a view to this very complexion of things. Because, an interval of three hundred and sixty-five days and nights was before him; an interval which, instead of impatiently enduring ashore, he would spend in a miscellaneous hunt. (*WHM*, 6:201)

This passage, which goes on to describe the "circumnavigating wake" of the *Pequod*, simultaneously highlights another anomaly in the novel: originally it seems clear from several early references to Cape Horn that the ship is destined for the whaler's traditional route to the Pacific by way of the tip of South America.[9] But the *Pequod* rounds the Cape of Good Hope instead and cruises the Indian Ocean and the Sea of Japan before sailing to the equatorial cruising ground in the mid-Pacific.

Shortly following this passage, there is another shanty chapter (chapter 46, "Surmises") devoted to a psychological rationale for the abeyance of Ahab's hunt for Moby Dick and the long period of time the *Pequod* spends in pursuit of the ordinary business of whaling. This rationale, briefly summarized, is that Ahab, who is "far too wedded" to the traditional whaleman's ways to give up the normal activities of the fishery, fears lest Starbuck and the crew will rebel if their minds are not occupied with their ordinary pursuits and also fears that he could be open to the charge of usurpation if he does not engage in whaling as usual (*WHM*, 6:211–13). The commander of the *Pequod* is thus presented as at once recklessly monomaniacal and cautiously observant of tradition, and he is put in the somewhat implausible position of working the crew up to a fever pitch to hunt Moby Dick in chapter 36 and then going about the normal activities of whaling for a year or more before expecting to encounter him.

This weak and somewhat tenuous rationale for Ahab's action (or lack of it) suggests that Melville wrote much of the whaling material (and thus the original novel) before conceiving either Ahab or his particular crusade.[10] Since *Moby-Dick* is so clearly Ahab's book, it may be difficult to imagine that the novel existed at some point without him. Nevertheless, evidence in the text suggests that this was the case and that the radical revision of principal characters extended beyond Ahab to the mates, the harpooners, and even some of the crew, for a tragedy on the Shakespearean model requires a far different cast of ancillary characters than does a novel of adventure about whaling.

The shanty passage that introduces Ahab—as one of a number of what Harrison Hayford calls "'hide out'" characters—suggests both his late addition and his difference from the original commanding officer(s) of the *Pequod*.[11] In chapter 16, "The Ship," Ishmael has signed on and then left the *Pequod*, when he has second thoughts and decides it would be a good idea to go back and ask to see Captain Ahab. In addition to its being rather egregiously an afterthought, this passage is illogical, for Ishmael has already been on the ship and even in the captain's cabin and knows Ahab is not there. The officer he has met and dealt with, Captain Peleg, explains that he will not be able to see Ahab but then launches into a description that limns the other captain's tragic and elevated character. Ahab is "'a grand, ungodly, god-like man,'" he has "'been in colleges, as well as 'mong the cannibals,'" and he has "'fixed his fiery lance in mightier, stranger foes than whales.'" Other portentous hints of a sort not likely to calm Ishmael's concerns follow from Peleg: the dark biblical symbolism of Ahab's name, the prophecy of the old squaw Tistig, the fact that Ahab is "'desperate moody, and savage sometimes,'" and that, "'stricken, blasted, if he be, Ahab has his humanities'" (*WHM*, 6:79). This afterthought passage at the end of "The Ship" is strikingly different in theme and language from Peleg's other utterances in the chapter, which reveal him as profane and blustering—hardly of a reflective or philosophical turn.

Another anomalous passage earlier in this chapter describes Ahab's qualifications as a tragic hero (though without naming him) and seems equally a later insertion, for it appears in the middle of the portrayal of Captain Bildad, Peleg's fellow Quaker and owner/agent. Bildad has none of the characteristics enumerated in the passage except the archaic Quaker diction. The interpolation refers to "a man of greatly superior natural force, with a globular brain and a ponderous heart; who has also . . . been led to think untraditionally and independently." This character has "learn[ed] a bold and nervous lofty language," and he is "a mighty pageant creature, formed for noble tragedies," with "a half wilful overruling morbidness at the bottom of his nature." In order to segue back to Bildad, a narrator, breaking into Ishmael's first-person account, comments, "But, as yet we have not to do with such an one, but with quite another" (*WHM*, 6:73–74).

These descriptions of the offstage Ahab stand out from the surrounding text by virtue of their diction and theme (the chapter is otherwise primarily comic), their lack of internal connection to their context, and the strained transitions that do connect them (Ishmael's decision to return to the ship, the narrator's "But, as yet . . ."). If these disjunctures, along with the fact that Ahab remains offstage until chapter 28, well into the voyage, suggest that he was a relatively late addition, they imply at the same time—as Hayford and others have noted—that Peleg and Bildad were originally much more important characters, perhaps the principal officers not merely onshore but at sea as well. For if Ahab was not the original captain, who was? The most obvious candidates among the existing cast are the two captains who dominate the *Pequod* during the shore chapters and in setting out to sea.

When Ishmael first goes aboard the *Pequod,* he addresses Peleg as the captain: "'Is this the Captain of the Pequod?'" Peleg equivocates, replying, "'Supposing it be the Captain of the Pequod, what dost thou want of him?'" When Ishmael says he wants to go whaling "'to see the world,'" Peleg reveals that Ahab is the captain and that he has lost a leg to a whale. Curiously, however, this description of Ahab's lost leg follows a reference to *Peleg's* leg. When Ishmael volunteers that he has been to sea in the merchant service, Peleg silences him: "'Marchant service be damned. Talk not that lingo to me. Dost see that leg?—I'll take that leg away from thy stern, if ever thou talkest of the marchant service to me again'" (*WHM,* 6:71). Why does Peleg call attention to his leg unless there is something unusual about it?

A number of other details in the novel—in addition to his name itself—reinforce the notion that Peleg may have been the original one-legged captain (or first mate—more on this possibility later) of the *Pequod.* In chapter 20, "All Astir," just before the *Pequod* sails, Peleg is described "running out of his whalebone den" (*WHM,* 6:96). In the first American edition, however, whose sheets Melville was not able to correct, Peleg comes "hobbling" from his den. Additionally, when the *Pequod* is weighing anchor, Ishmael feels "a sudden sharp poke in [his] rear" and turns around to see Captain Peleg "in the act of withdrawing his leg from [Ishmael's] immediate vicinity" (*WHM,* 6:103). Once again, Peleg's leg is emphasized, and his kick is termed a "poke," a word more appropriate for a jab with a peg leg than a kick with a human foot. Finally, when Peleg describes the loss of Ahab's leg to Ishmael—just after calling attention to his own—his emotion seems in keeping with a man lamenting his own injury rather than another's: "'Lost by a whale! Young man, come nearer to me: it was devoured, chewed up, crunched by the monstrousest parmacetty that ever chipped a boat!—ah, ah!'" (*WHM*, 6:72).

Perhaps the most tangible evidence of Peleg's importance to the original story lies in recently deciphered marginalia in Melville's copy of Thomas Beale's *The Natural History of the Sperm Whale* (1835), an important source for the cetology in *Moby-Dick* that Melville acquired in July 1850. A pencil notation on page 184 of Melville's copy of Beale reads "'Old Thunder'/Peleg/" giving Peleg the epithet used to describe Ahab by the crazy prophet Elijah in chapter 19 (*WHM*, 6:92).[12]

The passage that suggests most clearly what Peleg's and Bildad's original roles might have been—as well as hinting at some elements of the original plot—occurs right at the moment of Peleg's crucial kick (or "poke") at Ishmael's rear. Ishmael is slacking off at the capstan because he is imagining what the voyage has in store: "Meantime . . . Captain Peleg ripped and swore astern in the most frightful manner. I almost thought he would sink the ship before the anchor could be got up; involuntarily I paused on my handspike, and told Queequeg to do the same, thinking of the perils we both ran, in starting on the voyage with such a devil for a pilot. I was comforting myself, however, with the thought that in pious Bildad might be found some salvation" (*WHM*, 6:103). It makes no sense for Ishmael to have such concerns about undertaking the voyage "with such a devil for a pilot," since the pilot leaves the ship as soon as it gains an offing. Nor does it make sense for him to take consolation in the thought that Bildad will offer "some salvation," for he, too, is acting as pilot and will debark at the same time. However, if we imagine that the original passage read "captain," or even "first mate" (ordinarily the officer directly responsible for seeing the captain's orders carried out), instead of "pilot," Ishmael's apprehension becomes both reasonable and justified. The contrast between Peleg and Bildad, between the profane blusterer and the pious, parsimonious taskmaster, is elaborately described and dramatized in "The Ship" and then reinforced by their behavior as the *Pequod* sets out to sea. Ishmael's apprehensions about shipboard cruelty ("That was my first kick," he says of Peleg's poke [*WHM*, 6:103], though he is never kicked again), combined with the potentially explosive differences between the primary officers, could well have served as blueprint for the original novel's principal conflict. When Ishmael remarks that in setting out Peleg and Bildad were carrying on "as if they were to be joint-commanders at sea, as well as to all appearances in port" (*WHM*, 6:102), his observation may well signal another of Melville's shanty passages tying the original to the revised novel.

Hayford, analyzing this same evidence in the early chapters, concludes that Peleg was the original captain but Bildad was not intended to play an ongoing role. He bases this hypothesis on Peleg's longstanding relationship with the *Pequod* as mate and on the scene in which Peleg and Bildad leave the ship, noting that the long handshake they share seems to be a farewell. "'Come, come, Captain Bildad,'" Peleg then urges; "'stop palavering,—away!'" And Ishmael continues, "with that, Peleg hurried him over the side, and both dropt into the boat." Hayford observes that the addition of just two words, "both dropt," could have changed the scene from Peleg as commander to Peleg and Bildad as now-superfluous pilots (158; *WHM*, 6:105).

However, Ishmael's concerns about the voyage, embracing both Peleg and Bildad, as well as the careful elaboration of their character differences in "The Ship," argue in favor of both having originally been designed as continuing and important characters. Their precise roles in the ship's hierarchy, nonetheless, seem less certain. If they were major figures in the original novel, there are three possibilities for their relationship: (1) they were both captains and part owners and truly "joint-commanders at sea" as well as on land, as Ishmael suggests; (2) Peleg was captain and Bildad was first mate; or (3) Bildad was captain and Peleg was mate. Much of the evidence, as Hayford shows, seems to point to Peleg, with his possible ivory leg and somewhat sacrilegious attitudes, as the original captain and precursor to Ahab. Again, however, the evidence is not of a sort that allows conclusions to be drawn confidently, and the other two possibilities need to be kept in mind.

The appearances onshore and on board as the ship sets out suggest a joint command, and, while such an arrangement would have been unusual to say the least, since Peleg and Bildad were principal owners there could be some rationale for this arrangement. Such a relationship would have heightened the possibility of conflict between them, particularly if Peleg's desire to slay the whale that maimed him clashed with Bildad's religious and profit-oriented motives. An echo of this conflict survives in an encounter between Ahab and Starbuck, when Ahab accuses his first mate of "'always prating'" about the "'miserly owners'" in chapter 109,

"Ahab and Starbuck in the Cabin," despite the fact that we never hear Starbuck "prating" (*WHM,* 6:474).

Evidence also suggests that Peleg may have been the mate, as James Barbour has remarked as well.[13] In "The Ship," Peleg is described as the longtime first mate of the *Pequod,* and his direct physical oppression of the crew (Ishmael's kick) is more characteristic of a first mate than a captain. Although one passage asserts that he has "commanded another vessel of his own, and [is] now a retired seaman" (*WHM,* 6:69), other testimony contradicts this history and puts him aboard the *Pequod* as mate on the previous voyage when a whale took the leg. The Gay-Head Indian says of Ahab that "'he was dismasted off Japan . . . but like his dismasted craft, he shipped another mast without coming home for it'" (*WHM,* 6:124).[14] So the loss of the leg took place during the *Pequod's* last voyage in conjunction with the typhoon off Japan that is repeatedly mentioned. And Bildad confirms that it was Peleg who was mate on this voyage: "'Tell me, when this same Pequod here had her three masts overboard in that typhoon on Japan, that same voyage when thou went mate with Captain Ahab, did'st thou not think of Death and the Judgment then?'" (*WHM,* 6:90).

Additionally, in both of the interpolated chapters concerning encounters with Moby Dick, "The Jeroboam's Story" and "The Town-Ho's Story," it is the mate who rashly attacks the whale and pays with his life. As Barbour has persuasively argued, "The Town-Ho's Story" in particular contains a number of plot details that complete or complement the hints of the original story, and Radney, the rash mate who strikes a crew member and seeks to kill Moby Dick, bears more than a passing resemblance to Peleg.[15] Finally, one additional minor detail points to the role of mate for Peleg. In chapter 87, "The Grand Armada," the *Pequod* is pursued by Malay pirates. Ahab spots them and issues an order: "Levelling his glass at this sight, Ahab quickly revolved in his pivot-hole, crying, 'Aloft there, and rig whips and buckets to wet the sails;—Malays, sir, and after us!'" (*WHM,* 6:383). To whom does Ahab address this remark (no response or interlocutor is mentioned), and why does he address him as "sir"? Ahab, who would "strike the sun if it insulted [him]," can hardly be imagined addressing anyone aboard the *Pequod* as "sir." Nor would such a breach of nautical custom be expected even if Ahab were not so "sultan[ic]" (*WHM,* 6:164, 6:149). Since the attack by the pirates has no bearing on the plot, and nothing ensues from it (the pirates, like Cooper's Indians, simply fall behind and give up the chase), it may be a vestigial scene from the original story, in which someone (Peleg?) rotates his leg in his pivot hole and says to the captain "'Malays, sir, and after us!'"

Whatever Peleg's actual rank, if he was the original officer whose leg had been lost to a whale, one can imagine how Ahab's character may have grown organically from this earlier figure. In fact, Peleg himself provides the hint when, in his afterthought characterization of Ahab to Ishmael, he says that Ahab is "'something like [Peleg himself]— only there's a good deal more of him'" (*WHM*, 6:79). It was Peleg who outfitted the *Pequod* with her whalebone appurtenances, making her "a cannibal of a craft, tricking herself forth in the chased bones of her enemies" (*WHM*, 6:70). Like Ahab, Peleg is fierce and irreligious (he mocks Bildad's scripture study later in the chapter), and if he had lost a leg to a whale he might have harbored a thirst for revenge for which the whalebone-studded *Pequod* would be an apt instrument and that might partly propel the plot of an adventure novel. But Peleg "care[s] not a rush for what are called serious things" and is obviously not a vessel equipped to support the tonnage of the Promethean and Faustian tragic elements of Ahab's quest, the "fiery hunt" for which the whale becomes a symbol (*WHM*, 6:74, 6:195).

❦ ❦

If the foregoing speculations are tenable, then it follows that the second-ary characters—the mates and harpooners, chiefly—would also have been radically revised in order to provide suitable complements and foils to Ahab. To begin at the top, there is a good deal of evidence to suggest that Starbuck, like Ahab, was added at a relatively late stage of composition and may have evolved or metamorphosed from Bildad. At the most obvious level, both are Nantucket Quakers, and they share a number of physical characteristics. Compare Bildad:

> His own person was the exact embodiment of his utilitarian character. On his long, gaunt body, he carried no spare flesh, no superfluous beard, his chin having a soft, economical nap to it, like the worn nap of his broad-brimmed hat. (*WHM*, 6:75)

to Starbuck:

Only some thirty arid summers had he seen; those summers had dried up all his physical superfluousness. But this, his thinness, so to speak, seemed no more the token of wasting anxieties and cares, than it seemed the indication of any bodily blight. It was merely the condensation of the man. (*WHM*, 6:115)

Starbuck, like Ahab, is a "hide out character" in the shore chapters, mentioned but not actually present until well after the *Pequod* sails. In fact, he does not speak a line (except during the account of dining protocol in chapter 34, "The Cabin-Table") until he responds to Ahab's declamation to the crew in chapter 36, "The Quarter-Deck," asking if it was Moby Dick that took Ahab's leg and questioning the captain's desire for vengeance. The first scene in which Starbuck participates, then, also initiates his principal role: it is he who requires "the little lower layer" of philosophical explanation, serving both as foil and potential antagonist to Ahab (*WHM*, 6:163).

That Starbuck was a late addition is also suggested by his general lack of participation in the routine activities of whaling during the bulk of the voyage. When the first whale is killed (by Stubb) and then processed, there are what I take to be two shanty passages explaining why neither Ahab, as captain, nor Starbuck, as first mate, oversees this quintessential whaling activity. Ahab is said to evince some "vague dissatisfaction" that although a whale is dead Moby Dick still lives—thus the captain's mood is "now all quiescence." And Stubb is in such a bustle "that the staid Starbuck, his official superior, quietly resign[s] to him for the time the sole management of affairs" (*WHM*, 6:291, 6:292). Similarly, when the tryworks are first set up, many chapters later, "it belong[s] to Stubb to oversee the business" (*WHM*, 6:422). And when the *Pequod* meets the *Rose Bud*, it is Stubb who, apparently on his own authority, takes his boat and crew to "diddle" the Frenchman and secure the ambergris. It may be generalized that in the chapters dealing with routine whaling activity and encounters with ships of other nations (usually comic in tone), which probably belong to the earlier stages of the novel, neither Ahab nor Starbuck typically takes a prominent role.

Perhaps the clearest indication of Starbuck's probable later addition appears in the chapter that introduces him, the first one (in printed sequence) titled "Knights and Squires." Not only is he given a chapter to himself, separate from the other mates and the harpooners, but that chapter also contains the long passage constituting a sort of invocation to the democratic muse in which Melville attempts to justify his ambition to make great art out of the humble materials of "meanest mariners, and renegades and castaways," "weav[ing] round them tragic graces." It is a passage that seems to belong, in other words, to the later, more ambitious conception of the novel as both a tragedy and a democratic epic, particularly since, though ostensibly about Starbuck, it features Ahab, too, "the most mournful, perchance the most abased, amongst them all" (*WHM*, 6:117).

If Starbuck came in later to provide a foil and in some sense an intellectually worthy antagonist for Ahab, then it follows that Stubb, as already hinted, played a much more prominent role in the original narrative. In the same way that viewing Ahab as a later addition throws light on the roles of Peleg and Bildad, viewing Starbuck in this way tends to move Stubb into the foreground. It is primarily through Stubb, as noted, that we view the principal whaling activities of pursuit, capture, and processing. He kills the first whale in the most extended description of a hunt, supervises the securing and the cutting up of the whale, and, again, supervises the operation of the tryworks. In keeping with the seriocomic tone of much of the putatively original material, it is also Stubb who takes center stage in "Stubb's Supper" and "The Whale as a Dish," and in the *Pequod*'s comic encounters with the German and French whale ships.

One other anomalous detail suggests that Stubb was originally designed for a more important part than the one he finally assumes. The shore chapters introduce Aunt Charity, who helps provision the ship, as Bildad's sister and owner of a few shares in the vessel. When the *Pequod* is about to sail, she visits one last time with a gift of "a night-cap for Stubb, the second mate, her brother-in-law" (*WHM*, 6:102). As the editors of the Northwestern-Newberry edition note: "If Stubb is the brother-in-law of Aunt Charity, he is also Bildad's. . . . Since no such family relationships are again referred to in the book, some discrepancy seems to be involved here" (*WHM*, 6:846). Again, a number of possibilities suggest themselves (for example, did Melville simply add "in-law" to "brother" to mask an obvious discrepancy?), but if Stubb was related to Bildad (or even to Charity), then he had a connection by blood or marriage to the owners that was a possible "plot point" in the original narrative, perhaps again of the sort that mate and part-owner Radney represents in "The Town-Ho's Story."

Another major character who was also almost certainly and rather obviously an add-on foil to Ahab is Fedallah. A telling clue is the varying number of the *Pequod*'s boats. In chapter 48, "The First Lowering," in which Fedallah and his crew first appear, his whaleboat makes a fourth—an addition to those headed by Starbuck, Stubb, and Flask—and the reader learns the identity of the stowaways hinted at earlier. No whale is secured, however, and several chapters later when Stubb makes the first kill, there is no mention of Fedallah and his crew during the chase, and "a tandem of three boats" tows the carcass back to the ship (*WHM*, 6:291). Fedallah and the fourth boat play no part, again, in the many chapters dealing with the "presentment of the Whale Fishery" that follow. When the *Pequod* meets the German whaler *Jungfrau*, for example, specific reference is made to "the Pequod's three boats" (*WHM*, 6:354), and even as late as chapter 93, "The Castaway," when Pip leaps from Stubb's boat, the narrator partly excuses Stubb for his seeming heartlessness in leaving the boy behind "because there were two boats in his wake" (*WHM*, 6:414). So, like Ahab and Starbuck, Fedallah is mostly a nonpresence in the many episodes dealing with the routine business of whaling, and his character, though intimated in the early chapters, does not become significant until the novel's final section. The very brief shanty chapter, chapter 21 ("Going Aboard"), in which the mad prophet Elijah hints at stowaways onboard, serves to plant the seed of Fedallah's presence and add to the aura of mystery and portentousness that Melville cultivated in revising the shore chapters to reflect the ultimate thrust and atmosphere of the novel.

The "Castaway" chapter in which Pip jumps from Stubb's boat may also mark the juncture between the boy's earlier and later roles. Originally, it would seem, he was not to be rescued but to die, for in revising sheets of the first American edition for the first English edition Melville deleted the phrase "—oh no! he went before" from a description of Pip's fate in the context of the crew's collective doom (*WHM*, 6:121; 6:852). Conveniently if improbably rescued by the ship itself after the boats abandon him, Pip is resurrected to play the fool to Ahab's Lear in the novel's final stretches.

In many ways, the most interesting major character whose role seems to have undergone radical revision is Queequeg. However, evidence within the text suggests that his metamorphosis may have proceeded in a manner the reverse of the pattern observed for the other characters. In the cases of Ahab, Starbuck, and Fedallah, each is a "hide out" in the early chapters, with sufficient hints and predictions to allow him to take up his principal part in later sections. This process of planting literary stowaways enabled Melville, as his conception of the novel enlarged, to continue to use material he had already written. A great deal of the whaling matter, like the accounts of life aboard a navy vessel in *White-Jacket,* is primarily descriptive or meditative and bears no direct relation to plot. Thus, it continued to be available and would have required relatively little (if any) revision as the focus shifted from adventure story to Ahab's quest to grapple with that which lay behind the mask. In the case of Queequeg, however, the evidence points toward a major rewriting and amplification of his character *in the early chapters,* for he clearly plays a diminished role as the novel develops, losing almost entirely his purported status as Ishmael's boon companion and cutting no significant figure in the revised action. This hypothesis is admittedly counterintuitive; that is, one would normally infer that, since Queequeg takes a major part early on and nearly disappears later, he belongs to the original conception of the novel. However, as Hayford first observed, the evidence pulls in the other direction, and this reworking of Queequeg's character, while deleterious to conceptual unity, allowed Melville to achieve a kind of balance in the expression of important themes whose resonance for him transcended consistency of character (145–46).

Queequeg has a role throughout the novel, obviously, but it is not the one elaborated for him in the shore chapters. There is virtually no carry-through of the bosom-friend and whaling-mentor relationships that he and Ishmael develop while they are together and become "married" in New Bedford. The episode in which Queequeg appears most prominently in the later section of *Moby-Dick*—his near-fatal illness and the building of his coffin—illustrates this disjuncture between his projected part and the actual one he plays.

Queequeg takes ill while working in the damp hold of the *Pequod* trying to find the source of a serious leak in the oil casks already stowed.

This leak first causes a confrontation between Starbuck and Ahab, who initially refuses to attend to it because the *Pequod* is nearing the Japanese cruising ground, but then relents and orders the ship to heave to while the hold is searched. This episode would seem to be a carry-over from the earlier stage of the novel. There is no reason for Ahab's concern about losing time on the Japanese cruising ground if he does not expect to encounter Moby Dick until the "Season-on-the-Line"—but off Japan is where the original "dismasting" occurred, according to the Gay-Head Indian, and where Peleg, if he was the original seeker after the whale, might have expected to encounter him again. More important, like the Malay pirate episode, the leak itself, which seems so urgent, has no resolution and no consequences. We never learn the source of the leak, what measures are taken to make repairs, or what effect the incident has on the voyage. As Barbour conjectures, the *Pequod*'s leak may have been a major plot device in the original narrative, operating the way the leak does in "The Town-Ho's Story" to precipitate a conflict between officers and crew and possibly to force a landing (113–14). Whether this is the case or not, it seems likely that the disconnected incident was a component of the early narrative and that Queequeg's involvement reflects his place in the cast of characters as originally conceived.

Leaving aside for a moment the fact that once established as Ishmael's bosom friend and whaling mentor Queequeg appears only rarely and hardly ever in these roles in the rest of the novel, two aspects of Queequeg's situation and character in the leak episode are particularly discordant. First, he inhabits the forecastle where the ordinary seamen live, rather than the after part of the ship—between the captain's cabin and the forecastle—where harpooners always reside and where the narrator earlier places them (*WHM,* 6:478, 6:147). As the editors of the Northwestern-Newberry edition say, this is "a major unemendable discrepancy," raising the possibility "that at the stage when Melville first wrote Queequeg's 'death' scene he had not yet made him one of the harpooneers" (*WHM,* 6:900). This possibility is strengthened if, as I conjecture, the entire episode beginning with the mysterious leak belongs to the original narrative. Queequeg's duty to search the hold for the leak does not seem to square with his rank as harpooner, either. Similarly, when he is put to work fending off sharks in chapter 66 with "a forecastle seaman," Queequeg and his companion (not Ishmael) are referred to as "these two mariners" with no distinctions of rank (*WHM,* 6:302).

Most discordantly, though, Ishmael himself is not present at nor apparently concerned about his bosom friend's near-fatal illness. When Queequeg wants his coffin made, he calls some unnamed crew member to him to request the favor, not Ishmael. Except for one sentence at the beginning of the chapter in Ishmael's voice that would have been easy to insert, referring to his "fast bosom-friend, Queequeg" (*WHM*, 6:476), Ishmael never appears during Queequeg's illness and recovery, and the rest of the chapter is narrated in the third person. It seems remarkable that this crisis should have occurred without any expression of concern or assistance from Ishmael, strengthening the likelihood that the episode was part of the original narrative and written before the "marriage" of Ishmael and Queequeg. It is probable, too, that Queequeg did not survive his illness in the original version. There seems to be a Shakespearean add-on in the chapter following the preparation of his coffin: Pip in his later incarnation as wise fool speaks over him, and Starbuck then soliloquizes over Pip, following which Queequeg miraculously recovers and goes about his business.

There is also a shanty passage in the shore chapters that in purporting to account for a logical discrepancy further bolsters the probability that Queequeg as the reader knows him was a late addition. Following the blossoming of Ishmael and Queequeg's deep friendship, they resolve to throw in together on the forthcoming whaling voyage, and Ishmael, who is "wholly ignorant of the mysteries of whaling," particularly welcomes this development because, as an experienced harpooner, Queequeg can help him (*WHM*, 6:57).

Yet, when the time comes to choose a ship, Queequeg stays behind and the greenhorn Ishmael goes alone. Obviously, if Queequeg is to be Ishmael's guide, he should play a role in the selection of the ship that is to be their home for the next three years. The shanty passage explaining this discrepancy, the first paragraph of chapter 16, "The Ship," assigns responsibility for the illogical turn of events to Yojo, Queequeg's idol, who declares that Ishmael, if left to his own devices, will "infallibly" pick the right ship (*WHM*, 6:68). This divine intervention seems a fairly obvious ploy enabling Melville to keep intact the scene in which Ishmael signs on board the *Pequod* and becomes acquainted with Peleg and Bildad, but it necessitates another signing-on scene for Queequeg later, in chapter 18.

If the several chapters devoted to Queequeg and to Ishmael and Queequeg's friendship in the shore section of *Moby-Dick* are products of a later rather than the earliest phase of composition, what motive could Melville have had for adding at this stage a major relationship destined not to be developed and sustained in the rest of the narrative? Answering this question requires a little lower layer of speculation that rests on the totality of Melville's feelings and aspirations and relationships while he was writing the novel. As "Hawthorne and His Mosses" demonstrates, Melville's rereading of Shakespeare and his discovery of Hawthorne gave him a powerful impetus to reconceive his work in more ambitious terms and to "tea[r] off the mask, and spea[k] the sane madness of vital truth" through Ahab's tragic quest (*WHM*, 9:244). But this dark ontological and religious drive was only half of his characteristic mood at this time; the other half was an almost giddy happiness at the profound spiritual friendship he felt for Hawthorne himself—an affection that seems not to have been returned with anything like the same warmth but that was sustained with intensity on Melville's part in his letters to and visits with Hawthorne while working on *Moby-Dick* (and through his dedication of the book to Hawthorne) in late 1850 and 1851. Here, for example, is a passage from the most fervid letter, dated November 17, 1851: "Whence come you, Hawthorne? By what right do you drink from my flagon of life? And when I put it to my lips—lo, they are yours and not mine. I feel that the Godhead is broken up like the bread at the Supper, and that we are the pieces. Hence this infinite fraternity of feeling" (*WHM*, 14:212). Earlier, in "Hawthorne and His Mosses," Melville had written: "But already I feel that this Hawthorne has dropped germinous seeds into my soul. He expands and deepens down, the more I contemplate him; and further, and further, shoots his strong New-England roots into the hot soil of my Southern soul" (*WHM*, 9:250).

As Robert K. Martin and Leland S. Person have recently observed, as long ago as 1950 Newton Arvin called attention to this "astonishingly sexual image," and in recent decades it has become common to analyze the Melville-Hawthorne relationship in terms of homoerotic attraction.[16] It goes beyond the scope of this essay to speculate on the precise nature of this attraction, but if the sexually charged imagery of the Ishmael-Queequeg friendship was a later addition to the plot, then it seems natural to infer that Melville's powerful feelings of friendship (or something stronger) for Hawthorne provided the stimulus for this portrait. Martin and Person connect the dots: "The question is not so much whether such language points to a sexual relationship between the two men as it is how Melville's 'astonishingly sexual' response to Hawthorne helped him to represent a same-sex relationship in his novel and perhaps even revise that novel to make that relationship (not to mention the similar feelings expressed in 'A Squeeze of the Hand') such an important counterpoint to Ahab's monomaniacal quest for Moby Dick" (110).

I do not mean to suggest, of course, that Queequeg is intended literally to represent Hawthorne. The South Sea islander is certainly sufficiently "Other" to mask any such identification by readers. The audacity of Melville's reach in *Moby-Dick,* on the other hand, along with his well-known penchant for thrusting into novels-in-progress like *Mardi* and *Pierre* his immediate concerns (to the detriment of coherent plot) make it quite plausible that his idyllic picture of an intense, and in some respects taboo, male relationship stems from his feelings for Hawthorne. As in the case of Bulkington, Melville was not averse to inserting material that would clash with the rest of the novel if it suited his larger thematic purposes. Additionally, there are some elements of Ishmael and Queequeg's friendship that, once we allow for the boldness of Melville's conception, do hint at his relationship with Hawthorne. Their friendship initially warms as they turn over the leaves of a book together, stay up late in profound conversation, and—in the spirit of real taboo violation—smoke together in bed. One of Melville's letters anticipates getting Hawthorne "up in [his] snug room . . . & discussing the Universe with a bottle of brandy & cigars" (*WHM,* 14:180), and Hawthorne notes that, during a visit by Melville while his (Hawthorne's) wife was absent, they stayed up nearly all night and smoked cigars in the sitting room, which was strictly off-limits to tobacco.[17]

Most significant, however, as Martin and Person suggest, is the balance this ideal friendship offers to Ahab's quest. Through friendship with Queequeg, Ishmael's own quest is in fact triumphantly resolved before the *Pequod* sets out to sea, and he is transformed from a man with an Ahab-like alienation to a man at peace with himself and the world: "I began to be sensible of strange feelings. I felt a melting in me. No more my splintered heart and maddened hand were turned against the wolfish world. This soothing savage had redeemed it" (*WHM,* 6:51).

Melville's feelings of special kinship with Hawthorne sustained and inspired him during the turbulent period of *Moby-Dick*'s composition and allowed him to strike, if only momentarily, a counterpoise between the self-destructive and annihilating drive of Ahab and the drive toward merger and love represented by Queequeg's tattooed arm hugging Ishmael in bed. Indeed, through Ishmael and Queequeg's "marriage" Melville came close to realizing an ideal vision of social, racial, and sexual relations. As Martin aptly puts it in *Hero, Captain, and Stranger*: "The marriage of Queequeg and Ishmael is a vision of a triumphant miscegenation that can overcome the racial and sexual structures of American society. The novel is indeed tragic from the perspective of Ahab . . . but it is worth pointing out that it is also a pastoral vision of a restored harmony that might be achieved if only men would learn to love each other (individually and socially)."[18]

This vision is not sustained, of course, in the rest of the novel, but its relative lateness in the chronology of composition is supported by its only other transgressive depiction, Ishmael's mutual masturbation fantasy in chapter 94, "A Squeeze of the Hand," in which he kneads globules of sperm until "a strange sort of insanity" comes over him, and he begins squeezing the hands of his fellow workers. Then, "such an abounding, affectionate, friendly, loving feeling did this avocation beget; that at last I was continually squeezing their hands, and looking up into their eyes sentimentally; as much as to say . . . come; let us squeeze hands all round; nay, let us all squeeze ourselves into each other; let us squeeze ourselves universally into the very milk and sperm of kindness" (*WHM*, 6:416). This episode is rather clearly a later addition, interpolated in the beginning of the chapter and separated by a row of asterisks from the body of the text, which treats in a different tone and more technical way other aspects of preparing various parts of the whale for the tryworks—and thus probably belongs to the earlier whale fishery material.

One final implication of Queequeg's expanded early role has to do with the character of Ishmael himself: the friendship with Queequeg, their activities together, and Ishmael's religious, social, and racial musings about their relationship greatly extend his own part in the early narrative too. It seems unlikely that the original story devoted some twenty-one chapters and a hundred pages or so to activities that precede the ship's sailing, and Hayford is certainly correct in noting the many "unnecessary duplicates" that mark this section. The sheer length of the introductory section suggests that Melville probably reworked and added to it greatly, even to the degree that he altered the projected ending and changed the entire novel from an adventure story to a tragedy. In this context Ishmael qua Ishmael—that is, the outcast and orphan who survives to tell the tale—seems himself a later avatar of the original narrator, and his name, too, a late creation (as every reader notices, it almost never appears after the early chapters). If this is so, Melville may well have chosen the name for its racial suggestiveness as well as its biblical associations of outcast and exile: Ishmael was the son of Hagar, whose ethnic identity was often portrayed as African in nineteenth-century American popular culture and fiction.[19] For a contemporaneous audience, Ishmael's name would have had profound racial as well as religious connotations, strengthening his identification with the other outcast of color, Queequeg.

When it comes to charting the *Pequod*'s original course and the novel's original plot, there are fewer navigational aids than for determining how characters were modified or added. A number of factors contribute to this difference, but chief among them is the simple fact that a plot needs its conclusion or denouement to be complete, and there is no evidence that Melville had worked this out entirely at the point when his book was "mostly done"; his reconception of the novel may have begun before he had reached this crucial stage, particularly if the original plot involved a sudden turn attendant on a whale striking the ship. Additionally, a large portion of the original novel consisted, as Evert Duyckinck observed and as the evidence adduced earlier suggests, of a "presentment of the Whale Fishery," which could be worked up in fanciful, comic, or meditative ways (as in "The Monkey-Rope" or "The Whale as a Dish") without much need for a plot at all. Indeed, as Melville's previous novel *White-Jacket* had demonstrated, a successful book could be made of such details and incidents with but a very slender narrative thread.

These strictures notwithstanding, there are some indications of what the fate of the *Pequod* and its crew might have been had Ahab's doomed quest not become the book's driving concern. First, as mentioned before, it seems likely that if Peleg and Bildad were the original principal officers then the explicit tension between them—between the profane, irreligious, and possibly maimed Peleg and the parsimonious, profit- and religion-centered Bildad—would have been a major source of conflict in the plot. Peleg's abusive behavior toward the crew and Ishmael's reference to his "first kick," along with similar details in "The Town-Ho's Story," all suggest that, as in Melville's earlier novels, antagonism between the crew and the officers was a motive force in *Moby-Dick*'s original plot.

Sketch of the *Essex* being struck by the whale that sank it. By Thomas Nickerson, a survivor (November 20, 1820). Courtesy of the Nantucket Historical Association, T385.

It also seems probable that not all the crew perished in the original. To begin with, there is the implausibility of Ishmael's Ancient Mariner-like lone survival in the final version. And even if the previous plot had a whale striking the ship, there is no reason to think that this accident would have been fatal to the entire crew. In Melville's principal source for that episode, the sinking of the *Essex* by a whale in 1820, there is nothing to suggest the sort of cataclysmic vortex that ends *Moby-Dick:* indeed, as Nathaniel Philbrick's recent work on the *Essex* tragedy, *In the Heart of the Sea,* makes clear, the wooden ship naturally remained afloat for a couple of days, until it broke up in heavy seas, and the crew had plenty of time to modify the whaleboats and outfit them with supplies.[20] The tragedy as well as the notoriety of the *Essex* were due not so much to its being sunk by a whale as to the fate of its crew in the boats, who were rescued only after a long voyage during which some of them died of starvation and the survivors resorted to cannibalism.

Nor is it likely that the entire action of the novel was intended to take place on the ship alone. Melville emphasizes (in what is probably another shanty passage) the *Pequod*'s ability to sail almost indefinitely without touching land (chapter 87, "The Grand Armada"), but in fact whalers made landfall frequently to replenish water supplies, procure fresh food, and recruit new crew members. As Melville's own experience showed, deserting from whalers at such times was also common practice. It is fitting that the *Pequod* remain entirely at sea, emphasizing the solitary and concentrated nature of its commander's quest, but the plot of the original novel likely would have involved landfall(s), either as a matter of course ("If ye touch at the islands, Mr. Flask, beware of fornication," Bildad warns [*WHM*, 6:105]), or due to some emergency, such as the need to repair a leaky ship or one damaged by a whale. Again, the conclusion of "The Town-Ho's Story" holds clues to possible elements of the original plot. After Moby Dick kills the mate, Radney, the mistreated sailors, led by their champion Steelkilt, desert when the ship lands on a tropical island to mend a serious leak. The captain sets out in a whaleboat to Tahiti to recruit new crew members but is stopped on the high seas by Steelkilt, who makes him promise to wait six days before continuing, giving Steelkilt time to sail to Tahiti and enlist on a French ship about to sail. Eventually the captain arrives in Tahiti, takes on new crew members, and resumes his whaling cruise.

It has long been a commonplace that the sinking of the *Essex* provided Melville with the factual basis for a whale sinking a ship, especially since he read Owen Chase's narrative of the disaster while he was a sailor in the Pacific and actually saw Chase and met his son. However, less attention has accrued to the larger story of the *Essex* as a potential source for the *plot* of *Moby-Dick*—especially the possibility that the original may have featured, like the story of the *Essex,* the long-term consequences of the whale strike. The fact that both the mutineers and the captain of the *Town-Ho* sail directly to Tahiti after their encounter with Moby Dick and beach the ship for repairs corrects in fact what Melville himself surmised (in his manuscript notes) was the fatal error of the Essex crew: "All the sufferings of these miserable men of the Essex might, in all human probability, have been avoided, had they, immediately after leaving the wreck, steered straight for Tahiti" (*WHM*, 6:992).

There is further evidence that Melville made a direct connection between the aftermath of the sinking of the *Essex* and his own novel-in-progress, for one of his erased pencil marginal notes to page 184 of Beale's *Natural History of the Sperm Whale,* recently recovered by Steven Olsen-Smith, reads "'Killers' dragging the whale away from the vortex (Ex —?—])," which seems to suggest that the whale killers or mates managed to tow the dead whale out of the vortex in which the ship sank, with a reference to the *Essex* ("Ex"). If this is the case, the crew of the *Pequod* would have been, like the crew of the *Essex,* left on the ocean with only the whaleboats after the attack on the ship.[21]

Since Melville attempted to procure both Chase's narrative of the sinking of the *Essex* and another volume titled *A Narrative of the Mutiny, on Board the Ship Globe* some time in late 1850, he likely was thinking about such incidents in relation to the plot of his novel then under way (*WHM,* 6:972). The *Globe* narrative recounts the captain's cruelty toward the crew, followed by a brutal mutiny and the crew's eventual capture by Pacific islanders—all of which could plausibly have furnished details for early versions of a plot resembling "The Town-Ho's Story." The possibility of cannibalism pursuant to a long voyage in open boats may even explain the existence of such a character as Queequeg in the original narrative, before he underwent his metamorphosis into Ishmael's noble friend.

There was still another source for a *Town-Ho*-like plot that Melville knew from personal experience, as related in *Mardi* in the chapter on the swordfish, "Xiphius Platypterus": "With the Rousseau, of Nantucket, it fared worse. She was almost mortally stabbed [by a swordfish]; her assailant withdrawing his blade. And it was only by keeping the pumps clanging, that she managed to swim into a Tahitian harbor, 'heave down,' and have her wound dressed by a ship-surgeon with tar and oakum. This ship I met with at sea, shortly after the disaster" (*WHM,* 3:105). How far such a plot—if it ever existed in the narrative—was developed before Melville fixed on the cataclysmic conclusion to his tragedy can probably never be known. So much of the novel is unrelated to any plot—either actual or hypothetical—that this question appears less significant than the metamorphosis the main characters apparently underwent. The principal evidence, insofar as I have been able to isolate and analyze it here, suggests the addition or revision of characters who were capable of embodying Melville's desire to write a heroically ambitious book that was at once epic, democratic, and tragic. Enough of this overarching energy and ambition is present throughout the novel to render the experience of reading it (depending upon the reader, of course) a unified and not a fragmentary experience. Once the "great flood-gates of the wonder-world" have "swung open" (*WHM,* 6:7), the reader is not likely to be distracted by the fact that the *Pequod* sometimes has four boats and sometimes three, or that Queequeg lives adjacent to the officers' cabin at one point and in the forecastle at another. In the Melvillean world, to notice such things makes one a bit of a sub-sub-librarian.

Melville's own literary theory that, as he put it in "Hawthorne and His Mosses," "it is better to fail in originality, than to succeed in imitation" (*WHM*, 9:247) authorized his ambitious experiments in *Moby-Dick* and doubtless tended to make him rest somewhat easier about the rough edges and tool marks he left behind. There are even places, as in Bulkington's "six-inch chapter," where he flaunts the inconsistency of the text, confidently subsuming it under a higher goal of striving for an originality of thought that avoids the "slavish shore," not so implicitly suggesting that, in good romantic fashion, the real hero is the artist himself. To be understood by the ideal friend and reader, hypothesized as Nathaniel Hawthorne, was his dearest hope—amply realized, it appears, in Hawthorne's famously missing letter to Melville about *Moby-Dick*. Hawthorne's praise, reflected in Melville's well-known response to this missing letter, enabled him to close the circle—at least momentarily—both on the book with which he had struggled for two years and on his yearning for closeness with Hawthorne: "A sense of unspeakable security is in me this moment, on account of your having understood the book. I have written a wicked book, and feel spotless as the lamb" (*WHM*, 14:212).

Notes

1. Duyckinck was presumably the author of the two-part review of *Moby-Dick* that appeared in the *Literary World* on November 15 and 22, 1851. There, he continued to praise the description of the whale fishery and the book's romantic and humorous aspects while expressing reservations about the symbolic and allegorical elements in Ahab's story and about Ishmael's philosophical and religious musings.

2. Parker, *Herman Melville*, 1:839–40.

3. Emerson, *Journals and Miscellaneous Notebooks*, 9:71.

4. Twain, *Tragedy of Pudd'nhead Wilson*, 311.

5. Bryant, "Politics, Imagination, and the Fluid Text," 91; Bryant, *Fluid Text*, 9.

6. The history of scholarship on this topic is detailed in section 5 of the "Historical Note" to the Northwestern-Newberry edition of *Moby-Dick* (*WHM*,

6:648–59), but major interpretations deserve special mention. Howard first called attention to the extended gestation of the book in "Melville's Struggle with the Angel"; George R. Stewart coined the term "Ur-*Moby-Dick*" in "The Two *Moby-Dicks*" and established the pattern of looking at various sections of the novel as belonging to the earliest or the later stages of composition. Stewart's work was expanded and challenged by James Barbour in his 1970 dissertation, later redacted as "The Composition of *Moby-Dick*"; working primarily with Melville's use of source material, Barbour discerned not two but three *Moby-Dicks* (345), but he still emphasized the more or less discrete and self-contained nature of the different sections. My work is closest and most indebted to Hayford's in "Unnecessary Duplicates." Hayford pointed out the striking number of "unnecessary duplicates" in the novel's early chapters (duplicate captains, duplicate companions for Ishmael, duplicate whaling towns, and so on) as a key to figuring out the changing character roles in the novel's development. An inference I draw from Hayford's observations is that it is likely the early chapters were much more heavily revised than previous accounts have assumed and thus belong to both the earliest and the latest stages of composition. Not all scholars have accepted the notion that different versions can be inferred from the completed text; see especially Milder, "Composition of *Moby-Dick*," and Markels, "*Moby-Dick* White Elephant."

7. Melville had *Moby-Dick* stereotyped himself, and these plates served as the basis for the first American edition. He then had proof sheets struck to send to England for the first English edition. He was able to make changes on these proof sheets for the English edition—published first for copyright reasons—that he was unable to make for the first American edition, since they would have involved considerable replating expense. Thus the unusual situation of revisions appearing in an earlier edition (English) that do not appear in a later edition (American).

8. Parker, *Herman Melville*, 1:843.

9. Whalers bound for the Pacific normally took advantage of prevailing trade winds and sailed southeasterly across the Atlantic to the Azores and/or the Cape Verde islands, where they would take on supplies and sometimes additional crew members. They would then double back across the Atlantic on the corresponding trade winds of the Southern Hemisphere to round Cape Horn and enter the Pacific. The *Pequod* follows this route as far as the coast of South America (she is sited off the Rio de la Plata near Argentina in chapter 51), then without explanation reverses course and sails east again to round the Cape of Good Hope (*WHM*, 6:232–35).

10. It must also be noted that Melville added whaling material after changing his conception of the work, for as Barbour has indicated he did not acquire

his principal cetological source, Thomas Beale's *Natural History of the Sperm Whale,* until the summer of 1850 and probably was not able to use the Beale material until resuming work on the novel in the fall ("'All My Books Are Botches,'" 41–43).

11. Hayford, "Unnecessary Duplicates," 130; hereafter cited parenthetically.

12. See Melville's Marginalia Online, ed. Olsen-Smith, http://www.boisestate .edu/melville (accessed August 7, 2007).

13. Barbour, "'All My Books Are Botches,'" 45.

14. This is another anomaly in the text, for in chapter 44, "The Chart," we are told it was during the "Season-on-the-Line" (that is, on the equator) that Ahab lost his leg to Moby Dick (*WHM,* 6:201).

15. Barbour, "*Town-Ho's* Story," 111–15; hereafter cited parenthetically. Vincent was the first to make this suggestion, in *Trying-Out of "Moby-Dick,"* 46.

16. Arvin, *Herman Melville,* 138; Martin and Person, "Missing Letters," esp. 100. The Martin/Person essay, hereafter cited parenthetically, is the afterword to a special issue devoted to the Hawthorne-Melville relationship. For extended treatments of this subject, see also Miller, *Melville;* Martin, *Hero, Captain, and Stranger;* and Milder, "'Ugly Socrates,'" originally published in the issue of *ESQ* just cited and revised for the present volume.

17. Parker, *Herman Melville,* 1:853.

18. Martin, *Hero, Captain, and Stranger,* 94.

19. See Gabler-Hover, *Dreaming Black/Writing White.*

20. Philbrick, *In the Heart of the Sea,* 92–103.

21. Melville's Marginalia Online; http://www.boisestate.edu/melville (accessed August 7, 2007).

Genealogical Fictions

Race in *The House of the Seven Gables* and *Pierre*

ROBERT S. LEVINE

HAWTHORNE'S *The House of the Seven Gables* and Melville's *Pierre* pose challenges to cultural memory by questioning the genealogical histories and legacies of the fathers. Both novels depict what appears to be a thriving, prosperous, democratic United States, and both ultimately suggest that beneath that happy surface lies an ambiguous history of violation, deceit, and racial entanglement. In *House*, we learn that the esteemed Judge Pyncheon, like his esteemed distant forbear Colonel Pyncheon, is a thief, and that the thievery of both men props up a white genealogical line that is more mixed and provisional than either is willing to allow. In *Pierre*, there are suggestions that Pierre's father may have had a daughter out of wedlock who may be "black" and that his grandfather, a Revolutionary War hero, may have had sexual relations with his slaves. Like William Wells Brown, Hannah Crafts, Harriet Beecher Stowe, and other antislavery writers of the period, Hawthorne and Melville encourage the reader to take seriously the talk and perspectives of those on the margins. For as Hawthorne remarks in *House*, access to sites of exclusion and repression, to the truths of conflict and power, may best be found in "private diurnal gossip" (*CE*, 2:122).

To some extent, "gossip" has dominated discussions of the interconnections between *House* and *Pierre*, with the focus being on the story line, adumbrated by Edwin Haviland Miller and others, of Melville's unrequited love for Hawthorne. To take two representative instances: John Seelye argues that *Pierre* expresses Melville's "passionate feelings for Hawthorne," while Robert Milder proclaims that the novel allowed

The House of the Seven Gables in Salem, Massachusetts (c. 1918). Courtesy of the Library of Congress, Prints and Photographs Division, LC-USZ62-115767.

Melville "to excavate the foundations of his attachment to Hawthorne." Criticism on Melville's impact on *House* tends similarly toward the personal. Thomas Mitchell argues that *House* constitutes Hawthorne's peeved rejection of the "darkness Melville had admired" in "Hawthorne and His Mosses," and Brenda Wineapple sees Melville in Hawthorne's characterization of Holgrave. While I do not dispute that the intense short-term friendship between Hawthorne and Melville had an impact on their writing, I'm concerned that an overly biographical focus on the respective writers' "feelings" about each other obscures the fact that their novels embraced actual contemporary subjects and concerns and were about something other than each other. When read together, *House* and *Pierre* emerge as part of a literary conversation between these great writers on questions of racial and national identity. I reject the notion that *Pierre*, as Wineapple puts it, is an "inversion" of *House* and contend that *House* prompted Melville to think more deeply about race. In *Pierre,* Melville does not subvert but rather extends Hawthorne's designs by opening some doors of the "fine old chamber" (Melville's playful term for *House*) that Hawthorne may have preferred to keep closed.[1] The current critical binary that conceives of Hawthorne as an inveterate racist and Melville as a visionary progressive is in need of reconsideration.

Hawthorne of course embraced Jacksonian democracy during the early 1820s, became friends with a number of the men who would emerge as the leading Democrats of their time, found employment with the help of Democrats, and eventually wrote the campaign biography of his friend Franklin Pierce, which led to a plum political appointment as U.S. consul to Liverpool in 1853. Much to the detriment of his reputation, Hawthorne has been reviled by a number of critics for his apparent commitment to the racist, compromising Unionism of the majority wing of the Democratic party and for his earlier association with the jingoistic and racist writers of the *Democratic Review*. While I readily concede that anyone reading through all of Hawthorne's journals and letters would be able to find troubling statements about slavery and race, I want to raise questions about the ahistorical flattening of Hawthorne's views by complicating our sense of his Democratic politics.[2]

Though it is conventionally argued that the Democrats supported the slavery system, the fact is that there was much dissent among Democrats about slavery, and that dissent was consistent with the radical energies that contributed to the founding of the Democratic party. Influential Democratic writers of the 1820s and 1830s, such as William Leggett, George Henry Evans, and Thomas Morris, attacked monopolies and other forms of concentrated power and saw connections between the "monstrous" First Bank of America and the slave power. In a recent revisionary study, the historian Jonathan Earle provides substantial evidence that Free Soil politics, and not the expansionism of John O'Sullivan's *Democratic Review*, can be taken as the culmination of the Jacksonian principles that Hawthorne and many others had initially found so inspiring during the 1820s. David Wilmot, the Pennsylvania congressman whose proviso came close to banning slavery from the territories taken from Mexico, was a Democrat. His proviso passed the House on a vote of 77-58, and, though it was eventually defeated, there was significant support for the proviso in the Senate as well. Numerous Democrats who had fought the First Bank and other monopolies found themselves moving toward the emerging Free Soil party, and these Free Soilers, Earle writes, "opposed the perpetuation of slavery wherever it existed, rejected racist arguments justifying bondage, and insisted on the basic humanity of African Americans."[3]

While Hawthorne remained true to his close friend Franklin Pierce, there is evidence that he was increasingly sympathetic to the Free Soil

position. During the late 1840s Hawthorne was the corresponding secretary for the Salem Lyceum, and in January 1849 he arranged for Free
Soiler Charles Sumner to give a lecture titled "The Law of Human Progress." Sumner had delivered the same lecture in July 1848 before the Phi
Beta Kappa Society of Union College in Schenectady, New York, one
month after he had condemned "that combination of persons, or, perhaps, of politicians, whose animating principle is the perpetuation and
extension of Slavery, with the advancement of Slaveholders." In "The Law
of Human Progress," Sumner, known for his radicalism, urges a patient
antislavery course in the manner that Hawthorne would adopt in his
campaign biography of Pierce: "Nothing is accomplished except by time
and exertion. Nature abhors violence and suddenness."[4]

Though there is no record of Hawthorne's response to this lecture,
he maintained his admiration for Sumner into the 1850s. Writing Longfellow on May 8, 1851, Hawthorne remarks that he is dismayed by the
Fugitive Slave Law, which Pierce had supported, and that he is therefore
heartened by Sumner's successful campaign for the Senate: "How glad
I am that Sumner is at last elected!" (CE, 16:431). Two months later, in
a letter of July 15, 1851, that is regularly cited as evidence for his racism,
Hawthorne elaborates to his friend Zachariah Burchmore on the politics
of slavery, race, and Free Soil: "I have not, as you suggest, the slightest
sympathy for the slaves; or, at least, not half so much as for the laboring
whites, who, I believe, as a general thing, are ten times worse off than the
Southern negros. Still, whenever I am absolutely cornered, I shall go for
New England rather than the South;—and this Fugitive Law cornered
me. Of course, I knew what I was doing when I signed that Free-Soil
document, and bade farewell to all ideas of foreign consulships, or other
official stations" (CE, 16:456). This is a contradictory letter that reveals a
more progressive Hawthorne than we usually imagine. His avowed lack
of sympathy for the slaves is qualified with respect to the white working
class (with the suggestion that that "lack" is relative and not absolute),
and then is further qualified by a statement of his opposition to the Fugitive Slave Law (which suggests some commitment to antislavery), and
then is qualified even further by the surprising revelation, which is usually not noted by those intent on putting Hawthorne's racism on display,
that he had signed a Free Soil document that threatened to keep him
permanently unemployed. Significantly, he signed that document shortly
after he published The House of the Seven Gables and right around the
time he met Herman Melville.

Although Hawthorne and Melville are often presented in the critical literature as diametrical opposites on the political spectrum (Hawthorne as "conservative" Democrat, Melville as "radical" cosmopolitan), there is no equivalent in Melville's life to Hawthorne's signing of a Free Soil petition. To be sure, Melville mocked the expansionism of General Zachary Taylor in his 1847 "Authentic Anecdotes of 'Old Zack'" and pointed to the historical and social evils of slavery in *Typee, Mardi, Redburn,* and *White-Jacket.* Still, he was hardly known as a political firebrand. Like Hawthorne, who was celebrated by O'Sullivan in the *Democratic Review,* Melville had a place in the American literary nationalist program of the writers and editors associated with the "Young America" circles of the *Democratic Review* and the *Literary World.* Melville's first novel, *Typee,* was published by O'Sullivan's New York friend Evert A. Duyckinck in Wiley and Putnam's Library of American Books series. It was Duyckinck and his friends who arranged for Melville to meet Hawthorne at a Stockbridge picnic on August 5, 1850, and it was Duyckinck who arranged later that month for the publication in the *Literary World* of Melville's literary nationalist "Hawthorne and His Mosses."[5]

A relatively short and intense friendship ensued between Hawthorne and Melville from late 1850 through 1852. Melville shared with Hawthorne his struggles over *Moby-Dick,* which he dedicated to Hawthorne, and Hawthorne, like Melville, was chagrined by Duyckinck's unappreciative review of *Moby-Dick* in the *Literary World.*[6] If Melville had second thoughts about the literary program of Young America, that review certainly helped him to make his break, and he would satirize Duyckinck's tame version of American literary nationalism in *Pierre.* Meanwhile, Hawthorne shared *The House of the Seven Gables* with Melville, and though we do not have Hawthorne's side of the correspondence, we do have Melville's letter to Hawthorne on his initial reading of *House.* For those who see *House* as a genteel performance, Melville seems to be reading something other than *House,* or else (as I prefer to think) reading it more deeply than most. In his April 16, 1851, letter on the novel, Melville declares in the spirit of "Hawthorne and His Mosses": "There is the grand truth about Nathaniel Hawthorne. He says NO! in thunder; but the Devil himself cannot make him say *yes.*" Melville's most specific comment on the novel comes in the letter's P.S.: "The marriage of Phoebe with the daguerreotypist is a fine stroke, because of his turning out to be a *Maule.* If you pass Hepzibah's cent-shop, buy me a Jim Crow (fresh) and send it *to* me by Ned Higgins" (*WHM,* 14:187). It is noteworthy that

Melville invokes Jim Crow without specifically referring to issues of slavery and race. And yet his conjoining of the marriage and Jim Crow suggests that Melville was interested in the conjunction of genealogical history and race, issues that, as he well understood, were central to Hawthorne's *House*.

The House of the Seven Gables has traditionally been regarded as Hawthorne's most upbeat celebration of the nation's middle-class values. But as a genealogical fiction, it deserves to be better understood as a novel that poses considerable challenges to the orthodoxies of the day. Begun right around the time the Fugitive Slave Law was adopted as the law of the land, and completed shortly before Hawthorne expressed a surprising solidarity with the Free Soilers, *House* can be read, in part, as a questioning of the blood-based Anglo-Saxonist nationalism and expansionism of the O'Sullivan Young American crowd and of the many others, Democrat or otherwise, who shared their views. Whereas writers in the *Democratic Review* had argued in support of the War with Mexico and other expansionist ventures by invoking what one writer proclaimed as the "inevitable destiny" and "virtues of the Anglo-Saxon race,"[7] *House* challenges beliefs in the superiority of Anglo-Saxon "blood" and remains highly unclear, even suspicious, about whether race even exists as a workable category of human identity and difference. In this and other respects, the novel is unrelentingly *political* in its vision of race and nation. The novel's narrative strategies encourage resistant readings of the "accepted" social truths of racial and class hierarchies and thus can be tied to a democratic reading practice that we tend to undervalue in Hawthorne and that has its sources in the radical antiaristocratic Jacksonianism of the 1820s and 1830s that attracted him to the party in the first place.

As presented by the narrator, there are two genealogically figured "racial" families in the novel, the Pyncheons and the Maules, and one of these families, or races, would seem to have triumphed over the other. But how biologically distinct or distinctive are these racially described families? And to what extent is Hawthorne invested in a blood-based or racial politics of heredity? In influential early analyses of the topic, Roy Male argued that Hawthorne "assumed that heredity factors are somehow transmitted 'in the blood,'" and Frank Kermode similarly argued that Hawthorne believed in different and separate racial "types."[8] And yet if *House* emphasizes anything, it is just how difficult it is to trace the flow of blood in order to make such "scientific" distinctions. In language that Melville would draw on for *Pierre*, the narrator compares the "original" Maule's bloodlines to the ebbing flow of a river: "His blood might possibly exist elsewhere; here, where its lowly current could be traced so far back, it had ceased to keep an onward course" (*CE*, 2:26). In this regard, it is crucial to note that the Pyncheons over the decades have married outside of their family, and the Pyncheons central to the present of the story—Hepzibah, Clifford, Jaffrey, and Phoebe—are not in the direct line of Colonel Pyncheon; instead, they are various "little offshoot[s] of the Pyncheon race" (*CE*, 2:69). Their blood already has been dispersed, mixed, dissipated. Heredity may provide one possible way of understanding Judge Jaffrey Pyncheon's similarities to Colonel Pyncheon, but the narrator more crucially emphasizes that the key connection between the judge and the colonel is their similar imbrication in their respective culture's institutions of power, as manifested by the apoplexy that plagues so many in the genealogical house of Pyncheon (but not the marginalized Hepzibah, Clifford, or Phoebe).

As Hawthorne makes clear, the narrator and the purveyors of "gossip" are critically distant from the Pyncheon elites, the blood thinkers whose "eugenicism" and expansionism must therefore be taken as one of the novel's *subjects*, not its donnée. Rather than subscribing to blood thinking in the manner of the Pyncheons, Hawthorne takes pains throughout the novel to raise questions about the very notion of blood purity and superiority that the Pyncheons deploy to legitimate their power over others. A key image of their prideful ambition is the portrait of Colonel Pyncheon hanging in the House of the Seven Gables, which puts on perpetual display the Pyncheon desire to naturalize connections between blood (the genealogical house) and rank (the house itself and the additional money and property that such connections between blood and rank enable). In some respects that portrait does help to suggest the resemblances between the current principal representative of the Pyncheon line, Judge Jaffrey Pyncheon, and Colonel Pyncheon. But even as Hepzibah and Phoebe see connections between the flesh-and-blood judge and the portrait of the colonel, the narrator takes pains to present the genealogical (or blood) basis of their insights as fanciful. When Hepzibah, for instance, believes she discerns a blood transmission of character from the founding Pyncheon to the judge, the narrator, by inserting a parenthetical "at least, she fancied so" and by mocking her "hereditary reverence" (CE, 2:59), raises questions about the validity of thinking in such terms. After all, if her theory of blood transmission makes sense, it would have equal implications for Hepzibah and Clifford, who are just as much in the genealogical line of Colonel Pyncheon as Jaffrey.

Hawthorne did turn to contemporaneous genetic thought for two main figures of inheritance and transmission in the novel: the garden (with its imagery of planting and seeds) and the animals within the garden (Chanticleer and the family of fowl). But even here, Hawthorne seeks to show that genetics complicates rather than clarifies questions of bloodlines. The description of the garden's confusion, and a submerged confusion at that, emphasizes that the seeds and roots of various flowers mix with the seeds and roots of other flowers and that the waters of Maule's Well take on other waters. In this light, the merging of Alice's poesies with Maule's Well, viewed by some readers as Hawthorne's forecasting of a purifying happy ending of the novel, might more accurately be taken as a figuring of a mysteriously lurid intermixture of that which is already intermixed. Where purity does seem to be preserved is in the novel's most insistently eugenicist figure, that of the Pyncheons' Chanticleer and his fellow fowl, who are presented as a familial "race" bred in the way that Colonel Pyncheon hoped to breed the Pyncheons: through a form of inbreeding that would preserve the aristocratic blood purity that he regarded as legitimating the Pyncheons' claims on Maule's and the Indians' lands. Hawthorne underscores the parallels between the Pyncheons and their "self-important" fowl (CE, 2:152) by comically exaggerating Chanticleer's Pyncheon-like qualities, and in this way, Shawn Michelle Smith notes, he casts "an obsession with blood purity and ancestral inheritance as the cornerstone of aristocratic malady."[9] Both the fowl and the Pyncheons are presented as degenerating, but the Pyncheons' degeneration has nothing to do with inbreeding but instead with their conception of themselves as aristocrats who shouldn't have to exert themselves because of their claims on the extensive lands supposedly deeded them by Indians. Concepts of genetic purity might be vaguely workable with a controlled animal population, but the emphasis in House is on how bloodlines in human populations become too mixed up, too hidden, to account in easy ways for the behavior that supposedly is passed along through a house or "race."

In The House of the Seven Gables, racial imagery is everywhere, and Hawthorne's use of that imagery, I am arguing, generally destabilizes

racial categories, whether he is addressing matters of family (the respective "races" of the Pyncheons and the Maules) or the binary of whiteness
and nonwhiteness underpinning American literary nationalist and expansionist projects of the period. Whereas Colonel Pyncheon aspires to
fix "his race and future generations" on the stable basis of "the Pyncheon
blood" (*CE*, 2:17, 2:18), Hawthorne suggests just how unstable, mixed, or
even "black" that blood is. Jaffrey, we are told, inherited from the "dark,
high-featured countenance" of the colonel, indeed, from the "black and
heavy-browed" House of the Seven Gables itself, a "black stain of blood"
(*CE*, 2:43, 2:81, 2:23); and throughout the novel there is an emphasis on
the "blackness" that lurks beneath Judge Jaffrey Pyncheon's display of
whiteness. Thus while Jaffrey regularly displays "a white neckcloth of
the utmost snowy purity" (*CE*, 2:116), it is the darkness or blackness that
prevails. Like the house itself, he is "dark-browed," and like the founding
patriarch, he has a "dark, full-fed physiognomy" (*CE*, 2:118).

This vision of the fluid, shifting, and uncertain nature of race in-
forms one of the cruxes of the novel: Holgrave's (Maule's) story of Alice
Pyncheon as told to Phoebe Pyncheon. There are obvious and much-
discussed parallels between Holgrave's telling of his story to Phoebe and
the story's account of Matthew Maule's "enslavement" of Alice. In both
cases, we have characters who are using their "Black Art" against para-
gons of white femininity (*CE*, 2:84), with Holgrave choosing ultimately
to resist the temptation to exert his powers over the mesmerized Phoebe.
It is significant in this regard that Matthew Maule is linked with black
Scipio and in certain respects is depicted as "blacker" than Scipio. As David Anthony notes, Scipio is presented for the most part in terms of the
"basic tropes of minstrelsy and racial performance."[10] But it is precisely
the sense that race is performed, or mediated by mass-circulated images,
that makes race such a provisional and hard-to-define category in the
story (and overall novel). What is clear is that Scipio exhibits the class superiority of his master by challenging Maule's use of the front entrance,
which only stokes the anger of Maule to the point that he is described as
"black." Unnerved by his effrontery, Scipio demands of Maule, "[W]hat
for do you look so black at me?" Maule's response only further undercuts
fixed notions of race: "Do you think nobody is to look black but yourself?" (*CE*, 2:188). If anyone can look or even be "black," then what exactly does the term mean? And if the Maules are presented as one "race"
and the Pyncheons as another, then what is the difference between the

two when Gervayse Pyncheon, a slaveholder himself, is willing to "sell" his daughter to Maule with the hope of recovering the lost Indian deed, while Maule, angered by his misperception of Alice's class superiority, is willing to use his mesmerical skills to make her into what Holgrave calls "Maule's slave" (*CE*, 2:208). The two "races" seem at one here; they are both drinking each other's blood. In a Hegelian mode, Hawthorne powerfully underscores the enslaving dimensions of mastery itself.

With his account of the rape of Alice by "black" Maule (with the help of Alice's "black" father), Holgrave further complicates questions of bloodlines both within and beyond the frame of the story. Remarking that Gervayse married a "lady of fortune" while in England (*CE*, 2:190), he chooses not to convey details of the new Mrs. Pyncheon's genealogical history. It remains unclear whether she is even English, for she and Gervayse educate their daughter, termed "an exotic" (*CE*, 2:191), in Italy. Given that their daughter dies, that would seem to be the end of the direct flow of the Pyncheon bloodlines. So the question given new impetus by this story is where did the other Pyncheons of the novel come from? What exactly is their connection to the founding line, and how "pure" was that founding line anyway?

The death of Judge Jaffrey Pyncheon shortly after the telling of the story brings these questions sharply into focus but, as anticipated in the tangled imagery of the Pyncheon garden, with no clear answer in sight. Presented as the very embodiment of what his allegedly murdered uncle had regarded as the "black stain of blood" in the Pyncheon family tree, Judge Pyncheon would appear to be in the genealogical line of the colonel, given the nature of his actions and the "blackness" that matches the "dark countenance" of the colonel's portrait (*CE*, 2:36). Like the colonel, the judge himself dies of apoplexy while in the throes of greed, and thus Hawthorne holds onto notions of biological determinism or heritability as a possible way of thinking about Pyncheon genealogies while also signaling in no uncertain terms that greed can do great damage to the body. The one thing that Hawthorne clearly is *not* suggesting in the racial imagery of the overall novel is that Anglo-Saxon whiteness transmits itself across the centuries in a "pure" form that makes one family, or "race," better than or essentially different from another. Sitting beneath the dark portrait of Colonel Pyncheon, the dead judge initially exhibits what the narrator terms a "singularly white" countenance (*CE*, 2:276). But that countenance changes as the narrator gazes upon the dead body, turning from white to what the narrator calls a "swarthy whiteness" and a "swarthily white visage" (*CE*, 2:276, 2:295). Anthony nicely posits that the narrative descriptions of the dead judge's transformation from whiteness to swarthy whiteness are meant to represent "a failed last moment in the maintenance of upper-class whiteness" (264). From beginning to end, I would suggest, the novel suggests precisely the difficulty, indeed the impossibility, of maintaining such a genealogical fiction given the unknowability of bloodlines and the inevitability of blood intermixture.

But if Hawthorne uses his descriptions of the judge's blackening white face to undercut the fictions of whiteness, what are we to make of the novel's ending, which, in its happy and escapist marriage of Holgrave/Maule and Phoebe, has been regarded by many readers as Hawthorne's own escape from the darker and more challenging implications of his novel? Punningly stating that Hawthorne "plants the seed of a theory of biological inheritance newly articulated by biological racialists in the first half of the nineteenth century" (50), Smith links Hawthorne by association to Colonel Pyncheon but also, through the image of the seed, to what she describes as the "eugenicists' romance of Anglo-Saxon superiority at the turn of the century" (41). And yet if we resist linking *House* to the cultural narratives that we know will sprout from the seeds of mid-nineteenth-century Anglo-Saxonism and instead, as I have been urging, read the novel at its moment of production as a critical engagement with the genealogical fictions of a "pure" and "better" Anglo-Saxonism, the ending is not as conventional as it seems. After all, Hawthorne leaves us not with two characters—a loving couple—choosing to live together happily ever after but with five characters, three of whom are elderly and two of whom are brother and sister. In the prophetic pictures evoked at the end of the novel, there is no mention of the children to come from Holgrave/Maule and Phoebe or of the desire to "plant" a family. Moreover, given that Holgrave and Phoebe are presented in the novel as exemplars of two different "races," it is difficult not to see some hinting at cross-racial mixing in Hawthorne's final disposition of the lovers. Significantly, the only progeny mentioned at the novel's end are those that will be produced by the Pyncheon fowls at the judge's country seat, the suggestion being that Holgrave and Phoebe represent the possibility of something much different from the fowl, especially given Phoebe's genealogical distance from the founding Pyncheon. The five characters moving to the judge's former home do not engage in blood talk; they have no immediate aspirations to do anything other than begin to make sense of their rapidly transformed situations. Family, community, and national histories remain to be written; new seeds may be in the process of being planted; but no one can declare with any sort of confidence what those seeds are, how they are to be nourished, or what will sprout. Entanglement and confusion remain the order of the day, and there's nothing necessarily poisonous about that.

Or would Melville beg to differ on precisely this point, given that his novel of genealogical entanglement and confusion ends with poison? Published less than a year after *The House of the Seven Gables*, Melville's *Pierre*, in part because of that ending, has generally been taken as a novel that "responds" to *House* by pointing to its limitations. The argument that Melville to some extent parodies *House* through a series of strategic inversions could be supported, for example, by noting that Hawthorne's announced generational theme of *House* is revoiced in *Pierre* by the morally shallow and hypocritical Reverend Falsgrave: "'The sins of the father shall be visited upon the children to the third generation'" (*WHM*, 7:100). But that revoicing could also be taken as Melville's wink to Hawthorne on what he and Hawthorne both knew were the sorts of moral bromides that Hawthorne felt he had to offer his readers in a preface. Rather than seeing Melville as trying to subvert or "invert" Hawthorne, I will be arguing that in crucial respects *Pierre* develops some of the more complex and culturally adversarial dimensions of *House*.

There are numerous parallels between *House* and *Pierre* as genealogical fictions, such as the use of portraiture to illuminate (and call into doubt) family history, the importance of rumor in unfixing that history, and the broad consideration of American (literary) nationalism and race. Both novels frame questions of blood in relation to what Hawthorne presents as aspirations to "plant" a family through a kind of eugenicist breeding. Given the importance of motifs of breeding to both novels, I would suggest that the "seed" of *Pierre* may well have been the description in *House* of Chanticleer's "two wives" and their one chicken, which "looked small enough to be still in the egg, and, at the same time, sufficiently old, withered, wizened, and experienced, to have been the founder of the antiquated race" (*CE*, 2:88, 2:152, 2:151). That bred chicken can be taken as a prefiguration of Pierre. Invested in her chicken as both the exemplar and possibly last of the "illustrious race" (*CE*, 2:152), the mother hen of *House* speaks to the Pyncheons' pride in their "race" but also anticipates *Pierre*'s Mary Glendinning, who obsessively regards Pierre as the last best hope of her "race" (the Glendinnings). From the opening of the novel to the point of her despairing renunciation of her son, Mary "glorifie[s] the rare and absolute merits of Pierre," seeing him as "the choicest guild of his race" and thus in need of constant guidance so that he would remain true to what she would like to believe is a genealogy "wherein is no *flaw*" (*WHM*, 7:15, 7:16, 7:11). But let us not forget about Chanticleer's second wife!

The possibility that his heretofore highly revered father may himself have had a second "wife," or mistress, haunts Pierre, and nowhere are his concerns more acutely on display than in a scene at the midpoint of the novel that to some extent parallels the moment late in *House* in which the dead Judge Pyncheon is transformed from white to "swarthy" beneath the ambiguous portrait of the colonel. Preparing to journey to New York City with the black-haired, "olive"-complected Isabel Banford (*WHM*, 7:46), Pierre at the Black Swan Inn contemplates a chair portrait of his father from his happier bachelor days. Convinced by the circumstantial evidence of Isabel's story that his father had had a premarital affair and fathered Isabel, Pierre suddenly comes to see all that his mother has been celebrating—the glorious Glendinning family genealogy, and indeed his own identity as exemplar of the race—as little more than a fraud. Enraged at his father, Pierre drops the canvas into a flaming hearth, taking satisfaction in "the first crispings and blackenings of the painted scroll." But when his father's blackened face on the canvas seems to look at him "in beseeching horror," Pierre makes a last-minute unsuccessful effort to save the portrait, which leaves one of his hands "burnt and blackened" (*WHM*, 7:198). He later notices that Isabel's hand too is mysteriously blackened. At the Black Swan Inn, Pierre discovers (or so he thinks he discovers, for the novel remains forever ambiguous on the matter) that what joins him to Isabel is not just that they have a common father (if in fact they do) but, as suggested by their mutually blackened hands, that they are of a common "race" (if in fact one can ever know one's racial identity). Melville's subtle troubling of the connections between whiteness and familial identity in early national and antebellum culture, his exploration of the connections among genealogical history, racial identity, and ultimately national identity, particularly in the first

half of the novel, emerged in significant ways from his imaginative response to Hawthorne's *House*.[11]

Both *Pierre* and *House* begin with detailed genealogical histories, and
Melville's use of such history anticipates the novel's depictions of Pierre's
and Isabel's blackened hands. Initially speaking in the jingoistic voice of
the American literary nationalist, Melville in the opening book patrioti-
cally mocks the English "Peerage Book" (*WHM*, 7:9), comically undercutting the very notion of pure, heroic, and known English genealogies
of royalty and aristocracy by reminding his readers of the branches extending forward from Charles II and his mistress Nell Gwynne and then
back to the "thief knights of the Norman" (*WHM*, 7:10). And yet the first
American genealogies that the narrator discusses after his comical remarks on the miscegenated character of the English Peerage Book reveal
a confluence of sources that raise questions about national purity. The
narrator refers to "the old and oriental-like English planter families of
Virginia and the South; the Randolphs for example, one of whose ancestors, in King James' time, married Pocahontas the Indian Princess, and
in whose blood therefore an underived aboriginal royalty was flowing
over two hundred years ago" (*WHM*, 7:10). As with the river imagery
Hawthorne deploys in describing the Maules, the emphasis here is on the
ebb and flow and mixing of blood, with the ironically developed notion
that the Randolph blood is both miscegenated and pure. In the context
of such paralleling accounts of both English and American mixing of
blood, the narrator then turns to the house of Glendinning, declaring,
as Hawthorne would declare about the Pyncheons, that the family aims
to "perpetuate itself," despite the difficulties of transmitting traits and
property from generation to generation in a country lacking in a "char-
tered aristocracy, and . . . law of entail" (*WHM*, 7:8). Appearances pro-
claim that they have succeeded in their quest, for their "special family
distinction" (*WHM*, 7:12) has become both the joy and onus of Pierre's
strong-willed mother, who remains committed to "the fair succession of
an honorable race!" (*WHM*, 7:194). But in the crucial subsequent genealogical account of Pierre's paternal grandfather, a slave master, Melville
suggests that that race may not be so fair or honorable after all.

In *House*, there is an emphasis on the Pyncheons' legal deeds with
Indians; in *Pierre*, the emphasis is initially on the Glendinnings' deeds
against Indians, specifically, the violent actions along "the historic line of
Glendinning" that, to Pierre's young mind, helped to establish the great-

ness of "his race" (*WHM*, 7:5, 7:6). Telling a story that has become central to Pierre's own sense of family and self, the narrator comments on how Pierre's paternal great-grandfather had fought Indians for possession of the land and how his paternal grandfather, General Glendinning, "had annihilated two Indian savages by making reciprocal bludgeons of their heads" (*WHM*, 7:29–30).[12] In addition to establishing a violent racial authority over the Indians, the general also exerted authority over his black slaves, though in the narrator's evocative discussion of the Glendinning estate around the time of the American Revolution, the violence of ownership is ironically romanticized as a love altogether similar to the love that the general has for his horses. The general, we are told, loves his slaves and horses, has the slaves watch over his horses, and insists that "no man loved his horses, unless his own hands grained them" (*WHM*, 7:30). But what exactly does the master do to the horses/slaves with "his own hands"? Or, to put the question differently: how does a patriarchal master express his "love"?

Melville hints at answers to these questions in his description of the general later in life after he has decided to forgo his morning ride of his beloved "saddle beast" because of the changes time has wrought on his body: "But time glides on, and grand old Pierre grows old: his life's glorious grape now swells with fatness; he has not the conscience to saddle his majestic beast with such a mighty load of manliness" (*WHM*, 7:31). The implication of the phallic imagery here is that, not unlike the southern slave master, the general when in vital health, during the time in his younger days when his "glorious grape" swelled with something other than "fatness," saddled his "beast" with his "mighty load of manliness"; and the implication, given that the general is representative of a long line of Glendinning patriarchs, and given the novel's blending of the slaves and horses as interchangeable property, is that Pierre and other Glendinnings and the horses/slaves themselves may all be thought of as "one branch" or "family cousins," nurtured as they all are by the "same fountain" (*WHM*, 7:21). As with the English Peerage Book, when one looks closely at genealogical histories, one discerns mixture and shared origins among high and low (in this case, Pierre and the colts/slaves). But that sexual and racial history can only be hinted at, for as the historian Joel Williamson writes, "[t]he great difference between miscegenation by white men and that by white women was, of course, that maternity could not be hidden with the same ease as paternity."[13] Hidden paternity, one of the central tropes of antislavery discourse, is central to the unfolding of *Pierre*'s plot as well. Through this tantalizingly enigmatic genealogical history, Melville suggests that Pierre's blackened hand should perhaps be regarded as having the force of a revelation.

In the manner of Hawthorne's emphasis on the hidden streams of the Pyncheons' and Maules' genealogical bloodlines, then, Melville, too, points to the reality of miscegenated (and unknown) genealogies, what Pierre refers to as that "darker, though truer aspect of things" (*WHM*, 7:69). As in *House,* "darker" things are suggested through pictures, even as pictures are presented as ambiguous and highly mediated markers of genealogical histories that cannot be completely recovered or known. In a series of narrative set pieces that in similarly tantalizing and enigmatic fashion help to suggest the origins of Isabel's blackened hand, Pierre is depicted at age twelve overhearing his father on his deathbed asking after a daughter, and then is depicted several years later contemplating the two surviving portraits of his father: a large formal portrait painted when the father was married and of middle age, and a premarriage smaller, informal chair portrait surreptitiously sketched by a cousin. It is the small one, much beloved by Pierre's Aunt Dorothea and loathed by Mary Glendinning, that, until he chooses to burn it, fascinates Pierre, who regularly gazes at it in an attempt to discern what his aunt describes as the father's "secret published in a portrait" (*WHM*, 7:79). There are clues to that secret, for Dorothea tells Pierre that the portrait was sketched at a time when Pierre's father had become involved with a young French woman who had fled her "native land, because of the cruel, blood-shedding times there" (*WHM*, 7:75). The narrative offers no specific information about the young lady, who eventually disappears from sight (with the suggestion that she may have become pregnant with Pierre's father's daughter), and no specific information about the revolution from which she fled, which could just as easily have been the revolution in Saint Domingue as the one in Paris. Given that the father's friends regularly mutter "dark things" (*WHM*, 7:76) about what Anna Brickhouse terms the "Franco-Africanist figure of Isabel," we could speculate that Pierre's father (whose own racial identity remains ambiguous) was happily in love with a "black" woman.[14] The chair portrait that Pierre views for the last time before going to New York City thus possibly attests to an interracial love far more provocative than the cross-"racial" love between a Pyncheon and a Maule.

In her fine analysis of intersecting domestic motifs and themes in *Pierre* and *House,* Wyn Kelley takes Pierre's and Isabel's rebellious departure for New York as that point in the novel when "Melville leaves Hawthorne and the world of middle-class house and home far behind."[15] As my close attention to *Pierre's* first half suggests, I am in general agreement with Kelley's assessment. And yet if we read that domestic world in relation to the Young American nationalism that I am arguing both Hawthorne and Melville respond to in their genealogical fictions, Melville does not leave that world as far behind as it might seem. It is significant, for example, that Pierre's first great success in Manhattan as a Young American author comes about through the publication of what the narrator calls his "delightful love-sonnet, entitled 'The Tropical Summer'" (*WHM,* 7:245). Here the literary work clearly invokes U.S. expansionist aspirations of the period for an "American" Caribbean, a point underscored by the fact that Pierre uses the profits from his sonnets to purchase cigars "perfumed with the sweet leaf of Havanna" (*WHM,* 7:262).[16] Of course Pierre quickly turns against his facile success as a genteel author, lighting his cigars "by the sale of his sonnets, and . . . by the printed sonnets themselves" (*WHM,* 7:263). But Melville's amusing parody of Young American gentility and "Perfect Taste" should not obscure the fact that he is also raising larger questions about the nation's program of hemispheric expansion, linking it, in certain respects, to the amoral "virtuous expediency" described in "Chronometricals & Horologicals," wherein the possible author Plotinus Plinlimmon declaims on how "professed Christian nations" greedily extend their rule and "glory in the owning" (*WHM,* 7:245, 7:214, 7:207).

The *House*-inspired blood themes and motifs of *Pierre's* domestic first half also remain of crucial importance to the novel's urban chapters. Melville continues to work with a sense of racial instabilities and inversion, reminiscent of Hawthorne's treatment of the Pyncheons, by comically presenting the enraged and out-of-control Pierre, with his maniacal jealousies and "black vein" (*WHM,* 7:358), as a sort of American Othello. And, like Hawthorne, he works with portraits to explore and ambiguate matters of identity. In yet another moment when, as in *House,* portraits *seem* to disclose hidden realities, Pierre and the "ebon" Isabel (*WHM,* 7:314) view a copy of Guido's "Cenci" and an unknown painter's rendition of "The Stranger." Isabel and Pierre are particularly drawn to the image of the stranger, fascinated as they are by his "dark head, with its crisp, curly, jetty hair, . . . disentangling itself from out of curtains and clouds." In the ambiguously dark face of the stranger, Isabel detects "certain shadowy traces of her own unmistakable likeness; while to Pierre, this face [is] in part as the resurrection of the one he had burnt at the Inn" (*WHM*, 7:351). In gazing at the dark stranger, who "gazes" at the conventionally light Beatrice Cenci, they believe they are viewing a version of a union that gave rise to their own incestuous predicament. Arguably, what these characters are also witnessing in the cross-gazing of the seemingly light Cenci and the seemingly dark stranger is a figuration of racial crossing that, as long as the portraits remain positioned face to face, perpetually implies not only Pierre's and Isabel's miscegenated identities but the miscegenated identities of unknown men and women of preceding, current, and subsequent generations.

Whereas Hawthorne at the end of *House* attempts to find some solace in the mysteriously hopeful coming together of two "races" (families), Melville raises the conceptual stakes in his depiction of miscegenation as the ultimate reality of race. Consider that when Isabel offers Pierre poison, she takes it from "the secret vial nesting" at her bosom (*WHM*, 7:360). To some extent that "vial" serves as a metonym of her secret "black" vein. But by referring to Isabel's hidden "nest" of poison, Melville also associates her with Shakespeare's Cleopatra, who suicidally placed a poisonous asp at her breast. Pierre too is associated with an Egyptian forbear, as he had given the name "Memnon Stone" to the stone he fancifully enjoyed imagining as a sort of tombstone, thereby honoring Memnon, "that dewey, royal boy, son of Aurora, and born King of Egypt" (*WHM*, 7:35). In associating his blackened heroes with Egypt, Melville underscores the "miscegenated" origins not only of the United States but also of Western culture and thus participates in a larger antebellum cultural conversation on race. Insistent on establishing absolute racial differences between blacks and whites, but aware that Western civilization had crucial sources in Egypt, white racial ethnologists of the American school argued, in the words of Samuel Morton, that Egypt "was originally peopled by a branch of the Caucasian race," and that "the complexion of the Egyptians did not differ from that of the other Caucasian races." Numerous African Americans of the period objected to this whitening of an African nation, and in a compelling response, "The Claims of the Negro Ethnologically Understood" (1854), Frederick Douglass attacked Morton and his followers while asserting "a near relationship between the present enslaved and degraded negroes, and the ancient highly civilized and wonderfully endowed Egyptians." In associating his blackened heroes with Egypt, Melville, like Douglass, underscores the "miscegenated" origins of Western culture, thereby suggesting the representativeness of Pierre's "blackness."[17] It is in this broader conception of Western culture that Melville extends the racial thematics of *House,* though it is noteworthy that in *The Marble Faun* Hawthorne would suggest an alliance with Melville on this historical vision of the centrality of blackness to Western culture when his narrator praises Kenyon for the realism of his sculpture of Cleopatra: "The face was a miraculous success. The sculptor had not shunned to give the full Nubian lips, and other characteristics of the Egyptian physiognomy. His courage and integrity had been abundantly rewarded; for Cleopatra's beauty shone out richer . . . than if, shrinking timidly from the truth, he had chosen the tame Grecian type" (*CE,* 4:126).

The Civil War years following the publication of *The Marble Faun* exposed a certain reactionary temperament in both Hawthorne and Melville. In "Chiefly about War-Matters," Hawthorne, while conveying his skepticism about the idealism of the northern war effort, refers to the "monstrous birth" resulting from the linkage of "the Puritans with these Africans of Virginia," implying that he feels some revulsion about the nation's miscegenated origins even as he proclaims that blacks are "our brethren" (*CE,* 23:420). Two years later (and two years after Hawthorne's death in 1864), Melville in the "Supplement" to *Battle-Pieces* makes a similar observation on the nation's mixed origins, but, in his attempt to promote reconciliation between the sections, reaches out not to the freed blacks but to southern whites, whom he claims are "nearer to us in nature."[18] In their genealogical fictions of the early 1850s, Hawthorne and Melville convey a far more capacious and challenging view of race and nation by raising questions about the "nature" of race and the historical roots of kinship. Etienne Balibar writes that the "symbolic kernel of the idea of race (and of its demographic and cultural equivalents) is the schema of genealogy, that is, quite simply the idea that the filiation of individuals transmits from generation to generation a substance both biological and spiritual and thereby inscribes them in a temporal community known as 'kinship.'"[19] In *House* and *Pierre,* Hawthorne and Melville show how race was deployed in the service of defining and regulating the national family, distinguishing between the whiteness inside and the "blackness" without. But in their complementary genealogical fictions, racial and, by extension, national identity are depicted as incoherent and tottering on the point of collapse. Hawthorne may not have developed his thoughts on race and nation quite as provocatively as Melville, and he may have taken refuge in an improbable conclusion, but during a time when their friendship was at its most intense, this divided Democrat inspired Melville to write one of his most complex and troubling fictions.

Notes

1. Seelye, "'Ungraspable Phantom,'" 438; Milder, "'Ugly Socrates,'" 25; Mitchell, "In the Whale's Wake," 59; Wineapple, "Hawthorne and Melville," 77 (see also 90 on Holgrave and Melville); Melville to Hawthorne, letter of April 1851 (*WHM*, 14:185). See also Miller, *Melville*, esp. 20–44, 178–91, 234–50.

2. For representative (and influential) attacks on Hawthorne for his alleged racism, expediency, and acceptance of slavery, see Cheyfitz, "Irresistibleness of Great Literature," and Yellin, "Hawthorne and the Slavery Question." In a recent essay, Riss argues that Hawthorne regarded blacks as "nonpersons" ("Art of Discrimination," 277). For a very different perspective, see Reynolds's fine (and sympathetic) historicist analysis of Hawthorne on slavery and race, "'Strangely Ajar with the Human Race,'" which, among other things, takes note of Hawthorne's efforts to help fugitive slaves during the early months of the Civil War.

3. Earle, *Jacksonian Antislavery*, 15.

4. Sumner, "Union among Men of all Parties," in *Works*, 2:77; Sumner, "Law of Human Progress," in *Works*, 2:125. Hawthorne wrote Sumner on January 8, 1849, to confirm that he would be speaking on the "Law of Progress" at the Salem Lyceum (*CE*, 16:258).

5. On the Young American literary nationalism associated with the *Democratic Review*, see Miller, *The Raven and the Whale*; and Widmer, *Young America*.

6. Hawthorne voiced his complaints to Duyckinck himself in a letter of December 1, 1851 (*CE*, 16:508).

7. See, for example, "The War."

8. Male, *Hawthorne's Tragic Vision*, 122; Kermode, *The Classic*, 104.

9. Smith, *American Archives*, 29; hereafter cited parenthetically.

10. Anthony, "Class, Culture, and the Trouble with White Skin," 261; hereafter cited parenthetically. On minstrelsy and *House*, see also Gilmore, *Genuine Article*, 125–50.

11. This and several other paragraphs on *Pierre* draw on Levine, "Pierre's Blackened Hand." On Melville and race, see Morrison, "Unspeakable Things Unspoken"; and Otter, "'Race' in *Typee* and *White-Jacket*."

12. On landscape and race, see Otter, "Eden of Saddle Meadows," esp. 67.

13. Williamson, *New People,* 52.

14. Brickhouse, *Transamerican Literary Relations,* 244. On Isabel's "mottled . . . racial identity," see also Dayan, "Amorous Bondage," 201.

15. Kelley, "*Pierre*'s Domestic Ambiguities," 103. On race in *House* and *Pierre,* see also Weinauer, "Hawthorne and Race"; and for a provocative discussion of family and nation in the novel, see Weinstein, *Family, Kinship, and Sympathy,* 59–84.

16. On cigars and literary imperialism, see Merish, *Sentimental Materialism,* ch. 6, 270–303.

17. Morton, *Crania Ægyptiaca* (1844), cited in Nott and Gliddon, *Types of Mankind,* 214, 218; Douglass, "The Claims of the Negro Ethnologically Considered: An Address Delivered in Hudson, Ohio, on 12 July 1854," 517. For helpful discussions of antebellum racial ethnology, see Gossett, *Race,* 54–83; and Nelson, *National Manhood.*

18. Melville, *Battle-Pieces,* 267.

19. Balibar, "The Nation Form: History and Ideology," 143.

In the Whale's Wake

Melville and
The Blithedale Romance

Thomas R. Mitchell

THE HAWTHORNE-MELVILLE FRIENDSHIP in the Berkshires in 1850–
51 has received enormous attention, but most of it has understandably
focused on the transformative power of Hawthorne's influence on Melville as he wrestled with *Moby-Dick*.[1] Hawthorne, after all, had written
the greatest work he would ever write months before meeting Melville,
but Melville's greatest work would be forged to some debatable degree
by—as well as during—the heat of that momentous friendship. Writing
The House of the Seven Gables and *A Wonder Book for Girls and Boys*
in the midst of their Berkshire friendship and beginning *The Blithedale
Romance* at its close, Hawthorne does not seem to have been notably
inspired, much less influenced, by Melville's personal presence or his
literary example. He does not seem to have been, but I think that he most
certainly was. A closer examination of that moment in Hawthorne's life
and literary career suggests that Melville's friendship had complex and
contradictory influences on his work.[2]

Immediately before Hawthorne moved to Lenox and met Melville,
he had left Salem in disgrace and in thorough disgust had moved into
a Boston boardinghouse while his wife and two small children put up
with his in-laws. Though he had just published his masterpiece, he was
forty-five-years old and unable to support himself or his family: he had
no great hopes that sales of *The Scarlet Letter* would transform his fortunes; he was indebted to George Hillard for a five-hundred-dollar chari-
table gift raised to help the Hawthornes; he had been ill periodically over
the past year; and, he wrote confidentially to Horatio Bridge that year,

he had hidden from Sophia increasing anxiety about his deteriorating health and especially his "lack of physical vigor and energy" (*CE*, 16:312). He had begun his marriage just eight years previously in the spacious manse, left it owing several months' rent, moved his family back into the home of his mother and sisters in Salem, and now, in Lenox, found himself taking refuge in the tight quarters of the Tappan's red farmhouse. Arriving in Lenox, Hawthorne became very ill with another "nervous fever," as Sophia called it in a letter to her mother, describing his eyes as "two immense spheres of troubled light" and judging that he was "harassed in spirit" by "brain work and disquiet."[3] As this summary of his situation at forty-five suggests, Hawthorne had much to cause him "disquiet." Because of the publication in March of *The Scarlet Letter* and the beginning in August of his friendship with Melville, we think of 1850 as Hawthorne's year of triumph. In retrospect, it was. In the lived experience of his life, it most certainly was not.[4]

When Hillard sent Hawthorne the five-hundred-dollar check in January, Hawthorne had written back that he accepted his plight as a consequence of his own failures and vowed to redeem himself through arduous exertions in the future (*CE*, 16:309). Driven by financial need, by the desire to reclaim his honor as a successful American man and family breadwinner, and by the encouragement of James T. Fields, Hawthorne began in August, just days after meeting Melville, to redouble his exertions by writing works meant to please readers and pay royalties. To achieve that aim, he felt he had to avoid writing another *Scarlet Letter*. Hawthorne had worried, of course, that *The Scarlet Letter* was too "hell-fired," too lacking in "sunshine," and would thus "disgust" rather than please readers (*CE*, 16:307–8, 16:311–12), and indeed, as he feared, it garnered condemnation as well as praise. But what he had not counted on was that it would stimulate disturbing speculation about his own character. In fact, he had only recently expressed confidence that writers need not be anxious over the possibility of casual readers detecting the autobiographical origins of their work. In the same month that *The Scarlet Letter* reached the public, Hawthorne reassured would-be poet L. W. Mansfield about the supposed "indelicacy" of expressing his most intimate feelings through his work:

> To whom should you speak of matters near your heart, if not to these
> invisible friends [readers]? You need not dread being overheard, how-

ever loudly you may speak. Your voice—or, at least, your meaning—will reach only those who are privileged to hear and understand it, and what sense is there in caring one fig about the helter-skelter judgments of those who cannot understand you. It might be, that only one person in the whole world would understand, while all the rest would ridicule you; but it would be worth a life's labor to be understood by that one. . . . My theory is, that there is less indelicacy in speaking out your highest, deepest, tenderest emotions to the world at large, than to almost any individual. You may be mistaken in the individual; but you cannot be mistaken in thinking that, somewhere among your fellow-creatures, there is a heart that will receive yours into itself. And those who do not receive it, cannot, in fact, hear it; so that your delicacy is not infringed upon. This is my theory; and if I were a less sophisticated man, I suppose I should act upon it more perfectly than I ever yet have. (*CE*, 16:325)

Hawthorne here reiterated more privately and informally his recent statement in the opening paragraph of "The Custom-House":

The truth seems to be . . . that, when he casts his leaves forth upon the wind, the author addresses, not the many who will fling aside his volume, or never take it up, but the few who will understand him, better than most of his schoolmates and lifemates. Some authors, indeed, do far more than this, and indulge themselves in such confidential depths of revelation as could fittingly be addressed, only and exclusively, to the one heart and mind of perfect sympathy; as if the printed book, thrown at large on the wide world, were certain to find out the divided segment of the writer's own nature, and complete his circle of existence by bringing him into communion with it. (*CE*, 1:3–4)

That Hawthorne would restate this aesthetic of the autobiographical in private correspondence suggests that he not only was not disdainful of such authors, as many have supposed, but in fact numbered himself among them.

Hawthorne had worried that *The Scarlet Letter* lacked sunshine but not that its darkness would be attributable by the general reading public to a darkness within himself. To make matters worse, the conjecture about his character sparked by *The Scarlet Letter* was not limited to ordinary, impersonal readers but included family and the closest of friends.

From Hawthorne's February 4, 1850, letter to Horatio Bridge. Reproduced by permission from coll. 77, box 1, folder 46, in the collections of the Maine Historical Society.

Elizabeth Peabody, for example, reported to her sister Sophia the remark of a friend—and she endorsed the interpretation—that in writing *The Scarlet Letter* Hawthorne had "purified himself by casting out a legion of devils into imaginary beings." In the same letter, she reported a similar comment made by Hawthorne's friend Ellery Channing.[5] Sophia's sister Mary Peabody Mann likely endorsed Elizabeth's views also, for though she left no record of her immediate reaction to *The Scarlet Letter,* she did write later to her son Horace that incidents in Hawthorne's life inevitably found themselves "'bye and bye in books, for he always put[s] himself into his books; he cannot help it.'" More unsettling for Hawthorne than the opinion of his sisters-in-law, or of Ellery Channing, was that of his great friend and recent benefactor, George Hillard. Hillard wrote to him that the Hawthorne he knew seemed hardly capable of such dark tales, causing him to wonder pointedly about the source of such a "'morbid anatomy of the human heart'" and leading him to conclude, "'you were burdened with some secret sorrow; . . . you had some blue chamber in your soul into which you hardly dared to enter yourself.'"[6]

Hawthorne did not defend himself against these charges, but Sophia certainly did. Justifying Hawthorne's belief in the inability of "lifemates" to detect the man behind or within the fiction, Sophia defended Hawthorne to her sister Elizabeth with a vehement bluntness: "It was a work of the imagination wholly & no personal experience, as you well know." However, she did concede, "doubtless all the tendencies of powerful, great natures lie deep in his soul; but they have not been waked, & sleep fixedly, because the noblest only have been called into action." He is able to see "passions & crimes & sorrows by the intuition of genius, & all the better for the calm, cool, serene height from which he looks." When Cornelius Mathews typed Hawthorne as "Mr. Noble Melancholy" in an account of his August 1850 Berkshire adventures with authors, Sophia felt the necessity to write to her mother an even stronger defense of her husband's character, one that totally separated him from his works and from the fallen state of ordinary humanity itself. Not only was he free from the taint of the dark emotions about which he wrote, but he was "like a stray Seraph, who had experienced in his life no evil." He had "literally been so pure from the smallest taint of earthiness" that it could "only be because he [was] a seer that he kn[ew] of crime," only be because he possessed "the intuition of a divine intellect" that did not experience but only "saw and sorrowed over all evil." Sophia, in fact, proceeded to link her faith in Hawthorne's purity with her faith in the absolute separation of good and evil: "Not Julian's little (no, great) angel heart and life are freer from any intention or act of wrong than [Hawthorne's]. And this is best proof to me of the absurdity of the prevalent idea that it is necessary to go through the fiery ordeal of sin to become wise and good. I think such an idea is blasphemy and the unpardonable sin."[7] Given Sophia's willingness to stake the foundation of her religious convictions on the spotlessness of Hawthorne's life and the total absence of autobiographical investment in his works, the stakes were clearly very high for Hawthorne at home. Sophia's supernal faith in Hawthorne may have been incapable of admitting the possibility that Hawthorne had known the dark experiences he described, but Hawthorne's faith in the inability of readers to detect autobiographical origins must have been shaken during the immediate aftermath of speculations over *The Scarlet Letter*. Pouring more "sunshine" into his fiction now seemed a personal as well as a commercial necessity.

At this critical juncture, Melville entered Hawthorne's life, and the two began a friendship, the story of which is well known. To be idolized as both a man and a writer by a fellow writer fifteen years his junior must have been extremely flattering and encouraging to Hawthorne at first. Hawthorne, for his part, clearly took to Melville as a man and greatly respected his work.[8] The reclusive Hawthorne extended the much younger writer the extraordinary hospitality of inviting him for extended visits, accepted similar invitations from Melville, and engaged in heady and lengthy conversations over cigars and brandy. Even before Melville's identity as author was known—and certainly afterward—"Hawthorne and His Mosses" had earned him Hawthorne's gratitude and Sophia's extravagant praise. For Hawthorne, the writer of the review had a "truly generous heart" and was "no common man." "Next to deserving his praise," Hawthorne wrote to Evert Duyckinck, "it is good to have beguiled or bewitched such a man into praising me more than I deserve" (*CE*, 16:362). For Sophia, however, the writer seemed almost preternatural in his capacity to appreciate the greatness she saw in her husband. To Duyckinck, she wrote: "I keep constantly reading over & over the inspired utterances, & marvel more & more that the word has at last been said which I have so long hoped to hear, & so well said. . . . The freshness of primeval nature is in that man, & the true Promethean fire is in him. Who can he be, so fearless, so rich in heart, of such fine intuition?" (*CE*, 16:361). What made Sophia ecstatic was the reviewer's fearlessly placing Hawthorne in the same company as Shakespeare and promoting him as America's greatest author. "'I have been wearied & annoyed hitherto with hearing him compared to Washington Irving & other American writers—& put generally second,'" she wrote to her sister Elizabeth. "'At last some one dares to say what in my secret mind I have often thought—that he is only to be mentioned with the Swan of Avon—The Great Heart and the Grand Intellect combined.'"[9]

Such extravagant praise of Hawthorne from another beguiled Sophia into ignoring that its very foundation had been constructed on a reading of Hawthorne's works that she was to condemn vehemently only days later in a letter to her mother. Melville's praise of the courageous "blackness" that he found in Hawthorne's works was precisely the kind of praise that Hawthorne did not want to hear—even if he was grateful for Melville's general encomium. Worse, Melville read—and encouraged others to read—Hawthorne's tales for their intimate revelations of the author's interior life: "Such touches as these . . . furnish clews, whereby we enter a little way into the intricate, profound heart where they originated. And we see, that suffering, some time or other and in some shape or other,—this only can enable any man to depict it in others. All over him, Hawthorne's melancholy rests like an Indian Summer" (*WHM*, 9:242). But Melville saw in Hawthorne's tales more than just a melancholy author who had suffered the common afflictions of humanity and turned that suffering into art. "The Christmas Banquet" and "The Bosom Serpent," for instance, Melville proclaimed "fine subjects for a curious and elaborate analysis, touching the conjectural parts of the mind that produced them. For spite of all the Indian-summer sunlight on the hither side of Hawthorne's soul, the other side—like the dark half of the physical sphere—is shrouded in a blackness, ten times black" (*WHM*, 9:243). If Hillard had been troubled by a "blue chamber" that he suspected within Hawthorne and questioned him privately, Melville was positively exhilarated to find in Hawthorne a "blackness, ten times black," and to trumpet its existence to the world.

Ironically, in celebrating the darkness within Hawthorne and within his work, Melville sought to rescue him from his reputation as "a sequestered, harmless man, from whom any deep and weighty thing would hardly be anticipated:—a man who means no meanings." Indeed, Hawthorne had been considered "a pleasant writer, with a pleasant style" (*WHM*, 9:242), but the disturbing speculations about his character attending the publication of *The Scarlet Letter* had seemed to threaten to supplant that benign image with precisely the one that Melville sought to promote. Melville thus unwittingly contributed greatly to a problem that Hawthorne felt he must avoid if he were to make his exertions as a writer more commercially successful than they had yet been.

Having begun *The House of the Seven Gables* just a couple of weeks before Melville's review, Hawthorne became determined to succeed better than he had with *The Scarlet Letter* in dispelling the darkness that Melville admired. He would turn from the disturbing Hester and her subversive challenge to conventions to the reassuring Phoebe and her power to tame the radical Holgrave into acquiescence with the "sunshine" of her redemptive domesticity. In so doing, Hawthorne would prove, as he had implicitly promised Hillard when accepting the five-hundred-dollar collection, that he was "strong and able" enough to apply "his ability to good purpose"—the good purpose, that is, of meeting the expectations of his most important audiences: wife, friends (those like Hillard, if not Melville), and general reading public.

It was not easy going. If Hawthorne wrote *The Scarlet Letter* in the white heat and fury of an inspiration that frightened Sophia, he wrote *The House of the Seven Gables* in a slow, sentence-by-sentence, page-by-page frustration born of grim determination, not inspiration. Again and again in his letters to Fields, Hawthorne complained of his struggle writing this less troubling romance. He apologized to Fields for his lack of progress as early as August 23. Though he claimed to "seclude" himself "religiously" each morning "much against [his] will," he reported but "little progress," blaming the summer for not being conducive to inspiration, but vowed "to lumber along with accelerated velocity" in order to finish by November (*CE*, 16:359). By October 1, Hawthorne had to retract the promise, saying that he was "never good for anything in the literary way till after the first autumnal frost," which, he claimed, affected his imagination as it does the foliage, "multiplying and brightening its hues; though they are likely to be sober and shabby enough after all" (*CE*, 16:369).

Brightening the soberness of his imagination continued to be a slow process for Hawthorne. On November 3, he wrote Fields that though he worked "diligently" he was not getting on "so rapidly as [he] had hoped." Unlike *The Scarlet Letter,* this new romance, he said, took "more care and thought" and required waiting "oftener for a mood." He explained, "*The Scarlet Letter* being all in one tone, I had only to get my pitch, and could then go on interminably." Hawthorne's contrast of the new romance with *The Scarlet Letter,* his need to depend more on "care and thought" than erratic inspiration, and his admission that he "sometimes" got "tired of it" and saw "the whole [as] an absurdity"—all suggest that when he then characterized "writing a romance" as "careering on the utmost verge of a precipitous absurdity," he was locating the source of his difficulties in the twin fears of "tumbling over" into darkness again or of appearing "absurd" in determined efforts to avoid doing just that (*CE*, 16:371).

Absurd or not, the effort was designed to pay off. "My prevailing idea is, that the book ought to succeed better than the Scarlet Letter," he assured Fields (*CE*, 16:371). Three weeks later, on November 29, the book still not finished but projected for completion in two to four weeks, he identified the remaining threat to its "success" and in so doing the problem he had been contending with all along: "It darkens damnably towards the close," he wrote Fields, "but I shall try hard to pour some setting sunshine over it" (*CE*, 16:376). Attempting to force light into his tale led him, two weeks later, to report to Fields that he had been "in a Slough of Despond, for some days past," and unable to write. He was "bewildered" and did not know "what to do next" (*CE*, 16:378). Even after he had apparently finished in mid-January and begun reading the book to Sophia, he had to spend another ten days revising the concluding chapters before disclosing them to her.

The "sunshine" of the ending may have seemed forced to generations of later readers, but Sophia probably spoke for many readers of her time who applauded Holgrave's disavowal of radical thought and his acquiescence to Phoebe's redemptively domestic and unquestioning love. At the close of this romance, Sophia wrote, "the flowers of Paradise scattered over all the dark places, the sweet wall-flower scent of Phoebe's character." As Hawthorne had intended, Sophia found the ending one of "unspeakable grace and beauty" that cast "upon the sterner tragedy of the commencement an ethereal light, and a dear home-loveliness and satisfaction."[10] Giving artistic substance to Sophia's faith in his spotless character, Hawthorne was quick to claim to all that he too preferred the lighter romance to its more shadowed predecessor and considered it more indicative of his own character and temperament. Thanking Evert Duyckinck for his positive review of *The House of the Seven Gables*, Hawthorne, for instance, wrote, "It appears to me that you like the book better than the Scarlet Letter; and I certainly think it a more natural and healthy product of my mind, and felt less reluctance in publishing it." Yet he worried that Duyckinck (perhaps like others) was not fully persuaded that the domestic sunshine of this romance was indeed the "natural . . . product" of his mind; in an effort at reassurance, Hawthorne made it clear to Duyckinck that his overriding purpose from the beginning was to avoid writing another disturbing tale with a dark ending: "I cannot quite understand why everything that I write takes so melancholy an aspect in your eyes. As regards this particular story, I really had an idea that it was rather a cheerful one than otherwise; but, in writing it, I suppose I was illuminated by my purpose to bring it to a prosperous close; while the gloom of the past threw its shadow along the reader's pathway" (*CE*, 16:421).[11] If Hawthorne seemed frustrated that Duyckinck would persist in seeing this romance as "melancholy," he must have been completely baffled and frustrated by Melville's extracting, from this romance at least, the "grand truth" that Hawthorne "says NO! in thunder; but the Devil himself cannot make him say *yes*" (*WHM,* 14:186). "Yes," in fact, was precisely what Hawthorne had struggled so hard to say.

In his efforts to transform his personal and professional image into something more broadly appealing, Hawthorne had found the writing more difficult, but, as he had hoped, it did prove more lucrative. Even as he struggled to force sunshine over his tribute to Sophia in the character of Phoebe, he had already begun to make his appeal to the audience that he hoped to address, and placate, in *The House of the Seven Gables.* His first effort to expand his audience and answer questions about his character generated by *The Scarlet Letter* was to release in November a compilation of previously published historical sketches for children in *True Stories from History and Biography.* The success of *True Stories* confirmed at least the commercial value of Hawthorne's efforts and encouraged him to write the even more successful *A Wonder Book for Girls and Boys* immediately after *The House of the Seven Gables.* Within its first six months, *True Stories* had been issued twice in a total press run of 4,500 copies, a mere 500 fewer than *The Scarlet Letter* during its first six months. As Hawthorne had predicted to Fields, *The House of the Seven Gables* was better received by contemporary readers than *The Scarlet Letter.* Within its first six months, *Seven Gables* had generated a press run of 6,710 copies, 810 more than had been printed of *The Scarlet Letter* by August 1851, a full seventeen months after its emergence on the market. The press run for *A Wonder Book* would reach 4,667 copies just two months after its November 1851 release (significantly, by contrast, the same month as the release of *Moby-Dick*), but a third edition of *Twice-Told Tales* in March 1851 would have a press run of only 2,000 copies and the collection of Hawthorne's previously uncollected tales, *The Snow-Image,* would have an initial run in December 1851 of only 2,425 copies, an additional printing of 1,000 copies not being needed for another twelve months.[12]

The message seemed clear to the forty-seven-year-old writer who had had difficulty supporting himself, much less his wife and three children, through his writing. Avoiding the darker predilections of his genius and writing "dear home-loveliness and satisfaction" could be counted on to generate greater royalties, earn him even greater praise at home, and provide a measure of protection from unwanted public curiosity. "The only sensible ends of literature," Hawthorne wrote his friend Bridge as *The House of the Seven Gables* was being printed, "are, first, the pleasurable toil of writing, secondly, the gratification of one's family and friends, and lastly the solid cash" (*CE,* 16:407). Certainly his turn toward a more domestic fiction of affirmation had helped him achieve the second and third ends, but as his frustrations with writing *Seven Gables* and as other evidence throughout 1851 suggest, his very attempt to gratify family and friends and to achieve commercial success had taken some of the pleasure out of the toil. At the end of his labors on *The House of the Seven Gables,* for instance, he wrote his sister Elizabeth that, "except from necessity," he now hated "the thought of writing" (*CE,* 16:402). Concluding *A Wonder Book,* he confessed to his other sister, Louisa, that he had come to "abominate the sight" of a pen (*CE,* 16:453).

Such grumbling could be read as the expected complaints of an exhausted writer at the end of a major project, but other evidence suggests the complaints were part of Hawthorne's general discontent with his life and his work. While this is not the place to enter into the complicated terrain of Hawthorne's domestic frustrations, his discontent with his work is linked to a significant degree, I believe, to his relationship with Melville.[13] Entering his late forties during the year and a half of his friendship with Melville, Hawthorne was continually reminded by the presence and the example of an enormously gifted writer barely thirty years old that he was now decidedly middle-aged and had few years of creative work ahead, that he lacked the enthusiasm and energy of youth (certainly that heady enthusiasm of Melville's), and that he had attempted, in fact, to become a very different writer from the one his young friend persisted in celebrating, despite his best efforts. Melville's letters to Hawthorne in 1851 are the effusions of a writer filled to overflowing with a creative energy and excitement stimulated by his work on *Moby-Dick* and his intense feelings for Hawthorne, but Hawthorne gives evidence throughout the year of a weary, middle-aged discontent with his own career. In his March 15, 1851, letter to Bridge, Hawthorne laments: "How slowly I have made my way in life! How much is still to be done! How little worth (outwardly, I mean) is all that I have achieved! The 'bubble Reputation' is as much a bubble in literature as in war; and I should not be one whit the happier if mine were world-wide and time-long, than I was when nobody but yourself had faith in me" (*CE,* 16:407).

In his preface to the third edition of *Twice-Told Tales,* published the month of his letter to Bridge, Hawthorne looked back longingly on his early obscurity, when he had no "reasonable prospect of reputation or profit" and wrote for "nothing but the pleasure itself of composition" (*CE*, 9:3). Though nostalgic about the pleasure he then found in writing, he was not at all satisfied with the achievement of that time. Melville had applauded him in "Hawthorne and His Mosses" for allowing his work to originate from an "intricate, profound heart" with its "depth of tenderness . . . boundless sympathy [and] omnipresent love" (*WHM*, 9:242). Hawthorne, however, can only lament that even his youthful work lacks heart, that it is "tame," that "[i]nstead of passion, there is sentiment," that "even in what purport to be pictures of actual life, we have allegory, not always so warmly dressed in its habiliments of flesh and blood" (*CE*, 9:5).[14] Nine months later, in the preface to the December 1851 publication of *The Snow-Image*, Hawthorne, inspired perhaps by his influence on Melville's confidence, wrote a nostalgic tribute to his glorious youthful friendship with Bridge and to Bridge's early and crucial faith in his work. In the preface to *Twice-Told Tales*, Hawthorne had expressed discontent with his early work, and here, looking backward, he claimed to find few signs of progress to vivify the labors of middle age. Those tales, he said, "come so nearly up to the standard of the best that I can achieve now" that "the ripened autumnal fruit tastes but little better than the early windfalls." Hawthorne's was the voice that he would give to the self-deprecating Coverdale beginning the very month in which this preface was published: "It would, indeed, be mortifying to believe that the summertime of life has passed away, without any greater progress and improvement than is indicated here." Contemplating that lost summer of his career, Hawthorne consoled himself, "in youth, men are apt to write more wisely than they really know or feel; and the remainder of life may be not idly spent in realizing and convincing themselves of the wisdom which they uttered long ago" (*CE*, 11:6).

When he read the decidedly "wise" and undomestic *Moby-Dick* in November 1851, Hawthorne immediately recognized its greatness, writing Melville a now-lost letter of accolade that elicited Melville's famously ecstatic response proclaiming an "infinite fraternity of feeling" with this man, who drank from his "flagon of life," whose "divine magnet" attracted his own magnet (*WHM*, 14:212–13). Before reading the novel, Hawthorne had alluded in *A Wonder Book* to Melville's "shaping out the gigantic conception of his 'White Whale,' while the gigantic shape of Graylock loom[ed] upon him from his study-window" (*CE*, 7:169), but Hawthorne was not to write a public review, as Melville himself had requested that he not (*WHM*, 14:213). To Duyckinck, Hawthorne simply wrote: "What a book Melville has written! It gives me an idea of much greater power than his preceding ones. It hardly seemed to me that the review of it, in the Literary World, did justice to its best points" (*CE*, 16:508). The phrases "gigantic conception" and "much greater power," however, suggest that Hawthorne was taken with the passion of the book, a passion whose absence from his own work he had recently lamented.

That is all we know with any certainty about Hawthorne's reaction to the novel that was dedicated to him and, to some extent at least, inspired by him. *The Blithedale Romance,* however, provides some intimations of the impact of both Melville and *Moby-Dick* on Hawthorne.

Three months after reading Melville's praise of his ability to capture the "visable [sic] truth" and say "NO! in thunder" and three months before reading *Moby-Dick,* which he had heard about all year, Hawthorne signaled his restlessness with the increasing domesticity of his fiction by informing Fields that, when he wrote his next romance, it would not be another "quiet book," as he phrased it. He intended "to put an extra touch of the devil into it" (*CE*, 16:462). A year earlier, he had recoiled from the "blue chamber" in his soul that had created Hester and provoked questions about his own character, but now, having placated his friends, family, and readers by embracing the "sunshine" of Phoebe and of innocuous children's stories, Hawthorne desired to revive the writer that Melville had seen in him—or perhaps, by the extraordinary example of *Moby-Dick* as well as by praise, had shamed him into becoming again. Just five days after the first anniversary of Margaret Fuller's tragic drowning at sea and two days after his letter to Fields, Hawthorne suggested to his friend William Pike that he would put that "extra devil" into a tale about his experiences at Brook Farm, where Hawthorne had spent much time with Fuller (*CE*, 16:465). When Hawthorne actually began *The Blithedale Romance* in December 1851, he looked backward nostalgically to his earlier, more hopeful days in Concord as much as he did to Brook Farm.[15] With Fuller now dead, he reexamined her character and his relationship to her, to Sophia, and to Emerson in the characters of, respectively, Zenobia, Priscilla, and Hollingsworth.

The Blithedale Romance is thus not about Hawthorne's relationship with Melville or his days in the Berkshires, but it bears important traces of their influence. The "devil" that Hawthorne would put into *The Blithedale Romance* is a first cousin to the "devil" that Melville put into

Moby-Dick. Hawthorne's works had heretofore buried any sources that they may have had in his personal life under thick layers of fictional displacements and prefatory denials. Melville, on the other hand, had built and sustained his reputation on the very well known and exotic autobiographical origins of his tales of the sea. For the first time, Hawthorne was ready to risk doing the same by writing about what he admitted to be "the most romantic episode of his own life" (*CE,* 3:2). He was now willing to act upon the aesthetic principles he had recommended to L. W. Mansfield "more perfectly" than he "ever yet" had. He advertised in the preface his personal connection with the now-famous Brook Farm experiment while at the same time he teasingly disavowed any living model for his characters, knowing full well that his vivid portrait in Zenobia of the still-scandalous Margaret Fuller would be recognized immediately, as indeed it was.[16] He went a step further, however, and here Melville's influence should be obvious. With Ishmael's voice still ringing in his ears, Hawthorne chose for the first time to tell his tale through a first-person participant narrator. And Coverdale, like Ishmael but to a significantly greater extent, is more observer than actor in the theatrical tale he narrates—a tale, by the way, driven by Coverdale's need to understand his own white-shrouded mystery, the veiled lady. For Hawthorne, unlike Melville, the mystery that bedeviled him into obsession was not what lay behind the "mask" concealing God but the less cosmic, more immediate mysteries veiled behind the complexities of human relationships. The desire for knowledge and power over another, particularly man's desire to define and master woman, Hawthorne suggests, destroys us just as thoroughly as does Ahab's flight from woman and his quest to strike through the "mask" that is Moby Dick.

Melville may have first unwittingly helped spur Hawthorne into fleeing from "blackness" toward the "sunshine" of redemptive domesticity and later may have inspired him, through praise and example and even shame, to seek a return to something darker and more disquieting, but in the end the unbridled intensity and passion of both this much younger writer and his powerful *Moby-Dick* served but to strengthen Hawthorne's restless disaffection with his life and his work.[17] In one of many passages in *The Blithedale Romance* drawing on images of bodies of water and voyages, Coverdale suggests the contrast Hawthorne must have felt between himself and the books that had lately flowed out of his life, on the one hand, and Melville and his *Moby-Dick,* on the other: "My book was of the dullest, yet had a sort of sluggish flow, like that of a stream in which your boat is as often aground as afloat. Had there been a more impetuous rush, a more absorbing passion of the narrative, I should the sooner have struggled out of its uneasy current, and have given myself up to the swell and subsidence of my thoughts. But, as it was, the torpid life of the book served as an unobtrusive accompaniment to the life within me and about me" (*CE,* 3:147). Ishmael on the *Pequod* narrates the sublime chase on the high seas for the "grand hooded phantom" (*WHM,* 6:7), Melville giving himself up to the swell and subsidence of his passionate imagination, his "gigantic conception," while Coverdale's book and his life float sluggishly in a little boat on a stream like the Concord River, Hawthorne feeling decidedly middle aged and torpid. The self-contempt of this failed poet, Coverdale, is not Hawthorne's vision of what he could have become had he remained a bachelor, as has often been suggested, but Hawthorne's vision of what he in fact felt himself to be at forty-seven.

While *Blithedale* suggests that Hawthorne mourned his lack of Melville's passion and creative energy, it also bears traces of a recoil from Melville's passionate overtures of intimacy. In *Hawthorne's Fuller Mystery,* I explore ways in which Hollingsworth functions at different levels as a representative of both Hawthorne and Emerson in the autobiographical dimensions of the romance (190–98). Deleted in revisions of that study, however, was the notion that Hawthorne, to some extent, also had Melville in mind, as Edwin Haviland Miller has argued.[18] Hollingsworth, who is "two men," as Coverdale tells us (*CE,* 3:42), contains in his relationship with Coverdale the traits of the "two men" who had sought to enlist Hawthorne as friend and supporter in their own self-absorbing projects, the two men to whom Hawthorne was drawn but whom he rejected—most recently Melville, most importantly Emerson. When Hollingsworth implores Coverdale to "join" with him and ignore their relationships with the women in their lives—"devote yourself, and sacrifice all to this great end," he urges, "and be my friend of friends, forever" (*CE,* 16:135)—he calls up not only the flight from relationship lived by Ahab but also the rhetoric and ritual of Ahab's imposition of will on his men in the "Quarter-Deck" chapter (particularly of his courting of Starbuck there and elsewhere) as he absorbs them into his megalomaniacal mission:

"Take it up with me! Be my brother in it! It offers you (what you have told me, over and over again, that you most need) a purpose in life, worthy of the extremest self-devotion—worthy of martyrdom, should God so order it! . . . You can greatly benefit mankind. Your peculiar faculties, as I shall direct them, are capable of being so wrought into this enterprise, that not one of them need lie idle. Strike hands with me; and, from this moment, you shall never again feel the languor and vague wretchedness of an indolent or half-occupied man! There may be no more aimless beauty in your life; but, in its stead, there shall be strength, courage, immitigable will—everything that a manly and generous nature should desire! We shall succeed!" (CE, 3:133)

Hollingsworth demands of Coverdale, as Ahab did of Starbuck:"'Be with me . . . or be against me! There is no third choice for you.'" When Hollingsworth insists that he choose, offering fraternity one last time, Coverdale says the word that costs him "an absolute torture of the breast": "'No!'" (CE, 3:135). This refusal echoes—and deflects—the "NO!" that "thunders" in the recent memory of both Hawthorne and Melville.

For Miller, the "crisis" between Coverdale and Hollingsworth restages Hawthorne's recoil from the homoerotic nature of his young friend's appeal to an intimate artistic brotherhood, Hollingsworth being an embodiment of "Melville's aggression and need of a 'brother'" (357). I would propose that, in Coverdale's insistence on standing "upon his right, as an individual being," and looking "at matters through his own optics" instead of Hollingsworth's (CE, 3:135), Hawthorne inscribes his resistance not only to Melville's aggressive personal advances but also to Melville's vision of their joint literary enterprise. Moby-Dick may have emboldened Hawthorne in Blithedale to return to the "intellectual forge" of a "hell-fired" imagination, but its passionate epic of the all-absorbing masculine will may also have frightened him with a shock of recognition—of what he most feared in himself and of what he saw in Melville (CE, 1:34, 16:312). Coverdale characterizes Hollingsworth as something of a philanthropic Ahab who has "conjured up" a "cold, spectral monster" (CE, 3:55), "surrendered" himself "to an over-ruling purpose," sacrificing everything and everyone to this "false deity" that is but "a spectrum of the very priest himself, projected upon the surrounding darkness" (CE, 3:70–71).

Hollingsworth's former occupation as a blacksmith links him both to Melville's working-class days as a sailor and to the imagery of iron and fire so pervasive in Melville's characterization of Ahab. Hollingsworth's grand scheme of collecting "out of a thousand human hearts" a "great, black ugliness of sin" that he and Coverdale would "spend [their] lives in an experiment of transmuting . . . into virtue" (*CE*, 3:134) parallels to some extent Melville's view of Hawthorne's literary exploration of "blackness"; Coverdale's response may be read, in a sense, as Hawthorne's resistance to Melville's unconscious attempt to enlist the older writer by naming his own literary mission as Hawthorne's. Hollingsworth's tearful plea, "'Do not forsake me!'" (*CE*, 3:133), echoes not only Christ's appeal to God on the cross but also Ahab's demand of his sailors, as well as his own crucifixion on the white whale. Perhaps, too, it imagines Melville's reaction to Hawthorne's rejection in the very religious language in which Melville characterized his friendship with the "archangel" Hawthorne, as a form of holy communion in which the two mutually absorb each other's Christlike spirit (*WHM*, 14:212–13).

Hawthorne's magnet may have drawn Melville to him, but Melville's magnet had a negative as well as a positive pole for Hawthorne. Both attracted and repelled, he refused to absorb or be absorbed by Melville. What he could not do, however, was escape his influence.

Notes

1. See Wilson, ed., *Hawthorne and Melville Friendship*, 24.

2. With apologies for the title allusion to Clark Davis, author of *After the Whale: Melville in the Wake of "Moby-Dick,"* the present essay elaborates a suggested connection between Melville and the writing of *The Blithedale Romance* made in Mitchell, *Hawthorne's Fuller Mystery*, 178–79. Davis, in his 1999 article "Hawthorne's Shyness," examines the Melville-Hawthorne friendship from Hawthorne's perspective; while his study begins with the biographical, it shifts quickly to Davis's main focus—the contrasting ways in which Melville and Hawthorne viewed the quest for truth.

3. Sophia Peabody Hawthorne to her mother, Mrs. Elizabeth Peabody, June 9–16, 1850, in Sophia Hawthorne, Letters, Berg Collection.

4. Sophia certainly did not think so either. Writing two months after initially reporting his "nervous fever" and only days before Hawthorne met Melville, Sophia reported to her mother that Hawthorne had "not recovered his pristine

vigor" because he felt Salem "dragging at his heels still." The past year, she wrote, had been "the trying year of his life, as well as of mine—I have not yet found again all my wings—neither is his tread yet again elastic" (August 1, 1850, in Sophia Hawthorne, Letters, Berg Collection).

5. Sophia repeated the charge and responded to her sister Elizabeth in a June 21, 1850, letter, in Sophia Hawthorne, Letters, Berg Collection.

6. Mary Peabody Mann to Horace Mann, quoted in Miller, *Salem Is My Dwelling Place*, 9; George Hillard to Nathaniel Hawthorne, March 28, 1850, quoted in Lathrop, "The Hawthornes in Lenox," 88.

7. Sophia Hawthorne to her sister Elizabeth Palmer Peabody, June 21, 1850, in Sophia Hawthorne, Letters, Berg Collection; Sophia Hawthorne to Mrs. Elizabeth Peabody, September 4, 1850, in Sophia Hawthorne, Letters, Berg Collection.

8. Of his first impression of Melville, Hawthorne wrote his friend Horatio Bridge on August 7, 1850, "I met Melville, the other day, and liked him so much that I have asked him to spend a few days with me before leaving these parts" (*CE*, 16:355). For the most recent accounts of the friendship, see the following: Parker, *Herman Melville*, 1:729–883; Robertson-Lorant, *Melville*, 257–97; and Miller, *Salem Is My Dwelling Place*, 299–318.

9. Sophia Hawthorne to Elizabeth Palmer Peabody, August 29, 1850, quoted in Parker, *Herman Melville*, 1:769.

10. Sophia Hawthorne to Mrs. Elizabeth Peabody, January 27, 1851, in Sophia Hawthorne, Letters, Berg Collection.

11. Hawthorne seems to have gone out of his way to reassure his friends that *Seven Gables* was more reflective of his nature than was *The Scarlet Letter*. In a July 24, 1851, letter to his friend William Pike, Hawthorne complains that Pike has not told him what he thought of his new romance and then proceeds to write: "At any rate, it has sold finely, and seems to have pleased a good many people better than the others, and I must confess that I myself am among the number. It is more characteristic of the author, and a more natural book for me to write, than *The Scarlet Letter* was" (*CE*, 16:465).

12. Clark's *Nathaniel Hawthorne* is the source of all bibliographic information.

13. For an exploration of Hawthorne's domestic life at this period, see Mitchell, *Hawthorne's Fuller Mystery*, 159–79. Herbert's *Dearest Beloved* is, of course, the most thorough study of the tensions within the Hawthorne marriage. See also Miller's *Salem Is My Dwelling Place*, 338–52.

14. Hawthorne's criticism of his own work was influenced by Margaret Fuller. See her *Dial* review of *Twice-Told Tales*.

15. For an extended argument to this effect, see Mitchell, *Hawthorne's Fuller Mystery*, 180–219.

16. See Mitchell, *Hawthorne's Fuller Mystery,* 292n1; hereafter cited parenthetically.

17. Buford Jones in a paper at the 1996 Hawthorne Society meeting in Concord argued, in fact, through references and allusions in "The Old Manse," that
Melville's *Typee* had begun to have this effect on Hawthorne as early as 1846.

18. See Miller, *Salem Is My Dwelling Place,* 357–58; hereafter cited parenthetically.

"In Old Rome's Pantheon"

Hawthorne, Melville, and the Two Republics

Richard Hardack

IN *THE MARBLE FAUN*, Hawthorne uses Rome to develop his final critique of a transcendental American pantheism he associates with Catholicism—what he considers two correlative threats to a distinct Puritan/Protestant American identity. But Hawthorne's final published novel is as concerned with its own narrative displacement, its recursive trajectory from Rome to New England, as it is with its ostensible subject of old world decadence. In Rome, Hawthorne locates a genuine historical palimpsest, and now surrogate for New England, to describe a deification of nature initially indistinguishable from, but finally preferable to, Catholicism. Hawthorne uses one city on a hill (or hills) to critique another; Catholicism serves as a malleable feint for pantheism, its predecessor in Italy and successor in America.

Hawthorne tries to discredit transcendental pantheism—a discourse most routinely attributed to Emerson but most systematically dramatized in Melville—by making a thinly veiled Pan the focal point of his narrative. Hawthorne incorporates not only several of Melville's texts into *The Marble Faun* but the "Rome"-inflected pantheism the heterodox Melville dedicated to him. Hawthorne especially uses *Pierre*, and its merger of an American pantheism with its European sources, to set up a false contest between old and new world "nature religions." As a text of displaced homologies, *The Marble Faun* asks that we choose between the two alternatives while simultaneously undercutting the distinctions it offers. In a previously published article, I argued that Hawthorne's and Melville's correspondence helps structure the intertextuality of some of their works, particularly "Rappaccini's Daughter," *Moby-Dick,* and *Pierre.* I now focus on Hawthorne's final attempt to differentiate his views of American transcendentalism from Melville's. While I track the specific influence of Melville on Hawthorne, I also want to elucidate the cultural contexts for that interplay, and the reasons Hawthorne incorporates some aspects of Melville's works and repudiates others.

Hawthorne formulated some of his perceptions of American nature, transcendentalism, and Rome through his experiences at Brook Farm and his reading of Emerson and *The Dial,* as well as popular sensational literature, which often featured anti-Catholic, nativist caricatures. But he also developed a series of responses to specific transcendental influences on Americans through his relationship with Melville, and especially his reading of Melville's later novels. Like *Moby-Dick, The Marble Faun* at first becomes a "hideous allegory" whose central figure has no definite shape. But unlike Melville's novels, *The Marble Faun* reifies and personifies the presence of pantheism in the figure of an actual, and highly sexual, Pan. Through his reading of Melville, Hawthorne asserts that the Catholicism of Rome represents a form of vestigial nature worship, as well as a discourse of transhistorical universality, that closely resembles American transcendentalism. *The Marble Faun* represents a fictional exchange of correspondence, or novels, with Melville, a reply both to *Pierre* and to Melville's letters concerning transcendental pantheism, divine fraternity, male identity, Rome, and the All of nature.

Through images in popular media, and especially through his correspondence with and reading of Melville, Hawthorne would have been aware of a connection between Rome and a pervasive American pantheism. Corresponding with Hawthorne, Melville repeatedly espouses and then apologizes for pantheism—the merger of men with one another in a sacralized nature. Melville couches that pantheism as a translation of Greek egalitarianism and Roman animism into an American idiom. Some years after breaking off his relationship with his correspondent, Hawthorne uses Rome as a way to address Melville's pantheism and the "foreign" transcendentalism that had colonized his New England. Unlike many writers, though, Hawthorne is not assimilating the "modern Faun" to America but trying to deport him or trace him back to his origins in Europe, where he is admittedly all but extinct (*CE,* 4:463). But while he changes locales, Hawthorne maintains strict homologies: if the old republic, and the Catholic Church in its wake, failed wholly to eradicate the faun, the new republic has failed to eradicate its transcendental Pan. In that sense, Pan emerges as a kind of totem of republican empire, a symbol that must be discredited and relegated to the past: the epigram of Hawthorne's novel could be "great Pan is dead, long live the new republic."

As Nancy Armstrong and Leonard Tennenhouse suggest with regard to captivity narratives, Hawthorne here writes a narrative that generates its own origins by "producing a world of things and people that see[m] to be outside and prior to writing, however long ago [they] vanished into the past." In other words, Hawthorne finally composes Melville's "original" American fiction by creating a displaced origin myth about the new world and obfuscating the origins and ends of the aboriginal races of that world (*CE,* 4:216). It is as if Hawthorne must affirm that the new world is partly predicated on forms of "primitive" nature worship—both in the aboriginal cultures his nation has wiped out and in the transcendental ghosts haunted by those cultures—but then must disavow and reject those beliefs as a foundation for his country. As displaced through time, space, and Hawthorne's reading of Melville, Catholicism serves as the heuristic through which Hawthorne differentiates a "pure," fantasized new-world Protestant identity from an old-world identity oddly conjoined with that of aboriginal America. For much of Hawthorne's novel, however, that very opposition turns out to be insupportable, a false contrast that Hawthorne belies before finally reifying it in unconvincing ways.

Before turning my attention to Hawthorne's specific responses to Melville, I wish to address the role Catholicism played in antebellum culture, and particularly the ways it elicited vehement censure. What was at stake in antebellum representations of Catholicism from Hawthorne's perspective? In what context was Hawthorne belatedly addressing the sacramental and political appeal and shortcomings of the Catholic Church in a predominantly Protestant New England? In a variety of ways, the Church afforded Hawthorne a pointedly "anachronistic" vocabulary with which to address contemporary issues from a remove. According to Jenny Franchot:

Nativist "religious" purity powerfully supplemented appeals to ethnic supremacism and racial purity, projecting contaminations of the Republic. . . . The widening controversy over the validity or permissible extent of slavery clarified this focus on Catholicism, the "foreign" religion a powerful surrogate for the "foreign race" enclosed in white America. The image of captivity to Rome, then, not only expressed the slave's captivity for the Protestant abolitionist and the slave conspirator's for the planter class but also revised the estrangements of a modernizing economy and social space into the righteous simplicities of filial revolt against Rome.[1]

In relation to Catholicism, Hawthorne was then caught in the middle of a series of conflicting positions; for example, if Hawthorne did not believe in the pragmatic or philosophical cause of abolitionism, he also did not ally himself with the Church on the issue. As the Civil War approached, concern regarding foreign natures, religions, and races dramatically increased. In unstable but engaging ways, the Church could serve as a universal sign for these anxieties: it could be used to represent slavery/race; slavery/race could be used to represent the Church; and a universal transcendental nature could emblematize universal Catholicism and vice versa.

Catholicism was especially resonant for Hawthorne when it touched on issues of race and national identity. As Robert Levine writes, "Rome was regularly imaged in Whig and Republican 'free labor' rhetoric as the embodiment of a corrupt 'slave power.'"[2] Southerners often compared American slaves to those of the ancient world, inaccurately claiming that their new-world manumission procedures were comparable to those of late imperial Rome.[3] Rome could therefore be invoked to rationalize slavery, to compare the Church as an institution unfavorably to Southern slavery, or to cast racial bigotry against religious or ethnic bigotry. As Franchot documents:

> In 1841, the nativist Joseph Berg uttered a revealing diatribe against the confessional:
>> "We hear a great deal said about slavery in our day; and I abhor oppression in every shape; but I count the poor slave ... a freeman, when compared with the man who breathes the atmosphere of liberty, and yet voluntarily fetters his soul, and surrenders himself, bound hand and foot, to the sovereign will and pleasure of a popish priest."
>
> Berg was not alone in his astonishing opinion that the slave was better off than the Roman Catholic. His statement reveals a depressing capacity

to rationalize chattel slavery as one (and not the worst) among a series of enslavements, a reasoning that suggests how images of bondage to papal captivity could minimalize objections to race slavery. (171–72)

Perhaps ironically, Hawthorne does not contrast but conflates the Catholic with the slave, racializing the Roman and Catholicizing "nonwhite" Americans.

A form of "nativism" could even be invoked against Native Americans, who were in limited contexts bizarrely associated with Catholics. Native Americans, slaves, and racially ambiguous figures within the Republic threatened its "true" and somehow ulterior character; those groups were often associated with Catholics as too close to nature. In a form of inversion and reification, Catholics and Native Americans were particularly conflated through the issue of captivity as threats to the liberty of white Protestants: "As the genre of Indian captivity narratives shows," Franchot argues, "the experience of 'Roman' captivity was a highly self-conscious one in colonial America, a trauma of ethnic confrontation that attracted intense religious and aesthetic responses. . . . Roman Catholicism played a crucial historical and symbolic role in this simultaneous extraction of the pure from the corruptions of Europe and assertion of European purity against the seductions of Indian America" (88). As a coming civil war threatened to destroy the formed American self, the ghosts of these former putative threats are resurrected to play new roles in Hawthorne's imagination.

Catholicism also served as a focus for anxieties about immigration that overlapped with concerns about slavery, expansion, and national identity. In the colonial period, most Catholics settled in Maryland, and priests as well as laymen owned slaves. By 1785, approximately 15,800 Catholics owned 3000 black slaves in Maryland. As H. Shelton Smith observes, though some Catholics lamented the existence of slavery, Catholic doctrine only disavowed abuses in slavery and never the institution of slavery itself, which violated neither natural nor divine law; Catholic spokesmen adamantly dissociated themselves from the abolitionist notion that slavery was inherently sinful.[4]

Still, by the mid-nineteenth century few Catholics owned slaves, and in the Protestant South the Catholic Church itself had little contact with slaves. While not necessarily thought of as slaveholders, however, Catholics were increasingly identified as opponents of emancipation; during the Civil War, for example, "one of the severest critics of abolitionism was Courtney Jenkins, editor of the Baltimore *Catholic Mirror*," who wrote that "[i]t is fanaticism or hypocrisy to condemn slavery as in itself criminal, or opposed to the laws of God."[5] Before the Civil War, many immigrant Catholics, politically marginalized and wary of radical movements, felt that abolitionism was disloyal to the existing government of the North; many were also deterred by the sense that abolitionism was closely allied to rationalism and to virulently anti-Catholic enlightenment propositions about the equality of men. While Daniel O'Connell was able to stir European Catholics against slavery, he largely failed with Irish Americans, who found Archbishop Hughes of New York and even the reformist Bishop England of Charleston more politically palatable. The former, while opposed to slavery, was perceived in his arguments with Orestes Brownson to favor the slave trade: he wrote, "sometimes it has appeared to us that abolitionism . . . stands in need of a strait jacket and the humane protection of a lunatic asylum."[6]

Northerners, however, could oppose both slavery and Catholicism without being abolitionists. As the Boston Irish paper the *Pilot* intimates in an editorial titled "Abolitionism and Popery," resistance to one form of "oppression" did not automatically translate to others, meaning in effect that one could support abolition for the wrong reasons. As Noel Ignatiev argues, "opposition to slavery did not imply approval of abolitionism, which it said was 'thronged with bigoted and persecuting religionists; with men who . . . desire the extermination of Catholics by fire and sword.'"[7] In Franchot's estimation, "New England hostility to immigrant Catholicism in the three decades prior to the Civil War facilitated the mounting regional attack on slavery by popularizing a usefully improbable and clearly regional rhetoric of purity and contamination. . . . One could attack the South for the Romanism of its slaveholding practices rather than the white supremacism of such customs" (103). Against this background in the United States, abolitionism was imagined to have a largely Protestant base of support in Britain. With such an array of fantasies and inconsistent associations, it is easier to see how Hawthorne came to associate nonwhites with Catholicism, Rome, transcendentalism, nature, and a litany of threats/lures to a Protestant American identity.

Hawthorne's novel does not directly or literally treat much of the historical context addressed above but invokes or deflects many of these political issues in philosophical contexts, linking Catholicism to transcendentalism, which then forms a kind of bookend to the Puritanism with which he was most concerned earlier in his career. To Hawthorne, transcendentalism represented such an extreme and atavistic form of Protestant idealism that it circled back to and overlapped with paganism and Catholicism; more specifically, transcendentalism became a kind of "gateway" religion that inevitably led Protestants back to Catholicism. Further, given Hawthorne's complicated attitude toward slavery and abolitionism, he might have been attracted to Catholicism not for any overt or literal proslavery sentiments attached to it but heuristically for the ways Catholicism, along with transcendentalism, allowed him a symbolic use of race to portray nature and sin as triangulated among old world, contemporary Rome, and new world. Much as he uses pre-Etruscan and Roman settings to comment on contemporary American identity, Hawthorne deliberately uses anachronistic representations of Catholicism in the new world to comment on contemporary American spirituality.

Critics have long noted that *The Marble Faun* underscores a polarity between North American and European history. Conrad Shumaker, for example, argues that this "romance as a whole defines the difference between American history, which has created the spotless daughter of the Puritans, and Old World history, which is illustrated in the fall and redemption of Donatello."[8] I instead propose that this seeming opposition forms an inversion, a mutually defining, contiguous sequence. Through contemporary Catholicism, Hawthorne emphasizes the hybridity of pagan Rome and pagan transcendentalism and insinuates that they are aspects of the same vice. His Puritan daughter is neither spotless nor entirely Puritan, and the ambiguous "transformation" of the faun reflects the way his atavistic Pan figure moves from symbolizing the old pagan world to representing contemporary America.

Hawthorne makes detailed use of his Roman setting to chronicle cultural differences from his contemporary New England. For Michael Colacurcio, "Europe would challenge both Hawthorne's religious sympathies and his literary imagination; but the 'myth' of *The Marble Faun* would turn out to be, after all, a version of the 'fable' of 'The May-Pole of Merry Mount.'" However, where Colacurcio claims "all the elaborate Catholicism of *The Marble Faun* would turn out to mean just nothing at all," I would counter that it clarifies everything.[9] Hawthorne's belated romance reflects his fear that American idealism could degenerate into perversion and that acceptance of the All of nature would lead to acceptance of the universal of religion. Nancy Bentley demonstrates the significance of an American primitivism to Hawthorne's putatively foreign text; for "while the dominant vocabulary of *The Marble Faun* is derived from the art and history of Rome . . . its faun is still linked to American anxieties about a 'social system thoroughly disturbed.'"[10] Bentley's reading, however, doesn't fully take into account how American transcendentalism inflects the image of an "African faun" as well as the novel's representation of race, Catholicism, and "nativist" identity. *The Marble Faun* defers and deflects; its Catholicism is really American transcendentalism, but its transcendentalism is really Catholicism. Catholicism and transcendentalism are situated as equivalent insofar as they are racialized, primitive, universal, and closely associated with nature.

The question of location remains crucial in approaching Hawthorne's text. Hawthorne's allegorical setting, the ahistorical eternal city, is at times overwhelmed by the particular, degraded reality of the present Rome. The "temporal disjunctions" Bentley notes between the preserved splendors of Rome's past and its contemporary overlay are matched by a geographical fugue; Hawthorne is contrasting not just epochs but shores. According to Franchot, "The Eternal city's aggressive, finally unassimilable, materiality in *The Marble Faun* suggests that its difference is entirely other than that of Hester Prynne's Boston. . . . Italy, it turns out, is not a 'faery precinct' but the opposite: a region of excessive representation," overly embodied, mordant, and decadent (352).

As Leonardo Buonomo contends, Hawthorne downplays Rome's contemporary political travails and the "country's" civil war. Against the reading of critics like Robert Levine, Buonomo argues that Hawthorne's "critique [of the pervasive influence of the Church] is not grounded in the specificity of the historical period in which the story is set," and its Rome "might never have seen the revolution of 1849. . . . [T]he reader . . . may even fail to realize that the city . . . is under occupation."[11] Beneath the superficially "timeless" facade of Rome, however, we also find a racially conscious depiction of antebellum American culture and an impending civil war.

In this context, Rome's status as eternal city partly reifies a transcendental sense of universal correspondences and a denial of differences between cultures. The figure of Pan, like America itself, stands outside history. Characterizing pantheism, Donatello has little sense of past or future (*CE*, 4:428, 4:15). He is an incarnation of Emerson's Americanized figures of Pan and Bacchus, who would have an almost original relationship with nature and almost none with society or history. Hawthorne is replying to a variety of Emersonian claims that, for example, "the belt of wampum, and the commerce of America, are alike" to the transcendental mind. With language resonant for Hawthorne's family, Emerson lectured that "[a]n everlasting Now reigns in Nature that produces on our bushes the selfsame Rose which charmed the Roman." If Emerson believes that "Greece, Rome, Gaul, Britain, America lie folded already in the first man" and sees "not only this equality between new and old countries . . . but also a certain equivalence of the ages of history," Hawthorne demonizes the consequences by making his displaced Native/African American an irredeemable Italian faun.[12]

Throughout his life, Hawthorne was suspicious of, yet attracted to, transcendental idealism and beliefs that could purify sin in nature or a universal church. Levine persuasively argues that Hawthorne early in his career had been affronted by the corruption of Roman Catholicism as a political power, but in *The Marble Faun*, while still concerned about "tendencies toward despotism," he expresses an attraction to an "'artistic' Catholicism" (20–21). Levine concludes that Hawthorne becomes less nativist, "correspond[ing] to a similar wavering in American culture during the 1850s" (23).

But Hawthorne also transforms his personal attraction to "artistic" or confessional Catholicism, as most fully expressed in his journals, to his narrator's suspicion of Catholicism as a form of transcendental decadence. In that process, Hawthorne's narrator remains obsessed with the most influential, early period of transcendentalism. Just as a literal Puritanism no longer influenced the nation but became a metaphor for Hawthorne's contemporary anxieties, pantheism served as a locus for his concerns about American religion, race, and social relations. In 1857, the antipantheist tract writer James Buchanan notes, "In its Ideal or Spiritual form [pantheism] may be seductive to some ardent, imaginative minds; but it is a wretched creed notwithstanding."[13] Reverend Morgan Dix similarly declaims in 1864, "[I]f the age be full of pantheistic tendencies . . . though their maintainers and teachers ignore or conceal the fact, then [we] must . . . show how men may have been tempted, seduced . . . by it almost at unawares."[14] Such representative statements, flanking the production of *The Marble Faun*, help further contextualize why Hawthorne was still ruminating on the seductiveness of transcendentalism. In any case, though transcendentalism remained a more pervasive influence than is usually imagined, Hawthorne's concern with it was more heuristic than realistic.[15]

For Hawthorne, Catholic discourse and the nature worship it unsuccessfully suppresses are perilous to an American sensibility: "Had the Jesuits known the situation of this troubled heart, [Hilda's] inheritance of New England puritanism would hardly have protected the poor girl from the pious strategy of those good fathers" (*CE*, 4:344). The sins of these fathers supplant those of Hawthorne's own Puritan ancestors. We should remember that this good father's daughter Rose eventually converted to Catholicism and became Mother Mary Alphonsa, while Hawthorne wrote of Una when she was fourteen—as he began preliminary work on *The Marble Faun*—"we shall have done the poor child no good office in bringing her here, if the rest of her life is to be a dream of this 'city of the soul,' and an unsatisfied yearning to come back" (*CE*, 14:230). In Hawthorne's imagination, Catholicism and transcendentalism seduce and poison young women's bodies and souls and young men's minds. By the novel's turning point, when Hilda is asked if she is a Catholic, she responds, "I don't quite know what I am." With charged terminology, Hawthorne emphasizes the danger of such ambiguity, admonishing that "the New England girl would permanently succumb to the scarlet superstitions" of Italy (*CE*, 4:368, 4:416). As Bentley claims, "At times Catholicism serves as a figure of universal religious spirit; at other moments the same Roman Catholic signs are dead forms behind which are 'scarlet superstitions' or worse" (906). That "worse," the new scarlet letter, is the revenant pantheism for which Catholicism serves as a kind of laundering or pandering service. Well before D. H. Lawrence, Hawthorne traces how the horned, tailed, and cloven-hooved devil devolves from Pan, the original shepherd; yet Pan and Mephistopheles remain inextricable from one another as well as the mythology of Catholicism.

Hilda is so frequently described as a "faithful Protestant, and daughter of the Puritans" that the reader can only become suspicious of her alleged religious singularity (*CE*, 4:399). As Franchot suggests, Hilda winds up in a "liminal position between New England Protestantism and Italian Catholicism," her identity and origin destabilized (357). Hilda is nearly seduced by this scarlet Catholicism. Her theological "seduction" parallels Miriam's fall with, and seduction by, Donatello; as Miriam observes:

"The Great God Pan." An illustration by Frederic Leighton for "A Musical
Instrument," by Elizabeth Barrett Browning, *Cornhill Magazine* 2 (July 1860): 84.

"[H]ow close he stands to nature! . . . He shall make me as natural as himself"—or in other words convert her to nature (*CE*, 4:83).

However, in the theological and popular discourse of the day, in a rhetoric developed from earlier American sentimental novels, one is also "seduced" by American pantheism—the peril abroad displaces the peril at home. Writers with whom Hawthorne would have been familiar invoke pantheism as the most "seductive" force to the American mind. Titling *successive* chapters of *Democracy in America* "The Progress of Roman Catholicism in the United States" and "What Inclines Democratic Nations towards Pantheism," Alexis de Tocqueville considers these covalent belief systems ontological lures for Americans and pantheism "one of [the philosophies] most fitted to seduce the human mind in democratic times."[16] Even Emerson feared "the Woodgod who solicits the wandering poet. . . . Very seductive are the first steps from the town to the woods, but the End is want & madness."[17] These rhetorical associations were neither isolated nor culturally marginal. Hawthorne would have noted that in *Moby-Dick* Melville repeatedly advises, "[Y]ou needs must own the seductive god, bowing your head to Pan" (*WHM*, 6:483). For Hawthorne, such emblematic seduction by nature or universality is more perilous than seduction by desire. The seducer in his last novel is notably different from that of *The Scarlet Letter;* partially but significantly, it is because Melville's sense of transcendentalism has interposed. Through geographic and temporal displacement, Hawthorne's nativism comes to be directed against his own transcendental compatriots as "foreign Catholics" out to seduce the national character.

Against the above historical backdrop, and under the overdetermined conceit of writing a romance in Rome, Hawthorne reproves Catholicism's ulterior guise of New World transcendentalism. But he continues to do so without engaging with politics, slavery, or race in realistic contexts. In his introduction to the novel, Hawthorne highlights the Latin derivation of the romance, claiming that Italy, as "fairy precinct," is the perfect site where "actualities would not be so terribly insisted upon, as they . . . must needs be, in America" (*CE*, 4:3). But Hawthorne also follows a transposition made by transcendentalists like William Ellery Channing, who, as Franchot notes, identifies Rome as the site of "Transcendentalist romance" in "To the Reader": "[L]et us see Rome, / As she stands firm within the Fancy's home. / . . . The sands of Europe gleam on Salem's shore" (259).

Such a geographic and philosophical fugue is most evident in miniature in Hawthorne's "The Celestial Railroad," where lived "two cruel giants, Pope and Pagan. . . . These vile old troglodytes are *no longer there; but* into their deserted cave another terrible giant has thrust himself. . . . He is a German by birth, and is called Giant Transcendentalist; but as to his form, his features, his substance, and his nature generally, it is the chief peculiarity . . . that neither he for himself, nor anybody for him, has ever been able to describe them" (*CE,* 10:196–97; emphasis added). Pope and pagan are supplanted not just by a generic transcendentalism but a typically unnamed Emersonian Pan. In Hawthorne's reference to the explicit successor to pope and pagan in the new world, the absence of the name verifies the identity. As Emerson writes in "The Natural History of Intellect," Pan is by definition the indescribable master of transformation: "Pan, that is, All. His habit was to dwell in mountains. . . . [H]e was in the secret of nature and . . . was only seen under disguises." For Hawthorne, Pan's disguises complement those of Rome. Emersonian transcendentalism was inexorably associated with German romanticism and Goethe, as *Pierre* bears out: Hawthorne then reassociates transcendentalism with a Catholic paganism, bringing Pan full circle. Emerson also describes "Pan . . . [as] a shapeless giant . . . without hands or fingers or articulating lips or teeth or tongue."[18] As Lawrence retrospectively writes, "Alas, poor Pan! . . . Legless, hornless, faceless, even smileless, you are less than everything or anything. . . . And yet here, in America . . . old Pan is still alive."[19] Yet why would Hawthorne still disguise that Pan in the equally unrepresentable Donatello twenty-five years after "The Celestial Railroad"?

In part, we sometimes overlook the animosity these two discourses aroused during the American Renaissance, when "Giant Transcendentalis[m]" was endemically situated in *relation to* Catholicism, as its ally, predecessor, and potential successor in a stock progression from nature to trinity and back. (Their priority/sequence is unstable throughout Hawthorne's novel, which could be subtitled "Peter-Pan.") Part of the historical context involves philosophical debates that might seem arcane or unintelligible from our remove but that were heatedly contested at that time. For example, the transcendental preacher Theodore Parker writes: "Pantheism seems to be the bugbear of some excellent persons. They see it everywhere except on the dark walls of their own churches. . . . [Maret] finds it the *natural result of Protestantism,* and places before us the pleasant alternatives, *either the Catholic Church or Pantheism!*"[20] In order to combat the specter of an impersonal science, people turn to pantheism, which, ironically, winds up being attacked as a form of "rationalism." Paraphrasing Bronson Alcott, Emerson avers that, in the woods, "it seemed plain to me that most men were pantheists at heart" (*JMN,* 10:175).

For even its Catholic critics, pantheism serves as a halfway house between Protestantism and Catholicism. Among scores of writers promoting or denouncing pantheism in the mid-nineteenth century, Reverend Januarius De Concilio, author of the 1873 *Catholicity and Pantheism,* concludes that in America "Pantheism is more prevalent at the present time than ever it was."[21] Following Brownson and presaging Annie Dillard, critics worry as late as 1884 "that Pantheism is [also] the inevitable goal of Protestantism."[22] Especially at the height of the American Renaissance, new-world writers are accused of leading readers into unorthodoxy: the *Athenaeum,* for example, calls *Pierre* "one of the most diffuse doses of transcendentalism offered for a very long time to the public" (*Log,* 464). Complaining of the novel's "supersensuousness," Duyckinck's *Literary World* concludes that "the combined power of New England transcendentalism and Spanish Jesuitical casuistry could not have more completely befogged nature and truth, than this confounded *Pierre* has done."[23] Such comments are relevant to *The Marble Faun:* the pantheism of Hawthorne's competitors and even his former acolyte can be identified in the conjoined "transcendental" paganism and Catholicism of Rome.

To the Hawthorne critical of transcendental experimentalism, pantheism would pose a more specific threat to the American character. As De Concilio adds, "Pantheism is the real practical error of the day, the last logical consequence of the principle of free examination" (9). De Concilio is unusually vituperative, but his following diatribe epitomizes the charges brought against pantheists from many quarters:

> It is the intelligence, the will of man, of society, of the state which are independent, self-existing, absolute, which are the only God; . . . What is this but Pantheism carried to its farthest consequences? Pantheism . . . is a living, quickening, tremendous reality . . . which is drying up and exhausting the very life of man, sapping the very foundation of society, demolishing the strongest and the most powerful state. (11)

"And let none, especially Americans, think they can grapple with it by any other means" (11), he concludes, than the Catholic Church, the "only solution" for this particularly American form of free thinking (26). To the Catholic—especially one trying to distinguish Catholicism from transcendentalism—pantheism represents a false merger of all forms of post-Kantian rationalism. Going beyond Unitarianism, pantheism incorporates the mysticism of the Catholic Church—the belief in a power in nature to transform and transcend matter that Protestantism lacks—but without any of its rituals or hierarchic structures of authority. In the context of their putative antagonism, Hawthorne shares Tocqueville's apprehension that America "is the country in which the Roman Catholic religion makes most progress" and his sense that Catholicism and pantheism play the same role for people living in republics: they fulfill their need for an "idea of unity" (29, 32).

Hawthorne would have been aware of the continued influence of even a waning transcendentalism. From the 1830s to the 1860s, the already imperfect homogeneity of American religion dissolved: in 1833, Massachusetts "became the last in the Union to abandon an official religious establishment," allowing for what Mary Kupiec Cayton calls a competition for souls.[24] Among these new sects, Unitarianism is identified as the precursor to pantheism; for De Concilio, only the trinity stands between Catholicism and the "class of disguised Pantheists—disguised even to themselves—that is, the Unitarians" (71). Hawthorne is thus being mimetic in disguising pantheism in the structures of Catholicism; like Melville, he was fascinated by subterfuge, dissembling, and masquerades. Rome, the city of the trinity and disguise, represents Hawthorne's version of *The Confidence-Man* cast as the Confidence City.

It is most of all Melville who distills transcendental pantheism for Hawthorne, identifying its seductive allure as well as its ultimate failure. In reaction to Melville's pantheism, most often voiced in his letters to Hawthorne but also embedded in the novels from *Mardi* to *Pierre,* Hawthorne comes to imagine Rome as the fitting location for his renunciation of American religious speculation. Hawthorne's use of Italy is most of all a response to the obsession with the "soft social Pantheism" that structures *Pierre* (*WHM,* 7:250). Pierre is cast as the quintessential young American transcendentalist in literature. Yet as connoted by his name, and by Isabel's imputed French origin, this Peter is not "purely" American: their foreignness, however, is as ambiguous as their familial relationship.[25] Where Melville seeks to create an American Cenci—a woman whose European "sin" becomes emblematic of American identity—Hawthorne seeks to extradite her back to Europe. Through her knowledge of Miriam's guilt, Hilda, the quintessential American daughter, becomes the novel's "channeler" for the foreign expression of the Cenci. Following Melville, Hawthorne blurs the racial, and possibly incestuous, origins of one of his primary female characters—he even begins his tale by claiming there "was an ambiguity about this young lady" (*CE*, 4:20)—and as in "Benito Cereno," Hawthorne conjoins blackness and racial mixture with Catholicism as well as pantheism. Hawthorne emphasizes Miriam's "ambiguity" throughout the book, again suggesting her affinity with Pierre's Isabel, who in many ways embodies the subtitular, transcendental "ambiguities" of Melville's novel. As filtered through Melville's representations of pantheistic reverie, Catholicism and transcendentalism in Hawthorne's mind are ambiguously Christian, of ambiguous racial origin, and of ambiguous moral valence.

Tellingly, when Melville stayed with the Hawthornes in September 1850, Sophia noted, in for us an overdetermined fashion, that "one morning [Melville] shut himself in the boudoir and read Mr. Emerson's Essays in presence of our beautiful picture," an engraving of Raphael's "The Transfiguration," itself a gift from Emerson.[26] This scene triangulates American transcendentalism with Roman Catholicism and pre-Western beliefs. Symbolically, Hawthorne receives Melville's transfiguration of Emersonian transcendentalism in his own bedroom. But where Melville dramatizes his sense that an old-world animism seeps through the surface of American capitalism, Hawthorne remains intermittently detached; Melville narrativizes the consequences of his beliefs, while Hawthorne stages the consequences as refutation.

The Marble Faun can be read partly as Hawthorne's synthetic response to his numerous exchanges with and reading of Melville. When Melville writes to Hawthorne in November 1851 of his pantheism, he begins to suggest to Hawthorne the form and forum for his final novel:

> So now I can't write what I felt. But I felt pantheistic then—your heart beat in my ribs and mine in yours, and both in God's. . . . I would sit down and dine with you and all the gods in old Rome's Pantheon. . . . Whence come you Hawthorne? By what right do you drink from my flagon of life? And when I put it to my lips—lo, they are yours and not

mine. I feel that the Godhead is broken up like the bread at the Supper, and that we are the pieces. Hence this infinite fraternity of feeling. (*WHM*, 14:212–13)

Melville correlates pantheism, his desire to transcend Protestant individuality and merge his body with other men through a divine nature, with Rome's Pantheon, Catholic communion, and Hawthorne himself. Merger with a universal nature winds up occurring not in Emerson's woods, nor the grassy fields of Melville's pantheistic letters, but near the Field of Mars.

Hawthorne likely associated Melville with the pagan world in a variety of overlapping contexts. In 1857, Melville spent a month in Rome a year before Hawthorne's residence there. Commenting on his subsequent lectures on Roman statuary, the *Ohio Farmer* describes Melville's disquieting "affection for heathenism [as] profound and sincere. He speaks of the *heathenism of Rome* as if the world were little indebted to Christianity."[27] Melville's nostalgia for pre-Christian religions of nature fills Hawthorne with a mixture of curiosity, admiration, and suspicion.

Hawthorne tracks the return of this repressed pre-Christian animism through contemporary American representations of nature. In "Nature," originally titled "Pan," Emerson famously wrote of being "bathed by the blithe air and uplifted into infinite space—all mean egotism vanishes": "I become a transparent eyeball. I am nothing; I see all."[28] Even more than in *The Blithedale Romance*—a novel that derides this "blithe air" of transcendentalism—Hawthorne in *The Marble Faun* reifies Emerson's conceit of the open-air sepulchre of nature and his attendant notion that he could be nowhere but see all. Melville had linked pantheism, sight, and invisibility throughout *Moby-Dick* and *Pierre*: the self-proclaimed pantheist Ishmael, for example, vanishes from his own tale as he becomes its invisible all-seeing narrator, able to chronicle even Ahab's soliloquies. But Ishmael also warns the transparent transcendentalist who "takes the mystic ocean at his feet for the visible image of that deep, blue, bottomless soul, pervading mankind and nature. . . . And perhaps . . . with one-half throttled shriek you drop through that transparent air into the summer sea, no more to rise for ever. Heed it well, ye Pantheists!" (*WHM*, 6:159). Hawthorne recuperates that oscillation from pantheistic reverie to dissolution in Donatello's dramatic fall.

After Emerson, who transcends individuality in the domain of the wood-god, Melville positively associates all aspects of nature and transcendental oversight with pantheism. Like Donatello, Pierre seeks "the refuge of the god-like population of the trees": their high foliage shall drop heavenliness" upon him; when his feet entwine "with their mighty roots, immortal vigor" will steal into him. Pierre at first tries to "lose [his] sharp individuality, and become delightfully merged into that soft social Pantheism[,] . . . that rosy melting of all into one," precisely Melville's fantasy of merger with Hawthorne (*WHM*, 7:106, 7:250). Melville writes to Hawthorne that in reading "Goethe's sayings . . . [he] came across this, '*Live in the all*.' . . . [B]ring to yourself the tinglings of life that are felt in the flowers and the woods." Melville emblematically describes such pantheistic feelings as "nonsense!" before immediately recanting to say, "there is some truth in [it]. You must often have felt it" (*WHM*, 14:193–94). It is with regard to this pantheism that, as Hawthorne generally describes him, Melville can neither believe nor be comfortable in his unbelief (*Log*, 529).

By *Pierre*, however, Melville winds up bitterly rebuking Goethe for deifying nature. Pierre, whose transcendental eyesight deteriorates throughout the novel, writes on a scrap of paper: "Away, ye . . . inconceivable coxcomb of a Goethe. . . . Corporations have no souls, and thy Pantheism, what was that? Thou wert but the pretentious, heartless part of a man." Eventually, "the only visible outward symbols of [Pierre's] soul—his eyes—did also turn downright traitors to him, and with more success than the rebellious blood. . . . The pupils of his eyes rolled away from him in their own orbits" (*WHM*, 7:302, 7:341–42). Such is Melville's resolution of merger with transcendental nature: his pupil, like giant Pan and the Enceladus of the novel, is blinded and dismembered.

❦ ❧

Transcendental sight is another motif Hawthorne uses to link pantheism with the Church. Just as Melville and Hawthorne construct several novels around the character poles of Pan and the Cenci, the latter orchestrates his drama around two key structures in Rome, the Pantheon and St. Peter's, competing sites of religious and "ocular" universality. It is no accident that Hawthorne's novel opens with the eye of the public but closes with that of Rome's Pantheon; the familiar "great eye"/I forms another quintessential transcendental circle.[29] When Hawthorne early in his novel describes "the circular roof of the Pantheon looking heavenward with its ever-open eye," he goes beyond even Melville in relocating an All-seeing Pan-opticon from the Emersonian woods to the center of the Catholic world (*CE*, 4:110). Kenyon claims "it is to the aperture in the Dome—that great Eye, gazing heavenward—that the Pantheon owes the peculiarity of its effect." With moss covering its center, the Pantheon is cast as nature's cathedral, the old world equivalent of Emerson's "plantations" of god. Hilda, for example, while watching a penitent kneeling "beneath the great central Eye," half expects to see angels floating above the aperture. Kenyon had gravely implored Hilda to worship beneath that eye because to pray at a saint's shrine, "tempting" as it would be, would only express "earthly wishes" (*CE*, 4:457–59). That great eye of the Pantheon recalls Emerson's transparent eyeball in nature, the obsession with being an unobserved transcendental observer narrativized in *The Blithedale Romance*. Choosing here between pantheism and Catholicism, Hawthorne partly validates what he sees as the former's more acceptably nativist vice.

In contrast, St. Peter's lacks the Pantheon's eye of heaven in its dome. Yet "perverted" Catholicism is equally associated with the eye of transcendentalism, much as the voyeurism of *The Blithedale Romance* correlates the universal eye with the sexual transgressions of New England free thinking. For example, while the protagonists look down from St. Peter's—the one site in Rome they could be nowhere and see all— Hilda's "every movement [has previously been] watched and investigated far more thoroughly by the priestly rulers than by her dearest friends" (*CE*, 4:465). The universal Catholic eye—Hawthorne's social version of the transparent eyeball—sees All, but with more pernicious consequences than even transcendentalism. Catholicism momentarily turns out to be the appropriate affiliation for Hawthorne's overly observant, all-seeing narrators.

It is against these backdrops—notions of a romanticized nature religion and primitive races, the exchange of ideas and letters with Melville—that Hawthorne situates his characters. Hawthorne's obsession with pantheistic "interminglings of identity"—geographic, literary, and racial—structures much of *The Marble Faun*: we are early on told that the "characteristics of creatures that dwell in woods and fields, will seem to be mingled and kneaded into one substance, along with the kindred qualities in the human soul. Trees, grass, flowers . . . and unsophisticated man." Hawthorne's characters obtain "a glimpse far backward into Arcadian life, or, farther still, into the Golden Age": "'It is your kinsman Pan, most likely, . . . playing on his pipe,'" Miriam says to Donatello at the sound of sylvan music (*CE*, 4:188, 4:10, 4:84). The faux faun is so bluntly cast as a contemporary incarnation of primitive Pan—possessing furry ears and a purely animal nature, belonging to an entirely different race—that Hawthorne is surely aiming his satire at Emerson via his understanding of Melville and his unsocialized wild-child Isabel.

In a variety of contexts, transcendentalists configure nature as pre-Western and nonwhite. Emerson, for example, consistently codes the All not just as primitive but as black—"pre-Anglo-Saxon"—claiming: "Such homage did the Greek pay to the unscrutable force we call Instinct, or Nature. . . . [Pan] could intoxicate by the strain of his shepherd's pipe. . . . [He was] aboriginal, old as Nature, and saying, like poor Topsy, 'Never was born; growed.'"[30] Emerson's Pan resembles Stowe's parthenogenetic black girl Topsy, a conceit Hawthorne reifies in "Chiefly about War Matters" in imagining a group of runaway slaves, in their "primeval simplicity," as "not altogether human . . . and akin to the fauns and rustic deities of olden times" (*CE*, 23:420). The aboriginal blackness of transcendentalism thus provides a subtext for Hawthorne's voicing of pre-Western beliefs in general and Donatello in particular. As if offering a blueprint for the faun, Emerson writes in his *Journals* that "the negro must be very old & belongs . . . to the fossil formations. What right has he to be intruding into the late & civil daylight of this dynasty of the Caucasians and Saxons? . . . [S]o inferior a race must perish shortly like the poor Indians" (*JMN*, 7:393).[31] Donatello's bust even possesses something "very much resembling a fossil countenance" (*CE*, 4:380). For Hawthorne, "[t]he faun is a natural and delightful link betwixt human and brute life, with something of a divine character intermingled."[32] Through such fantasies, blacks are equated with Native Americans, and both "intermingled" with the vanishing race of "pre-Etruscan" fauns. Their successors are transcendental white men in the New England woods, writing about their predecessors in Arcadia. In this historical context the antebellum association of Catholicism with slavery makes overdetermined sense.

Melville again intermediates for Hawthorne, having effectively situated Babo as a "dark Satyr in a mask" in "Benito Cereno" and Pip as the character—after the black-identified, self-designated Ishmael—most susceptible to pantheism in *Moby-Dick*. Pip suffers the complete loss of self in a pantheistic nature coded as black (*WHM*, 6:414). Roman/

Dionysian nature and race are so overdeterminedly intertwined for Melville that, as Parker notes, a shipmate from the *Acushnet* inscribed in the copy of *Moby-Dick* Melville gave him: "Pip—Backus—his real name. I was in the boat at the time he made the leap overboard" (2:151). Ishmael also warns that a "Pantheistic vitality seems[s] to lurk in [sharks'] very joints and bones, after what might be called the individual life ha[s] departed." These sharks consume their own rebellious body parts because—like Emerson, Ishmael, Pierre, and Melville when writing Hawthorne—they cannot tell where their own bodies begin and end in nature. As Queequeg discovers when a detached "pantheistic" shark head nearly bites off his hand, it is "unsafe to meddle with the[ir] corpses and ghosts: "'de god wat made shark must be one dam Ingin'" (*WHM*, 6:302). On the edge not of civil daylight but of civil war, Hawthorne then incongruously transposes all the elements of this intoxicating, non-white, transindividual pantheistic nature divinity onto a surrogate Native American in the pope's court.

For the transcendentalist Merrill Richardson in 1843, aboriginal or pre-Christian religion is the truth of the new world: "Pantheism, a word full of denial and skepticism to superficial minds, is one of the highest products of the devout spirit of man." Richardson's invocation of Native American pantheism is reminiscent of Hawthorne's rendition of the faun's worldview and Melville's enactment of transcendentalism: God "is constantly operating every where and in every thing[.] . . . Those you call *heathen*[,] the wild Indian . . . sees God in the forest."[33] Like Native Americans in Jefferson's view, or blacks in Emerson's, Donatello has "a great deal of animal nature in him; as if he had been born in the woods . . . and were as yet but imperfectly domesticated": he "call[s] the woodland inhabitants, the furry people and the feathered people, in a language that they see[m] to understand." A "creature of the happy tribes below us," Hawthorne's faun is destined for extinction, recapitulating what Ronald Takaki and Wai Chee Dimock identify respectively as Jeffersonian and Jacksonian rhetorics of genocide (*CE*, 4:104, 4:247, 4:79). As Kristie Hamilton demonstrates, for Hawthorne modernity itself involved the erasure of Native Americans.[34] Under the logic of American expansion, Native Americans were members of now melancholy prelapsarian tribes who could not survive in the contemporary world.

In Hawthorne's synthetic and imitative imagination, Pan connotes all Native and African American cultures, the world before the new world that still lies beneath its Protestant veneer. Hawthorne found another surrogate for those cultures in the conjoined faun and Roman Catholic. As Bentley argues, tracing the way Donatello reverts to the flaws of his ancestors, "the Faun was apt to become, in other words, an Italian priest—or rather the Italian priest as he appeared in Anglo-American travel descriptions. Countless travel accounts show that the Roman Catholic clergyman served as America's Old World savage" (916). Such an association would again be inflected for Hawthorne through Melville, whose greatest notoriety came through his attacks on missionaries, who are characterized in *Typee* as far more savage than the "primitives" they purported to convert. Bentley also suggests that American travelers imagined Catholics, and monks especially, as closer "to the lower order of animals" (917). If we correlate this prejudice to Emerson's, we see how Catholic priest, pagan Pan, and African American are conjoined for Hawthorne. Emerson orated in an early lecture that "the free negro . . . stand[s] as he does in nature below the series of thought, and in the plane of vegetable and animal existence."[35] In the fantasy of a wild blackness, the contradictions of transcendental self-representation are powerfully brought to bear on the bodies of slaves, on those who cannot occupy the position of self-reliant white males. If Catholics are imagined in popular discourse as not just racially mixed, but "primitives," their use as surrogates for Pan by those who wish to extirpate transcendental influences makes perverse sense.

Like Emerson, then, Hawthorne is talking not simply about nature or Catholics in Rome but about nature in the new world: and most of all, about the difference between Protestantism and all prior, "primitive" religions. The aboriginals of Rome would be Donatello's transcendental race, supplanted by Etruscans, Italians, and finally displaced Protestants. In America, the equivalent natives are also ironically displaced not just by whites but (allegedly) by African Americans. Hawthorne utilizes pantheism as a doctrine of racial homologies; hence the move to Rome contains cultural logic: few Native Americans are left to write about in New England, at least not in the ways Hawthorne wants to situate them in society.

Melville began this process of "Catholic transformation" in *Pierre:* the transcendental Church of the Apostles, though a "relic of a more primitive time," is "converted from its original purpose to one widely contrasting," and it "usurp[s] an unoccupied space formerly sacred as the old church's burial inclosure" (*WHM,* 7:266, 7:268). This transformation is as charged for Melville as Hilda's religious conversion: for Melville, transfigurations of identity raise vexed issues of confidence, unbelief, and self-alienation. Similarly, in "Statues in Rome," Melville asserts, "Many of those ideas from heathen personages[,] [Milton] afterwards appropriated to his celestials, just as the Pope's artists converted the old heathen Pantheon into a Christian Church."[36] Melville chronicles only the appearance of such "conversions," for beneath each supposedly Christian church resides the Pantheon of nature.

After Melville, Rome for Hawthorne represents the impersonal *conversions* of pantheism, where one man's life is merged with the All in a sequence of death and rebirth; as Catholicism supplanted pantheism in Europe, pantheism now again supplants Catholicism in America. Pantheists' belief in fated repetition is oddly more compatible with Hawthorne's sense of psychological and narrative recursion than a Protestant notion of progress. Melville prepares us for such sentiments in *Redburn*: "as St. Peter's church was built in great part of the ruins of old Rome, so in all our erections . . . we but form quarries and supply ignoble materials for the grander domes of posterity" (*WHM*, 4:149). Pantheism is the ghost in this machine, the hidden foundation on which the new republic stands. Hawthorne begins his novel with a paraphrase of this passage, noting that throughout Rome "the domes of Christian churches [are] built on the old pavements of heathen temples, and supported by the very pillars that once upheld them" (*CE*, 4:6). In a doctrine of transcendental impersonality, history overlays individual identity. Hawthorne then echoes Melville's premise that the ruined figure of Rome personifies an impersonal history but again uses the city and the faun to intimate that Catholicism and transcendentalism have the same twisted roots and branches. Rome's cycle of decay particularly repulses Hawthorne's narrator: trampled, soiled bouquets, "these they sell again, and yet once more, and ten times over, defiled as they all are with the wicked filth of Rome." Hawthorne here rails against the indiscriminate merger of bodies and identities that defines pantheism, what almost becomes a traffic in women: these ruined flowers "may symbolize . . . crumpled and crushed . . . hearts . . . [and bodies] passed from hand to hand." (So much for exchanging his heart and ribs with Melville in a floral nature.) In nature, much as in Catholic Rome, all things are reused and transformed, all bodies "passed around," without any Protestant virtue or divinity to safeguard their chastity or resurrection. Perhaps in anticipation of a lost Rose, to Hawthorne these flowers represent an irretrievable Arcadia and the ineluctable repetitions of history. Instead of Pan's nature, we are left with imitation: "instead of blossoms on the shrub, or freshly gathered . . . [the Romans'] worship, now-a-days, is best symbolized by the artificial flower" (*CE*, 4:440–41, 4:298).

That flower personified, a transcendental Pan remains associated with plants and trees, and binds and blends men with them. As Emerson would have it, "[t]he world, the universe, is a gigantic flower,—but the flower is one function or state of the plant, and the world but a stage or state of the Pan" (*JMN*, 11:187). Such a passage remains impenetrably mystical, but Emerson invokes Pan's botanical configuration as a model for the stages of existence and the operation of all natural law, including his notion that all evolution begins with primal organs and forms. The Catholic or universal flower moves us from Emerson's Pan to Hawthorne's Rose.

At least part of *The Marble Faun* represents Hawthorne's response to Melville's literary and personal pantheism, in which Donatello figures as a mixture of Melville and his transcendental characters, especially the tree-sanctifying Pierre. For example, Donatello, as "intoxicated" and "exhilarat[ed]" as Emerson in the woods, "[i]n a sudden rapture . . . embraced the trunk of a sturdy tree, and seemed to imagine it a creature worthy of affection and capable of a tender response" (*CE*, 4:74). This passage probably contains a specific reference not just to Pierre but to Melville himself. On a trip with Hawthorne and a watchful Oliver Wendell Holmes, Maunsell Field commemorates, Melville "took us to a particular spot on his place to show us some superb trees. He told me that he spent much time there *patting them upon the back*" (*Log*, 506). Hawthorne may also belatedly be replying to Melville's epistolary proposals that they "cross [their] celestial legs in the celestial grass . . . . lying on the grass on a warm summer's day": "Your legs seem to send out shoots into the earth. Your hair feels like leaves upon your head. This is the *all* feeling" (*WHM*, 14:191, 194). Hawthorne's invocation of "leafy patriarchs" reflects Emerson's, Pierre's, and pantheism's embrace of a divine nature: literalizing Melville in his fantasy of grassy repose, or Emerson in his depiction of Topsy as parthenogenetic black Nature "jes growing" from the soil, Donatello may "have sprouted out of the earth." Birds recognize Donatello "as something akin to themselves; or else they fanc[y] that he was rooted and grew there" (*CE*, 4:71, 74–76). So does Hawthorne describe southern blacks as so primevally natural it was "as if their garb had grown upon them spontaneously" (*CE*, 23:419–20).

For all Hawthorne's intimations otherwise, however, Rome can no longer serve as the haunt of a contemporary Pan or divine nature: "In Miriam's remembrance, the scene had a character of fantasy" as if "a company of satyrs, fauns, and nymphs, with Pan in the midst of them, had been disporting themselves in these venerable woods. . . . The spell being broken," we awake to a Rome decaying "as if it were a corpse" (*CE,* 4:90, 4:149). Miriam says to Donatello, "this melancholy and sickly Rome is stealing away the rich, joyous life that belongs to you" (*CE,* 4:149). Yet against Hawthorne's wishful thinking, but also his own structural set-up, Pan remains more alive in New England than old Arcadia: as Kenyon tells Hilda, "Great Pan is not dead, then, after all! The whole tribe of mythical creatures yet live in the moonlight seclusion of a young girl's fancy" (*CE,* 4:103). Such a revenance and warning returns us to Morton of Merrymount, his celebration of nature in the midst of an infant Puritan culture. But Hawthorne inverts *Pierre's* gender configurations: the repository of transcendental fancy is America's young woman, not its representative young man.

As historical epochs merge into the present, Hawthorne's Italian moonlight "scarcely show[s] what portion of it was man's work, and what was Nature's, but left it all in very much the same kind of ambiguity and half-knowledge, in which antiquarians generally leave the identity of Roman ruins." The overlap between ambiguous pantheism and Catholicism recurs even in St. Peter's climate; as Kenyon ventures: "The best thing I know of St. Peter's is its equable temperature. . . . Winter and summer are married at the high altar, and dwell together in perfect harmony," to which Hilda adds that she has "always felt this soft, unchanging climate of St. Peter's to be another manifestation of its sanctity" (*CE,* 4:168, 4:368–69). St. Peter's has stolen the Pantheon's weather pattern, merging all nature's climates in harmony. This is another conceit Hawthorne develops from *Moby-Dick,* where Ishmael advises, "[L]ike the great dome of St. Peter's, and like the great whale, retain, o man! in all seasons a temperature of thine own." Melville begins the circle joining Catholicism and nature and also compares tracing the whale's unreadable visage to manipulating "the Dome of the Pantheon" (*WHM,* 6:307, 6:345). St. Peter's then becomes Hawthorne's own bête blanc.

In *Pierre,* Melville's incarnation of a Christ without a church fails, and Hawthorne decides instead to investigate the failures of a church without a Christ: he uses Catholicism to question whether transcendentalism is Christian in any recognizable way. Now much like the Pantheon, St. Peter's is "a magnificent, comprehensive, majestic symbol of religious faith": "All splendour was included within [St. Peter's] verge, and there was space for all." Further, in its "Cathedral, worthy to be the religious heart of the whole world, there was room for all nations. . . . [Hilda thought that] beneath the sweep of its great Dome, there should be space for all forms of Christian truth; room both for the faithful and the heretic to kneel" (*CE*, 4:350, 4:356, 4:348). While Hawthorne's Church remains a Catholic icon, its dome connects it to the Pantheon. Hawthorne insists that St. Peter can "appeal as much to Puritans as Catholics," and that his all-representative edifice contains not just historical Catholicism but the universal nature and cultural geography of the new world (*CE*, 4:352). Peter's rock remains the cornerstone of Pan's open-air church.

When Hawthorne equates the two structures, he destabilizes the distinction between historical and present-day Rome, much as he interrogates distinctions between Puritan and contemporary New England. Not St. Peter's, but the Pantheon "stands almost at the central point of the . . . modern city," that "great circle . . . formerly dedicated to heathen gods, but Christianized. . . . The world has nothing else like the Pantheon."[37] It is here the story ends just after Hilda reemerges: in the Pantheon, "all these things make an impression of solemnity, which St. Peter's itself fails to produce" (*CE*, 4:457). The novel finally recants the Catholicism with which it periodically flirts for the "nativist" Pantheon, leaving Hawthorne almost willing to pay the piper. Melville dreamed of merging with Hawthorne and of a transcendental American literature that would become universal. But Hawthorne annuls that merger, casting one Satan against another, Catholicism against pantheism, a Romanized St. Peter against his own half brother Pan, in the universal church in the universal city, to denigrate the excesses of American transcendentalism. When Hawthorne finally sits down to dine with Melville and all the gods in old Rome's Pantheon, he agrees the fare is preferable to that of St. Peter, but he still makes it their last supper.

Notes

I presented a different version of a paper on Hawthorne and Rome for the Nathaniel Hawthorne Society panel, MLA, Washington, D.C., 1996. My thanks to Millicent Bell, T. Walker Herbert, and the panel members.

1. Franchot, *Roads to Rome*, 104; hereafter cited parenthetically.

2. Levine, "'Antebellum Rome,'" 23; hereafter cited parenthetically.

3. LeBlanc, "Context of Manumission," 266–67.

4. Smith, *In His Image*, 7.

5. Smith, *In His Image*, 200. See also Gillard, *Catholic Church*, 25

6. Qtd. in Reverend Benjamin Blied, *Catholics and the Civil War*, 32. One should also remember that the white family most associated with abolitionism, the Beecher family, was also noted for preaching notoriously anti-Catholic sermons. See Blied, 20–21.

7. Ignatiev, *How the Irish Became White*, 13.

8. Shumaker, "'Daughter of the Puritans,'" 65.

9. Colacurcio, *Province of Piety*, 31, 261.

10. Bentley, "Slaves and Fauns," 902; hereafter cited parenthetically.

11. Buonomo, *Backward Glances*, 54–55.

12. Emerson, "The Poet," in *Complete Works*, 3:12; "The Naturalist," in *Early Lectures*, 1:71; "History," in *Complete Works*, 2:34; "Progress of Culture," *Complete Works*, 8:213.

13. Buchanan, *Modern Atheism*, 184.

14. Dix, *Lectures on the Pantheistic Idea*, 34.

15. Still, Perry Miller notes that Emerson exerted his greatest influence, as a lecturer, between 1850–60 (*Errand into the Wilderness*, 204). Looking back, Henry Adams confesses he was damaged by "pantheism, but the Schools were pantheist; at least as pantheistic as the *Energetik* of the Germans" (*Education of Henry Adams*, 429).

16. Tocqueville, *Democracy in America*, 32; hereafter cited parenthetically.

17. Emerson, *Journals and Miscellaneous Notebooks*, 10:344; hereafter cited parenthetically as *JMN*.

18. Emerson, "Natural History of Intellect," in *Complete Works*, 12:36, 12:35.

19. Lawrence, "Pan in America," 24.

20. Parker, *Discourse of Matters Pertaining to Religion*, 77; emphasis added.

21. De Concilio, *Catholicity and Pantheism*, 23; hereafter cited parenthetically.

22. Hunt, *Pantheism and Christianity*, 25.

23. [Duyckinck], review of *Pierre*, 118.

24. Cayton, *Emerson's Emergence*, 134–35.

25. "France, indeed! whose Catholic millions still worship Mary Queen of Heaven," serves some of the same purpose for Melville as Italy does for Hawthorne (*WHM*, 7:24). Isabel's "mixture" is facetiously cast against Lucy's Protestant purity much as Miriam's is cast against Hilda's. Emily Miller Budick notes that Miriam's ambiguously mixed race is not only Jewish but African; with Donatello's, her status should be situated in the context of how "human" identity

was defined through American slavery ("Perplexity, Sympathy, and the Question of the Human," 237).

26. Parker, *Herman Melville*, 1:776; hereafter cited parenthetically.

27. Sealts, *Melville as Lecturer*, 34.

28. Emerson, "Nature," in *Complete Works*, 1:10–11.

29. Hawthorne may renounce "transcendental" Catholicism even further because, unlike Melville, he was still in the eye of the public. As Hawthorne writes in his preface to *The Marble Faun*, remarking on his own absence from the literary field, the reader potentially becomes a kind of "mythic character," perhaps equivalent to the faun. Hawthorne's implied author claims that he wrote for that gentle reader "year after year, during which the great eye of the Public (as well it might) almost utterly overlooked [his] small productions" (*CE*, 4:2). The female eye of the public was reading sentimental women, but even worse, the male eye that could have been reading Hawthorne might have been reading transcendentalists; Hawthorne repeatedly associates that public eye and Emerson's transcendental eyeball with the all-seeing, ever-open eye of the Pantheon.

30. Emerson, "Natural History of the Intellect," in *Complete Works*, 12:35–36.

31. As Lawrence writes, perhaps with Emerson's Topsy, Babo, and Donatello in mind: "Pan! All! That which is everything has goat's feet and a tail! With a black face! This really is curious" ("Pan in America," 23). John Carlos Rowe further suggests that the reference to plantations in Emerson's "Nature," originally titled "Pan," evokes the slaveholding estates of the South, which would further associate Pan with blackness (*At Emerson's Tomb*, 20). More darkly than for Emerson, however, the shadow of Hawthorne's civil daylight can only be civil war.

32. Hawthorne, *Notes of Travel*, 3:327.

33. Richardson, "Plain Discussion with a Transcendentalist," 75–76.

34. Hamilton, "Fauns and Mohicans," 42–43.

35. This lecture seems to survive only in excerpt in Cabot, *Memoir of Ralph Waldo Emerson* (see 429). Regarding the association of Catholicism with blacks, see Lepore, who describes a 1741 New York "slave rebellion" that was popularly perceived as a Papist plot in which blacks impersonated priests (*New York Burning*, 177–83).

36. Sealts, *Melville as Lecturer*, 137.

37. This passage is another partial transcription from Hawthorne's journals (*CE*, 14:195).

Hawthorne, Melville, and the Spirits

Ellen Weinauer

IN MARCH 1848, in their house in Hydesville, New York, Margaret and Kate Fox began communicating with the spirit of a dead man. The Hydesville "rappings" launched the modern spiritualist movement, which, in the years that followed, gained widespread credibility and large numbers of adherents. We might look askance at claims made in spiritualist journals throughout the 1850s that the movement had attracted upwards of three million followers; but as Daniel Cottom has noted, "even if this number was exaggerated, the influence of the movement was sufficiently widespread to inspire comments" about its popularity and significance.[1] In 1855, for example, diarist (and disbeliever) George Templeton Strong queried, "What would I have said six years ago to anybody who predicted that before the enlightened nineteenth century was ended hundreds of thousands of people in this country would believe themselves able to communicate with the ghosts of their grandfathers?"[2]

Strong was not alone in commenting on the spiritualist movement's rapidly growing influence. Periodicals such as the *International Monthly Magazine* (absorbed into *Harper's Monthly Magazine* in 1852), the *North American Review, Littell's Living Age,* and *Putnam's Monthly Magazine* engaged the debate, reviewing spiritualist tracts and testimonials and reporting on the many popular public demonstrations of "spiritual manifestations." These accounts were often skeptical, even harshly critical; at times, they were outright dismissive. Yet their proliferation testifies not only to the perceived influence of the movement but also to the hold its ideas had, even on disbelievers. An 1853 essay from *Littell's Living Age* provides a case in point. Published fully six years after the Fox sisters launched what many thought would be a brief craze, "Spiritual Manifestations" ends with the definitive declaration that "[h]umbug, and deliberate imposture, are the mildest terms we can apply to the American 'spiritual manifestations,' and with that expression of opinion we dismiss the subject."[3] But this "dismissal" comes after fourteen double-columned pages of critique and commentary, suggesting that spiritualism exerts a stronger imaginative hold on the writer than he or she might like to admit. Like an essay in the usually staid *North American Review,* which seeks to diminish the force of this "new form of necromancy" by citing its "*quasi* miracles" but which in fact underscores its consequence by citing its "epidemic" potential,[4] the essay in the *Living Age* is unable simply to "dismiss the subject." Clearly, spiritualism has gotten under its skin.

This intriguing combination of dismissal and compulsion circulates prominently in the nearly ubiquitous periodical accounts of spiritualism at midcentury. It also circulates in a variety of midcentury texts by both Hawthorne and Melville. Critics have long recognized Hawthorne's rather reluctant assent to the principles of the occult practice of mesmerism: whether discouraging his then-fiancée, Sophia Peabody, from undergoing mesmeric treatments for her chronic headaches or representing the power of Holgrave's "magnetic" glance over the susceptible Phoebe Pyncheon, Hawthorne appeared to find mesmerism, in the words of Samuel Chase Coale, "morally repellant" but "psychologically accurate."[5] So too, it would appear, did Melville, whose depictions of Ahab's galvanic influence over the compliant crew members on the *Pequod* or of Isabel's "magnetic" power over the eponymous Pierre draw on metaphors of mesmerism and echo the dynamic between Holgrave and Phoebe (or Hollingsworth and Coverdale, or virtually any pair of magnetically attracted characters in Hawthorne's corpus).

But while both writers accept, however ambivalently, the premises and psychological principles of mesmeric "suggestion," they appear to be far more dubious about the premises and principles of spiritualism, mesmerism's occult sibling. Writing in his notebook about Ada Shepard, the spirit-writing medium who served as the family's governess in Italy, for example, Hawthorne noted a "lack of substance in her talk, a want of gripe, a delusive show, a sentimental surface with no bottom beneath it. The same sort of thing has struck me in all the poetry and prose that I have read, from spiritual sources" (*CE,* 14:399). Melville, too, was a manifest doubter, poking fun at the "sentimental" belief in rapping "spirits" in such stories as "I and My Chimney" and "The Apple-Tree Table."

For all of their skepticism about what Hawthorne called the "flummery and delusion" (*CE*, 14:608) at work in spiritualism, however, neither writer seemed able to "dismiss the subject" altogether. "I should be glad to believe in the genuineness of these spirits, if I could," Hawthorne wrote in his notebook, in an admission of the movement's attraction and hold. Samuel Chase Coale has asserted, in a formulation that I would suggest equally applies to Melville, "however much Hawthorne detested the dogma of the spiritualists, he could not shake the belief in the reality of the power inherent in it."[6] Following Coale's lead, I want to try to understand the "reality of the power inherent" in spiritualism for both Hawthorne and Melville by examining two critically overlooked stories: Hawthorne's last published tale, "Feathertop"—written in 1851 just before Hawthorne left Lenox, Massachusetts, where his relationship with Melville had blossomed—and Melville's 1856 "The Apple-Tree Table." By reading these stories in the context both of the friendship between the two writers and of specific spiritualist principles, we begin to see a kind of fictional dialogue opening up between Hawthorne and Melville about spiritualism's challenge to the models of (sovereign, male) individualism at work in antebellum culture. The occult, as a look at spiritualist practice and belief indicates, embraces principles of ontological permeability and undermines the binary opposition between self and other on which the antebellum individual was constituted. So too, it would appear, did the friendship between Hawthorne and Melville—certainly, in any event, on the latter's part. "[Y]our heart beat in my ribs and mine in yours," wrote Melville to Hawthorne in November 1851, upon learning that the older writer had read, and more importantly understood, *Moby-Dick*. "By what right do you drink from my flagon of life?" he went on, effusing that "when I put it to my lips—lo, they are yours and not mine" (*WHM*, 14:212).

The "infinite fraternity of feeling" that Melville celebrates in this letter (*WHM*, 14:212) is one that would have been familiar to adherents of spiritualist practice, who celebrated the capacity for a spiritual brotherhood that crossed and recrossed lines of self and other even as it opened human beings to the world of the infinite. Hawthorne's exploration of occult boundary crossings in "Feathertop" was rendered both more compelling and more urgent, I want to suggest, by the boundary-crossing

Fannie Davis (a medium active from at least the 1860s), under the influence of a spirit. From *Life and Labor in the Spirit World* . . . , by M. T. Shelhamer (Boston: Colby and Rich, 1887).

relationship with Melville that was, by the time he penned the story, coming to its close. With its ironic, surprisingly jocular treatment of a narrator unmanned by "spirits," "The Apple-Tree Table" might be read as Melville's carnivalesque rejoinder to the anxieties that circulate through Hawthorne's pre-text, an indirect commentary on the pleasures of letting go, of allowing oneself to be possessed by another. Finally, then, the occult in general—spiritualism in particular—becomes a crucial site where Hawthorne and Melville engage one another and raise questions about the self's ontological foundations, inviting them, sometimes reluctantly and sometimes in the spirit of liberating play, to imagine new ways of "being" in the world.

It is difficult to find one definition of spiritualism, for the movement's embrace of individual authority and self-sovereignty legislated against doctrinal organization and dogma. Whether writing in the 1850s or the 1990s, however, most historians of the movement identify as common denominators in spiritualist belief faith in the immortality of every soul and, as a corollary, the ability of the "dead" and the living to communicate with one another across the relatively permeable boundary between "this world" and "the next." Responding, historian Ann Braude has explained, to a "crisis of faith experienced by many Americans at mid-century," spiritualism tried to bring people back to the Christian fold by providing "'scientific' evidence of religious truth. Initially, it required people to believe nothing. Rather, it asked them to become 'investigators,' to observe 'demonstrations' of the truth of Spiritualism produced under 'test conditions' in the séance room."[7] To bolster such demonstrations, spiritualists produced countless testimonials and tracts. One estimate provided by a spiritualist periodical—an estimate cited and endorsed by the otherwise skeptical *North American Review* in "Modern Necromancy"—gives the number of periodicals "devoted to the publication of its phenomena and the dissemination of its principles" at "[n]o less than twelve or fourteen" and notes that "[n]early every succeeding week brings through the press some new books treating exclusively upon this subject" (512). Spiritualism also drew numerous influential adherents, including, perhaps most notably, the respected scientist Robert Hare and Judge John W. Edmonds, a New York assemblyman and Supreme Court judge.

Spiritualism's rapidly growing popularity and increasing influence at midcentury can be attributed, at least in part, to its individualist premises. Like transcendentalism, its highborn and far more intellectual counterpart, spiritualism had a manifestly antiauthoritarian bent, positing, as Braude notes, that "divine truth was directly accessible to individual human beings through spirit communication" (6). Its embrace of antiauthoritarian religious principles and practices, Braude further points out, translated readily into "radical social program[s]" and reforms. Not surprisingly, then, spiritualists "led so-called ultraist wings of the movements for the abolition of slavery, for the reform of marriage, for children's rights, and for religious freedom, and they actively supported socialism, labor reform, vegetarianism, dress reform, health reform, temperance, and antisabbatarianism" (3).[8] Such commitment to radical reform troubled many of spiritualism's staunchest critics and motivated their often panic-stricken diatribes. In response to spiritualist editor Samuel Brittan's claim that the movement sought to "change the entire structure of society," for example, the Reverend Hiram Mattison declared that the spiritualist "creed" "embodies more elements of ruin than were ever before combined under any one system. Only let these views prevail, and they not only destroy every thing fair in religion and morals, but they upheave at once all the foundations of society; abolish the relations of husband and wife; and parents and children; annihilate all law; subvert all order; strike down all justice and right; and fill the land with anarchy, corruption, and bloodshed."[9]

Buttressing the distress of critics like Mattison were the movement's oft-noted inclusive and integrative tendencies. As a writer for *Putnam's* remarked in 1854, the "wrath" of the movement's adherents "burns hot against all 'sect and denomination.'"[10] The movement's detractors, by contrast, "burned hot" against the elimination of "all sect and denomination," both religious and social. Thus would Miles Grant, another agitated cleric, fret in his choicely titled treatise, *Spiritualism Unveiled, and Shown to Be the Work of Demons* (1866), "Its doors are open for Catholics and Protestants, Infidels and Atheists, the lewd and the virtuous, Mohammedans, Jews, and Pagans,—all are invited, all are welcome to this 'broad church.'"[11] Grant was not alone in seeing the "broadness" of the movement, and its "open" doors, as gateways to religious, moral, and social degeneration. As private sittings and public exhibitions alike brought together, often in settings of intense bodily intimacy, men and women, whites and blacks, the socially privileged and the laborers, the spiritual-ist movement seemed indeed to presage the "subversion" of "all order." "[W]ithout pretense, without parade," wrote William Howitt in 1863, spiritualism "has gone up from the middle ranks of life to the highest aris-tocratic regions, and down to the humblest abodes of working men."[12]

Even as spiritualist principles undermined prior forms of hierarchy and authority, however, practices of spirit possession and mediumship, like those at work in mesmerism, involved other forms of power and control—in particular, the individual's (lack of) control over his or her own privatized self—that added further layers of distress for those out-side the movement. Such practices concerned what Hawthorne called, in the now-famous letter to Sophia begging her *not* to take mesmeric treatments for her headaches, the "transfusion of one spirit into another" (*CE*, 15:588). In the case of mesmerism, this "transfusion" occurred be-tween living beings: the mesmerist used his powers of "magnetism" to gain control of the patient's, medium's, or clairvoyant's will. Spiritualism involved a fundamentally similar dynamic; the spirit of the dead was believed to take possession of the living medium and to use his or, more typically, her voice and/or body as a means of communicating with the living. In his effort to demonstrate that "the spirits use the same agency to move their mediums that is used by mesmerizers," Grant addresses precisely this "*modus operandi* of controlling a *medium*" in spiritualist practice. Quoting from the spiritualist journal the *Banner of Light*, Grant allows a spirit to explain that he or she "has no right to the medium's body" and must get permission from the "the spirit who owns the body" to take "control" of its "mortal form"; the acquiescing "spirit" is then "subjected to the entire control of the predominating spirit. It is, in a word, magnetized by the spirit; held in perfect subjection" (15–16).

This dynamic of absolute control and "perfect subjection" appears over and over again in accounts, by both detractors and believers, of the mechanisms of spirit communication. Adin Ballou, the founder of the utopian Hopedale community and one of spiritualism's most vocal proponents, provided an explanation of "spirit writing" that echoes the description of spirit possession that we find in Grant's treatise. When asked to describe the process of spirit writing, Ballou's dead son, Adin Augustus—whose communications from the spirit world through his own writing medium, Elizabeth "Alice" Reed, are relayed in Ballou's 1852 testimonial—explains: "I feel as though I enter into her for the time being, or as if my spirit entered into her. I am disencumbered of my spiritual form, and take hers. . . . I have my spiritual form or body when I communicate by tippings or rappings, but to *write* my spirit must enter the medium . . . otherwise I am unable to control her will or muscles. . . . The moment I leave Alice's [the Medium's] body, I assume my own."[13]

At work in the dynamic of willed passivity that we witness in both Ballou's and Grant's descriptions is, importantly, not only an exercise of power but also an undermining of the notion of self-sustaining, sovereign personhood—of the very individualism that was an ostensible hallmark of the spiritualist "creed." For, once Adin's "spirit" has "entered into" Alice, does Alice exist anymore? If so, who is she? And furthermore, who is he? In "Spiritual Materialism," a lengthy critique that appeared in the same 1854 issue of *Putnam's Monthly* as did Melville's "The Lightning-Rod Man" and several chapters of *Israel Potter,* the writer notes that in order for the spirits to "claim . . . credit" for "producing" the movement's spectacular "effect," they must "get rid of the *identity* of the agent, as an intelligent active cause, by the infusion into his organization of a new element, which shall thrust aside and take possession; of which the agent must necessarily be unconscious, but by which his physical man shall be controlled absolutely, as if by his own will consciously exercised. Under such control he is not he but the spirit is absolutely *he:* his actions are not his, but the actions of an infused, foreign, annihilating force, in fact, of *another being*" (160–61; emphasis in the original).

Not surprisingly, as the language of annihilation, "foreign" occupation, and loss of agency from "Spiritual Materialism" suggests, this undermining of the notion of autonomous "being" was, for many, profoundly unsettling. In his 1853 antioccult tract (attacking "Mesmerism, Clairvoyance, Visions, Revelations, Startling Phenomena," and the "Rapping Fraternity"), the Reverend James Porter styles himself a "watchman on the walls of Zion." The stated object of Porter's watchful eye is the "faith of the public in fundamental principles."[14] But he also claims guardianship over the self-possessed, autonomous individual. "Self-control," Porter declares, "is an elemental principle in the human character. It is here that we find our responsibility, and safety. Take this away, and we are mere machines, without judgment or will, subject to be driven and tossed at the dictation of others. . . . In so impure and dishonest a world as this," he goes on, "there is no security for our character and fortune, but in sleepless vigilance" (50).

In his efforts to demonstrate the ways in which such "vigilance" is our duty to ourselves and to God—"The Creator," Porter notes, "has endowed us with rational powers, which we are required to exercise to his glory, and our own good"—Porter compares the occult medium with an opium user or a drunkard who "unmans himself with alcohol" (50). Porter's linking of autonomous personhood and manhood is important, pointing as it does to the ways in which spiritualist practice may well have challenged antebellum assumptions not only about the "self-possessed" individual (whose boundaries are revealed to be permeable, unstable) but also about the essential differences between men and women (whose "spirits" can "transfuse" one into the other without regard to categorical gender distinctions). Note the anxiety that emerges, precisely around the issue of gender transformation, in Hiram Mattison's commentary on Adin Ballou. Making specific reference to the above-quoted description of spirit writing, which involves the "entering" of the male spirit into the female medium's body, Mattison attempts to poke fun at the ways in which this theory of "spirit-occupation"

> quite confounds the sexes, and obliterates all the distinctions of natural history. In the case cited by Mr. Ballou, the spirit of a deceased *gentleman* enters the body of a young *lady!* Adin's soul in Alice's body!! Well, then, which is it, Alice or Adin? a lady or a gentleman? Could the "medium" answer the question? Would she not find it as difficult to identify herself as a certain Mr. Ami, of whom we once heard? Awaking one morning after a night's lodging in the gutter, his clothes torn and muddy, and his person not a little disguised, he was heard thus to soliloquize: "Am I *Ami,* or am I *not* Ami? If I *am* Ami, *where* am I? And if I am *not* Ami, *what* am I?" So Miss Alice might have inquired: "Am I *Alice,* or am I *not* Alice?" Will some of our "seers" inform us who the medium was, under the circumstances, Adin or Alice? a lady or a gentleman? (69)

Mattison pretends to laugh at spiritualism's dissolution of the boundary between Alice and Adin, at the idea that identity in general, and gender identity in particular, could be "unfixed" in this way. Yet we might read the series of insistent "ors" in this passage as an effort to police the very boundaries that Ballou's description of "spirit writing" renders permeable. Mattison wants to derive humor from the idea that "Adin's soul" could be in "Alice's body"—but his nearly obsessive return to the "which is it?" question indicates that perhaps spiritualism's ability to put essentialist notions of (gender) identity into question is not really all that funny.

Spiritualism's challenge to such seemingly innate and "natural" differences—what Mattison anxiously calls its "obliteration" of "all the distinctions of natural history"—were rooted in the movement's universalist premises regarding the immortal soul. Most spiritualists would have agreed with mesmerist Charles Poyen, whose series of lectures and demonstrations across New England in 1836 did much to popularize spiritualism's precursor, when he insisted that the phenomenon of animal magnetism proved that "the human soul was gifted with the same primitive and essential faculties, under every climate, among every nation, and under whatever skin, black, red, or white, it may be concealed."[15] This emphasis on the "sameness" of all immortal souls put spiritualism on a collision course not only with conventional religious attitudes regarding sin and redemption but also with antebellum culture's increasingly taxonomic tendencies regarding human "difference." Even as an emergent antebellum race "science" sought to essentialize and differentiate human beings—"looked," as historian Reginald Horsman has noted, "for what was special and different"—occult practitioners looked for what was "general and alike," emphasizing spiritual qualities that were believed to cross seemingly indelible lines of gender, race, and social position.[16]

This principle of affiliation and the forms of spiritual "merger" it enables galvanizes, both negatively and positively, Hawthorne's and Melville's intersecting fictional engagements with spiritualism. For however skeptical about the "spiritual manifestations" and their social byproducts Hawthorne and Melville may have been, they could not, or would not, merely set the principles of occult possession and dispossession aside. Commenting on occult claims regarding the "miraculous power of one human being over the will and passions of another," Miles Coverdale, the narrator of *Blithedale,* declares, "It is unutterable, the horror and disgust with which I listened, and saw, that, if these things were to be believed, the individual soul was virtually annihilated. . . . But I would have perished on the spot, sooner than believe it" (*CE*, 3:198). The words "if" and "sooner" are significant in this passage, for they point, of course, to doubt. Coverdale would "sooner perish" than believe the "truth" to which occult practice testifies: that the seemingly inviolable "individual soul" is subject to penetration, appropriation, and annihilation. Yet he is not able, with complete certainty, to dismiss that truth either. So, too, for both Hawthorne and Melville, neither of whom can reject the notion that the boundaries of what Hawthorne called the "inmost Me" (*CE*, 1:4)—what Melville called, in *Pierre,* the "untrammeledly . . . ever-present self" (*WHM*, 7:199)—are far more fluid than they are fixed.

Complicating their response to such challenges is, I would suggest, the personal relationship between the two men. As virtually every critic and biographer who has attempted to tackle the subject admits, that relationship is deeply elusive, in large part because, apart from one brief and intriguingly domestic epistle (in March 1851, Hawthorne asks Melville to "inquire" after an errant box for him in Pittsfield and to purchase for his family a wooden "kitchen-clock . . . of Connecticut manufacture" if possible [*CE*, 16:412]), none of Hawthorne's letters to Melville survive. What evidence we do have suggests that the relationship involved both convivial family visits back and forth—Hawthorne remarks in his letter to Melville, for example, that his daughter, Una, has "very delightful reminiscences of our visit to Melville Castle" and sends his "regards to Mrs Melville and your sisters" (*CE*, 16:412)—and an intellectual intensity that both writers clearly enjoyed. In a June 1851 letter, Melville promises Hawthorne to come soon for a visit and a bout of the "ontological heroics" in which the two were inclined to engage (*WHM*, 14:196). Sophia Hawthorne herself reinforced this view of their conversational style, writing in a letter (likely to her sister Elizabeth), "Nothing pleases me more than to sit and hear this growing man dash his tumultuous waves of thought against Mr. Hawthorne's great, genial, comprehending silences."[17]

While Sophia's metaphor of crashing waves suggests a kind of natural and essential difference between the two men (Melville's wave, after all, dashes "against" Hawthorne's silences), Melville himself frequently described the two as ontologically connected. By the time Melville wrote to Hawthorne about his own out-of-body experience ("your heart beat in my ribs and mine in yours"), the latter knew that Melville was the "Virginian" who had penned the effusive "Hawthorne and His Mosses"—a text that describes Hawthorne as a "ravish[er]," a "wizard" who "stole over" the writer, a man who "shoots" his "strong . . . roots" into the "hot soil" of the writer's "soul" (*WHM*, 9:241, 9:250). Significantly, Melville's descriptions of his response to and feelings for Hawthorne echo occult descriptions of spirit possession. Perhaps more importantly, they indicate the pleasure that Melville, who elsewhere expressed his admiration for Hawthorne's self-sovereignty (*WHM*, 14:186), could find in the "loss" of self to another. It was a pleasure that Hawthorne did not seem particularly to share—yet, at the same time, it was a principle to which he offered his reluctant assent. Such ambivalence goes some distance toward explaining why, much like Coverdale himself, Hawthorne could not stop making fictional visits to the site of occult practice and belief.

Hawthorne makes one such visit in his last story, "Feathertop: A Moralized Lesson," which he was working hard to peddle in the fall and early winter of 1851. Intriguingly, Hawthorne first mentions the finished story in a letter written in November 1851 (*CE*, 16:506)—the very month Melville writes his letter to Hawthorne celebrating their transposed hearts and lips. "Feathertop" tells the story of Mother Rigby, "one of the most cunning and potent witches in New England," who creates a scarecrow, animates him, and sends him off into the world, reasoning that "many a fine gentleman has a pumpkin-head, as well as my scarecrow" (*CE*, 10:224–25). After seducing first the townspeople and then a young woman, Feathertop sees himself in a truth-telling mirror, discovers there his true, "sordid" nature, and runs back home to his "mother," where he collapses in despair and disintegrates.

At first glance, "Feathertop" seems little connected to the spiritualist movement or its particular occult claims. Mother Rigby is a witch, not a medium, and Feathertop is a product of conjuration, not a spirit who is able to move between "this sphere" and "the next." But, as both adherents and critics of the spiritualist movement suggested, the distance between witchcraft and spiritualist practices could seem small indeed. The issue of *Putnam's* in which Melville's "The Apple-Tree Table" appeared, for example, also prints an essay titled "The Spirits in 1692, and What They Did at Salem" that links the Salem witchcraft hysteria and the spiritualist craze. At the root of the Salem tragedy, the essay insists, was "an unwise and superstitious curiosity about devils and spirits"—a "belief" that has been "pressed upon us in our own day" and that is "presented" on equally "shallow proof."[18] Another essay, this one in the *North American Review*, refers to spiritualism as "Modern Necromancy." Considered in the context of such connections, the treatment of necromantic production and consumption in "Feathertop"—a witch conjures an illusory man who is mistaken for a "fine gentleman" and a "great nobleman" (*CE*, 10:237)—might well be read as a sharp poke at a gullible public that mistakes table-tipping and "rapping" for "proof" of contact between the living and the dead. Importantly, the entity that Mother Rigby sends forth into the streets is largely empty, lacking in substance or true meaning. "If we must needs pry closely into the matter," the tale's narrator coyly remarks as the scarecrow begins to "assum[e] a show of life," "it may be doubted whether there was any real change, after all, in the sordid, worn-out, worthless, and ill-joined substance of the scarecrow; but merely a spectral illusion, and a cunning effect of light and shade, so colored and contrived as to delude the eyes of most men." Thus, he goes on, "the miracles of witchcraft"—like the alleged "miracles" of spiritualism—"seem always to have had a very shallow subtlety" (*CE*, 10:228–29). Like the "talk" of the Hawthorne family governess-cum-medium, Feathertop is all "sentimental surface with no bottom beneath" him.[19]

In exposing the fraudulence of Mother Rigby and satirizing the credulous public that accepts her counterfeit product as genuine, "Feathertop" redacts Hawthorne's oft-expressed anxieties about the act of authorship—anxieties that were ratcheted up in 1852, while he was being pushed by James T. Fields to produce almost unceasingly and to flood the market with his productions. "Shall I confess the truth?" the narrator queries as Feathertop takes his first, jerky step; "the scarecrow reminds me of some of the lukewarm and abortive characters, composed of heterogeneous materials, used for the thousandth time, and never worth using, with which romance-writers (and myself, no doubt, among the rest) have so over-peopled the world of fiction" (*CE*, 10:230). Thus, while the narrator designates Feathertop a "work of art" (*CE*, 10:242), "in the context of the story," Brian Way has noted, "this phrase has so ironic an implication that, far from dignifying the work of Mother Rigby, it merely serves to devalue the idea of art. There is indeed a strong undercurrent of suggestion that created fictions are no better than miscellaneous rubbish masquerading as reality."[20] If Feathertop is a "work of art," then the artist is himself no better than the "modern necromancer," the spiritualist who turns out counterfeit "rubbish" for "the joke's sake," as Mother Rigby puts it (*CE*, 10:227)—or, perhaps worse, for the sake of a dollar. "Feathertop," Way asserts, takes "so weary and cynical a view of the process of artistic creation, that it is tempting to regard it as the author's farewell to the writing of short fiction" (26).

Hawthorne's negotiations over the publication of this story can certainly be seen to reinforce Way's reading, for they oddly devalue the product that Hawthorne is trying to sell. In the earliest letter that makes reference to "Feathertop," Hawthorne tells John Sullivan Dwight, working on behalf of John Sartain, that he can " supply" *Sartain's Union Magazine* "with an article" for a hundred dollars—a sum, he takes pains to point out, that "Dr. Bailey, of the National Era," had offered him for a story "a year since" (*CE*, 16:506). Yet ten days later, he writes to Sartain himself: "I should not at all wonder if you should not consider it worth, to you, the price named in my note to Mr. Dwight. Most certainly, I myself would not pay it, were I in the chair editorial" (*CE*, 16:513). He further disclaims the value of the story by suggesting that it is a kind of toss-off, written in offhand moments—a suggestion that is, incidentally, belied by the story's long trail in Hawthorne's notebooks: "I happened to have a little time, just before leaving Lenox, which I could not fill up better than by writing this story," Hawthorne claims, "otherwise I should not now have had it on hand" (*CE*, 16:513).[21] Here, Hawthorne presents himself as kin to his story's own witch-creator, Mother Rigby, who decides to "make a man of [her] scarecrow, were it only for the joke's sake!" (*CE*, 10:227). Like the (modern) necromancers and their fraudulent products, then, Hawthorne's story appears to have little value even to the author's own eye. But when Hawthorne moves to his next potential buyer—Sartain didn't bite at this particular "joke" of a tale—he offers a more positive (and presumably more persuasive) assessment of the story's value. In a letter to Rufus Griswold (whose *International Monthly Magazine* ended up printing the story in February and March 1852), Hawthorne explains, "I have by me a story which I wrote just before leaving Lenox, and which I thought of sending to Dr. Bailey of the National Era, who has offered me $100 for an article." He would be willing to send it to the *International*, he tells Griswold, "should you wish it at the price above-mentioned." Nor, in this case, does he hedge on that price or on the story's value: "I cannot afford it for less than $100, and would not write another for the same price," he writes as he brings the letter to a close (*CE*, 16:518–19).

These negotiations might be read in any number of ways: as a manifestation of Hawthorne's Hepzibah-like discomfort, even at this late stage, with commercial exchange, or—alternatively—of his often canny coyness precisely with regard to the mechanisms of such exchange.[22] But I want to suggest that they mirror Hawthorne's ambivalence not only about the story's value in the literary marketplace but also about its eponymous protagonist and the occult powers it sets out to satirize. For if on the one hand Hawthorne seems to identify with Mother Rigby—a casual conjurer of empty, meaningless forms—he also seems to identify with Feathertop himself. Here, the story's exploration of necromantic conjuring points to real concerns about the self's substantiality and integrity that appear throughout the Hawthorne corpus.

Importantly, the very forms of spirit possession and dispossession—and the gender inversions and substitutions—that we have seen enacted in spiritualist discourse circulate throughout this story, between Mother Rigby and Feathertop, Feathertop and the bewitched townspeople, Feathertop and "pretty Polly" Gookin. As Mother Rigby works to animate the passive, medium-like Feathertop, she "beckon[s]" to him with "so much magnetic potency . . . that it seem[s] as if [her gesture] must inevitably be obeyed, like the mystic call of the loadstone, when it summons the iron" (*CE*, 10:229). In her exercise of "magnetic potency," of course, Mother Rigby resembles Matthew Maule and Holgrave, the mesmerists we encounter in *The House of the Seven Gables,* published just a few months before "Feathertop" was written. And Feathertop (named for the rooster feather that his hat bears and that points parodically to his lack of masculine potency) resembles the mesmerized Alice Pyncheon, who is dispossessed by Maule and "constrained" by his foreign "will" to "do its grotesque and fantastic bidding" (*CE*, 2:208).

Enacting a series of echoes, doublings, and gender inversions, "Feathertop" might thus be said to enact in miniature Hawthorne's oft-expressed anxieties about the self's violability and, as Monika Elbert has argued, about the substantiality of antebellum manhood. These are anxieties, one could assume, that Melville's insistent elaboration of their identic transpositions, peaking at the time Hawthorne was composing "Feathertop," made more urgent. Yet, anxious and "cynical" as "Feathertop" is—about the shams of art, about masculine autonomy, about ancient and "modern necromancy"—there are a number of elements in the story that suggest a more fruitful relationship between Hawthorne's art and occult transgressions. Most importantly, the story's effort to discredit the products of "necromancy," whether in the form of "ancient" witchcraft or "modern" spiritualism, is undermined by its depiction of Feathertop's unexpected but profound revelatory capacities. Having looked in the mirror and seen himself "stript of all witchcraft," Feathertop recognizes himself for "the wretched, ragged, empty thing I am!" "I'll exist no longer," he declares in a supreme, if ironic, act of agency, throwing away the pipe that is the instrument of his conjuration and sinking "upon the floor, a medley of straw and tattered garments" (*CE*, 10:244, 10:245). "For perchance the only time, since this so often empty and deceptive life of mortals began its course," the narrator remarks of Feathertop's self-recognition, "an Illusion had seen and fully recognized itself" (*CE*, 10:244). But, the story forces us to ask, if Feathertop can "recognize" himself as illusory, is he indeed an "Illusion"? What, then, are the boundaries between that which is "real" and that which is "illusory," between the "man" and the "not-man"?

In forcing such questions, both Feathertop and "Feathertop" reveal the perhaps unwitting hold that "modern necromancy" exerts on its author, in its capacities not only to conjure forth meaningful and substantial anxieties about "autonomous" being and self-sustaining manhood but also to point simultaneously to forms of being that exceed conventional binary limits—between the "real" and the "illusory," the "sovereign" and the "slave," the "man" and the "not-man." T. Walter Herbert has noted Hawthorne's interest in what he calls a "frontier selfhood" that moves "beyond the boundaries that map conventional differences between manhood and womanhood"—or, we might add, between self and other, sovereign and subject, possessor and possessed.[23] Perhaps Hawthorne's desire to "believe in the genuineness of these spirits, if I could," like the story's desire to believe in Feathertop, indicates his sense that, for all the spiritualist movement's "flummery and delusion," its principles of inseparability and affinity open the door to the possibility of just such a frontier selfhood, of a kind of borderland being, a being-in-between. Nor is it coincidental that Hawthorne engages these questions at the very height of his relationship with Melville—for the door to a "frontier selfhood" is one that Melville repeatedly attempted to open in Hawthorne's presence.

Four years after "Feathertop" appeared, and long after the intensity of their relationship had waned, Melville published "The Apple-Tree Table," a story that might be read as a playful, if still ambivalent, rejoinder to Hawthorne's. Like "Feathertop," Melville's tale sets out to satirize the spiritualist movement. Its satire is more explicit, its humor more broad, and its ending even more inconclusive and wistful. Only slightly less neglected than "Feathertop" in critical discussion, "The Apple-Tree Table" recounts the efforts of an unnamed first-person narrator to discover the source of the ticking sounds that come from a "necromantic little old table" he has unearthed from his "haunted" attic (*WHM*, 9:378). Pulled between his credulous daughters, who are convinced that the table is possessed by "Spirits! spirits!" and his empirically minded wife, who insists that she "will see into this ticking," which "is something that can be found out, depend upon it," the narrator finds himself wavering between his own imaginative susceptibilities and his rational impulses (*WHM*, 9:385). His "problem" is in a way resolved when the source of the "ticking" reveals itself of its own accord: first one bug, then another, crawls out of the table, having hatched from an egg and eaten its way out of its wooden tomb. The bugs are beautiful—even "seraphical" (*WHM*, 9:395)—but short lived: one is put to death by a practical-minded servant, the other dies just a day after it appears.

Understandably, given its parodic treatment of the narrator's gullible daughters and its turn to a natural explanation of a seemingly supernatural phenomenon, "The Apple-Tree Table" has been read as a pointed and unambiguous "topical satire" of the spiritualist movement.[24] Whatever critical debate surrounds the story centers less on its perspective on spiritualism than on the religious and spiritual significance of the "seraphical" bugs.[25] But even as "The Apple-Tree Table" can be seen, like "Feathertop," to present spiritualism as a sham perpetrated on an impressionistic public willing to invest in, or too credulous to resist, its delusions, it is no more able than Hawthorne's story simply to dismiss the movement—not least, as in Hawthorne's case, because spiritualism addresses questions about autonomy and the substantiality of (male) personhood that so absorbed Melville.

Published in *Putnam's Monthly Magazine* in May 1856, "The Apple-Tree Table" follows nearly on the heels of Melville's March 1856 story, "I and My Chimney," which functions as an important thematic pre-text. Unambiguous in its treatment of masculinity under siege, "I and My Chimney" explores the efforts of a first-person narrator to protect his house's "royal old chimney"—a phallic symbol ad infinitum—against the efforts of his wife and two daughters to "abolish" it (*WHM*, 9:360, 9:356). The description of the massive chimney, which "stands, solitary and alone—not a council of ten flues, but, like his sacred majesty of Russia, a unit of an autocrat" (*WHM*, 9:358), echoes a description that Melville once offered of Hawthorne himself. In April 1851, in the throes of the intense sixteen months they spent as neighbors, Melville wrote Hawthorne a letter celebrating his achievement in the recently published

The House of the Seven Gables and commending him as a "man who, like Russia or the British Empire, declares himself a sovereign nature (in himself) amid the powers of heaven, hell, and earth" (*WHM,* 14:186). Even when that "sovereign nature" is represented by a massive structure of brick and mortar, however, it remains embattled. The narrator's wife and daughters, reinforced by outside troops in the shape of a "rough sort of architect" and "badgering" neighbors, continue to fight for the chimney's "abolition." "Assailed on all sides, and in all ways," the narrator complains, "small peace have I and my chimney" (*WHM,* 9:365, 9:376). The chimney's preservation, indeed, involves an eternal vigilance to which the narrator devotes himself: "it is now some seven years since I have stirred from home," he admits as the story comes to a close (*WHM,* 9:377). In his constant watchfulness, the narrator of this story would impress James Porter, the advocate of "sleepless vigilance" against spiritualism's incursions.

"The Apple-Tree Table" functions in many respects as a direct extension of "I and My Chimney." Like "Chimney" in its domestic focus, "The Apple-Tree Table" gives us another unnamed narrator who has an unnamed wife with whom he is at odds; in both stories, the daughters are named "Anna" and "Julia." But whereas in the earlier story our narrator is able to stand guard over "I and my chimney" and to fend off his assailants, in "The Apple-Tree Table" he loses his self-possession. Like the imagined drunkard in Porter's antispiritualist tract—the man who relaxes his vigilance over himself and hence loses his self-control and his capacities for self-government—the narrator of Melville's story is "unmanned." He is dispossessed by spirits.

As does "Feathertop," and with more explicitness, "The Apple-Tree Table" forges a link between modern day "spirits" and ancient "witchcraft." When he finds the "cloven foot[ed]" table in his "haunted" garret, the narrator also finds, sitting on its dust-laden surface, a "mouldy old book"—"Cotton Mather's 'Magnalia'" (*WHM,* 9:387, 9:380, 9:379). A key facilitator of the 1692 Salem witchcraft trials, Mather includes in the "Ecclesiastical History" that is the *Magnalia,* which appeared in a new edition in 1852, a treatment of the Salem outbreak and "detailed accounts of New England witchcraft" over which Melville's narrator pores (*WHM,* 9:382). Interestingly, Melville's story is not the only text in this issue of *Putnam's* that deals with Mather or the spiritualist-witchcraft connection. "The Spirits in 1692, and What They Did at Salem" minces no words about either Mather or the similarities between the witchcraft hysteria and the spiritualist craze. Mather, the anonymous author declares, was a "pedantic, painstaking, self-complacent, ill-balanced man" who cannot be defended "from the charge of slavishness and malignity" or of "credulity" (506). It "may be well to remember" the "misery" Mather encouraged and facilitated, the article warns, "for it grew out of an unwise and superstitious curiosity about devils and spirits"—a curiosity, the writer notes, that is dangerously present "in our own day" (511).

It would appear that the narrator of "The Apple-Tree Table" is far more susceptible than the *Putnam's* essayist to Mather's seductive accounts and their contemporary avatars. Sitting up late one night reading the *Magnalia* "before the little old apple-tree table," he tries to go to bed but cannot: "I was, in fact," he confesses, "under a sort of fascination" (*WHM,* 9:382). Like the mesmeric trance maiden or the spiritualist medium, like Feathertop or the narrator of "Feathertop" at his grandmother's knee, the narrator of "The Apple-Tree Table" finds himself "yielding" to Mather's "fascination." He is enthralled, bewitched, unable to tear himself away: "Nothing but fascination," he reiterates, "kept me from fleeing the room." It would appear that the narrator's dispossession by the ironically bewitching Mather prepares him for a further loss of autonomy, for while he sits in thrall to the "ghostly, ghastly Cotton Mather," the narrator suddenly hears, coming from the table, "a faint sort of inward rapping or rasping—a strange, inexplicable sound . . . Tick! Tick!" (*WHM,* 9:383). Over the next several days, the narrator attempts to regain his self-control; but he remains, much like the daughters with whom the story repeatedly and insistently associates him, unsettled by the "tickings." Nor does the appearance of the first bug, "wriggling" out of a crack in the table, still his beating heart; indeed, he seems to think he may have conjured the bug, which appears to be a "supernatural coruscation" that has, as with Feathertop and Mother Rigby, arisen in response to his repeated addresses (*WHM,* 9:389). Wavering between Mather and his other major influence, the Greek philosopher Democritus—whose rejection of supernatural causation establishes him as Mather's polar opposite—the narrator isn't ever able fully to banish his fears. Sitting up with his family to solve once and for all the mystery of the table, he "cower[s] in the corner," as frightened as his daughters, when they hear a "terrific, portentous rapping"; "'[y]ou fools!' his wife cries, 'it's the baker with the bread'" (*WHM,* 9:395). Clearly, unlike the narrator of "I and

My Chimney," the "fascinated" narrator of "The Apple-Tree Table" fails to maintain "himself a sovereign nature (in himself)." "Much midnight reading of Cotton Mather," he notes dryly, "was not good for a man" (*WHM*, 9:384).

In staging the unmaking of a man through the mechanisms of occult possession and dispossession, Melville certainly suggests that there is something more than mere satire at work in the story's treatment of spiritualism. Like Hawthorne, Melville uses the occult in his story to spectralize the antebellum man, to reveal that man as itself a delusive and contingent production. Yet he does so, it has to be noted, with a great deal of humor and play. Unlike, say, the brooding *Pierre*, published just a few months after "Feathertop" and sharing some of that text's fatigued pessimism about both reliable manhood and the literary marketplace, "The Apple-Tree Table" takes a certain amount of pleasure in contingency, in-betweenness, and manly-self-*un*making. Throughout the story, the narrator inhabits a sort of liminal zone, "oscillat[ing]" in what he calls "a strange and not unpleasing way" between "panic and philosophy," "foolish imaginations" and materialist practicality, Cotton Mather and Democritus; he also oscillates, it should be noted, between masculinity and femininity (*WHM*, 9:388, 9:394). Significantly, "The Apple-Tree Table" derives not just humor but a "not unpleasing" pleasure from the sorts of inversions and disruptions effected by the "Spirits! spirits!" Indeed, the story might be read as a sort of domestic carnivalesque, where the once-sovereign husband is (dis)possessed and liberated into a kind of riotous free play of "feminine" emotion, while his wife proceeds to function as what is, in essence, a rational man—a "female Democritus," counterpart to the "cool, collected," and manifestly unimaginative "naturalist" who is brought in to explain the mystery of the bugs—or who, more precisely, comes to demonstrate that the bugs are not mysterious at all (*WHM*, 9:394, 9:396).

The story's treatment of Professor Johnson, the man of science, suggests Melville's rather playful treatment of the limits of masculine forms of being and knowing. "Look[ing] hard at the table" and "scrap[ing] with his pen-knife into the holes" made by the bugs, Professor Johnson mocks Anna and Julia for "associat[ing] this purely natural phenomenon with any crude, spiritual hypothesis." The narrator tries to take up the naturalist's banner but admits that he doesn't "exactly understand" the "scientific statement of the case" (*WHM*, 9:396–97). Working with his phallic penknife, the "cool, collected" scientific observer threatens to do a kind of violence to the "glorious, lustrous, flashing, live opal" (*WHM*, 9:397) that is the "seraphical bug"; at the very least, his methods fail to capture the rapturous wonder that the bug inspires. The narrator may not be able fully to endorse his daughter's easy conversion of the bug from a "spirit" to a more orthodox emblem of the soul's immortality, but he certainly seems to find her recognition of the bug's ineffability more appealing than the naturalist's flat, and flatly disappointing, explanation. However "crude," the "spiritual hypothesis" at least acknowledges an experiential dimension that is inexplicable, that requires our imaginative faith—a dimension to which the narrator is opened by his unwitting and even unwilling "feminine" investment in "Spirits!"

In the penultimate paragraph of *Walden,* Henry David Thoreau turns to a story that "[e]very one has heard . . . of a strong and beautiful bug which came out of the dry leaf of an old table of apple-tree wood." Not surprisingly, Thoreau uses the story as an emblem for the awakened, (re)born self that he seeks to inspire: "Who knows what beautiful and winged life . . . may unexpectedly come forth from amidst society's most trivial . . . furniture," he wonders.[26] Thoreau's remark provides an apt summation of what I am suggesting might be at work in Hawthorne's and Melville's treatment of spiritualism—a treatment that points to something more than dismissal, and even something more than disapproval. Both writers clearly saw much that was "trivial," and much that was troubling, in spiritualist practice. Yet, as we see in both "Feathertop" and "The Apple-Tree Table," from its seemingly "trivial furniture" something "unexpectedly come[s] forth"—something that reaches beyond convention and that opens the door to new, albeit inchoate, forms of selfhood that are liberated from the boundaries and binaries (imaginative, spiritual, ontological) of antebellum culture. Not surprisingly, Melville lets that door open a little further than does the more cautious Hawthorne—and enjoys himself a good deal in doing it, too.

Melville leaves an intriguing trace in "The Apple-Tree Table" that suggests he has his admired precursor very much on his mind: when the narrator goes up to the "haunted" attic where he finds the table and its companion, Mather's *Magnalia,* he sees a chest "full of mildewed old documents; one of which, with a faded red ink-blot at the end, looked as

if it might have been the original bond that Doctor Faust gave to Mephistopheles" (*WHM*, 9:380). Recalling the "documents" of Hester Prynne's
story, tied up with "faded red tape" (*CE*, 1:30), and the scarlet letter itself, both of which are found in Hawthorne's own dusty, haunted attic
in "The Custom-House," the gesture to Hawthorne suggests the ways in
which Melville imagined them as still, even in 1856, engaged in a joint
project. The primary object of that project is not, of course, spiritualism.
But at its heart is an exploration into the meaning of selfhood that, as I
have been trying to suggest, the relationship between the two men brings
to the fore and to which the discourse of spiritualism gives shape. The
antebellum spiritualist embraces, in many respects, T. Walter Herbert's
"frontier selfhood," fluid, permeable, and unbound by temporal, spatial,
and gender categories. Like *Pierre*'s mystical, magnetic Isabel, the spiritualist might well have agreed that "there can be no perfect peace in indi-
vidualness" (*WHM*, 7:119). Throughout their corpus, and—as Melville's
impassioned letters to Hawthorne suggest—throughout their relationship, both of these writers are at once fearful about the loss of "individu-
alness" and desirous, on some level, of letting it go, along with all of its
"unceasing . . . competition," "systematic cruelties," and demand for constant vigilance.[27] Melville's nod to Hawthorne in "The Apple-Tree Table"
indicates an awareness of a shared ambivalence regarding the haunted
confines of American individualism in general, and American masculinity in particular, that their relationship renders more urgent. To what
extent spiritualism had a place in the "ontological heroics" in which the
two writers engaged we can never be certain. What is clear is that while
neither writer can say "yes" to spiritualism's challenge to conventional
forms of being, neither writer can say "no" either.

Notes

1. Cottom, *Abyss of Reason*, 4.
2. Qtd. in Isaacs, "Fox Sisters and American Spiritualism," 79.
3. "Spiritual Manifestations," 820.
4. "Modern Necromancy," 523, 524; hereafter cited parenthetically.
5. Coale, *Mesmerism and Hawthorne*, 3.
6. Coale, "Spiritualism and Hawthorne's Romance," 35. For Coale, the
"power" of the occult for Hawthorne is rooted primarily in the writer's (albeit
troubled) conviction that its techniques were virtually identical to the tech-

niques of romance. See, along with "Spiritualism and Hawthorne's Romance," *Mesmerism and Hawthorne* and "Mysteries of Mesmerism."

7. Braude, *Radical Spirits,* 4; hereafter cited parenthetically.

8. For recent, more skeptical, readings of the reformist impulses of spiritualist and occult belief, see Carroll, *Spiritualism in Antebellum America*; and Castronovo, *Necro-Citizenship* and "'That Half-Living Corpse.'"

9. Mattison, *Spirit-Rapping Unveiled!,* 104; hereafter cited parenthetically.

10. "Spiritual Materialism," 166; hereafter cited parenthetically.

11. Grant, *Spiritualism Unveiled,* 1; hereafter cited parenthetically.

12. Qtd. in Cottom, *Abyss of Reason,* 4.

13. Ballou, *Exposition of Views,* 222, 224. Brackets and emphasis in the original.

14. Porter, *Spirit Rappings,* 3; hereafter cited parenthetically.

15. Poyen, *Progress of Animal Magnetism,* 41. As Castronovo notes, "The unconscious—or at least Poyen's map of it—eradicates difference by discovering a hidden realm of egalitarian spiritual relations" (*Necro-Citizenship,* 163).

16. Horsman, *Race and Manifest Destiny,* 159.

17. Qtd. in Mellow, *Nathaniel Hawthorne in His Times,* 344.

18. "Spirits in 1692," 506; hereafter cited parenthetically.

19. Monika Elbert offers a careful excavation of the treatment of masculinity in "Feathertop"; see "Hawthorne's 'Hollow' Men." Also see T. Walter Herbert's analysis of Hawthorne's complex attitudes toward the gender conventions of his time in "Hawthorne and American Masculinity." My reading of this story is indebted to both of these extraordinarily helpful essays.

20. Way, "Art and the Spirit of Anarchy," 27; hereafter cited parenthetically.

21. As early as 1840, Hawthorne explores the possibility of making "a story out of a scarecrow, giving it odd attributes": "From different points of view, it should appear to change,—now an old man, now an old woman,—a gunner, a farmer, or the Old Nick" (*CE,* 8:185). He returns to the idea sometime in 1849, offering a skeleton of what will become, two years later, "Feathertop": "A modern magician to make the semblance of a human being, with two laths for legs, a pumpkin for a head &c—of the rudest and most meagre materials. Then a tailor helps him to finish his work, and transforms this scarecrow into quite a fashionable figure. . . . At the end of the story, after deceiving the world for a long time, the spell should be broken; and the gray dandy be discovered to be nothing but a suit of clothes, with these few sticks inside of it. All through his seeming existence as a human being, there shall be some characteristics, some tokens, that, to the man of close observation and insight, betray him to be a mere thing of laths and clothes, without heart, soul, or intellect. And so this wretched old thing shall become the symbol of a large class" (*CE,* 8:286).

22. For Elbert, "Feathertop" and the negotiations surrounding it indicate that "Hawthorne finds himself at a crossroad—a financial one of sorts, about which business is more lucrative: story-telling or novel-writing." His choice of the more lucrative novel writing—a choice, Elbert points out, that situates Hawthorne with the "scribbling women" he so frequently disparaged—indicates for her that "[m]asculine concerns with economics finally overwhelm [him]" ("Hawthorne's 'Hollow' Men," 180).

23. Herbert, "Hawthorne and American Masculinity," 76.

24. Karcher, "'Spiritual Lesson,'" 101. Howard Kerr also sees Melville's attitude toward spiritualism as unambiguously satirical, putting his analysis of the story in a chapter titled "Humorous Literary Reactions to Spiritualism"; see *Mediums, and Spirit-Rappers, and Roaring Radicals,* 22–54.

25. For representative alternative views, see Karcher, "'Spiritual Lesson'"; and Davidson, "Melville, Thoreau, and 'The Apple-Tree Table.'"

26. Thoreau, *"Walden" and "Resistance to Civil Government,"* 222–23. For a reading that situates "The Apple-Tree Table" in the context of Thoreau's treatment of the episode and of the treatment that Melville found in a local guidebook, *A History of the County of Berkshire, Massachusetts,* see Davidson, "Melville, Thoreau, and 'The Apple-Tree Table.'"

27. Herbert, "Hawthorne and American Masculinity," 76, 63.

Alienated Affections

Hawthorne and Melville's Trans-intimate Relationship

CHRISTOPHER CASTIGLIA

MELVILLE'S WARNING IN *Pierre* that the "strongest and fiercest emotions of life defy all analytical insight" has certainly proven true for efforts to discern what transpired between Nathaniel Hawthorne and Herman Melville on their rambles through the Berkshire woods in 1850–51 (*WHM*, 7:67). The bond between the two authors has proven, to use Melville's word, "ineffable," in part because the archival record is spotty and in part because the terms through which we understand intimacy—"love," "rejection," "desire," "friendship"—were inflected by a different age and culture, as well as by the two men's individual histories. Without imposing our own terms (and the values they carry) on their relationship, however, we can learn much from the metaphors through which the two men made sense of their attachment. Although we can never know what these men *felt*, in other words, we can learn something about the discursive practices through which men—particularly complexly imaginative men—understood intimate attachments to other men in mid-nineteenth-century New England. In particular, geopolitical metaphors—national, imperial, and universalist—suffuse accounts of the Hawthorne-Melville relationship, suggesting how changing conceptions of place and belonging shaped and reflected the most personal relations. In their use of such metaphors, Melville and Hawthorne allowed intimacy to test the limits of geopolitical concepts dominating public discourse in the mid-nineteenth century. In exploring how Melville and Hawthorne moved through and beyond national metaphors to explore the possibilities of imperialism, universalism, and what I will call

The gam: a friendly, fleeting encounter between two ships at sea. From the frontispiece to *The Yankee Whaler*, by Clifford W. Ashley (Boston: Houghton Mifflin, 1926).

trans-intimacy, we might learn to avoid judging intimate relationships by the criteria of nationalism and start judging nationalism by the criteria of intimacy.

The United States underwent profound reinvention during the late 1840s and early 1850s, when the nation, still struggling to assert its cultural autonomy from Europe, undertook massive growth through global trade and imperial conquest. As national borders were made and unmade, the meanings of domestic and foreign, intimate and alien, friend and foe, became ever more unstable. Few American authors in 1850 were as well acquainted with the dynamics of national and global exchange as these two men: both sons of old New England families, Hawthorne was, until his dismissal in June 1849, Salem's customs officer, while Melville, as a sailor, participated throughout his young life in transatlantic trade. Noting that his name graced both the pages of literary journals and crates traveling inland from the port, Hawthorne well understood that identity is never free of the taxonomies of citizenship, national or global. That such taxonomies inadequately express the full range of human imagination (or anything close to it), he also understood. When, toward the end of "The Custom-House," Hawthorne exclaims, "I am a citizen of somewhere else," he conveys the inescapability of national belonging—of citizenship—in understanding even the most "private" matters of desire (*CE*, 1:44). In characterizing their relationship, Melville and Hawthorne also used the language of citizenship, building on a historical connection of "friendship" and "nationalism" central to Federalism in the United States. Hawthorne's wish for a "somewhere else" where he might belong indicates an elasticity to nationalism's hold on intimacy, however. If citizens can never escape, as Hester fantasizes doing, into a wilderness where the body will be freed from the letter of the law, one *can* travel. It is through itinerancy, between the conventional taxonomies of sexuality and nationhood, of commitment and loyalty, that new relational opportunities arise.

The nationalist rhetoric underlying the relationship of Melville and Hawthorne is most evident in the review of the latter's *Mosses from an Old Manse* that Evert Duyckinck encouraged Melville to write soon after the two authors first met on August 5, 1850. A guest of the Melvilles at the time, Duyckinck published the review in his *Literary World* on August 17 and 24, 1850, under the title "Hawthorne and His Mosses, by a Virginian

Spending July in Vermont." Duyckinck wished to establish an American canon with Hawthorne at its head, and Melville's review performed that task skillfully. Challenging his readers' belief in the unparalleled genius of Shakespeare, Melville asks, "[W]hat sort of belief is this for an American, a man who is bound to carry republican progressiveness into Literature, as well as into Life?" "Believe me, my friends," Melville continues, "that Shakespeares are this day being born on the banks of the Ohio." Not only are American authors born *on* the national landscape; they *embody* that landscape, as Melville's characterization of Hawthorne demonstrates: "He is one of the new, and far better generation of your writers. The smell of your beeches and hemlocks is upon him; your own broad praries [sic] are in his soul; and if you travel away inland into his deep and noble nature, you will hear the far roar of his Niagara." If U.S. writers do not immediately attain the genius of Shakespeare, Melville is not troubled, for it is better, he contends, for Americans to cherish "mediocrity even, in her own children," than to praise "the best excellence in the children of any other land." While America "has good kith and kin of her own, to take to her bosom," Melville enjoins, "let her not lavish her embraces upon the household of an alien" (*WHM*, 9:245, 9:249, 9:247).

If this review is, as Edwin Haviland Miller has claimed, a "love letter" to Hawthorne, then Melville's love was deeply jingoistic, giving way to a jealous defense against intruding outsiders in the form of alien "households." While Melville resists claiming that "all American writers should studiously cleave to nationality in their writings," he would contend that "no American writer should write like an Englishman, or a Frenchman." Happily, they need only "write like a man" in order to "write like an American," for they effortlessly "breathe that unshackled, democratic spirit of Christianity in all things." Even as he naturalizes Christian nationalism as the effortless effulgence of manly nature, Melville shows its less savory side: "The truth is," he admits, that "this matter of a national literature has come to such a pass with us, that in some sense we must turn bullies, else the day is lost, or superiority so far beyond us, that we can hardly say it will ever be ours" (*WHM*, 9:248). The evolution of genius, for Melville, appears as the growth of neglected postcolonial children into full-grown imperial bullies.

The heavy-handed patriotism of "Hawthorne and His Mosses" is part and parcel of the more subtle nationalism animating the two men's friendship from its start. Melville and Hawthorne met when they, along with a host of other literary figures, climbed Monument Mountain, dining afterward at the Stockbridge home of local historian David Dudley Fields. Over dinner, Oliver Wendell Holmes opined on the superiority of British gentlemen to their American counterparts, to which Melville strenuously objected, and Hawthorne, usually aloof in such debates, vigorously joined Melville's side, cementing the connection they had begun on the climb. In retrospect, it seems possible that Duyckinck, friend and publisher of both writers, set up their meeting to establish, in the form of an intimate friendship, the literary nationalism he publicized in Melville's review. If so, the shared response to Holmes shows the success of the strategy. This raises the question, however, of why, if Duyckinck could establish his national canon in print, he needed the two men to form an emotional attachment, a friendship? The "nationalization" of a literary canon is understandable, but why the nationalization of a *friendship*? The answer to that question lies in the early federal debates in the United States, during which friendship became a prevailing *national* fascination.

The early success of the United States as an "imagined community" required correspondences between individual bodies and national interest. Responding, for instance, to anti-Federalists such as William Findley who cautioned that the new system of governance was "not merely (as it ought to be) a Confederation of States, but a Government of Individuals," Alexander Hamilton turned his attention in "Federalist 27" to citizens' everyday (sensational) lives.[1]

> Man is very much a creature of habit. A thing that rarely strikes his senses, will have but a transient influence upon his mind. A government continually at a distance and out of sight, can hardly be expected to interest the sensations of the people. The inference is, that the authority of the union, and the affections of the citizens towards it, will be strengthened, rather than weakened, by its extension to what are called matters of internal concern; and that it will have less occasion to recur to force, in proportion to the familiarity and comprehensiveness of its agency.

The "more the operations of the national authority are intermingled in the ordinary exercise of government," Hamilton continues, "the more citizens are accustomed to meet with it in the common occurrences of their political life; the more it is familiarized to their sight, and to their feelings, the further it enters into those objects, which touch the most sensible cords, and put in motion the most active strings of the human heart; the greater will be the probability, that it will conciliate the respect and attachment of the community" (176). Hamilton understood that in order to turn people into citizens, one needed to reach them where they lived, which was not yet in a nation but in local associations where the affective bonds of loyalty and affection already existed. Hamilton saw that social feelings precede the law, rendering it palatable to citizens who might otherwise see little profit in consenting to its restrictions.

Hamilton's call for a national pedagogy of orderly affect found its fulfillment in the social reform movements that flourished in the 1830s and 1840s. "Legislature may enact laws, but education must originate their conception, and interpret their meaning," Jonathan Blanchard told the American Institute of Instruction in 1835: "Government may check and restrain, but duty and obedience are the result of instruction. The hopes of our country depend on the bias which the minds of our children and youth receive." Blanchard surpasses Hamilton in placing national pedagogy in the hands, not of government, but of civil institutions—family, church, fraternal and reform organizations, and schools—that precede law in making acceptable to citizens social orders whose goal is not the enhancement of liberty but its constraint, justified through the deferred potential ("hopes") of an abstract national association ("our country"). For Blanchard, the education required to ensure order is fundamentally training in proper affect, presented as the fundamental human desire for social relationships such as friendship: "Desire of society is as truly a part of our nature, as the dread of anguish or the love of life. This simple original desire, finds its gratification in the exercise of those natural affections, which interest us in the welfare of our kindred, our friends, our acquaintances, and our race; and, together with these affections, it forms that complex class of emotion, which we call the social feelings; and these, again, being constantly excited by the circumstances and relations of life, grow into a permanent habit, and become the all-pervading, master-feeling of the soul."[2] Without obviously proscribing the basis of a citizen's affiliations (which might otherwise take forms other than an abstract and exclusionary "race") or prescribing the modes of participatory consent (the family, which is based on nonconsensual relations of obligation and hierarchy, becomes the affective original of which the civil sphere, nominally based on more evenly distributed consent, is simply a reflection), Blanchard yokes public order and private affect, a conjoining central to federalization in a culture newly versant in the revolutionary rhetoric of democratic self-determination.

In Blanchard's account of the chain of equivalences that generate affective order, friendship occupies the pivotal space between the biological categories of individual desire and family relations and the abstract and nationalized category of "race." Friendship's role in federalizing "social feelings" is discernable, as well, in the Constitution's emergence from the Articles of Confederation. While the Constitution from the outset asserts a unified national entity ("we, the people"), the Articles locate juridical power among bodies assembled in a particular space and time: "Whereas the Delegates of the United States of America, in Congress assembled, did, on the 15th day of November, in the Year of Our Lord One thousand Seven Hundred and Seventy seven, and in the Second Year of Independence of America, agree to certain articles of Confederation."[3] Through the primary authority of locally and historically situated individuals, the states take on the qualities nominally possessed by autonomous citizens, each state maintaining "its sovereignty, freedom, and independence, and every Power, Jurisdiction and right, which is not by this confederation expressly delegated to the United States, in Congress assembled." Having figured the states as autonomous citizens, the Articles set forth their association as the affective give-and-take of friendship: "The said states hereby severally enter into a firm league of friendship with each other, for their common defense, the security of their Liberties, and their mutual and general welfare" (86). Figuring the confederation of state power through a metaphoric equivalence with friendship, the Articles bridge the widening gap between local assembly and abstract legality. Having established this affective rationale, the legal apparatus no longer required its metaphorical equivalences: the primary purpose of law in the Constitution was no longer to guarantee friendship but to ensure its own jurisdiction. The language of rights and immunities, of juridical purview, therefore carries over from the Articles to the Constitution, but the affective rationale—the references to friendship—disappears.[4]

In the Articles, friendship gives way to mobility—the movement between states—tied not only to a growing market economy but to the presumed *stability* of private life. Article 4, for instance, yokes friendship to commercial mobility: "The better to secure and perpetuate mutual friendship and intercourse among the people of the different states in this union, the free inhabitants of each of these states, paupers, vagabonds and fugitives from justice excepted, shall be entitled to all privileges and immunities of free citizens in the several states; and the people of each state shall have free ingress and regress to and from any other state, and shall enjoy therein all the privileges of trade and commerce, subject to the same duties, impositions and restrictions as the inhabitants thereof respectively" (86). Vagabonds, paupers, and fugitives from justice shape friendship's outer boundaries, creating an ideal citizen who, economically engaged and living in a definable home, willingly (mis)understands the nation's laws as effective guarantors of justice. The only bridge between a newly stabilized "privacy" and a rapidly mobilized "public" is friendship, which bears elements of negotiation, contingency, and dissent that are traces of a potentially more full public participation.

The federalization of affect found critics, however, among early American authors such as Hannah Foster and Washington Irving, for whom friendship remained an ideal against which to evaluate competing models of citizenship. Friendship exposed the links between geographical mobility and abstract codes of intimate rectitude, revealing America's growth into a global empire comprised of private and self-managing citizens. The tense relationship in early American literature between federal affect and inventive friendship, between physical mobility and fixed standards of virtue, presaged both the literary works of and (trans-)intimate relationship between Nathaniel Hawthorne and Herman Melville.

Hannah Foster's 1797 epistolary novel, *The Coquette*, is on one level a typical Richardsonian seduction-and-abandonment plot, in which the heroine, Eliza Wharton, freed from a loveless marriage by the death of her betrothed, struggles between the virtuous path (represented by her second respectable but boring suitor, John Boyer) and exhilarating pleasure (in the person of the bankrupt libertine, Peter Sanford). In the end, of course, Eliza makes the "wrong" choice and ends up pregnant, abandoned, and finally dead. Weaving through this predictable plot, however, is the story of a girl seduced and abandoned not by a handsome libertine but by the alluring promise and ultimate betrayals of friendship. Eliza's friends leave much to be desired, serving mostly, as Julia Stern notes, to "keep the voices of dead male authorities alive."[5] Eliza has grave doubts about her friendships, as when she challenges the "correspondence"— and the word is significant—between herself and one of her friends: "[I]s it time for me to talk again of conquests, or must I only enjoy them in silence? I must write to you the impulses of my mind; or I must not write at all." In this letter, Eliza draws a contrast between silence and what she calls her friends' "monitorial lessons."[6]

Eliza's resistance to her friends' efforts to "confine virtue to a cell" becomes tied to her skepticism about mobility. Initially, Eliza believes freedom to be synonymous with mobility. Released from "those shackles, which parental authority had imposed on my mind," Eliza prepares to "enjoy that freedom which I so highly prize": "Let me have opportunity, unbiased by opinion, to gratify my natural disposition in a participation of those pleasures which youth and innocence afford" (114, 113). Eliza's yoking of freedom-as-mobility and freedom-as-pleasure becomes painfully insupportable, however, as her friends marry and move away, provoking the written circulation of abstract virtue against which she struggles. Foster's keenest insight may lie in this connection of mobility and the conventional intimacies that force virtue to travel in the tightly maintained yet transportable units of the couple and the nuclear family. While virtue may be safeguarded by the family circle, however, mobility erodes other forms of contact, sacrificing the inventive freedom of friendship in favor of the managed privacy of conventional intimacy. Smarting with disappointment as her friends settle down and move on, leaving her feeling more abandoned than any libertine could possibly do, Eliza exclaims: "Marriage is the tomb of friendship. It appears to me a very selfish state. Why do people, in general, as soon as they are married, centre all their cares, their concerns, and pleasures in their own families? former acquaintances are neglected or forgotten. The tenderest ties between friends are weakened, or dissolved; and benevolence itself moves in a very limited sphere" (123).

Against Eliza's assumption that democracy is strengthened by increasing, through friendships, the number of people who share the responsibilities ("cares" and "concerns") and pleasures that constitute public intimacy, her friends defend their "limited sphere." While it is true that married women "cannot always pay that attention to former associates, which we may wish," Mrs. Richman insists, "the little community which we superintend is quite as important as others, and certainly renders us more beneficial to the public. True benevolence, though it may change its objects, is not limited by time or place. Its effects are the same, and aided by a second self, are rendered more diffusive and salutary" (123).

When a male admirer declares Mrs. Richman "truly republican," he suggests not only that her civic concern makes her a good citizen but that there is something "republican" about the location of the affairs of the commonweal in the normative privacy of hearth and home (139).

Even as she debates her friends, however, Eliza maintains her faith in friendship. Stating at the novel's outset, "I wish for no other connection than that of friendship," Eliza distinguishes that relationship from those, like Mrs. Richman's, built on federal affect (108). There are no laws governing friendship, few financial contracts, even a relatively small number of informal rituals to give it shape. In the absence of abstract patterns, friends, as Michel Foucault observes, "face each other without terms or convenient words, with nothing to assure them about the meaning of the movement that carries them towards each other. They have to invent, from A to Z, a relationship that is still formless, which is friendship: that is to say, the sum of everything through which they can give each other pleasure." Generating alliances based on the inventive pleasures negotiated—and renegotiated—in a spirit of historical contingency, friendship holds the potential power to "yield a culture and an ethics" that compete with nationalism itself.[7] Yet friendship, in Eliza's lifetime, was already being consigned to nostalgia, a live feeling visible only through a dead convention. "Oh that you were near me, as formerly," she writes to one childhood friend, "to share and alleviate my cares! to have some friend to whom I could repose confidence, and with whom I could freely converse, and advise, on this occasion, would be an unspeakable comfort!" (190).

While Foster contrasted friendship and mobility, Irving's 1819 "Rip Van Winkle" represents a more ambivalent relationship, beginning with the tale's "discovery" by Diedrich Knickerbocker, who, riding off atop a "hobby," kicks dust "in the eyes of his neighbors, and grieve[s] the spirit of some friends for whom he felt the truest deference and affection."[8] Though Irving seemingly consigns all bonds that compete with federal affect to a trivial (romantic, fantastic, and superstitious) "past" (never entirely) supplanted by the factual (and nationalized) present, his humor softens Foster's tragic conclusions. Affective bonds live on in Rip's melancholy memory (his neighbors remember Knickerbocker "'more in sorrow than in anger'"), vestiges of a more idiosyncratic and inventive social "past" (37). Despite Irving's tongue-in-cheek tone, however, grief persists in "Rip Van Winkle" as the relational supplement that, ever mobile, goes on crossing the borders of civic virtue and national belonging.

Rip's curse, at the outset of the tale, is precisely his lack of mobility. Henpecked by his shrewish Dame, Rip seems incapable of escaping her "petticoat government," rooted in place, like Hawthorne's narrators, by the local myths of ghosts, witches, and Indians. Rip's movement into the mountains, however, allows a shift from identification with the victims of imperial conquest (ghosts, witches, and Indians) to a new identification with the Dutch agents of imperial expansion. Although Rip's new mobile identification appears to put him at odds with the electoral democracy of postwar America, which bewilders and alienates him, the "rip" caused by expansive mobility is quickly repaired, as his fellow citizens, listening to Rip's tale, embrace him as one of their own. In so doing, the townspeople suggest that his seemingly extraordinary experiences are familiar to them as well: what Rip learns through the haunting history of imperialism, the townspeople learn through an expansive sympathy that enables them to embrace Rip for the good character they recognize, more than local history or electoral participation, as the true marker of civic belonging. From the beginning of the tale, Rip is described as "kind," full of "patience" (39), tolerant, and above all sympathetic: "'Poor Wolf,' he would say, 'thy mistress leads thee a dog's life of it; but never mind, my lad, whilst I live thou shalt never want a friend to stand by thee!' Wolf would wag his tail, look wistfully in his master's face, and if dogs could feel pity, I verily believe he reciprocated the sentiment with all his heart" (42). The tale affirms that federal affect like Rip's was not a new phenomenon but a nascent potential, its articulation not a disciplinary ritual but a fulfillment. After he has disclosed his "true" self—or rather, after he has learned to tell his "self" in ways consistent with the values of his audience—Rip is integrated into the community; as one of the townswomen says, "'Welcome home again, old neighbor'" (51).

Rip's homecoming remains haunted, however, by a grievous longing for lost friends, even a vanished wife. Irving's description of Rip's reactions might fit any number of displaced Americans who found themselves part of the newly mobile American public: "The very village was altered; it was larger and more populous. There were rows of houses which he had never seen before, and those which had been his familiar haunts had disappeared. Strange names were over the doors—strange faces at the windows—everything was strange" (47).[9] As he inquires after his former associates and learns that they have been killed or moved on, "Rip's heart die[s] away at hearing of these sad changes in his home and friends, and finding himself thus alone in the world" (50). Although "Rip Van Winkle" celebrates its hero's liberation from his shrewish wife, when he surveys his ruined home, he experiences grief: "This desolateness overcame all his connubial fears—he called loudly for his wife and children: the lonely chambers rang for a moment with his voice, then all again was silence" (48). Eliza Wharton's melancholy faith in friendship, never fully conquered in *The Coquette,* continues, in "Rip Van Winkle," to forestall the juridical force of federalized affect, suggesting in the process that relations that apparently die with Eliza Wharton or Dame Van Winkle may have only gone underground, preserving the affectively mobile, only ever partially visible, intimacies of friends who, like Rip Van Winkle, take to the hills.

Just as the language of friendship bonded the nation's contradictory impulses toward autonomy and expansion, mobility and sociality, so too it linked Hawthorne, who repeatedly declared himself rooted to his native soil, with Melville, whose narrators can't stop moving. Even as their relationship replicated a deeply national tension, however, both men expressed dissatisfaction with national belonging, yearning for something larger *and* more locally intimate. That paradoxical longing is the status of modern citizenship, which gains its affective rationale from local attachments while pointing outward to universal values (and imperial expansion). Caught between the narrow and the nowhere, citizens may soon recognize—as Hawthorne and Melville apparently did—that nationalism is a perpetual vanishing act. Never at rest in a definable location (even Melville's patriotic review acknowledges regional division between Virginia and Vermont), nationalism circulates between localism and universalism, generating in citizens a jerky affective choreography of contentment and restlessness.

Those terms characterize perfectly Hawthorne's and Melville's efforts, as the latter wrote in *Pierre,* "to denationalize the natural heavenliness of their souls" (*WHM,* 7:139). As Melville's side of their correspondence reveals, the relationship moved, like Rip's identification with the Dutch, beyond national metaphors, drawing instead on discourses of imperialism and universalism. Yet imperialism and universalism proved equally limited in representing democratic intimacy. While imperialism dampens intimacy by insisting on hierarchal values of difference, universalism, appearing to grant a general equality, disallows difference altogether.

As the intimacy between Hawthorne and Melville grew, it exceeded U.S. borders to include other nation-states. In a November 17, 1851, letter, Melville thanks Hawthorne for his praise of *Moby-Dick*, saying, "[Y]ou have now given me the crown of India"; on June 1, 1851, he compares himself to "one of those seeds taken out of the Egyptian Pyramids," and on April 16, 1851, he self-consciously quips, "You see, I began with a little criticism extracted for your benefit from the 'Pittsfield Secret Review,' and here I have landed in Africa" (*WHM*, 14:212, 14:193, 14:187). Responding to *The House of the Seven Gables*, Melville characterizes Hawthorne as one of the men who, saying "NO! in thunder," are like "judicious, unencumbered travelers in Europe," crossing "the frontiers into Eternity with nothing but a carpet-bag,—that is to say, the Ego" (*WHM*, 14:186). Sometimes Melville's nation crossings were more comical. On August 1, 1851, Hawthorne reports that, while he and son Julian sat in a field, they were approached by a "cavalier" on horseback who greeted them in Spanish. The "cavalier," of course, was Melville.[10]

These anecdotes suggest that for Melville and (perhaps to a lesser degree) Hawthorne, border crossing was a matter less of literal travel than of imagination (Melville described his review as a "poor fugitive scrawl" [*HMF*, 225]) and companionship (Melville promises to engage Hawthorne in "some little bit of vagabondism"), which together conspire to transform identity (*WHM*, 14:199). Melville described his all-night conversations with Hawthorne as "ontological heroics" (*WHM*, 14:196). Hawthorne's claim that those same conversations concerned "possible and impossible matters" suggests that the movement between the possible and the impossible, the here and the "somewhere else," the Ego and the Fantastic, allowed national and even individual identity ("ontology") to be, heroically, transgressed (*HMF*, 4).

At the same time, as Melville's references to Africa, Egypt, and India make clear, intimate border crossings could render "heroic" a disturbing history of imperial expansion. Melville praised Clifford Pyncheon, for instance, as "the man who, like Russia or the British Empire, declares himself a sovereign nature (in himself)" (*WHM*, 14:186). Even while translating Hawthorne's meek fugitive into the Imperial Self (Melville moves quickly from describing Clifford to referring to "myself" and "me"), Melville was well aware of the dangerous and dehumanizing hierarchies imperialism generated, especially in its most intimate relations. Finding himself, at the beginning of *Moby-Dick*, bedded with a tattooed harpooner who makes advances in the night, Ishmael quickly uses imperial logic to accommodate the breach in decorum: "In a country-man," Ishmael reasons, "this sudden flame of friendship would have seemed far too premature, a thing to be much distrusted; but in this simple savage those old rules would not apply" (*WHM*, 6:51). While his border crossing allows Ishmael to rethink social conventions, he does so only by asserting the binaries of native/foreign, civilized/savage, and complex/simple that impede, rather than enhance, intimacy.

Perhaps because he *was* aware of the dangers of imperial hierarchy, Melville more frequently represented international expansion as "this infinite fraternity of feeling" (*WHM*, 14:212). Melville concludes "Mosses," for instance, by speculating about "a boundless sympathy with all forms of being, such an omnipresent love," through which "genius, all over the world," shares "hand in hand" in a "great fullness and overflowing" that is "destined to be, shared by a plurality of men of genius" (*WHM*, 9:242, 9:249, 9:252). Coming close in its "ontological heroics" to what Emerson called the Oversoul, Melville's universalism connects not only men of genius but the animate and inanimate world as well: "your separate identity," he writes Hawthorne, "is but a wretched one,—good; but get out of yourself, spread and expand yourself, and bring to yourself the tinglings of life that are felt in the flowers and the woods, that are felt in the planets Saturn and Venus, and the Fixed Stars" (*WHM*, 14:193).

The potential benefits of translating imperialism into universalism become clear in Geoffrey Sanborn's analysis of how Melville avoids the pitfalls of imperial appropriation in *Moby-Dick* by introducing separation and equilibrium into the relationship of Queequeg and Ishmael. One can never know—or assimilate—the quirks of another's inviolable personality, Sanborn argues, but one can still count on a base set of values and behaviors common to all human beings. Suggesting "the value of distance and formal equality in global and interpersonal relations," Melville uses love to point us "toward a world in which human relationships neither emerge from nor justify the existing social order, a world of 'high qualities' and 'strange feelings.'"[11] What generates such "strange feelings" between people is not conventional desire, predicated on lack—"filling out one another's fantasies, substituting for something lost and nonexistent"—but *formal equivalence* that allows for "the appearance of sameness" across ephemeral differences of bodies and cultures (248).

The love that Sanborn describes in *Moby-Dick* seems close to what Melville describes, in his relationship with Hawthorne, as "the *all* feeling" (*WHM,* 14:194). Melville often used God to personify this expansive merger of identity-through-love, as when he writes Hawthorne, "your heart beat in my ribs and mine in yours, and both in God's" (*WHM,* 14:212). Just as Sanborn contends that universal love contests the "existing social order," so Melville's divine expansion stands counter to conventional life, as he makes clear in telling Hawthorne, "The reason the mass of men fear God, and *at bottom dislike* Him, is because they rather distrust His heart, and fancy Him all brain like a watch" (*WHM,* 14:192). Claiming that "what plays the mischief with the truth is that men will insist upon the universal application of a temporary feeling or opinion," Melville imposes the same distinction between "formal correspondence" and local ephemerality that Sanborn traces in Melville's great romance (*WHM,* 14:194).

Compared with imperial hierarchies that turn loved ones into simple savages, Sanborn's account of "a way of being alone in which we are nonetheless together and a way of being together in which we are no longer ourselves" seems appealing (251). Sanborn claims that Melville's love should make us "believe that a nonracist, nonhomophobic future is, if not within reach, at least within sight." Under what conditions, though, do these ideals remain always on the horizon, "within sight" but not within reach (229)? A "nonhomophobic" world is easy to imagine once one erases, as Sanborn wishes to do, the categories of sexuality. Melville, too, longed for such an erasure. Writing Hawthorne that he had found "content" and "irresponsibility," but "without licentious inclination," Melville harnesses stability and transgression only by bracketing the unruly impulses of the sexualized body (*WHM,* 14:212). When he characterizes this feeling as "my profoundest sense of being" rather than "an incidental feeling," furthermore, Melville aligns "licentiousness" with the ephemerality erased by "profound" correspondence. If sexuality becomes, in these accounts, the realm not only of particularity (the quirky fantasies and pleasures that refuse abstracting "equivalences") but also of demand (our fantasies are one of the few things modern citizens can aspire to live out materially), then removing sex from intimacy would indeed leave fulfillment perpetually deferred. While it is undoubtedly true, as Robert K. Martin and Leland S. Person argue, that critics must "raise the subject of sexual orientation and practice from gossip to politics," it is equally true that politics, so abstracted as to preclude all particularities, are not likely to prove transformative.[12] If we are drawn to others only through their manifestation of an abstract sameness—whether the sameness of our self-image or of purportedly "universal" values—we not only eliminate the differences that stimulate reconsideration and re-formulation, but we also generate a psychic order of sublimated dissent, or, rather, we take dissent out of the public realm and place it in the stormy unconscious. Melville never entirely disavowed the body's de-sires and the collectivities to which they lead, countering self-replication and sameness, the constitutive traits of Ahab's "monomania," with the collaborative intimacy most famously represented in "A Squeeze of the Hand." In those moments, exchanges of difference, of lack and fullness, virtue and sexuality, particularity and sociability, generate the often dis-ruptive but always transformative moments of social intimacy based on "strange feelings" neither nationalized nor fully alienated, but set, as it were, adrift.

If none of the geographical metaphors Melville used to describe his relationship with Hawthorne captured the nature of their intimacy, perhaps their failure expresses how intimacy disrupts and exceeds the ideological border drawing imposed by spatial metaphors. When Mel-ville famously asked, "Whence come you, Hawthorne?" (*WHM*, 14:212), rather than asking for a literal location he was setting Hawthorne in movement (if Hawthorne was coming, he was also, presumably, going). Love, for Melville and Hawthorne, was neither here nor there, but in the movements between, the imaginative efforts that it takes to make sense of difference, not by turning it into another version of the same, but by allowing it to *change* our conception of "sameness," to see how life might be under someone else's sense of normalcy, to recognize that morals, de-sires, conversations are not *things* in space (even the deep interior space of the individual or the expansive space of the Godhead) but thrive in the give-and-take *between* the known and the unknown, the self and the beloved.

Such moments of trans-intimacy characterize one of the most per-plexing episodes of the Hawthorne-Melville relationship. On August 13, 1852, after Hawthorne had left Lenox to resettle in Newton, Melville wrote to tell him about a story he had heard about a woman, Agatha, who nurses a shipwrecked sailor, Robertson (whom Melville renamed Robinson), back to health and marries him, only to be deserted when her beloved again takes to roaming. After seventeen years of awaiting his return, Agatha learns that her husband has married again. The story,

Melville cryptically tells Hawthorne, "lies very much in a vein, with which you are peculiarly familiar" (*WHM,* 14:234).

We might speculate, as Brenda Wineapple does, that Melville, left behind by his beloved Hawthorne and therefore identifying with the abandoned Agatha, was more "peculiarly familiar" with such tales than Hawthorne, but his gloss on the story suggests otherwise.[13] On October 25, Melville again wrote to Hawthorne: "In his previous sailor life Robinson had found a wife (for a night) in every port. The sense of the obligation of the marriage-vow to Agatha had little weight with him at first. *It* was only when some years of life ashore had passed that his moral sense on that point became develloped [sic]" (*WHM,* 14:240). Apparently, Melville identified not with abandonment but with a kind of intimate relativism, a notion that the constitutive terms of intimacy—commitment, loyalty, betrayal—are contingent on social practices and therefore open to comparative reinscription. Such intimate revisionism is possible, as the Agatha story makes clear, only in movement, in the travels *between* commitments, beyond the borders of home(lands). Melville carefully notes that Robinson never fully abandons Agatha but keeps coming back to her, offering companionship and financial support. What is missing in this story, then, is not intimacy so much as continuity and permanence, which make relationships appear steady in the same way they make nations and empires appear so. Perhaps Melville was drawn to Robinson because he seems to offer a model of intimacy built not on the supposed continuity of nation-states or the permanence of universal values but precisely on the crossings to which Melville repeatedly returns in his accounts of his friendship with Hawthorne. Perhaps, in other words, the best metaphor for intimacy is not citizenship but itinerancy.

Melville and Hawthorne, too, never quite abandoned one another, although their meetings became less frequent. The two men met for the last two times in Liverpool, where Hawthorne served as Franklin Pierce's consul, when Melville was traveling to and then back from the Holy Land. On Melville's way out they had what appears to have been an enjoyable visit, which Hawthorne recounts at length in his notebook. On the return, Melville wrote only "Saw Hawthorne," while Hawthorne made no mention of the visit at all (*HMF,* 13). Yet the two men *did* meet one more time, in the pages of Melville's epic 1876 poem, *Clarel,* in which the writer supposedly memorialized his troubled relationship with Hawthorne. While often read as a mournful lament, *Clarel* demonstrates how to recover alienated affections by making them, ironically, *more* alien; it is, in short, a manifesto on the value of trans-intimacy's vagabond desires.

In the poem, an American student, Clarel, travels to the Holy Land in a vain effort to resolve his spiritual doubts, discovering along the way that truth exists beyond the narrow provincialism of his upbringing in the United States. He can shake his "cultivated narrowness," Clarel understands, only when he "rove[s] / At last abroad among mankind" in order to "Forgo the state / Of local minds inveterate" (*WHM*, 12:6). At first, Clarel attempts to reduce difference to a harmonious sameness, as when, hearing "polyglot" Asian, African, and European voices at prayer, he imagines the different creeds "Tingling with kinship through and through— / Faith childlike and the tried humanity" (*WHM*, 12:14–15). Clarel can answer his urgent question, "What profound / Impulsion makes these tribes to range?" only by reducing historical difference to affective similitude:

Stable in time's incessant change
Now first he marks, now awed he heeds
The intersympathy of creeds
Alien or hostile tho' they seem—. (*WHM*, 12:23)

Ultimately, however, Clarel, abandoning the fantasy of "intersympathetic" harmony, allows himself to be

confronted so
By the true genius, friend or foe,
And actual visage of a place
Before but dreamed of in the glow
Of fancy's spiritual grace. (*WHM*, 12:6)

This is not a replication of "sameness" in others but a shattering confrontation of such projections ("fancy's spiritual grace") by "actual" differences. Neither peaceful nor comforting, such encounters remind Clarel of the "wrangles . . . which oft befall: / Contention for each holy place, / And jealousies how far from grace." "O bickering family bereft," he bitterly asks the polyglot pilgrims, "Was feud the heritage He left?" (*WHM*, 12:24). "Disturbed and troubled in estate" by the discord he encounters

in the Holy Land, where pilgrim faces seem "a book / Of disappointment" (*WHM,* 12:8), Clarel, undergoing a process not of projection but
of disruptive incorporation,

> took,
> In way but little modified,
> Part to himself; then stood in dream
> Of all which yet might hap to them. (*WHM,* 12:20)

The future, while (because) disconcertingly alien, shocks him out of the
familiar belief in sympathy and universal love, brought with him from
his homeland.

While Clarel's search is initially spatial ("Some other world to find.
But where?" he exclaims), the pilgrim, like his creator, realizes that geographic metaphors, imposing a choice between projection and incorporation, harmony and discord, must be abandoned. Instead, he seeks
"solacement in mate" (*WHM,* 12:8): only in other people does Clarel find
the promise of a world "re-imparadised" (*WHM,* 12:28). Thinking about
Luke's encounter with the resurrected Christ, Clarel imagines a

> novel sympathy, which said—
> I too, I too; could *I* but meet
> Some stranger of a lore replete,
> Who, marking how my looks betray
> The dumb thoughts clogging here my feet
> Would question me, expound and prove,
> And make my heart to burn with love—. (*WHM,* 12:26)

The move from "intersympathy"—seemingly natural and universal—
to "novel" sympathy—unique, contingent, and perhaps imaginary—
corresponds with the shift from projection to encounter, in which the
love-inspiring "stranger" does not confirm "sameness" but poses challenging questions that cause the lover to think, to grow, and to change.

The strangers Clarel meets in the Holy Land, like the figures Sanborn
describes, possess inviolable interiorities, refusing love's prying eyes.
Mystery is what prevents the American Clarel from gaining knowledge of the "other" that would allow him to hierarchize the cultures he
encounters into an imperial order. Beginning with the epigrammatic

pilgrim, Nehemiah, a "flitting tract-dispensing man" who invites Clarel "'With me divide the scrip of love'" (*WHM*, 12:28, 12:30), the young American encounters a series of men who excite his love without ever disclosing the secrets of their inner selves. Melville describes the first such encounter:

> Mutely for moment, face met face:
> But more perhaps between the two
> Was interchanged than e'en may pass
> In many a worded interview. (*WHM*, 12:35)

While this exchange feels deeply meaningful to Clarel ("A novel sympathy impressed"), he resolves not to "renew" the encounter (*WHM*, 12:35). Soon thereafter, he meets another dark stranger, Celio, whose "reserve," performing the task Clarel first expected of the landscape, disrupts the "habitual Past." As the "unexpected supervenes," Celio produces in Clarel "an upstart element," while remaining himself "Unpledged, unhampered" (*WHM*, 12:40, 12:37). These encounters climax when Clarel meets Vine, often read as a stand-in for Hawthorne. At his prayers, Vine suddenly

> looked up, and Clarel viewed,
> And they exchanged quick sympathies
> Though but in glance, moved by that act
> Of one whose faith transfigured fact.
> A bond seemed made between them there. (*WHM*, 12:90)

One might expect Vine's "manner shy," his "Ambiguous elfishness" and "austere control of self," to form "A clog, a hindrance" to connection, but once again it proves otherwise. Although Vine remains "shrunk / In privity," yet between him and Clarel an "excess of feeling pressed / Til ache to apathy was won" (*WHM*, 12:91, 12:94).

Despite this intense exchange of feeling, which leads Clarel to question the stories other pilgrims tell him and his prior beliefs about the Bible, the young student is plagued by self-doubts arising from impossible expectations of full disclosure and permanent attachment. Asking himself, "Would Vine disclaim / All sympathy the youth might share?"

or consent to "communion true / And close; let go each alien theme; / Give me thyself!" (*WHM*, 12:95), Clarel discovers in Vine a man all too typically self-occupied:

> Vine, at will
> Dwelling upon his wayward dream,
> Nor as suspecting Clarel's thrill
> Of personal longing, rambled still. (*WHM*, 12:226)

Caught between his romantic expectations and his realistic encounter with Vine's personality, Clarel talks himself into immanent disappointment.

> Divided mind knew Clarel here;
> The heart's desire did interfere.
> Thought he, How pleasant in another
> Such sallies, or in thee, if said
> After confidings that should wed
> Our souls in one:—Ah, call me *brother!*
> So feminine his passionate mood
> Which, long as hungering unfed,
> All else rejected or withstood.
>   Some inkling he let fall. But no:
> Here over Vine there slid a change—
> A shadow, such as thin may show. (*WHM*, 12:226–27)

It is important to note that Vine does not reject Clarel's advances, which the young American never permits himself to make. Rather, Clarel *imagines* Vine responding,

> But for thy fonder dream of love
> In man toward man—the soul's caress—
> The negatives of flesh should prove
> Analogies of non-cordialness
> In spirit.—E'en such conceits could cling
> To Clarel's dream of vain surmise
> And imputation full of sting. (*WHM*, 12:227)

The "sting" here is not Vine's rebuke, but Clarel's own inability to let go of his desire to make from contingent encounters a familial relation ("call me *brother*"), a permanent bond.

Clarel's "feminine . . . passionate mood" is paralleled by Agar and Ruth, who cast Clarel's desires in terms of geopolitical belonging and displacement. When an Illinois farmer, Nathan, marries the "Jewess" Agar, he soon becomes more ardent in the Jewish faith than his wife, transporting Agar and their infant daughter, Ruth, to the Holy Land where, devoting his time to study with the rabbis, he neglects his lonely and homesick wife and daughter. Ruth cares for the elderly Nehemiah, through whom Clarel comes in contact with the Jewish family. While the devout Nathan feels an instant dislike for the Christian student, his wife and daughter welcome Clarel, finding in him "A waftage from the fields of home" (*WHM*, 12:86). As Melville writes:

> Welcome the matron ever had
> For Clarel. Was the youth not one
> New from the clime she doted on
> And if indeed an exile sad
> By daisy in a letter laid
> Reminded be of home-delight,
> Tho' there first greeted by the sight
> Of that transmuted flower—how then
> Not feel a kin emotion bred
> At glimpse of face of countryman
> Tho' stranger?

A few lines later, Melville writes that Clarel, "sharing not her blood, / Nearer in tie of spirit stood / Than he she called Rabboni," since mother, like daughter, yearns "for freedom." "Happy was Agar ere the seas / She crossed for Zion" (*WHM*, 12:84, 12:85), Melville reports.

Clarel ultimately rejects Agar and Ruth, not, as Nina Baym argues, because they represent the embodied degeneration associated with women (after all, Clarel encounters more dramatic bodily degeneration in the form of male lepers), but because they represent (in a manner no less misogynistic) the degeneration associated with *nationalism*. The opposite of embodied womanhood, in Baym's ethos of naturalized heterosexuality, is a sterile celibacy or, worse (for her), homosexuality.[14]

The opposite of feminized nationalism, however, is a cosmopolitanism that still allows the passions of the flesh. While nationalism leads to nostalgic knowingness (sorrow, Melville writes, "Never eluded love, true love, / A deep diviner" [*WHM*, 12:85]), the furtive glances between men open *mystery*, precisely an *un*knowingness. It is this that Agar needs, not a nation-of-origin, when she muses, "how to give her feelings play?" (*WHM*, 12:86). Clarel's feelings, his imagination, are given "play" not by the nostalgic certainty provided by home(lands) but by the mysterious desires awakened by travel.

Have relationships "failed" because they are short lived? Are friends disloyal because they move on? When, to use a Melvillean metaphor, two ships pass in the night, does anything of value pass between them? Critics and historians have too often approached the Melville-Hawthorne relationship with the assumption that the intimacy between the two authors had some intrinsic flaw. Like Clarel, they assume that because intimacies do not fit the institutional rubrics of heterosexual privacy (marriage, family), they are "doomed" to meaninglessness and impermanence. What the moments of trans-intimacy—exchanges between persons who share their *un*knowability in ways that provoke imagination and change—demonstrate, however, is that meaninglessness and impermanence are synonyms only in a national ideology that equates fulfillment with continuity. If continuity is the sine qua non of national meaning, however, ephemerality is the moving experience of intimacy. Intimacy teaches us to be in transit, vagabonds (the "other" of citizenship in the Articles of Confederation but the heart of intimacy in Melville's letters to Hawthorne).

Given a choice between permanence and contingency, belonging and growth, space and movement, nationalism and intimacy, which should we choose? As the metaphors that Melville and Hawthorne used to describe their relationship teach us, the choice is rhetorical, since intimacy is often grounded in geopolitical metaphors, which themselves grow out of lived experiences of friendship and intimacy. If nationalism *grounds* intimacy, intimacy keeps citizenship unsettled, contingent, *moving*. Melville describes Agar's nostalgic longing for America as an impossible effort "to realise the unreal!" (*WHM*, 12:86). If Agar's movements between the real and the ideal do not produce a homeland, they nevertheless generate her intimate relationship with Clarel, just as Hawthorne's and Melville's conversational movements across the borders of the possible and impossible allowed for Hawthorne's intimacy with Melville. We might ask, as Melville did of Hawthorne, "Is love appreciated?" (*WHM*, 14:212). If we judge love as we judge nation-states, then the answer is probably "no." But if we judge nation-states as we might judge intimacies, asking for the same give-and-take, the same imaginative responses to *not* knowing, the same influx of the seemingly "impossible" into political common sense, then perhaps our answer will begin to change.

Notes

1. *Federalist Papers,* 98; hereafter cited parenthetically.

2. Blanchard, *Cultivating the Social Affections,* 24, 3.

3. "Articles of Confederation," 85, 86; hereafter cited parenthetically.

4. See Cox's introduction to *Four Pillars of Constitutionalism,* 62.

5. Stern, *Plight of Feeling,* 82.

6. Foster, *Coquette,* 109; hereafter cited parenthetically. "The only resolution is beyond the gaze of monitors," David Waldstreicher argues, "where a physically absent Eliza can stand in for the idea of virtue, apart from vision and the evaluation of virtue" ("'Fallen under My Observation,'" 216).

7. Foucault, "Friendship," 204–5, 207.

8. Irving, "Rip Van Winkle," 37; hereafter cited parenthetically.

9. Noting "the rapid migration of large parts of the population" in Irving's day, in which communities "were left behind, new ones begun and then abandoned for the promise of still greater opportunities," Rubin-Dorsky argues for "an undertow of anxiety about the breakdown and loss of community" in tales such as "Rip Van Winkle" (*Adrift in the Old World,* 4–5).

10. Wilson, ed., *Hawthorne and Melville Friendship,* 4; hereafter cited parenthetically as *HMF.*

11. Sanborn, "Whence Come You, Queequeg?" 240, 231; hereafter cited parenthetically.

12. Martin and Person, "Missing Letters," 113.

13. Wineapple, "Hawthorne and Melville," 83.

14. See Baym, "Erotic Motif in Melville's *Clarel.*"

Works Cited

Adams, Henry. *The Education of Henry Adams: An Autobiography.* Boston: Houghton Mifflin, 1961.

Adamson, Joseph. *Melville, Shame, and the Evil Eye: A Psychoanalytic Reading.* Albany: SUNY Press, 1997.

Albanese, Catherine. *Nature Religion in America: From the Algonkian Indians to the New Age.* Chicago: Univ. of Chicago Press, 1990.

Anthony, David. "Class, Culture, and the Trouble with White Skin in Hawthorne's *The House of the Seven Gables.*" *Yale Journal of Criticism* 12, no. 2 (1999): 249–68.

Armstrong, Nancy, and Leonard Tennenhouse. *The Imaginary Puritan.* Berkeley: Univ. of California Press, 1994.

"Articles of Confederation." In *Four Pillars of Constitutionalism: The Organic Laws of the United States,* edited by Richard H. Cox, 84–96. Amherst, N.Y.: Prometheus Books, 1998.

Arvin, Newton. *Hawthorne.* New York: Russell and Russell, 1929.

———. *Herman Melville.* New York: William Sloane, 1950.

Baker, Paul R. *The Fortunate Pilgrims: Americans in Italy, 1800–1860.* Cambridge, Mass.: Harvard Univ. Press, 1964.

Balibar, Etienne. "The Nation Form: History and Ideology." In *Becoming National: A Reader,* edited by Geoff Eley and Ronald Grigor Suny, 107–30. New York: Oxford Univ. Press, 1996.

Ballou, Adin. *An Exposition of Views Respecting the Principal Facts, Causes, and Peculiarities Involved in Spirit Manifestations.* Boston: Bela Marsh, 1852.

Barbour, James. "'All My Books Are Botches': Melville's Struggle with *The*

Whale." In *Writing the American Classics,* edited by James Barbour and Tom Quirk, 25–52. Chapel Hill: Univ. of North Carolina Press, 1990.

———. "The Composition of *Moby-Dick.*" *American Literature* 47, no. 3 (1975): 343–60.

———. "The *Town-Ho's* Story: Melville's Original Whale." *ESQ: A Journal of the American Renaissance* 21, no. 2 (1975): 111–15.

Baym, Nina. "The Erotic Motif in Melville's *Clarel.*" *Texas Studies in Literature and Language* 16, no. 2 (1974): 315–28.

Bell, Millicent, ed. *Hawthorne and the Real: Bicentennial Essays.* Columbus: Ohio State Univ. Press, 2004.

Bentley, Nancy. "Slaves and Fauns: Hawthorne and the Uses of Primitivism." *ELH* 57, no. 4 (1990): 901–37.

Bercaw, Mary K. *Melville's Sources.* Evanston, Ill.: Northwestern Univ. Press, 1987.

Bercovitch, Sacvan. *The Office of the Scarlet Letter.* Baltimore, Md.: Johns Hopkins Univ. Press, 1991.

Bergman, David. *Gaiety Transfigured: Gay Self-Representation in American Literature.* Madison: Univ. of Wisconsin Press, 1991.

Berlant, Lauren. "Fantasies of Utopia in *The Blithedale Romance.*" In *The "American Literary History" Reader,* edited by Gordon Hutner, 3–35. New York: Oxford Univ. Press, 1995.

Berlant, Lauren, and Michael Warner. "Sex in Public." *Critical Inquiry* 24, no. 2 (1998): 547–66.

Berthoff, Warner. *The Example of Melville.* Princeton, N.J.: Princeton Univ. Press, 1962.

Berthold, Dennis. "Melville, Garibaldi, and the Medusa of Revolution." *American Literary History* 9, no. 3 (1997): 425–59.

Blanchard, Jonathan. *On the Importance and Means of Cultivating the Social Affections Among Pupils; Delivered at the American Institute of Instruction at its Annual Meeting.* Boston, 1835.

Blied, Reverend Benjamin. *Catholics and the Civil War.* Milwaukee: published by the author, 1945.

Bowlby, John. *Loss: Sadness and Depression.* Vol. 3 of *Attachment and Loss.* New York: Basic Books, 1980.

Braude, Ann. *Radical Spirits: Spiritualism and Women's Rights in Nineteenth-Century America.* Boston: Beacon Press, 1989.

Brickhouse, Anna Campbell. "'I Do Abhor an Indian Story': Hawthorne and the Allegorization of Racial 'Commixture.'" *ESQ: A Journal of the American Renaissance* 42, no. 4 (1996): 233–52.

———. *Transamerican Literary Relations and the Nineteenth-Century Public Sphere.* New York: Cambridge Univ. Press, 2004.

Brodhead, Richard. *The School of Hawthorne.* New York: Oxford Univ. Press, 1986.

Brooks, Van Wyck. *The Dream of Arcadia: American Writers and Artists in Italy, 1760–1915.* New York: Dutton, 1958.

Bryant, John. *The Fluid Text: A Theory of Revision and Editing for Book and Screen.* Ann Arbor: Univ. of Michigan Press, 2002.

———. Introduction to *Typee: A Peep at Polynesian Life,* by Herman Melville, ix–xxx. New York: Penguin, 1996.

———. "Politics, Imagination, and the Fluid Text." *Studies in the Literary Imagination* 24, no. 2 (1996): 89–107.

Buchanan, James. *Modern Atheism: Under Its Forms of Pantheism, Materialism, Secularism, Development, and Natural Laws.* Boston: Gould and Lincoln, 1857.

Budick, Emily Miller. "Perplexity, Sympathy, and the Question of the Human: A Reading of *The Marble Faun.*" In *The Cambridge Companion to Nathaniel Hawthorne,* edited by Richard H. Millington, 230–50. Cambridge: Cambridge Univ. Press, 2004.

Buonomo, Leonardo. *Backward Glances: Exploring Italy, Reinterpreting America (1831–1866).* Madison, N.J.: Fairleigh Dickinson Univ. Press, 1996.

Cabot, James Elliot. *A Memoir of Ralph Waldo Emerson.* Boston: Houghton Mifflin, 1888.

Calder, Alexander. "Pacific Paradises." In *A Companion to Herman Melville,* edited by Wyn Kelley, 98–112. Malden, Mass.: Blackwell, 2006.

Carringer, Robert L. "Collaboration and Concepts of Authorship." *PMLA* 116, no. 2 (2001): 370–79.

Carroll, Bret E. *Spiritualism in Antebellum America.* Bloomington: Indiana Univ. Press, 1997.

Carton, Evan. *The Marble Faun: Hawthorne's Transformations.* New York: Twayne, 1992.

Casper, Scott. "The Two Lives of Franklin Pierce: Hawthorne, Political Culture, and the Literary Market." *American Literary History* 5, no. 2 (Summer 1993): 203–30.

Castronovo, Russ. *Necro-Citizenship: Death, Eroticism, and the Public Sphere in the Nineteenth-Century United States.* Durham, N.C.: Duke Univ. Press, 2001.

———. "'That Half-Living Corpse': Hawthorne and the Occult Public Sphere." *REAL: Yearbook of Research in English and American Literature* 18, 231–58. Tübingen: G. Narr, 2002.

Cayton, Mary Kupiec. *Emerson's Emergence: Self and Society in the Transformation of New England.* Chapel Hill: Univ. of North Carolina Press, 1989.

Charvat, William. *Literary Publishing in America, 1790–1850.* Amherst: Univ. of Massachusetts Press, 1993.

Chase, Richard. *Herman Melville: A Critical Study.* New York: Macmillan, 1949.

Chesler, Phyllis. *About Men.* New York: Simon and Schuster, 1978.

Chevigny, Bell Gale, ed. *The Woman and the Myth: Margaret Fuller's Life and Writings.* Old Westbury, N.Y.: Feminist Press, 1976.

Cheyfitz, Eric. "The Irresistibleness of Great Literature: Reconstructing Hawthorne's Politics." *American Literary History* 6, no. 3 (1994): 539–58.

Clark, C. E. Frazer, Jr. *Nathaniel Hawthorne: A Descriptive Bibliography.* Pittsburgh, Penn.: Univ. of Pittsburgh Press, 1978.

Clifford, James. "Traveling Cultures." In *Routes: Travel and Translation in the Late Twentieth Century,* 17–46. Cambridge, Mass.: Harvard Univ. Press, 1997.

Coale, Samuel Chase. *Mesmerism and Hawthorne: Mediums of American Romance.* Tuscaloosa: Univ. of Alabama Press, 1998.

———. "Mysteries of Mesmerism: Hawthorne's Haunted House." In *A Historical Guide to Nathaniel Hawthorne,* edited by Larry J. Reynolds, 49–77. Oxford, England: Oxford Univ. Press, 2001.

———. "Spiritualism and Hawthorne's Romance: The Blithedale Theater as False Consciousness." *Literature and Belief* 14 (1994): 31–56.

Colacurcio, Michael J. *The Province of Piety: Moral History in Hawthorne's Early Tales.* Durham, N.C.: Duke Univ. Press, 1995.

Cook, Robert. *Civil War America: Making a Nation, 1848–1877.* London: Longman, 2003.

Cottom, Daniel. *Abyss of Reason: Cultural Movements, Revelations, and Betrayals.* New York: Oxford Univ. Press, 1991.

Cottrell, Robert D. *Sexuality/Textuality: A Study of the Fabric of Montaigne's "Essais."* Columbus: Ohio State Univ. Press, 1981.

Cox, Richard H., ed. *Four Pillars of Constitutionalism.* Amherst, N.Y.: Prometheus Books, 1998.

Creech, James. *Closet Writing/Gay Reading: The Case of Melville's "Pierre."* Chicago: Univ. of Chicago Press, 1993.

Davidson, Frank. "Melville, Thoreau, and 'The Apple-Tree Table.'" *American Literature* 25, no. 4 (1954): 479–88.

Davis, Clark. *After the Whale: Melville in the Wake of "Moby-Dick."* Birmingham: Univ. of Alabama Press, 1995.

———. "Hawthorne's Shyness: Romance and the Forms of Truth." *ESQ: A Journal of the American Renaissance* 45, no. 1 (1999): 33–65.

Dayan, Joan. "Amorous Bondage: Poe, Ladies, and Slaves." In *The American Face of Edgar Allan Poe,* edited by Shawn Rosenheim and Stephen Rachman, 179–209. Baltimore, Md.: Johns Hopkins Univ. Press, 1995.

De Concilio, Reverend Januarius. *Catholicity and Pantheism.* New York: D. and J. Sadler, 1874.

Delbanco, Andrew. *Melville: His World and Work.* New York: Knopf, 2005.

Dening, Greg. *Beach Crossings: Voyaging across Times, Cultures, and Self.* Philadelphia: Univ. of Pennsylvania Press, 2004.

———. *Islands and Beaches: Discourse on a Silent Land: Marquesas, 1774–1880.* Chicago: Dorsey Press, 1980.

Derrick, Scott. *Monumental Anxieties: Homoerotic Desire and Feminine Influence in 19th-Century U.S. Literature.* New Brunswick, N.J.: Rutgers Univ. Press, 1997.

Dewey, Reverend Orville. "Blanco White-Rationalism." *Christian Examiner* 39 (July 1845): 195–219.

———. "Rights, Claims, and Duties of Opinions." *Christian Examiner* 39 (July 1845): 82–102.

Dickinson, Emily. *The Letters of Emily Dickinson.* Edited by Thomas H. Johnson. 3 vols. Cambridge, Mass.: Harvard University Press, 1958.

Dimock, Wai Chee. *Empire for Liberty: Melville and the Poetics of Individualism.* Princeton, N.J.: Princeton Univ. Press, 1989.

Dix, Reverend Morgan. *Lectures on the Pantheistic Idea of an Impersonal Deity.* New York: Hurd and Houghton, 1864.

Dobson, Joanne. *Quieter Than Sleep.* New York: Doubleday, 1997.

Douglas, Ann. *The Feminization of American Culture.* New York: Avon Books, 1978.

Douglass, Frederick. "The Claims of the Negro Ethnologically Considered: An Address Delivered in Hudson, Ohio, on 12 July 1854." In *The Frederick Douglass Papers; Series One: Speeches, Debates, and Interviews,* edited by John W. Blassingame et al., 2:497–524. New Haven, Conn.: Yale Univ. Press, 1982.

Dowling, Linda. *Hellenism and Homosexuality in Victorian Oxford.* Ithaca, N.Y.: Cornell Univ. Press, 1994.

Doyle, Don H. *Nations Divided: America, Italy, and the Southern Question.* Athens: Univ. of Georgia Press, 2002.

Duckam, Janet. "Melville and the M(Other): Object-Relations Theory and Melville's Metaphysical Quest." PhD diss., Washington University, 2001.

Duyckinck Collection, New York Public Library.

[Duyckinck, Evert]. Review of *Moby-Dick,* by Herman Melville. *Literary World,* November 15, 1851, 381–83; November 22, 1851, 403–4.

[———]. Review of *Pierre; or, The Ambiguities,* by Herman Melville. *Literary World,* August 21, 1852, 118–20.

Earle, Jonathan H. *Jacksonian Antislavery and the Politics of Free Soil, 1824–1854.* Chapel Hill: Univ. of North Carolina Press, 2004.

Eddy, D. Mathis. "Melville's Response to Beaumont and Fletcher: A New Source for *The Encantadas.*" *American Literature* 40 (1968): 374–80.

Ede, Lise, and Andrea A. Lunsford. "Collaboration and Concepts of Authorship." *PMLA* 116, no. 2 (2001): 354–69.

Elbert, Monika. "Hawthorne's 'Hollow' Men: Fabricating Masculinity in 'Feathertop.'" *ATQ* 5, no. 3 (1991): 169–82.

Eliot, T. S. "Tradition and the Individual Talent." In *Selected Prose of T. S. Eliot,* edited by Frank Kermode, 37–44. New York: Harcourt Brace Jovanovich, 1975.

Emerson, Ralph Waldo. *The Collected Works of Ralph Waldo Emerson.* Edited by Robert E. Spiller, Alfred R. Ferguson, et al. 6 vols. to date. Cambridge, Mass.: Harvard Univ. Press, 1971–.

———. *The Complete Sermons of Ralph Waldo Emerson.* Edited by Albert J. von Frank et al. 4 vols. Columbia: Univ. of Missouri Press, 1989–92.

———. *The Complete Works of Ralph Waldo Emerson.* 12 volumes. Boston: Houghton Mifflin, 1903–21.

———. *The Early Lectures of Ralph Waldo Emerson.* Edited by Stephen Whicher, Robert Spiller, and Wallace Williams. 3 vols. Cambridge, Mass.: Harvard Univ. Press, 1959–72.

———. *The Journals and Miscellaneous Notebooks of Ralph Waldo Emerson.* Edited by William H. Gilman, Ralph Orth, et al. 16 vols. Cambridge, Mass.: Harvard Univ. Press, 1960–82.

Emmers, Amy Puett. "Melville's Closet Skeleton: A New Letter about the Illegitimacy Incident in *Pierre.*" In *Studies in the American Renaissance* 1, edited by Joel Myerson, 339–43. Boston: Twayne, 1977.

Erlich, Gloria. *Family Themes and Hawthorne's Fiction: The Tenacious Web.* New Brunswick, N.J.: Rutgers Univ. Press, 1984.

Evelev, John. *Tolerable Entertainment: Herman Melville and Professionalism in Antebellum New York.* Amherst: Univ. of Massachusetts Press, 2006.

The Federalist Papers. New York: New American Library, 1961.

Fetterley, Judith. "Theorizing Regionalism: Celia Thaxter's *Among the Isles of Shoals.*" In *Breaking Boundaries: New Perspectives on Women's Regional Writing,* edited by Sherrie A. Inness and Diana Royer, 38–53. Iowa City: Univ. of Iowa Press, 1997.

Fields, James T. *Yesterdays with Authors.* Boston: James R. Osgood, 1877.

Foster, Hannah Webster. *The Coquette.* In *"The Power of Sympathy" and "The Coquette,"* edited by Carla Mulford. New York: Penguin, 1996.

Foster, Travis M. "Matthiessen's Public Privates: Homosexual Expression and the Aesthetics of Sexual Inversion." *American Literature* 78, no. 2 (2006): 235–62.

Foucault, Michel. "Friendship as a Way of Life." In *Foucault Live: Collected Interviews, 1961–1984,* edited by Sylvère Lotringer, translated by John Johnston, 203–10. New York: Semiotext(e), 1989.

———. *The History of Sexuality.* Vol. 1: *An Introduction.* Translated by Robert Hurley. New York: Pantheon, 1978.

Franchot, Jenny. *Roads to Rome: The Antebellum Protestant Encounter with Catholicism.* Berkeley: Univ. of California Press, 1994.

Freud, Sigmund. *Beyond the Pleasure Principle.* Translated by James Strachey. New York: Norton, 1961.

———. *Civilization and Its Discontents.* Translated by James Strachey. New York: Norton, 1961.

———. "Mourning and Melancholia." In *Complete Psychological Works of Sigmund Freud,* 14:243–58. Translated by James Strachey. London: Hogarth Press and the Institute of Psychoanalysis, 1964.

Fuller, Margaret. *Memoirs of Margaret Fuller Ossoli.* Edited by R. W. Emerson, W. H. Channing, and J. F. Clarke. 2 vols. Boston: Roberts, 1874.

———. Review of *Twice-Told Tales. Dial* 3 (1842–43): 130–31.

———. *"These Sad But Glorious Days": Dispatches From Europe, 1846–1850.* Edited by Larry J. Reynolds and Susan Belasco Smith. New Haven, Conn.: Yale Univ. Press, 1991.

Gable, Harvey Jr. "Inappeasable Longings: Hawthorne, Romance, and the Disintegration of Coverdale's Self in *The Blithedale Romance." New England Quarterly* 62, no. 2 (1994): 257–78.

Gabler-Hover, Janet. *Dreaming Black/Writing White: The Hagar Myth in American Cultural History.* Lexington: Univ. Press of Kentucky, 2000.

Gara, Larry. *The Presidency of Franklin Pierce.* Lawrence: Univ. Press of Kansas, 1991.

Garner, Stanton. *The Civil War World of Herman Melville.* Lawrence: Univ. Press of Kansas, 1993.

Garner, Stanton, et al. "Biographers on Biography: A Panel Discussion." In *Melville's Evermoving Dawn: Centennial Essays,* edited by John Bryant and Robert Milder, 225–59. Kent, Ohio: Kent State Univ. Press, 1997.

Gemme, Paola. *Domesticating Foreign Struggles: The Italian Risorgimento and Antebellum American Identity.* Athens: Univ. of Georgia Press, 2005.

Gibian, Peter. "Cosmopolitanism and Traveling Culture." In *A Companion to Herman Melville,* edited by Wyn Kelley, 19–34. Malden, Mass.: Blackwell, 2006.

Gillard, John T. *The Catholic Church and the American Negro.* Baltimore, Md.: St. Joseph's Society Press, 1929.

Gilman, William H. *Melville's Early Life and "Redburn."* New York: New York Univ. Press, 1951.

Gilmore, Michael. *American Romanticism and the Marketplace.* Chicago: Univ. of Chicago Press, 1985.

———. "Hawthorne and the Making of the Middle Class." In *Rethinking Class: Literary Studies and Social Formations,* edited by Wai Chee Dimock and Michael Gilmore, 215–38. New York: Columbia Univ. Press, 1994.

Gilmore, Paul. *The Genuine Article: Race, Mass Culture, and American Literary Manhood.* Durham, N.C.: Duke Univ. Press, 2001.

Goddu, Teresa A. "Letters Turned to Gold: Hawthorne, Authorship, and Slavery." *Studies in American Fiction* 29, no. 1 (2001): 48–75.

Gossett, Thomas F. *Race: The History of an Idea in America.* New York: Oxford Univ. Press, 1997.

Grant, Miles. *Spiritualism Unveiled, and Shown to Be the Work of Demons.* Boston: "Crisis" Office, 1866.

Greenblatt, Stephen. "Anti-Dictator: Montaigne Witnesses the Death of His Friend Étienne de La Boétie." In *A New History of French Literature,* edited by Denis Hollier, 223–27. Cambridge, Mass.: Harvard Univ. Press, 1989.

Grossberg, Benjamin Scott. "'The Tender Passion Was Very Rife among Us': Coverdale's Queer Utopia and *The Blithedale Romance.*" *Studies in American Fiction* 28, no. 1 (2000): 3–26.

Grossman, Jay. "The Canon in the Closet: Matthiessen's Whitman, Whitman's Matthiessen." *American Literature* 70, no. 4 (1998): 799–832.

Halperin, David M. *One Hundred Years of Homosexuality.* New York: Routledge, 1990.

Hamilton, Kristie. "Fauns and Mohicans: Narratives of Extinction and Hawthorne's Aesthetic of Modernity." In *Roman Holidays: American Writers and Artists in Nineteenth-Century Italy,* edited by Robert K. Martin and Leland S. Person, 41–59. Iowa City: Univ. of Iowa Press, 2002.

Hardack, Richard. "Bodies in Pieces, Letters Entwined: Correspondence and Intertextuality in Hawthorne and Melville." In *Epistolary Histories: Letters, Fiction, Culture,* edited by Amanda Gilroy and Wil Verhoeven, 126–51. Charlottesville: Univ. Press of Virginia, 2000.

———. "'The Slavery of Romanism': The Casting Out of the Irish in *The Douglass Monthly.*" In *A Liberating Sojourn: Frederick Douglass in Britain,* edited by Martin Crawford and Alan Rice, 115–40. Athens: Univ. of Georgia Press, 1999.

Hardwick, Elizabeth. "Melville in Love." *The New York Review of Books* 47 (June 15, 2000): 15–20.

Hawthorne, Julian. *Nathaniel Hawthorne and His Wife: A Biography.* 2 vols. Boston: James R. Osgood, 1884.

Hawthorne/Manning Family Letters. Phillips Library, Peabody Essex Museum, Salem, Massachusetts.

Hawthorne, Nathaniel. *Notes of Travel*. 4 vols. Cambridge, Mass.: Riverside Press, 1900.

Hawthorne, Sophia Peabody. Letters. Berg Collection of English and American Literature, New York Public Library, Astor, Lenox, and Tilden Foundations.

Hayford, Harrison. "Melville and Hawthorne: A Biographical and Critical Study." PhD diss., Yale Univ., 1945.

———. *Melville's "Monody": Really for Hawthorne?* Evanston: Northwestern Univ. Press, 1990. Reprinted, in an abridged form, as "Melville's 'Monody': For Hawthorne?" in *Clarel: A Poem and Pilgrimage in the Holy Land*, edited Harrison Hayford et al., 883–93. Vol. 12 of *The Writings of Herman Melville*. Evanston and Chicago: Northwestern Univ. Press and the Newberry Library, 1991.

———. "The Significance of Melville's 'Agatha' Letters." *ELH* 13, no. 4 (1946): 299–310.

———. "Unnecessary Duplicates: A Key to the Writing of *Moby-Dick*." In *New Perspectives on Melville*, edited by Faith Pullin, 128–61. Edinburgh: Edinburgh Univ. Press, 1978.

Hayford, Harrison, and Merrell Davis. "Herman Melville as Office-Seeker." *Modern Language Quarterly* 10 (June and September 1949): 168–83 (pt. 1); 377–88 (pt. 2).

Herbert, T. Walter. *Dearest Beloved: The Hawthornes and the Making of the Middle-Class Family*. Berkeley: Univ. of California Press, 1993.

———. "Hawthorne and American Masculinity." In *The Cambridge Companion to Nathaniel Hawthorne*, edited by Richard H. Millington, 60–78. Cambridge: Cambridge Univ. Press, 2004.

———. "Pornographic Manhood and *The Scarlet Letter*." *Studies in American Fiction* 29, no. 1 (2001): 113–21.

Hewitt, Elizabeth, "Scarlet Letters, Dead Letters: Correspondence and the Poetics of Democracy in Melville and Hawthorne." *Yale Journal of Criticism* 12, no. 2 (1999): 295–319.

Higgins, Brian, and Hershel Parker, eds. *Herman Melville: The Contemporary Reviews*. New York: Cambridge Univ. Press, 1995.

Higgins, Brian, and Hershel Parker. Introduction to *Critical Essays on Herman Melville's "Pierre; or, The Ambiguities,"* 1–27. Boston: Hall, 1983.

———. "Reading *Pierre*." In *A Companion to Melville Studies*, edited by John Bryant, 211–39. Westport, Conn.: Greenwood, 1986.

Hillard, George Stillman. *Six Months in Italy*. Boston: Houghton, Mifflin and Co., 1853.

Hirschfeld, Heather. "Early Modern Collaboration and Theories of Authorship." *PMLA* 116, no. 2 (2001): 609–22.

Horsman, Reginald. *Race and Manifest Destiny: The Origins of American Racial Anglo-Saxonism*. Cambridge, Mass.: Harvard Univ. Press, 1981.

Howard, Leon. *Herman Melville: A Biography*. Berkeley: Univ. of California Press, 1951.

———. "Melville's Struggle with the Angel." *Modern Language Quarterly* 1 (June 1940): 195–206.

Hunt, John. *Pantheism and Christianity*. 1884. Reprinted, Port Washington, N.Y.: Kennikat Press, 1970.

Idol, John J., Jr., Buford Jones, and M. Thomas Inge, eds. *Nathaniel Hawthorne: The Contemporary Reviews*. New York: Cambridge Univ. Press, 1994.

Ignatiev, Noel. *How the Irish Became White*. New York: Routledge, 1995.

Inge, M. Thomas. "Collaboration and Concepts of Authorship." *PMLA* 116, no. 3 (2001): 623–30.

Irving, Washington. "Rip Van Winkle." In *The Sketch Book*, 37–55. New York: Signet, 1961.

Isaacs, Ernest. "The Fox Sisters and American Spiritualism." In *The Occult in America: New Historical Perspectives*, edited by Howard Kerr and Charles L. Crow, 79–110. Urbana: Univ. of Illinois Press, 1983.

James, Henry. *Complete Stories of Henry James*. New York: Library of America, 1999.

———. *Literary Criticism*. Edited by Leon Edel. 2 vols. New York: Library of America, 1984.

Jamison, Kay Redfield. *Touched with Fire: Manic-Depressive Illness and the Artistic Temperament*. New York: Free Press, 1993.

Jones, Buford. "Some 'Mosses' from the *Literary World*: Critical and Bibliographical Survey of the Hawthorne-Melville Relationship." In *Ruined Eden of the Present: Hawthorne, Melville, and Poe*, edited by G. R. Thompson and Virgil L. Lokke, 173–203. West Lafayette, Ind.: Purdue Univ. Press, 1981.

Karcher, Carolyn L. "The Moderate and the Radical: Melville and Child on the Civil War and Reconstruction." *ESQ: A Journal of the American Renaissance* 45, nos. 3/4 (1999): 187–257.

———. *Shadow over the Promised Land: Slavery, Race, and Violence in Melville's America*. Baton Rouge: Louisiana State Univ. Press, 1980.

———. "The 'Spiritual Lesson' of Melville's 'The Apple-Tree Table.'" *American Quarterly* 23, no. 1 (1971): 101–9.

Katz, Jonathan Ned. *Love Stories: Sex between Men before Homosexuality*. Chicago: Univ. of Chicago Press, 2001.

Kelley, Wyn. "*Pierre*'s Domestic Ambiguities." In *The Cambridge Companion to Herman Melville*, edited by Robert S. Levine, 91–113. New York: Cambridge Univ. Press, 1998.

———. "Rozoko in the Pacific: Melville's Natural History of Creation." In *"Whole Oceans Away": Melville and the Pacific,* edited by Jill Barnum, Wyn Kelley, and Christopher Sten, 139–52. Kent, Ohio: Kent State Univ. Press, 2007.

Kemp, Mark A. R. "*The Marble Faun* and American Postcolonial Ambivalence." *Modern Fiction Studies* 43, no. 1 (1997): 209–36.

Kermode, Frank. *The Classic: Literary Images of Permanence and Change.* New York: Viking Press, 1975.

Kerr, Howard. *Mediums, and Spirit-Rappers, and Roaring Radicals: Spiritualism in American Literature, 1850–1900.* Champaign: Univ. of Illinois Press, 1972.

King, Bolton. *A History of Italian Unity: Being a Political History of Italy from 1814 to 1871.* 2 vols. London: James Nisbet, 1899.

Koestenbaum, Wayne. *Double Talk: The Erotics of Male Literary Collaboration.* New York: Routledge, 1989.

Kohut, Heinz, *The Analysis of the Self: A Systematic Approach to the Psychoanalytic Treatment of Narcissistic Personality Disorders.* New York: International Universities Press, 1971.

———. *The Restoration of the Self.* New York: International Universities Press, 1977.

Kovel, Joel. *The Age of Desire: Reflections of a Radical Psychoanalyst.* New York: Pantheon Books, 1981.

Langenscheidt New College Merriam-Webster. New York: Langenscheidt, 1998.

Lathrop, Rose Hawthorne. "The Hawthornes in Lenox: Told in Letters by Nathaniel and Mrs. Hawthorne." *Century Magazine* 49, no. 1 (1894): 86–98.

Lawrence, D. H. "Pan in America." In *Phoenix: The Posthumous Papers of D. H. Lawrence,* edited by Edward D. McDonald, 22–31. New York: Viking, 1936.

Lear, Jonathan. *Open Minded.* Cambridge, Mass.: Harvard Univ. Press, 1998.

LeBlanc, John R. "The Context of Manumission: Imperial Rome and Antebellum Alabama." *Alabama Review* 46, no. 4 (1993): 266–87.

Lepore, Jill. *New York Burning: Liberty, Slavery, and Conspiracy in Eighteenth-Century Manhattan.* New York: Knopf, 2005.

Leuders, Edward G. "The Melville-Hawthorne Relationship in *Pierre* and *Blithedale Romance*." *Western Humanities Review* 4 (Autumn 1950): 323–44.

Leverenz, David. *Manhood and the American Renaissance.* Ithaca, N.Y.: Cornell Univ. Press, 1989.

Levin, Harry. *The Power of Blackness: Hawthorne, Poe, Melville.* New York: Knopf, 1958.

Levine, Robert S. "'Antebellum Rome' in *The Marble Faun*." *American Literary History* 2, no. 1 (1990): 18–38.

———. "Pierre's Blackened Hand." *Leviathan* 1, no. 1 (2000): 23–44.

Mack Smith, Denis. *Mazzini*. New Haven, Conn.: Yale Univ. Press, 1994.

Macpherson, C. B. *The Political Theory of Possessive Individualism: Hobbes to Locke*. London: Oxford Univ. Press, 1962.

Male, Roy R. *Hawthorne's Tragic Vision*. 1957. Reprint, New York: W. W. Norton and Co., 1964.

Manning, Rev. J. M. *Half Truths and the Truth*. Boston: Lee and Shepard, 1871.

Markels, Julian. "The *Moby-Dick* White Elephant." *American Literature* 66, no. 1 (1994): 105–22.

Marraro, Howard R. *American Opinion on the Unification of Italy, 1846–1861*. New York: Columbia Univ. Press, 1932.

———. "Garibaldi in New York." *New York History* 27 (April 1946): 179–203.

———. "Lincoln's Offer of a Command to Garibaldi: Further Light on a Disputed Point of History." *Journal of the Illinois State Historical Society* 36 (September 1943): 237–70.

Martin, Robert K. *Hero, Captain, and Stranger: Male Friendship, Social Critique, and Literary Form in the Sea Novels of Herman Melville*. Chapel Hill: Univ. of North Carolina Press, 1986.

———. "Knights-Errant and Gothic Seducers: The Representation of Male Friendship in Mid-Nineteenth-Century America." In *Hidden from History: Reclaiming the Gay and Lesbian Past,* edited by Martin B. Duberman, Martha Vicinus, and George Chauncey Jr., 169–82. New York: Meridian, 1990.

———. "Melville and Sexuality." In *The Cambridge Companion to Herman Melville,* edited by Robert S. Levine, 186–201. Cambridge: Cambridge Univ. Press, 1998.

———. "Newton Arvin: Literary Critic and Lewd Person." *American Literary History* 16, no. 2 (2004): 290–317.

Martin, Robert K., and Leland S. Person. "Missing Letters: Hawthorne, Melville, and Scholarly Desire." In "The Hawthorne-Melville Relationship." Special issue of *ESQ: A Journal of the American Renaissance* 46, nos. 1/2 (2000): 99–122.

———, eds. "The Hawthorne-Melville Relationship." Special issue of *ESQ: A Journal of the American Renaissance* 46, nos. 1/2 (2000).

Marx, Karl. *Capital: A Critique of Political Economy*. Translated by Edward Aveling and Samuel Moore. New York: Modern Library, 1906.

———. "Economic and Philosophic Manuscripts of 1844." In *The Marx-Engels Reader,* edited by Robert C. Tucker, 66–125. 2nd ed. New York: Norton, 1978.

———. "Theses on Feuerbach." In *The Marx-Engels Reader*, edited by Robert C. Tucker, 143–45. 2nd ed. New York: Norton, 1978.

Masten, Jeffrey. *Textual Intercourse: Collaboration, Authorship, and Sexualities in Renaissance Drama*. Cambridge: Cambridge Univ. Press, 1997.

[Mathews, Cornelius]. "Several Days in Berkshire," *Literary World*, August 24, August 31, and September 7, 1850; 145–47; 166; 185–86.

Matthiessen, F. O. *American Renaissance: Art and Expression in the Age of Emerson and Whitman*. New York: Oxford Univ. Press, 1941.

Mattison, Hiram. *Spirit-Rapping Unveiled! An Exposé of the Origin, History, Theology and Philosophy of Certain Alleged Communications from the Spirit World, by Means of "Spirit Rapping," "Medium Writing," "Physical Demonstrations," etc.* New York: Mason Brothers, 1853.

McCarthy, Paul. *The Twisted Mind: Madness in Herman Melville's Fiction*. Iowa City: Univ. of Iowa Press, 1990.

McWilliams, John P., Jr. *Hawthorne, Melville, and the American Character: A Looking-Glass Business*. Cambridge: Cambridge Univ. Press, 1984.

Mead, David. *Yankee Eloquence in the Middle West: The Ohio Lyceum, 1850–1870*. East Lansing: Michigan State College Press, 1951.

Mellow, James R. *Nathaniel Hawthorne in His Times*. Baltimore, Md.: Johns Hopkins Univ. Press, 1980.

Melville Family Papers, New York Public Library.

Melville, Herman. *Battle-Pieces and Aspects of the War*. New York: Harper and Brothers, 1866.

———. *Billy Budd, Sailor (An Inside Narrative)*. Edited by Harrison Hayford and Merton M. Sealts Jr. Chicago: Univ. of Chicago Press, 1962.

———. *The Collected Poems of Herman Melville*. Edited by Howard Vincent. New York: Hendricks House, 1947.

[———]. "Hawthorne and His Mosses, by a Virginian spending July in Vermont." *Literary World*, August 17 and 24, 1850; 125–27; 145–47. Reprinted in *Nathaniel Hawthorne: The Contemporary Reviews*, edited by John L. Idol Jr., Buford Jones, and M. Thomas Inge, 104–15. New York: Cambridge Univ. Press, 1994.

———. *The Letters of Herman Melville*. Edited by Merrell Davis and W. H. Gilman. New Haven, Conn.: Yale Univ. Press, 1960.

———. *Melville's Marginalia*. Edited by W. Walker Cowen. New York: Garland, 1989.

———. Melville's Marginalia Online. Edited by Steven Olsen-Smith. http://www.boisestate.edu/melville/index.html (accessed August 7, 2007).

———. *The Poems of Herman Melville*. Edited by Douglas Robillard. Kent, Ohio: Kent State Univ. Press, 2000.

Merish, Lori. *Sentimental Materialism: Gender, Commodity Culture, and Nineteenth-Century American Literature.* Durham, N.C.: Duke Univ. Press, 2000.

Metcalf, Eleanor Melville. *Herman Melville: Cycle and Epicycle.* Cambridge, Mass.: Harvard Univ. Press, 1953.

Milder, Robert. "The Composition of '*Moby-Dick*': A Review and a Prospect." *ESQ: A Journal of the American Renaissance* 23, no. 4 (1977): 203–16.

———. "'The Connecting Link of Centuries': Melville, Rome, and the Mediterranean, 1856–1857." In *Roman Holidays: American Writers and Artists in Nineteenth-Century Italy,* edited by Robert K. Martin and Leland S. Person, 206–25. Iowa City: Univ. of Iowa Press, 2002.

———. "Editing Melville's Afterlife." *Text: An Interdisciplinary Journal of Textual Studies* 9 (1996): 389–407.

———. "'The Ugly Socrates': Melville, Hawthorne, and Homoeroticism." In "The Hawthorne-Melville Relationship." Special issue of *ESQ: A Journal of the American Renaissance* 46, nos. 1/2 (2000): 1–49.

Miller, Edwin Haviland. *Melville.* New York: George Braziller, 1975.

———. *Salem Is My Dwelling Place: A Life of Nathaniel Hawthorne.* Iowa City: Univ. of Iowa Press, 1991.

Miller, John N. "Eros and Ideology: At the Heart of Hawthorne's *Blithedale.*" *Nineteenth-Century Literature* 55, no. 1 (2000): 1–21.

Miller, Perry. *Errand into the Wilderness.* New York: Harper and Row, 1964.

———. *The Raven and the Whale: The War of Words and Wits in the Era of Poe and Melville.* New York: Harcourt, Brace and World, 1956.

Milton, John. *Paradise Lost.* In *John Milton: Complete Poems and Major Prose,* edited by Merritt Y. Hughes. New York: Odyssey Press, 1957.

Mitchell, Thomas R. *Hawthorne's Fuller Mystery.* Amherst: Univ. of Massachusetts Press, 1998.

———. "In the Whale's Wake: Melville and *The Blithedale Romance.*" In "The Hawthorne-Melville Relationship." Special issue of *ESQ: A Journal of the American Renaissance* 46, nos. 1/2 (2000): 51–73.

"Modern Necromancy." *North American Review* 80, no. 167 (1855): 512–28.

Mooney, James L. *Dictionary of American Naval Fighting Ships.* 8 vols. Washington, D.C.: Navy Department, Office of the Chief of Naval Operations, Naval History Division, 1968.

Moore, Frank, ed. *The Rebellion Record: A Diary of American Events.* 11 vols. New York: G. P. Putnam, 1861–68.

Morrison, Toni. "Unspeakable Things Unspoken: The Afro-American Presence in American Literature." *Michigan Quarterly Review* 28, no. 1 (1989): 1–34.

Mueller, Monika. *"This Infinite Fraternity of Feeling": Gender, Genre, and Homoerotic Crisis in Hawthorne's "The Blithedale Romance" and Melville's "Pierre."* Madison, N.J.: Fairleigh Dickinson Univ. Press, 1996.

Mumford, Lewis. *Herman Melville.* New York: Literary Guild of America, 1929.

Murray, Henry A. Introduction to *Pierre; or, The Ambiguities,* by Herman Melville, xiii–ciii. New York: Hendricks House, 1949.

Murray, Henry A., Harvey Myerson, and Eugene Taylor. "Allan Melvill's By-Blow." *Melville Society Extracts,* no. 61 (February 1985): 1–6.

Nelson, Dana D. *National Manhood: Capitalist Citizenship and the Imagined Fraternity of White Men.* Durham, N.C.: Duke Univ. Press, 1998.

Newbury, Michael. *Figuring Authorship in Antebellum America.* Stanford, Calif.: Stanford Univ. Press, 1997.

Nott, J. C., and George R. Gliddon. *Types of Mankind; or, Ethnological Researches.* Philadelphia: Lippincott, Grambo, 1854.

Otter, Samuel. "The Eden of Saddle Meadows: Landscape and Ideology in *Pierre.*" *American Literature* 66, no. 1 (1994): 55–81.

———. *Melville's Anatomies.* Berkeley: Univ. of California Press, 1999.

———. "'Race' in *Typee* and *White-Jacket.*" In *The Cambridge Companion to Herman Melville,* edited by Robert S. Levine, 12–36. New York: Cambridge Univ. Press, 1998.

The Oxford Dictionary of Quotations. 2nd ed. New York: Oxford Univ. Press, 1966.

Parker, Hershel. *Herman Melville: A Biography.* 2 vols. Baltimore, Md.: Johns Hopkins Univ. Press, 1996, 2002.

———. "Herman Melville's *The Isle of the Cross:* A Survey and a Chronology." *American Literature* 62, no. 1 (1990): 1–16.

Parker, Hershel, and Harrison Hayford, eds. *"Moby-Dick" as Doubloon: Essays and Extracts, 1851–1870.* New York: W. W. Norton and Company, 1970.

Parker, Theodore. *A Discourse of Matters Pertaining to Religion.* Boston: American Unitarian Association, 1907.

Patterson-Black, Gene. "On Herman Melville." In *American Novelists Revisited: Essays in Feminist Criticism,* edited by Fritz Fleischmann, 107–42. Boston: G. K. Hall, 1982.

Pearson, Norman Holmes. "Elizabeth Peabody on Hawthorne." *Essex Historical Collections,* July 1958.

Philbrick, Nathaniel. *In the Heart of the Sea: The Tragedy of the Whaleship "Essex."* New York: Viking, 2000.

Plato. *Symposium.* Translated by Benjamin Jowett. Indianapolis, Ind.: Bobbs-Merrill, 1956.

Poe, Edgar Allan. "Tale-Writing—Nathaniel Hawthorne." *Godey's Magazine and Lady's Book* 35 (November 1847): 252–56. Reprinted in *Nathaniel Hawthorne: The Contemporary Reviews*, edited by John L. Idol Jr., Buford Jones, and M. Thomas Inge, 98–104. New York: Cambridge Univ. Press, 1994.

Porte, Joel, ed. *Emerson in His Journals*. Cambridge, Mass.: Harvard Univ. Press, 1982.

Porter, James. *The Spirit Rappings, Mesmerism, Clairvoyance, Visions, Revelations, Startling Phenomena, and Infidelity of the Rapping Fraternity, Calmly Considered, and Exposed*. Boston: James P. Magee, 1853.

Post-Lauria, Sheila. *Correspondent Colorings: Melville in the Marketplace*. Amherst: Univ. of Massachusetts Press, 1996.

Poyen, Charles. *Progress of Animal Magnetism in New England*. Boston: Weeks, Jordan, 1837.

Ra'ad, Basem. "'The Encantadas' and 'The Isle of the Cross': Melvillean Dubieties, 1853–54." *American Literature* 63, no. 2 (1991): 316–23.

Reynolds, Larry J. *European Revolutions and the American Literary Renaissance*. New Haven, Conn.: Yale Univ. Press, 1988.

———. "'Strangely Ajar with the Human Race': Hawthorne, Slavery, and the Question of Moral Responsibility." In *Hawthorne and the Real: Bicentennial Essays*, edited by Millicent Bell, 40–69. Columbus: Ohio State Univ. Press, 2005.

Richardson, Merrill. "A Plain Discussion with a Transcendentalist." *New Englander* 1, no. 4 (1843): 502–16. Reprinted in *Critical Essays on American Transcendentalism*, edited by Philip Gura and Joel Myerson, 65–82. Boston: G. K. Hall, 1982.

Riss, Arthur. "The Art of Discrimination." *ELH* 71, no. 1 (2004): 251–87.

Robertson-Lorant, Laurie. *Melville: A Biography*. Amherst: Univ. of Massachusetts Press, 1996.

Rogin, Michael Paul. *Subversive Genealogy: The Politics and Art of Herman Melville*. Berkeley: Univ. of California Press, 1985.

Romero, Lora. *Home Fronts: Domesticity and Its Critics in the Antebellum United States*. Durham, N.C.: Duke Univ. Press, 1997.

Rowe, John Carlos. *At Emerson's Tomb: The Politics of Classic American Literature*. New York: Columbia Univ. Press, 1997.

Rubin, Gayle. "The Traffic in Women: Notes on the "Political Economy" of Sex." In *Toward an Anthropology of Women*, edited by Rayna Reiter, 157–210. New York: Monthly Review Press, 1975.

Rubin-Dorsky, Jeffrey. *Adrift in the Old World: The Psychological Pilgrimage of Washington Irving*. Chicago: Univ. of Chicago Press, 1988.

Ryan, Mary. *Cradle of the Middle Class: The Family in Oneida County, New York: 1790–1865*. Cambridge: Cambridge Univ. Press, 1981.

Sanborn, Geoffrey. "Whence Come You, Queequeg?" *American Literature* 77, no. 2 (2005): 227–57.

Sandberg, Robert Allen. "Melville's Unfinished 'Burgundy Club' Book: A Reading Edition Edited from the Manuscripts with Introduction and Notes." PhD diss., Northwestern Univ., 1989.

Sattelmeyer, Robert, and James Barbour. "The Sources and Genesis of Melville's 'Norfolk Isle and the Chola Widow.'" *American Literature* 50, no. 4 (1978): 398–417.

Sealts, Merton M., Jr. *Melville as Lecturer.* Cambridge, Mass.: Harvard Univ. Press, 1957.

———. *Melville's Reading.* Columbia: Univ. of South Carolina Press, 1988.

———. *Pursuing Melville: 1940–1980.* Madison: Univ. of Wisconsin Press, 1982.

Sealts, Merton M., Jr., ed. *The Early Lives of Melville: Nineteenth-Century Biographical Sketches and Their Authors.* Madison: Univ. of Wisconsin Press, 1974.

Sedgwick, Catharine Maria. *Hope Leslie.* Edited by Mary Kelley. New Brunswick, N.J.: Rutgers Univ. Press, 1990.

———. *The Life and Letters of Catharine Maria Sedgwick.* Edited by Mary E. Dewey. New York: Harper and Brothers, 1872.

Sedgwick, Eve Kosofsky. *Between Men: English Literature and Male Homosocial Desire.* New York: Columbia Univ. Press, 1985.

———. *Epistemology of the Closet.* Berkeley: Univ. of California Press, 1990.

Seelye, John D. "'Ungraspable Phantom': Reflections of Hawthorne in *Pierre* and *The Confidence-Man.*" *Studies in the Novel* 1, no. 4 (1969): 436–43.

Sellers, Charles. *The Market Revolution: Jacksonian America, 1815–1846.* New York: Oxford Univ. Press, 1991.

Shumaker, Conrad. "'A Daughter of the Puritans': History in Hawthorne's *The Marble Faun.*" *New England Quarterly* 57, no. 1 (1984): 65–83.

Silverman, Gillian. "Textual Sentimentalism: Incest and Authorship in Melville's *Pierre.*" *American Literature* 74, no. 2 (2002): 345–72.

Simon, Bruce Neal. "The Race for Hawthorne." PhD diss., Princeton Univ., 1988.

Smith, Harmon. *My Friend, My Friend: The Story of Thoreau's Relationship with Emerson.* Amherst: Univ. of Massachusetts Press, 1999.

Smith, H. Shelton. *In His Image, But . . . Racism in Southern Religion, 1780–1910.* Durham, N.C.: Duke Univ. Press, 1972.

Smith, J. E. A. "Herman Melville." In *The Early Lives of Melville: Nineteenth-Century Biographical Sketches and Their Authors,* edited by Merton M. Sealts Jr., 119–49. Madison: Univ. of Wisconsin Press, 1974.

Smith, Martha Nell. *Rowing in Eden: Rereading Emily Dickinson.* Austin: Univ. of Texas Press, 1992.

Smith, Shawn Michelle. *American Archives: Gender, Race, and Class in Visual Culture.* Princeton, N.J.: Princeton Univ. Press, 1999.

Smith-Rosenberg, Carroll. *Disorderly Conduct: Visions of Gender in Victorian America.* New York: Oxford Univ. Press, 1985.

Solomon, Maynard. *Mozart: A Life.* New York: HarperCollins, 1996.

"The Spirits in 1692, and What They Did at Salem." *Putnam's Monthly Magazine* 7, no. 41 (1856): 505–11.

"Spiritual Manifestations." *Littell's Living Age* 37, no. 475 (1853): 807–20.

"Spiritual Materialism." *Putnam's Monthly Magazine* 4, no. 20 (1854): 158–73.

Stauffer, John. "Melville, Slavery, and the American Dilemma." In *A Companion to Herman Melville,* edited by Wyn Kelley, 214–30. Malden, Mass.: Blackwell, 2006.

Stebbins, Richard P. "Berkshire Quartet: Hawthornes and Tappans at Tanglewood, 1850–51." *Nathaniel Hawthorne Review* 25, no. 1 (1999): 1–20.

Sten, Christopher W. "Vere's Use of the 'Forms': Means and Ends in *Billy Budd.*" *American Literature* 47, no. 1 (1975): 37–51.

Stern, Julia. *The Plight of Feeling: Sympathy and Dissent in the Early American Novel.* Chicago: Univ. of Chicago Press, 1997.

Stern, Milton R. *The Fine Hammered Steel of Herman Melville.* Urbana: Univ. of Illinois Press, 1957.

Stewart, George R. "The Two *Moby-Dicks.*" *American Literature* 25, no. 4 (1954): 414–48.

Stewart, Randall. *Nathaniel Hawthorne: A Biography.* New Haven, Conn.: Yale Univ. Press, 1948.

Stillinger, Jack. *Multiple Authorship and the Myth of Solitary Genius.* New York: Oxford Univ. Press, 1991.

Styron, William. *Darkness Visible: A Memoir of Madness.* New York: Random House, 1992.

Sumner, Charles S. *The Selected Letters of Charles Sumner.* Edited by Beverly Wilson Palmer. 2 vols. Boston: Northeastern Univ. Press, 1990.

———. *The Works of Charles Sumner.* 15 vols. Boston: Lee and Shepard, 1873.

Takaki, Ronald. *Iron Cages: Race and Culture in Nineteenth-Century America.* New York: Oxford Univ. Press, 1990.

Taylor, Olivia Gatti. "Cultural Confessions: Penance and Penitence in Nathaniel Hawthorne's *The Scarlet Letter* and *The Marble Faun.*" *Renascence* 58, no. 2 (2005): 135–54.

Thaxter, Celia. *Among the Isles of Shoals.* Hanover, N.H.: Univ. Press of New England, 2003.

Thoreau, Henry David. *"Walden" and "Resistance to Civil Government."* Edited by William Rossi. New York: Norton, 1992.

Tocqueville, Alexis de. *Democracy in America.* Henry Reeve Text as revised by Francis Bowen. Edited by Phillips Bradley. New York: Knopf, 1953.

Tolchin, Neal. *Mourning, Gender, and Creativity in the Art of Herman Melville.* New Haven, Conn.: Yale Univ. Press, 1988.

[Tuckerman, Henry T.] Review of *Italy in Transition; or, Public Events and Private Scenes in the Spring of 1860,* by William Arthur. *North American Review* 92, no. 190 (1861): 15–56.

Turner, Arlin. *Nathaniel Hawthorne: A Biography.* New York: Oxford Univ. Press, 1980.

Twain, Mark. *The Tragedy of Pudd'nhead Wilson and the Comedy Those Extraordinary Twins.* Edited by Shelly Fisher Fishkin. New York: Oxford Univ. Press, 1996.

Vallier, Jane E. *Poet on Demand: The Life, Letters, and Works of Celia Thaxter.* Portsmouth, N.H.: Peter E. Randall, 1994.

Vance, William L. *America's Rome.* 2 vols. New Haven, Conn.: Yale Univ. Press, 1989.

Vincent, Howard P. *The Trying-Out of "Moby-Dick."* Boston: Houghton Mifflin, 1949.

Vincent, Howard P., ed. *Melville and Hawthorne in the Berkshires: A Symposium.* Kent, Ohio: Kent State Univ. Press, 1966.

Waldstreicher, David. "'Fallen under My Observation': Vision and Virtue in *The Coquette.*" *Early American Literature* 27, no. 3 (1992): 204–18.

Wallace, Robert K. *Douglass and Melville: Anchored Together in Neighborly Style.* New Bedford, Mass.: Spinner Publications, 2005.

———. "Fugitive Justice: Douglass, Shaw, Melville." In *Frederick Douglass and Herman Melville: Essays in Relation,* edited by Robert S. Levine and Samuel Otter, 39–68. Chapel Hill: Univ. of North Carolina Press, 2008.

Walters, Ronald G., ed. *Primers for Prudery: Sexual Advice to Victorian America.* Baltimore, Md.: Johns Hopkins Univ. Press, 1974.

"The War." *Democratic Review* 20 (1847): 100.

Watson, Charles N., Jr., "The Estrangement of Hawthorne and Melville." *New England Quarterly* 46, no. 3 (1973): 380–402.

———. "Melville's Agatha and Hunilla: A Literary Reincarnation." *English Language Notes* 6 (December 1968): 114–18.

Way, Brian. "Art and the Spirit of Anarchy: A Reading of Hawthorne's Short Stories." In *Nathaniel Hawthorne: New Critical Essays,* edited by A. Robert Lee, 11–30. London: Vision Press, 1982.

Weaver, Raymond M. *Herman Melville: Mariner and Mystic.* New York: George H. Doran, 1921.

Weinauer, Ellen. "Hawthorne and Race." In *A Companion to Herman Melville*, edited by Wyn Kelly, 327–41. Oxford, U.K.: Blackwell, 2006.

———. "Plagiarism and the Proprietary Self: Policing the Boundaries of Authorship in Melville's 'Hawthorne and His Mosses.'" *American Literature* 69, no. 4 (1997): 697–717.

Weinstein, Cindy. *Family, Kinship, and Sympathy in Nineteenth-Century American Literature*. New York: Cambridge Univ. Press, 2004.

Werth, Barry. *The Scarlet Professor: Newton Arvin; A Literary Life Shattered by Scandal*. New York: Doubleday, 2001.

Whalen, Terence. *Edgar Allan Poe and the Masses: The Political Economy of Literature in Antebellum America*. Princeton, N.J.: Princeton Univ. Press, 1999.

Widmer, Edward L. *Young America: The Flowering of Democracy in New York City*. New York: Oxford Univ. Press, 1999.

Williamson, Joel. *New People: Miscegenation and Mulattoes in the United States*. New York: Free Press, 1980.

Wilson, James C. "An Essay in Bibliography." In *The Hawthorne and Melville Friendship: An Annotated Bibliography, Biographical and Critical Essays, and Correspondence between the Two*, edited by James C. Wilson, 19–39. Jefferson, N.C.: McFarland, 1991.

———. "Melville at Arrowhead: A Reevaluation of Melville's Relations with Hawthorne and with His Family." *ESQ: A Journal of the American Renaissance* 30, no. 4 (1984): 232–44. Reprinted in *The Hawthorne and Melville Friendship: An Annotated Bibliography, Biographical and Critical Essays, and Correspondence between the Two*, edited by James C. Wilson, 200–212. Jefferson, N.C.: McFarland, 1991.

———, ed. *The Hawthorne and Melville Friendship: An Annotated Bibliography, Biographical and Critical Essays, and Correspondence between the Two*. Jefferson, N.C.: McFarland, 1991.

Wineapple, Brenda. *Hawthorne: A Life*. New York: Knopf, 2003.

———. "Hawthorne and Melville; or, The Ambiguities." In "The Hawthorne-Melville Relationship." Special issue of *ESQ: A Journal of the American Renaissance* 46, nos. 1/2 (2000): 75–98.

Wolanin, Barbara A. "Constantino Brumidi's Frescoes in the United States Capitol." In *The Italian Presence in American Art, 1760–1860*, edited by Irma B. Jaffe, 150–64. New York: Fordham Univ. Press, 1989.

Woolf, Stuart. *A History of Italy, 1700–1860: The Social Constraints of Political Change*. London: Methuen, 1979.

Woolf, Virginia. *The Diary of Virginia Woolf: Volume Three: 1925–1930*. Edited by Anne Olivier Bell. New York: Harcourt Brace, 1980.

————. *Moments of Being.* Edited by Jeanne Schulkind. 2nd ed. New York: Harcourt Brace, 1985.

World Almanac and Book of Facts, 2001. Mahwah, N.J.: World Almanac Books, 2001.

Wright, Nathalia. *American Novelists in Italy; The Discoverers: Allston to James.* Philadelphia: Univ. of Pennsylvania Press, 1965.

Yellin, Jean Fagan. "Hawthorne and the Slavery Question." In *A Historical Guide to Nathaniel Hawthorne,* edited by Larry J. Reynolds, 135–64. New York: Oxford Univ. Press, 2001.

Žižek, Slavoj. *The Sublime Object of Ideology.* London: Verso, 1989.

Contributors

JANA L. ARGERSINGER coedits *ESQ: A Journal of the American Renaissance* and *Poe Studies/Dark Romanticism*, both published at Washington State University, and recently completed a term as president of the Council of Editors of Learned Journals. Her research interests include Elizabeth Stoddard, Sophia Hawthorne, and Susan Warner, among other nineteenth-century American women writers, and her essays have appeared in *American Literature*, the *Edgar Allan Poe Review*, *American History through Literature*, and *Writers of the American Renaissance*. Current projects include a coedited collection of essays on Poe and a book-length study of eccentricity and sympathetic identification in antebellum women's texts.

DENNIS BERTHOLD is a professor of English at Texas A&M University, where he teaches nineteenth-century American literature and literature of the sea. His scholarship emphasizes the cultural politics of iconography, transnationalism, and the visual arts and covers writers ranging from Charles Brockden Brown to the seafarer Joshua Slocum. He has coedited books on Whitman and Hawthorne, and his articles have appeared in *William and Mary Quarterly*, *American Literary History*, *American Literature*, *Nineteenth-Century Literature*, and numerous collections of essays on Melville and maritime fiction.

CHRISTOPHER CASTIGLIA is a professor of English and senior research fellow at the Center for American Literary Studies at Pennsylvania State University. He is the author of *Bound and Determined: Captivity, Culture-Crossing, and White Womanhood from Mary Rowlandson to Patty Hearst* and *Interior States: Institutional Consciousness and the Inner Life of Democracy in the Antebellum United*

States, as well as coeditor of Walt Whitman's *Franklin Evans, or the Inebriate: A Tale of the Times.*

RICHARD HARDACK was a visiting assistant professor of English at Bryn Mawr and Haverford Colleges (from which he also graduated), received his PhD in English and JD from the University of California, Berkeley, where he was a Javits Fellow, and currently teaches law at Santa Clara University. His most recent articles on Melville and/or Hawthorne have appeared or are forthcoming in *New Zealand, France and the Pacific; Leviathan; Melville among the Nations;* and *Epistolary Histories: Letters, Fiction, Culture,* and he has published on nineteenth- and twentieth-century American literature, African American studies, and legal cultural studies.

WYN KELLEY, a senior lecturer in the Literature Faculty at MIT, is the author of *Melville's City: Literary and Urban Form in Nineteenth-Century New York* and *Herman Melville: An Introduction;* she has edited the Blackwell *Companion to Herman Melville,* an edition of Melville's *Benito Cereno* for Bedford/St. Martin's, and, with Jill Barnum and Christopher Sten, a collection titled *"Whole Oceans Away": Melville and the Pacific.* Her essays have appeared in *Melville and Women, "Ungraspable Phantom": Essays on "Moby-Dick," The Cambridge Companion to Melville,* and *Savage Eye: Melville and the Visual Arts,* as well as in a number of journals. She is associate editor of the journal *Leviathan: A Journal of Melville Studies* and a founding member of the Melville Society Cultural Project.

ROBERT S. LEVINE is a professor of English and a faculty affiliate in American Studies at the University of Maryland, College Park. He is the author of *Conspiracy and Romance; Martin Delany, Frederick Douglass, and the Politics of Representative Identity;* and *Unsettling Race and Nation,* and the editor of a number of volumes, including *Martin R. Delany: A Documentary Reader, The Norton Anthology of American Literature, 1820–1865* (2007), and, with Samuel Otter, *Frederick Douglass and Herman Melville: Essays in Relation.*

ROBERT MILDER, professor of English at Washington University in St. Louis, has published widely on American Renaissance subjects and is the author of *Reimagining Thoreau* and *Exiled Royalties: Melville and the Life We Imagine.* He is currently working on a book on Hawthorne.

THOMAS R. MITCHELL, professor of English at Texas A&M International University, is the author of *Hawthorne's Fuller Mystery.* Currently a member of the executive board of the Nathaniel Hawthorne Society, he has served as the reviewer of the year's work on Hawthorne for *American Literary Scholarship* and has published journal articles on nineteenth-century authors, both American and British.

LELAND S. PERSON is a professor of English at the University of Cincinnati. His most recent books are *The Cambridge Introduction to Nathaniel Hawthorne, A Historical Guide to James Fenimore Cooper, Henry James and the Suspense of Masculinity*, and a Norton Critical Edition of *The Scarlet Letter, and Other Writings*. He has also published *Aesthetic Headaches: Women and a Masculine Poetics in Poe, Melville, and Hawthorne* and many articles on nineteenth-century writers, particularly Nathaniel Hawthorne, Henry James, Herman Melville, Edgar Allan Poe, and James Fenimore Cooper, in journals such as *PMLA, American Literature, American Quarterly, Nineteenth-Century Literature, American Literary History, Novel, Arizona Quarterly, ESQ, Studies in the Novel*, and the *Henry James Review*.

LAURIE ROBERTSON-LORANT is the author of *Melville: A Biography* and *The Man Who Lived among the Cannibals: Poems in the Voice of Herman Melville*. A graduate of Radcliffe College with an MA and PhD from New York University, Dr. Lorant is a full-time visiting lecturer in the Education Department at the University of Massachusetts Dartmouth.

ROBERT SATTELMEYER is Regents' Professor of English and director of the Honors Program at Georgia State University. His research focuses on nineteenth-century American literature and culture—especially transcendentalism, Melville, and Mark Twain. Recently, he coedited a three-volume encyclopedia titled *American History through Literature*.

GALE TEMPLE is an assistant professor of English at the University of Alabama at Birmingham, where he specializes in early American literature and culture. His publications focus on connections among literature, economic change, and social reform in antebellum America. He is currently working on a book manuscript about the portrayal of addiction in early American literature.

ELLEN WEINAUER is an associate professor of English at the University of Southern Mississippi, where she teaches courses on nineteenth-century American literature and gender studies. Coeditor of *American Culture, Canons, and the Case of Elizabeth Stoddard*, she has published essays on Hawthorne, Melville, Stoddard, and William and Ellen Craft and has a developing interest in literature of the American Civil War.

BRENDA WINEAPPLE is the author, most recently, of *Hawthorne: A Life,* which won the English-speaking Union's Ambassador Award in Biography and the Boston Book Club's Julia Howe Prize. She has also recently edited the John Greenleaf Whittier volume for the Library of America's American Poets Project. A recipient of awards from the John Simon Guggenheim Memorial Foundation, the American Council of Learned Societies, and the National Endowment for the Humanities, she was the chair of the Nonfiction Panel of the National Book Awards in 2005. Her essays and reviews regularly appear in such publications as the *American Scholar, Poetry,* the *Iowa Review,* the *New York Times,* the *Los Angeles Times,* the *Nation,* and the *Boston Review.* She teaches in the graduate School of the Arts at Columbia University and is currently writing a book about Emily Dickinson and Thomas Wentworth Higginson.

Index

Page references to illustrations appear in italics.

CPSIA information can be obtained
at www.ICGtesting.com
Printed in the USA
LVHW021645131020
668702LV00002B/136